Kaplan Publishing are constantly findi[ng] ...do
difference to your studies and our exc[...]
offer something different to students [...]

This book comes with free MyKaplan c[...]an
study anytime, anywhere. **This free on[line ...cannot be purchased]
separately and is included in the price of the book.**

Having purchased this book, you have access to the following online study materials:

CONTENT	ACCA (including FBT, FMA, FFA)		FIA (excluding FBT, FMA, FFA)	
	Text	Kit	Text	Kit
Electronic version of the book	✓	✓	✓	✓
Check Your Understanding Test with instant answers	✓			
Material updates	✓	✓	✓	✓
Latest official ACCA exam questions*		✓		
Extra question assistance using the signpost icon**		✓		
Timed questions with an online tutor debrief using clock icon***		✓		
Interim assessment including questions and answers	✓		✓	
Technical answers	✓	✓	✓	✓

* Excludes BT, MA, FA, FBT, FMA, FFA; for all other papers includes a selection of questions, as released by ACCA
** For ACCA SBL, SBR, AFM, APM, ATX, AAA only
*** Excludes BT, MA, FA, LW, FBT, FMA and FFA

How to access your online resources

Kaplan Financial students will already have a MyKaplan account and these extra resources will be available to you online. You do not need to register again, as this process was completed when you enrolled. If you are having problems accessing online materials, please ask your course administrator.

If you are not studying with Kaplan and did not purchase your book via a Kaplan website, to unlock your extra online resources please go to www.mykaplan.co.uk/addabook (even if you have set up an account and registered books previously). You will then need to enter the ISBN number (on the title page and back cover) and the unique pass key number contained in the scratch panel below to gain access. You will also be required to enter additional information during this process to set up or confirm your account details.

If you purchased through the Kaplan Publishing website you will automatically receive an e-mail invitation to MyKaplan. Please register your details using this email to gain access to your content. If you do not receive the e-mail or book content, please contact Kaplan Publishing.

Your Code and Information

This code can only be used once for the registration of one book online. This registration and your online content will expire when the final sittings for the examinations covered by this book have taken place. Please allow one hour from the time you submit your book details for us to process your request.

Please scratch the film to access your unique code.

Please be aware that this code is case-sensitive and you will need to include the dashes within the passcode, but not when entering the ISBN.

ACCA Award in Audit (RQF Level 4)

FAU

Foundations in Audit

STUDY TEXT

British Library Cataloguing-in-Publication Data

A catalogue record for this book is available from the British Library.

Published by:
Kaplan Publishing UK
Unit 2 The Business Centre
Molly Millar's Lane
Wokingham
Berkshire
RG41 2QZ

ISBN: 978-1-78740-850-0

Kaplan Financial Limited, 2021

Printed and bound in Great Britain

The text in this material and any others made available by any Kaplan Group company does not amount to advice on a particular matter and should not be taken as such. No reliance should be placed on the content as the basis for any investment or other decision or in connection with any advice given to third parties. Please consult your appropriate professional adviser as necessary. Kaplan Publishing Limited, all other Kaplan group companies, the International Accounting Standards Board, and the IFRS Foundation expressly disclaim all liability to any person in respect of any losses or other claims, whether direct, indirect, incidental, consequential or otherwise arising in relation to the use of such materials. Printed and bound in Great Britain.

Acknowledgements

These materials are reviewed by the ACCA examining team. The objective of the review is to ensure that the material properly covers the syllabus and study guide outcomes, used by the examining team in setting the exams, in the appropriate breadth and depth. The review does not ensure that every eventuality, combination or application of examinable topics is addressed by the ACCA Approved Content. Nor does the review comprise a detailed technical check of the content as the Approved Content Provider has its own quality assurance processes in place in this respect.

This Product includes content from the International Auditing and Assurance Standards Board (IAASB) and the International Ethics Standards Board for Accountants (IESBA), published by the International Federation of Accountants (IFAC) in 2020 and is used with permission of IFAC.

This Product includes propriety content of the International Accounting Standards Board which is overseen by the IFRS Foundation, and is used with the express permission of the IFRS Foundation under licence. All rights reserved. No part of this publication may be reproduced, stored in a retrieval system, or transmitted in any form or by any means, electronic, mechanical, photocopying, recording, or otherwise, without prior written permission of Kaplan Publishing and the IFRS Foundation.

The IFRS Foundation logo, the IASB logo, the IFRS for SMEs logo, the "Hexagon Device", "IFRS Foundation", "eIFRS", "IAS", "IASB", "IFRS for SMEs", "IFRS", "IASs", "IFRSs", "International Accounting Standards" and "International Financial Reporting Standards", "IFRIC" and "IFRS Taxonomy" are **Trade Marks** of the IFRS Foundation.

Trade Marks

The IFRS Foundation logo, the IASB logo, the IFRS for SMEs logo, the "Hexagon Device", "IFRS Foundation", "eIFRS", "IAS", "IASB", "IFRS for SMEs", "NIIF" IASs" "IFRS", "IFRSs", "International Accounting Standards", "International Financial Reporting Standards", "IFRIC", "SIC" and "IFRS Taxonomy".

Further details of the Trade Marks including details of countries where the Trade Marks are registered or applied for are available from the Foundation on request.

This product contains material that is ©Financial Reporting Council Ltd (FRC). Adapted and reproduced with the kind permission of the Financial Reporting Council. All rights reserved. For further information, please visit www.frc.org.uk or call +44 (0)20 7492 2300.

CONTENTS

		Page
Introduction		P.5
Syllabus and study guide		P.7
The examination		P.11
Study skills and revision guidance		P.13

Chapter

1	Auditing and the audit profession	1
2	Professional ethics	13
3	Statutory audits	31
4	Auditing concepts: true and fair, materiality	39
5	Audit risk and planning	51
6	Internal controls	87
7	The audit evidence process: tests of control	119
8	Sampling	145
9	Audit verification work 1 – General principles	161
10	Audit verification work 2 – Inventory	173
11	Audit verification work 3 – Non-current assets	189
12	Audit verification work 4 – Receivables and cash and bank	201
13	Audit verification work 5 – Liabilities	221
14	Computers in audit	233
15	The final review stage	265
16	The auditor's report	289
17	The auditor's liability	307
Answers to activities and questions		319
References		387
Index		389

This document references IFRS® Standards and IAS® Standards, which are authored by the International Accounting Standards Board (the Board), and published in the 2020 IFRS Standards Red Book.

Quality and accuracy are of the utmost importance to us so if you spot an error in any of our products, please send an email to mykaplanreporting@kaplan.com with full details.

Our Quality Coordinator will work with our technical team to verify the error and take action to ensure it is corrected in future editions.

INTRODUCTION

This is the new edition of the FIA study text for Foundations in Audit, approved by the ACCA and fully updated and revised according to the examiner's comments.

Tailored to fully cover the syllabus, this Study Text has been written specifically for FIA students. Clear and comprehensive style, numerous examples and highlighted key terms help you to acquire the information easily. Plenty of activities and self-test questions enable you to practise what you have learnt.

At the end of most of the chapters you will find practice questions. These are exam-style questions and will give you a very good idea of the way you will be tested.

ACCA SUPPORT

For additional support with your studies please also refer to the ACCA Global website.

SYLLABUS AND STUDY GUIDE

Position of the exam in the overall syllabus

The accounting knowledge that is assumed for FAU is the same as that examined in FA1 and FA2. Therefore, candidates studying for FAU should refer to the IFRS® Standards listed under FA1 and FA2. Candidates will also be expected to be familiar with FFA.

Syllabus

A **Business environment and audit framework** Chapters 1, 2, 3, 4, 17
- (a) The purpose and scope of an audit
- (b) The legal duties of auditors
- (c) Professional ethics and ACCA's Code of Ethics and Conduct
- (d) Auditor engagement and liability
- (e) Audit regulation
- (f) Internal audit

B **Audit planning and risk** Chapter 5
- (a) Audit risk
- (b) Understanding the entity, its environment and the applicable financial reporting framework
- (c) Audit strategy and the audit plan
- (d) Audit documentation

C **Internal control** Chapters 6, 7
- (a) General principles of internal control
- (b) Techniques to understand, record and evaluate accounting systems
- (c) Tests of controls
- (d) Communicating control deficiencies

D **Audit evidence and procedures** Chapters 8 – 14
- (a) Audit evidence
- (b) Audit procedures and assertions
- (c) Substantive procedures
- (d) Audit sampling
- (e) Automated tools and techniques

E **Audit completion** Chapters 15, 16
- (a) Going concern
- (b) Subsequent events
- (c) Written representations
- (d) Independent Auditor's Report

F **Employability and technology skills**
- (a) Use computer technology to efficiently access and manipulate relevant information
- (b) Work on relevant response options, using available functions and technology as would be required in the workplace
- (c) Navigate windows and computer screens to create and amend responses to exam requirements, using appropriate tools
- (d) Present data and information effectively, using appropriate tools

Study Guide

A BUSINESS ENVIRONMENT AND AUDIT FRAMEWORK

1. The purpose and scope of an audit

(a) Explain the nature of an audit.

(b) Explain the purpose of an audit, including the advantages and disadvantages of an audit.

(c) Explain the nature of accounting records, including proper records.

(d) Explain the concept of true and fair presentation, and reasonable assurance.

(e) Define professional scepticism and explain how it should be exercised during an audit.

(f) Define professional judgement and identify when it should be applied during an audit.

(g) Identify the form and content of the auditors' report.

2. The legal duties of auditors

(a) Describe the duties of auditors.

(b) Describe the rights of auditors.

3. Professional ethics and ACCA's Code of Ethics and Conduct

(a) Discuss the fundamental principles of professional ethics of integrity, objectivity, professional competence and due care, confidentiality, and professional behaviour.

(b) Describe the detailed requirements, and application of professional ethics, in the context of integrity, objectivity and independence.

(c) Describe the auditor's responsibility with regard to confidentiality.

4. Auditor engagement and liability

(a) Explain the factors that auditors should consider before accepting an audit engagement.

(b) Explain the purpose and nature of an engagement letter.

(c) Explain the liability of auditors under contract and negligence to clients.

(d) Explain the liability of auditors to third parties.

5. Audit regulation

(a) Explain the purpose and scope of ISAs.

6. Internal audit

(a) Explain the purpose and scope of an internal audit function

(b) Identify the factors that external auditors should consider when evaluating the internal audit function and the work of internal auditors.

B AUDIT PLANNING AND RISK ASSESSMENT

1. Audit risk

(a) Define audit risk, including inherent risk, control risk and detection risk.

(b) Explain the risk-based approach to the audit.

(c) Define the concept of materiality and how materiality levels are calculated from financial information.

2. Understanding the entity, its environment and the applicable financial reporting framework

(a) Explain how auditors obtain an initial understanding of the entity, its environment and the applicable financial reporting framework.

3. Audit strategy and the audit plan

(a) Identify and explain the need for planning an audit.

(b) Identify and describe the contents of the overall audit strategy and the audit plan.

(c) Explain the use of analytical procedures in planning.

(d) Describe planning issues including the availability and management of audit resources, the effect of information technology on audit procedure, the audit of complex areas and the need to use experts.

(e) Explain the role of audit programmes and the advantages and disadvantages of using standard audit programmes.

4. Audit documentation

(a) Describe the reasons for maintaining audit documentation.

(b) Explain the purpose and contents of the current file and the permanent file.

(c) Explain the quality control procedures that should exist over the review of audit working papers.

(d) Explain how information technology (IT) may be used in the documentation of audit work.

C INTERNAL CONTROL

1. General principles of internal control

(a) Describe the five components of a system of internal control.

(b) Describe the objectives of a system of internal control.

(c) Describe the inherent limitations of internal control.

(d) Explain the importance of internal control to auditors.

2. Techniques to understand, record and evaluate accounting systems

(a) Describe the techniques used by auditors to understand and record accounting systems including narrative notes and flowcharts.

(b) Describe the techniques used by auditors to evaluate accounting systems including internal control questionnaires (ICQs), internal control evaluation questionnaires (ICEQs) and checklists.

(c) Provide examples of, and explain the format and contents, ICQs and ICEQs.

(d) Evaluate the system of internal control.

3. Tests of controls

(a) Describe and provide examples of control procedures to meet specified objectives for each of the following areas:
- purchases and trade payables
- sales and trade receivables
- wages and salaries (payroll)
- tangible non-current assets
- inventory
- bank and cash.

(b) Explain the purpose of tests of controls.

(c) Identify and explain the testing of controls over the following areas:
- purchases and trade payables
- sales and trade receivables
- wages and salaries (payroll)
- tangible non-current assets
- inventory
- bank and cash.

(d) Distinguish between tests of controls and substantive procedures.

(e) Distinguish between information processing controls and general IT controls and identify the objectives of each control type.

(f) Provide examples of specific information processing controls and general IT controls.

4. Communicating control deficiencies

(a) Identify and define significant internal control; deficiencies and explain the requirements and methods for communicating significant deficiencies to management and those charged with governance.

D AUDIT EVIDENCE AND PROCEDURES

1. Audit evidence

(a) Explain the importance of audit evidence, including sufficient appropriate audit evidence.

(b) Identify the factors that influence the relevance and reliability of audit evidence.

2. Audit procedures and assertions

(a) Explain the importance of the use of the assertions by the auditor.

(b) Explain the assertions in relation to classes of transactions and related disclosures and, account balances and related disclosures.

(c) Describe and give examples of procedures used by auditors to obtain audit evidence, including inspection, observation, external confirmation, recalculation, reperformance, analytical procedures and inquiry.

3. Substantive procedures

(a) Explain the rationale for designing audit programmes by reference to audit objectives.

(b) Identify and explain the substantive procedures to meet the specific objectives for the audit of each of the following:
- tangible non-current assets
- trade receivables, prepayments and other receivables
- trade payables, accruals and other payables
- bank and cash
- non-current liabilities
- provisions.

(c) Explain why the audit of inventory is often an area of high inherent risk.

(d) Describe the audit procedures that should be undertaken before, during and after attending an inventory count.

(e) Explain the extent to which an auditor may rely on a system of perpetual inventory.

  (f) Identify and explain the substantive procedures to meet the specific objectives for the audit of inventory.

4. **Audit sampling**

  (a) Define audit sampling and the relevance of sampling to the auditor.

  (b) Identify sampling selection methods, including random selection, systematic selection and haphazard selection.

  (c) State the main factors affecting sample sizes.

5. **Automated tools and techniques**

  (a) Explain the use of automated tools and techniques in an audit including the use of audit software, test data and other data analytics tools.

  (b) Explain the advantages and disadvantages of the use of automated tools and techniques to the auditor.

E AUDIT COMPLETION

1. **Going concern**

  (a) Define and discuss the significance of going concern.

  (b) Discuss indicators of going concern problems.

  (c) Explain the procedures to be applied in performing going concern reviews.

2. **Subsequent events**

  (a) Explain the responsibilities of the auditor regarding subsequent events occurring up the date of the auditor's report.

  (b) Explain the procedures to be applied in performing subsequent event reviews.

3. **Written representations**

  (a) Explain the purpose of written representations.

  (b) Describe the circumstances where written representations are necessary.

4. **Independent Auditor's reports**

  (a) Describe the form and content of the independent auditor's report including an unmodified opinion.

  (b) State the circumstances, including those where there are identified uncorrected misstatements, in which an auditor should issue a modified audit opinion in the auditor's report.

  (c) Identify the type of opinion which it is appropriate for the auditor to express based on the given circumstances.

F Employability and technology skills

1. Use computer technology to efficiently access and manipulate relevant information

2. Work on relevant options, using available functions and technology as would be required in the workplace

3. Navigate windows and computer screen to create and amend responses to exam requirements, using the appropriate tools

4. Present data and information effectively, using the appropriate tools

THE EXAMINATION

Format of the examination

	Number of marks
Section A	
15 compulsory multiple choice questions (2 marks each)	30
Section B	
8 compulsory questions	
Q1 & 2 (15 marks each)	30
Q 3 & 4 (10 marks each)	20
Q 5 – 8 (5 marks each)	20
Total	100

Total time allowed: 2 hours

Approach to examining the syllabus

The syllabus is assessed by a two hour examination. Examination regulations issued or legislation passed on or before 31st August annually, will be examinable from 1st September of the following year to 31st August of the year after that.

In addition to reading the tips contained here, we recommend that you review the resources available on the ACCA Global Website before sitting the CBE. Here you will find guidance documents, videos and a link to the CBE question practice platform.

Examination tips

- Spend the first few minutes of the examination reading the questions.

- Unless you know exactly how to answer the question, spend some time **planning your answer**. Stick to the question and tailor your answer to what you are asked.

- **Fully explain all your points** but be concise. Set out all workings clearly and neatly, and state briefly what you are doing. Don't write out the question.

- If you do not understand what a question is asking, **state your assumptions**. Even if you do not answer precisely in the way the examiner hoped, you should be given some credit, if your assumptions are reasonable.

- **If you get stuck** with a question, return to it later.

A Specimen CBE examination can be accessed via the following link on the ACCA website:

www.accaglobal.com/my/en/student/exam-support-resources/foundation-level-study-resources/fau/fau-specimen-exams.html

Answering the questions

Essay questions: Make a quick plan and under each main point list all the relevant facts you can think of. Then write out your answer developing each point fully. Your essay should have a clear structure; it should contain a brief introduction, a main section and a conclusion. Be concise. It is better to write a little about a lot of different points than a great deal about one or two points.

Computations: It is essential to include all your workings in your answers. Many computational questions require the use of a standard format: company statement of profit or loss and other comprehensive income, statement of financial position and cash flow statement for example. Be sure you know these formats thoroughly before the examination and use the layouts that you see in the answers given in this book and in model answers. If you are asked to comment or make recommendations on a computation, you must do so. There are important marks to be gained here. Even if your computation contains mistakes, you may still gain marks if your reasoning is correct.

Please note that it is unlikely that you will be required to prepare computations in FAU.

Reports, memos and other documents: Some questions ask you to present your answer in the form of a report or a memo or other document. Use the correct format – there could be easy marks to gain here.

STUDY SKILLS AND REVISION GUIDANCE

Preparing to study

Set your objectives

Before starting to study decide what you want to achieve – the type of pass you wish to obtain.

This will decide the level of commitment and time you need to dedicate to your studies.

Devise a study plan

Determine when you will study.

Split these times into study sessions.

Put the sessions onto a study plan making sure you cover the course, course assignments and revision.

Stick to your plan!

Effective study techniques

Use the **SQR3** method

Survey the chapter – look at the headings and read the introduction, summary and objectives. Get an overview of what the text deals with.

Question – during the survey, ask yourself the questions that you hope the chapter will answer for you.

Read through the chapter thoroughly, answering the questions and meeting the objectives. Attempt the exercises and activities, and work through all the examples.

Recall – at the end of the chapter, try to recall the main ideas of the chapter without referring to the text. Do this a few minutes after the reading stage.

Review – check that your recall notes are correct.

Use the **MURDER** method

Mood – set the right mood.

Understand – issues covered and make note of any uncertain bits.

Recall – stop and put what you have learned into your own words.

Digest – go back and reconsider the information.

Expand – read relevant articles and newspapers.

Review – go over the material you covered to consolidate the knowledge.

While studying…

Summarise the key points of the chapter.

Make linear notes – a list of headings, divided up with subheadings listing the key points. Use different colours to highlight key points and keep topic areas together.

Try mind-maps – put the main heading in the centre of the paper and encircle it. Then draw short lines radiating from this to the main sub-headings, which again have circles around them. Continue the process from the sub-headings to sub-sub-headings, etc.

Revision

The best approach to revision is to **revise the course as you work through it**.

Also try to leave **four to six weeks before the exam for final revision**.

Make sure you **cover the whole syllabus**.

Pay special attention to **those areas where your knowledge is weak**.

If you are stuck on a topic find somebody (a tutor or a colleague) to explain it to you.

Read around the subject – read good newspapers and professional journals, especially ACCA's *Student Accountant* – this can give you an advantage in the exam.

Read through the text and your notes again. Maybe put key revision points onto index cards to look at when you have a few minutes to spare.

Practise exam standard questions under timed conditions. Attempt all the different styles of questions you may be asked to answer in your exam.

Review any assignments you have completed and look at where you lost marks – put more work into those areas where you were weak.

Ensure you **know the structure of the exam** – how many questions and of what type they are.

Chapter 1

AUDITING AND THE AUDIT PROFESSION

INTRODUCTION

This chapter provides an introduction to the role and function of auditing and considers the structure and regulation of the auditing profession.

This chapter covers syllabus areas A (1), A (5).

CONTENTS

1 The nature of accounting records and audit

2 The purpose of the external audit

3 International Standards on Auditing

4 The relationship between auditing and accounting

LEARNING OUTCOMES

At the end of this chapter, you should be able to:

- explain the nature, purpose and structure of an audit

- appreciate the main mechanisms which currently regulate the auditing profession

- explain the role of both auditing and accounting standards.

1 THE NATURE OF ACCOUNTING RECORDS AND AUDIT

1.1 THE NATURE OF ACCOUNTING RECORDS

Businesses, both sole traders and incorporated companies, need to satisfy the informational needs of a wide range of stakeholders. Examples of typical stakeholders and their informational requirements include:

- Shareholders – they need information about company performance to aid investment decisions

- Lenders/financial institutions – they need information about the liquidity of a business to make lending decisions

- Government institutions – they need information to support the calculation and payment of relevant corporation and income taxes

- Management – they need information to support operational decisions and business strategy

- Employees – they need information relating to the liquidity and performance of a business to assess job security and remuneration potential

- Customers/suppliers – need information about the liquidity of a business to decide whether to commit to long term trading partnerships

- The public – they require a wide range of data; environmental and corporate social responsibility information is currently popular.

Each stakeholder requires good quality information to assist their decisions, all of which are significant to the stakeholder in question. If the information they use is of poor quality then they are likely to make poor quality decisions. Therefore providing them with the correct quality of information is a significant undertaking.

In order to meet these requirements company directors/management prepare a number of reports for use by the stakeholders identified above. They are too numerous to prepare a comprehensive list so a summary of some of the key documents is included below:

- Management accounts – these are typically used internally by management and employees for internal, operational and financial decisions. They include budgets/targets, performance to date and management commentaries. These are occasionally provided to lenders, at the discretion of management, to support loan/finance applications.

- Taxation computations and returns – these include summaries of sales and purchases to support sales tax and corporate tax payments and payroll reconciliations to support the payment of income taxes and social security payments.

- Financial statements – these incorporate summaries of historical financial performance (statements of comprehensive income and cash flows) and summaries of year-end assets and liabilities (statement of financial position). These are usually required by law for most companies and are used primarily by shareholders, although they are available to the public.

Whilst there are different requirements for each piece of information produced there are two specific requirements of information reported in the financial statements that are significant; in accordance with the Conceptual Framework, information presented in the financial statements must:

- be relevant, meaning that the information must be capable of influencing the users' decisions; and

- faithfully represent the transactions and balances it is reporting; meaning it must be complete, neutral and free from error.

Financial information must also be understandable, produced on a timely basis, be comparable and be verifiable.

It is vital that management have systems in place that support the preparation of this information. They must ensure that they set up appropriate systems, including accounting, and that they design appropriate controls to reduce the risk of fraud and error and to detect such problems if they do occur. Management must also establish systems sufficient to keep such records as long as they are required by stakeholders. For example; in the UK business records must be kept for a minimum of six years to satisfy tax regulations.

See Chapter 16, section 1.4 for more of on what constitutes 'proper accounting records'.

1.2 WHAT IS AN AUDIT?

Whilst it is, of course, important to have a sound grasp of the meaning of the subject which you are studying you are not likely to be assessed directly on the definition of the word 'audit.' It is therefore more important to grasp an appreciation of the ideas involved in the audit concept than to attempt to learn a definition word for word.

One possible definition of an audit is:

"The independent examination of evidence from which the financial statements of an enterprise are derived in order to give the reader of those statements confidence as to the 'truth and fairness' of the state of affairs which they disclose."

An alternative view is presented by ISA 200 *the Overall Objectives of the Independent Auditor and the Conduct of an Audit in Accordance with ISAs*: the objective of an audit is 'to enable the auditor to express an opinion whether the financial statements are prepared, in all material respects, in accordance with an identified financial reporting framework'.

What can we see as the essential features of an audit from a combination of these definitions and explanation?

- An audit involves an examination of financial statements – the auditor is not responsible for the preparation of financial statements. In the case of a limited company, it is the responsibility of the directors to prepare the financial statements – the auditor then examines the financial statements and reports his opinion on the 'truth and fairness' of the state of affairs disclosed.

- The end result of an audit is an opinion to assist the user of the financial statements – auditing therefore relies heavily on professional judgement, not merely facts.

- The auditor's opinion makes reference to true and fair, or fair presentation – but true and fair is again a matter of judgement – it is not precisely defined for the auditor.

In order for the user of the information to feel confident in relying on the auditor's report, the auditor should be independent of the enterprise subject to audit – independent essentially means that the auditor has no significant personal interest in the enterprise. This allows an objective, professional view to be taken.

You will note that this is a wide concept of an audit which can be applied to any enterprise, not just to limited companies. However we are concerned here primarily with the annual audits of the financial statements of limited companies (often known as statutory or external audits). Any other audit applications will be clearly indicated for you in the text.

1.3 EXAMPLE OF AN AUDITOR'S REPORT

It is appropriate to consider in brief the format and content of an auditor's report. This will be considered in more detail in subsequent chapters of this publication.

You should note the following details within the specimen report as follows:

(a) a title identifying the person(s) to whom the report is addressed

(b) the auditors' opinion on the financial statements

(c) the basis of the auditors' opinion

(d) key audit matters

(e) responsibilities of management

(f) responsibilities of the auditor

(g) the auditors' signature and address

(h) the date of the auditor's report.

INDEPENDENT AUDITOR'S REPORT TO...................[appropriate addressee]

Opinion

We have audited the financial statements of ABC Company (the Company), which comprise the statement of financial position as at December 31, 20X1, and the statement of comprehensive income, statement of changes in equity and statement of cash flows for the year then ended, and notes to the financial statements, including a summary of significant accounting policies.

In our opinion, the accompanying financial statements present fairly, in all material respects, (*or give a true and fair view of*) the financial position of the Company as at December 31, 20X1, and (*of*) its financial performance and its cash flows for the year then ended in accordance with International Financial Reporting Standards (IFRSs).

Basis for Opinion

We conducted our audit in accordance with International Standards on Auditing (ISAs). Our responsibilities under those standards are further described in the Auditor's Responsibilities for the Audit of the Financial Statements section of our report. We are independent of the Company in accordance with the International Ethics Standards Board for Accountants' Code of Ethics for Professional Accountants (IESBA Code) together with the ethical requirements that are relevant to our audit of the financial statements in [jurisdiction], and have fulfilled our other ethical responsibilities in accordance with these requirements and the IESBA Code. We believe that the audit evidence we have obtained is sufficient and appropriate to provide a basis for our opinion.

Key Audit Matters

Key audit matters are those matters that, in our professional judgment, were of most significance in our audit of the financial statements of the current period. These matters were addressed in the context of our audit of the financial statements as a whole, and in forming our opinion thereon, and we do not provide a separate opinion on these matters.

[Description of each key audit matter in accordance with ISA 701]

Responsibilities of Management and Those Charged with Governance for the Financial Statements

Management is responsible for the preparation and fair presentation of these financial statements in accordance with IFRSs, and for such internal control as management determines is necessary to enable the preparation of financial statements that are free from material misstatement, whether due to fraud or error.

In preparing the financial statements, management is responsible for assessing the Company's ability to continue as a going concern, disclosing, as applicable, matters related to going concern and using the going concern basis of accounting unless management either intends to liquidate the Company or to cease operations, or has no realistic alternative but to do so.

Those charged with governance are responsible for overseeing the Company's financial reporting process.

Auditor's Responsibilities for the Audit of the Financial Statements

Our objectives are to obtain reasonable assurance about whether the financial statements as a whole are free from material misstatement, whether due to fraud or error, and to issue an auditor's report that includes our opinion. Reasonable assurance is a high level of assurance, but is not a guarantee that an audit conducted in accordance with ISAs will always detect a material misstatement when it exists. Misstatements can arise from fraud or error and are considered material if, individually or in the aggregate, they could reasonably be expected to influence the economic decisions of users taken on the basis of these financial statements.

[Auditor's signature]

[Date of the auditor's report]

[Auditor's address]

An **unmodified opinion** provides assurance (not a guarantee) that an independent examination of the accounts has not discovered any unadjusted material (i.e. significant) misstatements and that the financial statements give a true and fair view.

You should note that it is also possible for the auditor to issue a **modified auditor's opinion**. This may occur when the auditor is either of the opinion that there is a material misstatement in the financial statements, or when the auditor has been unable to obtain sufficient appropriate evidence upon as a basis for the audit opinion.

1.4 THE DEVELOPMENT OF MODERN EXTERNAL AUDITING

Modern auditing owes its origins to the development of a number of 'fiduciary' relationships, the most important for our purposes being the relationship between company directors and shareholders.

Definition   A **'fiduciary' relationship** is a relationship of 'trust and good faith' such as that between a trustee and a beneficiary, and between directors and shareholders.

It was recognised many years ago that whenever a fiduciary relationship with financial implications existed – think of the relationship between company directors and the shareholders in the company – there was a need for an outsider (what we would now refer to as an independent auditor) to review the accounts reflecting financial transactions and to express an opinion as to their honesty (we would now say truth and fairness) or otherwise.

These relationships in the context of companies can be shown as follows:

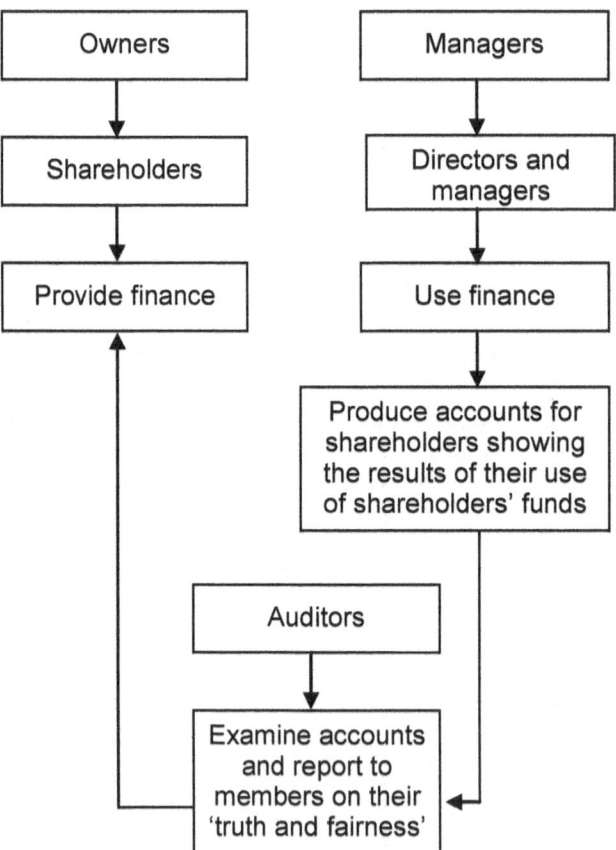

The relationship shown here is often described as depicting the **divorce of ownership from control**.

The shareholders own the company, but a different group, the directors, manage and control the company on behalf of the shareholders. This is an application of the agency principle (whereby the directors are acting as the agents of the shareholders) as the shareholders elect the directors to manage the company on their behalf. In effect, the directors have a responsibility of stewardship to account to the shareholders for the way they have managed the company. This is achieved by the directors preparing annual financial statements, which are audited, for presentation to the shareholders.

The auditor acts as an independent referee, reporting to the shareholders on the financial statements prepared by the directors.

Company legislation in most countries now requires auditors to express an opinion on the truth and fairness of the statement of comprehensive income and the statement of financial position, both of which should be prepared by directors and presented to the shareholders. In addition, it is generally required that auditors should possess a recognised professional qualification and detailed provisions can be laid down regarding their duties, powers and responsibilities.

2 THE PURPOSE OF THE EXTERNAL AUDIT

2.1 INTRODUCTION

As described above, the need for an external audit centres on the requirements of the users of the accounts who are primarily, but not solely, the shareholders in the case of company audits. There are also many other outside parties who use the financial statements as a basis for making decisions regarding a company. Bankers, suppliers and lenders as well as potential investors, customers and employees all have an interest in the state of the company's financial affairs. The independent audit requirement fulfils the need for a professional opinion on whether those financial statements are objective, free from bias and manipulation and relevant to the needs of the users.

2.2 ADVANTAGES OF AN AUDIT

As we have seen, the need for an external audit in the case of companies arises primarily from the existence of divorce of 'ownership from control'. There are however, certain advantages in having financial statements audited even where no statutory requirement exists for such an audit – in the case of a sole trader, partnership, club or society for example.

These advantages can be summarised as follows:

(a) Any audit will give assurance to readers of the accounts (e.g. current investors, potential investors, senior managers of the business) that the accounts have been properly drawn up and give a fair presentation of the financial position of the business. For example, the members of a sports club might choose to have the club's accounts audited each year, to give assurance to the members that their subscription paid had been used properly as set out in the published financial statements.

(b) Disputes between stakeholders may be more easily settled. For instance, a partnership which has complicated profit-sharing arrangements may require an independent examination of those accounts to ensure as far as possible an accurate assessment and division of those profits.

(c) Major changes in ownership may be facilitated if past accounts contain an independent auditor's report, for instance, where two sole traders merge their business to form a new partnership.

(d) Applications to third parties for finance may be strengthened by the submission of audited accounts, as it adds credibility to the figures. However, do remember that a bank, for instance, is likely to be far more concerned about the future of the business and available security, than by the past historical accounts, audited or otherwise.

(e) The audit is likely to involve an in-depth examination of the business and so may enable the auditor to give constructive advice to management on improving the efficiency of the business.

2.3 DISADVANTAGES OF AN AUDIT

Like most things in life, audits are not entirely without their disadvantages. There are two main points to make here:

(a) The audit fee! Clearly the services of an auditor must be paid for. It is for this reason that few partnerships and even fewer sole traders are likely to have their accounts audited.

(b) The audit involves the client's staff and management in giving time to providing information to the auditor. Professional auditors should therefore plan their audit carefully to minimise the disruption which their work will cause.

It is also worth pointing out that audits are only really useful when there is a separation of ownership and control. However, in many cases the directors may also be the majority shareholders, even in relatively large companies. In these circumstances is there any need for the financial statements to be audited?

ACTIVITY 1

A sole trader has just started a business and has asked you to explain whether his business will have to undergo a statutory audit and, if not, what benefits he may derive from having an audit performed on a voluntary basis.

Outline the main points which you would make in reply to his enquiry.

For a suggested answer, see the 'Answers' section at the end of the book.

3 INTERNATIONAL STANDARDS ON AUDITING

3.1 INTRODUCTION

The organisation and structure of the auditing profession will, of course, vary from country to country. Knowledge of how the profession operates in any given country is beyond the scope of this exam.

However, there is a clear movement towards harmonisation of both auditing and accounting standards throughout the world. All companies listed in the European Union have been required to use International Financial Reporting Standards (IFRSs) since January 2005 and the use of International Standards on Auditing (ISAs) has been a requirement in the EU since 2004.

The purpose of ISAs is twofold:

- **Harmonisation** of auditing procedures, so that users of audit services are confident in the nature of audits being conducted around the world.

- Focus on **audit quality,** so that the expectations of users are met.

The **IFAC Code of Ethics and Conduct** sets standards of conduct for professional accountants and states the fundamental principles that should be observed.

International Standards on Quality Control (ISQCs) provide guidance to auditors in their responsibilities to maintain good quality control over their audit engagements.

International Standards on Auditing (ISAs) provide guidance to auditors in carrying out their audit engagements. The basic principles and essential procedures (identified in each ISA in bold lettering) are mandatory guidance. Other guidance is only advisory in status.

International Auditing Practice Statements (IAPSs) provide practical assistance to auditors in interpreting and implementing standards and promote good practice. They are not intended to have the authority of standards.

International auditing and accounting standards do not at present override local regulations. Currently, organisations cannot be compelled to comply with international standards; nor are there specific IFAC sanctions where organisations claim to have complied with international standards, but have not done so. However, this situation will change as more and more countries adopt international standards rather than imposing their own domestic standards. For example, all listed European companies have been required to adopt international accounting standards since 2005, and the UK and Ireland have required all audits to be carried out in compliance with ISAs since December 2004.

3.2 SCOPE OF INTERNATIONAL STANDARDS ON AUDITING

The International Standards on Auditing (ISAs) are grouped into six main categories – General Principles, Risk Assessment and Response, Audit Evidence, Using the Works of Others, Conclusions and Reporting, and Specialised Areas.

Each ISA has a uniform style:

- Introduction – introductory material may include information regarding the purpose, scope and subject matter of the ISA, in addition to the responsibilities of the auditors and others in the context on which the ISA is set.

- Objective – each ISA contains a clear statement of the objective of the auditor in the audit area addressed by that ISA.

- Definitions – for greater understanding of the ISAs, applicable terms have been defined in each ISA.

- Requirements – each objective is supported by clearly stated requirements. Requirements are always expressed by the phrase 'the auditor shall'.

- Application and other explanatory material – this explains more precisely what a requirement means or is intended to cover, or includes examples of procedures that may be appropriate under given circumstances.

3.3 DEVELOPMENT OF INTERNATIONAL STANDARDS ON AUDITING

The stages are similar to those in developing accounting standards:

- an Exposure Draft is issued with a request for comments by a specified date
- the comments are reviewed and, where appropriate, the draft amended
- the ISA is issued with a specified implementation date.

4 THE RELATIONSHIP BETWEEN AUDITING AND ACCOUNTING

Auditing and accounting are closely connected but separate activities. The directors of a company are responsible for establishing records which will accurately record transactions and which are used for preparing the annual financial statements. It is similarly the responsibility of the directors to adopt consistent and appropriate accounting policies in order to prepare the financial statements. For the purposes of this exam, we assume that the financial statements have to comply with legislative requirements and International Accounting Standards (IASs) and International Financial Reporting Standards (IFRSs). The International Accounting Standards Board (IASB) assumed responsibility for setting these accounting standards from 1 April 2001. There is also a conceptual accounting framework in issue (the Framework) which sets out the concepts that underlie the preparation and presentation of the financial statements for users.

Auditors are primarily concerned with the end result of this work i.e. do the financial statements show a 'true and fair' view? In order to arrive at their conclusion the auditors must have a deep knowledge and understanding of accounting (including applicable accounting standards) and, in practice, the directors will consult with the auditors as to appropriate accounting policies to follow.

CONCLUSION

This chapter gives you a basis for studying the detail of audit regulation and procedures which are dealt with in later chapters.

As a result of studying the contents of this chapter you should have gained a general understanding of the role and structure of an audit.

You should note that most of what follows is dealing with the statutory (external) audit. The overriding objective of this is for an independent professional accountant to establish and be able to report whether the financial statements present a true and fair view.

KEY TERMS

Audit – The independent examination of evidence from which the financial statements of an enterprise are derived in order to give the reader of those statements confidence as to the 'truth and fairness' of the state of affairs which they disclose.

Fiduciary relationship – A relationship of 'trust and good faith' such as that between a trustee and a beneficiary, and between directors and shareholders.

International Standards on Auditing (ISAs) – Statements containing basic principles and essential procedures for the auditor to follow together with related guidance in the form of explanatory and other material.

International Financial Reporting Standards (IFRSs) – Pronouncements issued by the International Accounting Standards Board providing guidance in respect of the treatment and disclosure of accounting items in the financial statements.

SELF TEST QUESTIONS

		Paragraph
1	What is an audit?	1.2
2	What does the concept of divorce of ownership from control mean?	1.3
3	What are the main advantages of the typical external audit?	2.2
4	Distinguish between an ISA and an IAPS.	3.1

FAU: FOUNDATIONS IN AUDIT

PRACTICE QUESTION 1

KID BROTHER

Your younger brother has written to you stating that he is contemplating following your footsteps into the accountancy and auditing profession. However, he is finding difficulty in understanding the nature and purposes of an audit and he has asked for your assistance.

Write an appropriate letter, in language that a layperson can understand, describing an audit, with particular emphasis on its nature and purposes.

(Use fictitious names and addresses. Marks will be awarded specifically for style as well as for content.)

(Total: 20 marks)

For a suggested answer, see the 'Answers' section at the end of the book.

PRACTICE QUESTION 2

(a) Give a definition of an audit, and explain the significance of the terms therein.

(Total: 10 marks)

For a suggested answer, see the 'Answers' section at the end of the book.

Chapter 2
PROFESSIONAL ETHICS

INTRODUCTION

This chapter deals with the ethical framework within which auditors are required to operate. Ethics can be thought of as dealing with standards of acceptable behaviour, or questions of right and wrong. The statutory position of the external auditor, standing between the shareholders and the directors, means that it is important that both parties and society as a whole, can rely on the auditor to behave in a proper manner. The standard of behaviour expected of the auditor is the main subject matter of this chapter. The ACCA have issued a Code of Ethics and Conduct to give guidance to ACCA members on these difficult issues.

This chapter covers syllabus area A (3).

CONTENTS

1. The ethical base of auditing
2. Fundamental principles
3. Confidentiality
4. Integrity, objectivity and independence

LEARNING OUTCOMES

At the end of this chapter, you should be able to:

- apply the ethical guidelines and fundamental principles set down by ACCA
- appreciate the importance of confidentiality and security procedures and reflect these in carrying out audit assignments
- explain why independence is a fundamental concept to the auditor.

FAU: FOUNDATIONS IN AUDIT

1 THE ETHICAL BASE OF AUDITING

1.1 INTRODUCTION

There are a number of ethical matters which are extremely important for auditors to consider when performing their work. It is vital to the public image and credibility of the profession that the auditor is **seen** to be behaving in an acceptable manner in addition to actually complying with the ethical requirements. All the major accountancy bodies including ACCA have laid down their ethical guidelines which members (including student members!) are expected to adhere to. A summary of the guidance provided by ACCA's Rules of Professional Conduct is set out below.

1.2 GUIDELINES ON PROFESSIONAL ETHICS

It is important to recognise that many groups in society rely on the accountant's work, not just the shareholders on whose behalf the accountant is working. The accountant therefore has a public accountability.

In the light of this, the ACCA have issued a Code of Ethics and Conduct which emphasise the following key points about the characteristics of accountants.

The accounting profession, and this includes the accounting technician part of it, is distinguished by the following characteristics:

(a) mastering of particular skills and techniques acquired by training and education

(b) development of an ethical approach to the work, and to clients, acquired by experience and professional supervision under training and safeguarded by a strict disciplinary code

(c) acceptance of duties to society as a whole in addition to duties to the employer or the client

(d) an outlook which is essentially objective

(e) rendering personal services to a high standard of conduct and performance.

The key requirements that need to be met in order to achieve these objectives of the accountancy profession are seen to be:

(a) credibility – the public needs to be able to believe in the auditing profession

(b) professionalism – auditors should behave in a professional manner which emphasises client service

(c) quality of service – clients and others have a right to expect a service which is delivered to a high technical standard

(d) confidence – the public needs to be able to rely on the work of the auditing profession.

2 FUNDAMENTAL PRINCIPLES

The ACCA Code of Ethics and Conduct, which is derived from that of the International Federation of Accountants (IFAC), applies to both ACCA members and student members. The Code states that, in order to achieve the objectives of the accountancy profession as discussed above, ACCA members and student members should comply with a number of 'prerequisites' (fundamental principles) as detailed below:

(a) Integrity

Definition An accountant should be straightforward and honest in all professional and business relationships. Integrity implies fair dealing and truthfulness.

(b) Objectivity and independence

Definition An accountant should not compromise professional or business judgement because of bias, conflict of interest or undue influence of others.

(c) Professional competence and due care

Definition An accountant should:

(i) Attain and retain professional knowledge and skill at the level required to ensure that a client or employing organisation receives competent professional service, based on current technical and professional standards and relevant legislation; and

(ii) Act diligently and in accordance with applicable technical and professional standards.

(d) Confidentiality

Definition An accountant should respect the confidentiality of information acquired as a result of professional and business relationships.

An accountant should use or disclose any such information only with proper and specific authority or where there is a legal or professional right or duty to disclose.

(e) Professional behaviour

Definition An accountant should comply with relevant laws and regulations and avoid any conduct that the accountant knows or should know might discredit the profession.

An accountant should not knowingly engage in any business, occupation or activity that impairs or might impair the integrity, objectivity or good reputation of the profession, and as a result would be incompatible with the fundamental ethical principles.

ACTIVITY 1

You are an audit partner in a firm of registered Auditors. A client has invited you and your spouse, together with approximately 20 other business acquaintances to an evening social function for Christmas. Which of the above fundamental principles may be at risk in this situation? Should you accept the invitation?

For a suggested answer, see the 'Answers' section at the end of the book.

3 CONFIDENTIALITY

3.1 ACCA GUIDANCE

Accounting technicians have an obligation to respect the confidentiality of information about a client's or employer's affairs acquired in the course of professional work. This duty continues even after the end of the relationship between the accounting technician and the employer or client.

There are a number of exceptions to the principle described above:

- Disclosure is required by law, for example:

    (i) Production of documents or other provision of evidence in the course of legal proceedings; or

    (ii) Disclosure to the appropriate public authorities of infringements of the law that come to light

- Disclosure is permitted by law and is authorised by the client or the employing organisation; and

- There is a professional duty or right to disclose, when not prohibited by law:

    (i) To comply with the quality review of ACCA or another professional body;

    (ii) To respond to an inquiry or investigation by ACCA or another professional or regulatory body;

    (iii) To protect the professional interests of a professional accountant in legal proceedings; or

    (iv) To comply with technical and professional standards, including ethics requirements.

ACTIVITY 2

Your firm audits X, a privately owned company which is a customer of Y, another privately owned company. The Managing Director of Y has approached your firm and asked you to supply them with details of X's bank transactions for the last six months as they are concerned about their ability to pay. State whether or not you would supply this information and the reasons for your action(s).

For a suggested answer, see the 'Answers' section at the end of the book.

3.2 CONFLICT OF INTEREST

This arises when an auditor either audits two competing companies or is asked to become auditor of a company whilst at the same time auditing a competitor. There is a risk that sensitive commercial data could be passed from one company to the other via the audit team. Perhaps most importantly, clients may perceive this to be a risk.

If the auditor can implement appropriate safeguards, such as using separate audit teams and having clear instructions, then it is possible for the auditor to proceed with both engagements. However, both clients must be informed of the situation in writing and if they oppose the arrangement the auditor should decline at least one of the engagements.

3.3 SECURITY MEASURES

It is also vital that the auditor ensures that there are adequate security measures in place which maintain client confidentiality. In the absence of appropriate security measures, confidentiality will inevitably be at risk.

Typical examples of such measures are shown below:

(a) All audit files should be securely protected at all times – they will inevitably contain confidential information. They should never be left unattended at the client's premises or in an unsecured place – more than one auditor has left client files in his or her car, which has then been stolen!

(b) Information stored on computers should also be subject to appropriate security measures to prevent unauthorised access, loss or corruption of data such as use of passwords, firewalls etc.

(c) Any information gained whilst at the client's should never be used for personal advantage.

(d) All client matters should be treated as confidential and should not be discussed with any third party, friends or family.

4 INTEGRITY, OBJECTIVITY AND INDEPENDENCE

4.1 INTRODUCTION

Auditor integrity is essential to ensure that the work and professional opinion of the auditor can be relied upon. The auditor should ensure that they perform their work in a manner which is honest and straightforward.

Examples of situations when the auditor should be able to can demonstrate that they have acted in an honest and straightforward manner include:

(a) preparation, and agreement, of a letter of engagement with each client to confirm the nature and extent of services to be provided

(b) communication in advance of the basis upon which fees will be charged, which is normally included in the letter of engagement

(c) not having a personal interest in the business activities of a client, other than as auditor and professional accountant, for which fees will be charged on an agreed basis

(d) compliance with all relevant laws and professional regulations.

Additionally, auditor independence is essential to ensure that the auditor has the ability to satisfactorily perform the audit to the required standard. It is important that, not only are auditors independent, they are **seen to be independent**.

The following paragraphs indicate a number of situations which may impair auditor integrity and objectivity. Such threats need to be managed by either implementing acceptable safeguards or declining to perform work for the client in question.

4.2 THREATS TO INTEGRITY, OBJECTIVITY AND INDEPENDENCE

Self interest threats

The threat that a financial or other interest will inappropriately influence an accountant's judgment or behaviour.

(Section numbers in the tables below are references being made to the ACCA Code of Ethics and Conduct 2019)

Threat	Safeguards
Fee dependency Over-dependence on an audit client could lead the auditor to ignore adjustments required in the financial statements for fear of losing the client.	Non-listed clients If fees from an audit client represent a large proportion of the firm's total fees, the firm should implement safeguards such as: • Reducing dependency on the client • Consulting with a third party on key audit judgments • Having an external quality control review. [Section 410.3] Listed clients A firm's independence is threatened, and should be reviewed if total fees from a listed audit client exceed 15% of the firm's total fees for two consecutive years. • The firm should disclose the issue to those charged with governance at the client. • An independent engagement quality control review should be performed by a person not a member of the audit firm expressing the opinion or by the professional regulatory body. [Section 410.4]

PROFESSIONAL ETHICS : CHAPTER 2

Threat	Safeguards
Gifts and hospitality Acceptance of goods, services or hospitality from an audit client can create self-interest and familiarity threats as the auditor may feel indebted to the client.	Gifts may be accepted if: • Trivial and inconsequential. • Offered in the normal course of business without intention to influence decision-making. [Section 420.3] The offer of gifts and hospitality must be documented in the audit file even if refused.
Owning shares/financial interests The auditor will want to maximise return from the investment and overlook audit adjustments which would affect the value of their investment.	Any member of the audit team or their immediate family must not have a financial interest in the audit client therefore they must dispose of the shares immediately or be removed from the team. Any member of the audit team who has a close family member who owns shares should be removed from the audit team or the family member should dispose of their shares. A partner of the firm in the office connected with the audit engagement, or any partner providing non-audit services to the audit client should not have a financial interest in the client. [Section 510.4]
Loans and guarantees A loan or guarantee from (or deposit with) an assurance client will not create a threat to independence provided that: • it is on commercial terms, and • made in the normal course of business.	Loans and guarantees between audit clients and audit team members and their immediate family that are not in the normal course of business or not on commercial terms are not permitted. [Section 511.5] If the loan is made to the firm (rather than a member of the audit team), it must be immaterial to both the firm and the client. If it is material, a self-interest threat may arise and appropriate safeguards should be put into place. [Section 511.7]

Threat	Safeguards
Business relationships If audit firms (or members) enter into business relationships with clients (e.g. joint ventures, marketing arrangements), this leads to self-interest because the auditor would have an interest in the successful operation of the client. The purchase of goods and services from an assurance client would not normally give rise to a threat to independence, provided the transaction is in the normal course of business and on commercial terms.	A firm or audit team member should not have a close business relationship with an audit client unless any financial interest is immaterial and the business relationship is insignificant to the client, or the audit team member. [Section 520.4] If the purchase of goods and services by an audit team member represents a material amount, that person should be removed from the audit team or they should reduce the magnitude of the transactions. [Section 520.6]
Potential employment with an audit client If a member of the engagement team has reason to believe they may become an employee of the client they will not wish to do anything to affect their potential future employment.	The policies and procedures of the firm should require such individuals to notify the firm of the possibility of employment with the client. Remove the individual from the assurance engagement. Perform an independent review of any significant judgments made by that individual. [Section 524.5]
Overdue fees The overdue fees may be regarded as a loan (loans are not permitted to an audit client).	When a significant part of fees due from an audit client remains unpaid for a long time, the firm shall determine: (a) Whether the overdue fees might be equivalent to a loan to the client; and (b) Whether it is appropriate for the firm to be re-appointed or continue the audit engagement. An independent review of the work should be performed. [Section 410.8]
Contingent fees The auditor would have incentive to ensure a particular outcome is achieved in order to maximise the audit fee. E.g. overlook audit adjustments that would reduce profit if the fee is a percentage of the profit.	Fees based on a particular outcome, e.g. level of profits of the company, are not permitted for assurance services. [Section 410.12]

Threat	Safeguards
Compensation and evaluation policies A self-interest threat is created when a member of the audit team is evaluated on or compensated for selling non-assurance services to that audit client. The significance of the threat will depend on: • The proportion of the individual's compensation or performance evaluation that is based on the sale of such services. • The role of the individual on the audit team. • Whether promotion decisions are influenced by the sale of such services.	A key audit partner shall not be evaluated on or compensated based on that partner's success in selling non-assurance services to the partner's audit client. [Section 411.4] For other staff the firm shall either revise the compensation plan or evaluation process for that individual or apply safeguards such as: • Removing such members from the audit team. • Having a professional accountant review the work of the member of the audit team. [Section 411.3]
Actual or threatened litigation Litigation could represent a breakdown of trust in the relationship between auditor and client. This may affect the impartiality of the auditor, and lead to a reluctance of management to disclose relevant information to the auditor. The significance of the threat depends on the materiality of the litigation and whether the litigation relates to a prior assurance engagement.	It may be possible to continue other assurance engagements, depending on the significance of the threat by: • Discussing the matter with the client's audit committee. • If the litigation involves an individual, removing that individual from the engagement team. • Obtaining an external review of the work done. If adequate safeguards cannot be implemented the firm must withdraw from or decline the engagement. [Section 430.3]

Familiarity threats

The threat that due to a long or close relationship with a client, or employing organisation, an accountant will be too sympathetic to their interests or too accepting of their work.

Threat	Safeguards
Long association of senior personnel Using the same senior personnel in an engagement team over a long period may cause the auditor to become too trusting/less sceptical of the client resulting in material misstatements going undetected. The firm should consider: • The length of time on the audit team. • The structure of the firm. • Whether the client's management team has changed. • Whether the complexity of the subject matter has changed.	Non-listed clients • Rotate senior personnel. • Independent partner/quality control reviews. [Section 540.3] Listed clients • The engagement partner, Engagement Quality Control Reviewer (EQCR) or any other key audit partner must be rotated after no more than seven years (the 'time-on' period'). If the client becomes listed, the length of time the partner has served before becoming listed is taken into account. [Section 540.5] • In exceptional circumstances, a maximum one year extension is permitted where necessary to maintain audit quality. [Section 540.7] After the time-on period, the individual shall serve a 'cooling-off period'. – If the individual acted as the engagement partner for seven cumulative years, the cooling-off period shall be five consecutive years. [Section 540.11] – Where the individual has been appointed as responsible for the engagement quality control review and has acted in that capacity for seven cumulative years, the cooling-off period shall be three consecutive years. [Section 540.12] – If the individual has acted as a key audit partner other than in the capacities set out above, for seven cumulative years, the cooling-off period shall be two consecutive years. [Section 540.13] **Tutorial note:** Large listed companies must put the audit out to tender at least every ten years. However, this is the responsibility of the company not the audit firm.

PROFESSIONAL ETHICS : CHAPTER 2

Threat	Safeguards
Family and other personal relationships A familiarity threat (and self-interest threat or intimidation threat) may occur when a member of the engagement team has a family or personal relationship with someone at the client who is able to exert significant influence over the financial statements (or subject matter of another assurance engagement). Consideration should be given to the possibility that such a threat may also arise when a partner (or employee) of the firm has a family or personal relationship with someone at the client who is able to exert significant influence over the subject matter, even when the individual is not a member of the engagement team.	Remove the individual from the engagement team. Structure the engagement team so that the individual does not deal with matters that are the responsibility of the close family member. [Section 521.4]
Recruitment services Familiarity, self-interest and intimidation threats may occur if the firm is involved in recruiting senior personnel for the client. The firm may also be considered to be assuming management responsibilities. Reviewing qualifications and interviewing applicants to advise on financial competence is allowed.	Recruitment services may be provided to an audit client provided the client makes all management decisions including determining the suitability of the candidate, selecting a suitable candidate, determining employment terms and negotiating remuneration. [Section 609.4] The firm cannot provide recruitment services in respect of directors or senior management who would be in a position to exert significant influence over the financial statements. [Section 609.7]
Audit staff leave the firm to join the client A self-interest, familiarity or intimidation threat may arise where an employee of the firm becomes a director or employee of an assurance client (in a position to exert significant influence over the financial statements or subject matter of another assurance engagement). The threat is significant if significant connection remains between the employee and the firm such as entitlement to benefits or payments from the firm, or participation in the firm's business and professional activities. The firm should consider: • The position taken at the client. • The involvement the person is likely to have with the audit team. • The length of time since the individual was a member of the audit team.	Assign individuals to the audit team who have sufficient experience in relation to the individual who has joined the client. Perform a quality control review of the engagement. [Section 524.4] For partners joining public interest entities, independence would be deemed to be compromised unless, subsequent to the partner ceasing to be a key audit partner or senior partner, the public interest entity had issued audited financial statements covering a period of not less than twelve months and the partner was not a member of the audit team with respect to the audit of those financial statements. [Section 524.6]

KAPLAN PUBLISHING

Self-review threats

The threat that an accountant will not appropriately evaluate the results of a previous judgment made; or an activity performed by the accountant, or by another individual within the accountant's firm or employing organisation, on which the accountant will rely when forming a judgment as part of performing a current activity.

Threat	Safeguards
Accounting and bookkeeping services	Non-listed clients • A firm can provide a non-listed audit client with accounting and bookkeeping services, including payroll services, of a routine or mechanical nature. • Separate teams must be used.
	• Managerial decisions must not be made by the firm, and the source data, underlying assumptions, and subsequent adjustments must be originated or approved by the client. [Section 601.5] Listed clients • A firm cannot provide a listed audit client with accounting and bookkeeping services. [Section 601.6] • A firm can provide accounting services for divisions or related entities of a listed client if separate teams are used and the service relates to matters immaterial to the division/related entity. [Section 601.7]
Internal audit services In addition to the self-review threat, the auditor needs to be careful not to assume management responsibilities.	A firm cannot provide internal audit services for a listed audit client, where the service relates to internal controls over financial reporting, financial accounting systems, or in relation to amounts or disclosures that are material to the financial statements. Where services are provided, separate teams must be used. [Section 605.4]

Threat	Safeguards
Taxation services Tax calculations for inclusion in the financial statements and tax planning advice create a self-review threat. Completion of tax returns is **not** deemed to create a self-review threat.	Non-listed clients • Advice should be obtained from an external tax professional. • Where an audit team member performs the tax calculation the work should be reviewed by a senior person with appropriate expertise that has not been involved with the audit. [Section 604.5]
	Listed clients • A firm cannot prepare tax calculations for a listed audit client where the figures are material to the financial statements. Where the figures are immaterial, the safeguards for non-listed clients should be applied. [Section 604.6]
Tax advice	The firm should not provide tax advice that depends on a particular accounting treatment and is material to the financial statements. Other tax advice is allowable with safeguards. [Section 604.7]
IT services IT services may create a self-review threat and also be considered to be assuming management responsibilities. The firm can provide IT services which involve: • Design or implementation of IT systems unrelated to internal controls or financial reporting. • Implementation of off-the-shelf accounting software. • Evaluating and making recommendations on a system designed or operated by another service provider or by the entity.	All clients When providing such services, the firm should use professionals who are not audit team members to perform the service. The audit firm must be satisfied that management takes full responsibility for the IT controls and systems. [Section 606.3 Section 606.4] Listed clients A firm shall not provide IT systems services to a listed client that form a significant part of the internal controls over financial reporting or generate information that is significant to the financial statements. [Section 606.5]

FAU: FOUNDATIONS IN AUDIT

Threat	Safeguards
Valuation services	All clients • Use professionals who are not audit team members to perform the service. • Have an appropriate reviewer who was not involved in providing the service review the audit work or service performed. [Section 603.3] Non-listed clients Valuation services shall not be provided to audit clients if the valuation involves a significant degree of subjectivity and the valuation will have a material effect on the financial statements. [Section R603.4] Listed clients Valuation services that are material to the financial statements (regardless of subjectivity) should not be provided to listed audit clients. [Section R603.5]
Temporary staff assignments A self-review threat will be created if staff are loaned from the audit firm to the client. If the person was assigned to the audit they would be evaluating work for which they had been responsible during the temporary assignment and may not detect errors in their work.	Staff may be loaned to the client provided: • The loan period is short. • The person does not assume management responsibilities. • The client is responsible for directing and supervising the person. • The loaned staff member is not a member of the audit team. Additional review must be carried out of the work performed by the loaned personnel and the loaned personnel must not be on the audit team. [Section 525.3]

Threat	Safeguards

Corporate finance services
 	
Self-review and advocacy threats may be created if a firm:
 	
• Assists an audit client in developing corporate strategies
 	
• Identifies possible targets for the audit client to acquire
 	
• Advises on disposal transactions
 	
• Assists finance raising transactions
 	
• Provides structuring advice.
 	
Consideration should be given to:
 	
• The degree of subjectivity involved.
 	
• Whether the outcome will have a material impact on the financial statements.
 	
• Whether the effectiveness of the corporate finance advice depends on a particular accounting treatment.
	Where services can be provided:
	
	• Use professionals who are not audit team members to perform the service.
	
	• Have an appropriate reviewer who was not involved in providing the service review the audit work or service performed.
	
	[Section 610.3]
	
	Prohibited services
	
	• Corporate finance services that involve promoting, dealing in, or underwriting the audit client's shares.
	
	[Section 610.4]
	
	• Corporate finance services where
	
	   – the effectiveness of the advice depends on a particular accounting treatment or presentation in the financial statements
	
	   – the audit team has reasonable doubt as to the appropriateness of the accounting treatment, and
	
	   – the outcome will have a material effect of the financial statements.
	
	[Section 610.5]

Client staff joins audit firm A self-interest, self-review, or familiarity threat may arise where a director or employee of an assurance client (in a position to exert significant influence over the financial statements or subject matter of another assurance engagement) becomes an employee of the firm.	Such individuals should not be assigned to the audit if that person would be evaluating elements of the financial statements for which they had prepared accounting records. An employee or partner of a firm cannot also be an employee or director of an assurance client, as the self-interest and self-review threats created would be so significant that no safeguard could reduce the threats to an acceptable level. [Section 522.3]

Advocacy threats

The threat that an accountant will promote a client's or employing organisation's position to the point that the accountant's objectivity is compromised.

Examples include:

- Representing the client in court or in any dispute where the matter is material to the financial statements.

- Negotiating on the client's behalf for finance.

    Where the amounts are material the audit firm must not act for the audit client in this way. Any request for such services must be politely declined.

    Where the matter is not material to the financial statements the firm should:

- Use professionals who are not members of the audit team to perform the service, or

- Have a professional who was not involved in providing the legal services advise the audit team on the service and review any financial statement treatment.

Providing services involving promoting, dealing in, or underwriting an audit client's shares would create an advocacy or self-review threat so significant that no safeguards could reduce the threat to an acceptable level. Accordingly, a firm shall not provide such services to an audit client.

Intimidation threats

The threat that an accountant will be deterred from acting objectively because of actual or perceived pressures, including attempts to exercise undue influence over the accountant.

Intimidation can arise from some of the same situations mentioned above, for example:

- Fee dependency

- Personal relationships

- Audit partner joining the client

- Litigation between the audit firm and client.

The safeguards to address these threats are the same as to address the other threats.

If the threat cannot be eliminated or reduced to an acceptable level, the assurance provider must decline or resign from the engagement.

CONCLUSION

Independence and confidentiality are very important principles which have given rise to detailed rules set down by the ACCA and the IFAC to regulate the behaviour of auditors in these and in other areas of professional behaviour. It is important to remember that the auditor must not only behave ethically – the auditor must also be seen to behave ethically. The public perception of the auditor's standards of behaviour is vital to the credibility of the audit process.

In the case of listed and other large companies, the role of the audit committee is becoming an increasingly important element in the audit process.

KEY TERMS

Ethics – Standards of acceptable behaviour.

Integrity – Straightforwardness and honesty in carrying out professional work.

Objectivity and independence – Fairness and freedom from bias, prejudice and undue influence.

Confidentiality – Respect for the privacy of information relating to clients' affairs.

SELF TEST QUESTIONS

Paragraph

1 What are the key factors required to be met to achieve the ethical objectives of the accountancy profession?   1.2

2 What are the ACCA's fundamental principles that have been established to meet these ethical objectives?   2

3 What threat does the acceptance of gifts off clients create?   4

4 What threat might arise if an auditor provides other services to an audit client?

FAU: FOUNDATIONS IN AUDIT

EXAM-STYLE QUESTION 1

You are the junior auditor in a small audit firm. One of the audit partners has asked you to prepare a briefing document for distribution to the firm's employees regarding the independence of the auditor. The partner wants to make sure that the firm complies with the relevant ACCA rules.

Prepare a memo for distribution to the firm's staff stating the ACCA's Rules of Professional Conduct which strengthen the independence of the auditor. **(Total 15 marks)**

For a suggested answer, see the 'Answers' section at the end of the book.

EXAM-STYLE QUESTION 2

You are the junior auditor in a small audit firm. One of the audit partners has asked you to prepare a briefing document for distribution to the firm's employees regarding the independence of the auditor. The partner wants to make sure that the firm complies with the relevant ACCA rules.

Summarise, in a memorandum to the audit partner, further ways as to how the independence of the auditor could be improved. **(Total 10 marks)**

For a suggested answer, see the 'Answers' section at the end of the book.

Chapter 3
STATUTORY AUDITS

INTRODUCTION

This chapter deals with the statutory regulation of auditors and auditing. Together with the codes of conduct imposed on auditors by the professional accountancy bodies dealt with in the previous chapters, it provides a framework within which auditors operate.

It is, of course, the case that the statutory regulation of auditing will vary internationally. This chapter gives an overview of the typical statutory regime; this will vary by country. For examination purposes you will not be expected to have knowledge of the regime operating in any particular country.

This chapter covers syllabus areas A (2) and (5).

CONTENTS

1 The audit requirement

2 Auditors' rights and duties

3 Engagement considerations

LEARNING OUTCOMES

At the end of this chapter, you should be able to:

- understand the general legal framework within which auditors operate
- appreciate both the rights available to the auditor and the duties that the auditor is required to carry out.
- appreciate the duties of directors
- understand the factors to consider before an audit is accepted and the need for engagement letters.

1 THE AUDIT REQUIREMENT

In most countries, not all limited companies are required to have their financial statements audited. Nor are all companies required to produce financial statements in the same formats, as many exemptions may apply to small and medium-sized companies.

If the United Kingdom is used as an example, small companies are normally exempt from the audit requirement, small and medium-sized companies may file abbreviated accounts with the registrar of companies and small companies may prepare accounts with reduced disclosures for their members.

According to the Companies Act 2006 in the United Kingdom, all companies must keep proper accounting records which disclose the financial position of the company. This requires records of cash payments and receipts; assets; and liabilities. A private company must retain these accounting records for three years from the date on which they were made and a public company must retain the records for six years.

From these accounting records, financial statements can be produced for each financial period that give a true and fair view of the company at the end of the accounting period and of the profit and loss of the company for that period. This is the duty of directors and is discussed again in section 5.3.

2 AUDITORS' RIGHTS AND DUTIES

2.1 INTRODUCTION

The auditor will typically have various detailed duties to perform in order to achieve the overall duty to report on whether the financial statements present a true and fair view. In order to fulfil these duties, various rights (or powers) are often given to the auditor.

The terms 'rights' and 'duties' are frequently used legal terms. You may want to think of 'duties' in terms of 'what the auditor is expected to do' and 'rights' as 'the authority which the auditor possesses – the power to carry out his duties'.

2.2 DUTIES OF THE AUDITOR

The typical duties of the auditor are:

(a) To report to the members on whether the financial statements of the company show a true and fair view and have been properly prepared in accordance with appropriate legislation.

(b) To consider whether the information in published documents which have not been specifically audited, such as the Directors' Report (often required to be published as part of the company's annual report and accounts) is consistent with the financial statements and if not, to state the fact in his report.

(c) To give the details required by statute in the auditor's report, if not given in the financial statements themselves. These might include, for example:

   (i) particulars of directors' emoluments, pensions and compensation for loss of office

   (ii) details of loans to officers

   (iii) particulars of any directors' emoluments waived

   (iv) disclosure of transactions involving directors and other connected persons.

(d) To form an opinion as to whether certain defined statutory requirements have been complied with by the company. Examples from UK law include:

   (i) proper accounting records have been kept by the company

   (ii) proper returns adequate for their audit have been received from branches not visited by them (where applicable)

   (iii) the company's statements of financial position and comprehensive income are in agreement with the accounting records and returns

   (iv) such information and explanations as he (the auditor) thinks necessary for the performance of his duties have been received from the company's officers.

(e) To send a statement of the reasons for ceasing to hold office if the engagement relates to a company in the public interest. An auditor of a non-public interest company will also have to send a statement to the company unless the auditor's term of office has come to an end or the auditor's reasons for leaving are all 'exempt reasons' (e.g. the auditor is ceasing to act as an auditor) and there are no matters that need to be brought to the attention of members or creditors of the company.

The following was outlined in an earlier chapter, but it is important to remember that the auditor usually has **no** specific statutory duty to detect fraud. However, if a material fraud affects the truth and fairness of the financial statements then this should be detected by audit work; the auditor has a duty to design procedures to give reasonable assurance of detecting material misstatements whether caused by fraud or error.

2.3 DUTIES OF THE DIRECTORS

In the UK, for example, the directors' statutory duties primarily come from the responsibilities laid out in the Companies Act 2006. The principal duties are as follows:

(a) Safeguarding assets of the company. The directors must take reasonable steps for the prevention and detection of fraud and other irregularities.

(b) Keeping proper accounting records which disclose with reasonable accuracy at any time the financial position of the company. This requires records of: cash payments and receipts; assets; and liabilities.

(c) Preparing financial statements for each financial period that give a true and fair view of the affairs of the company at the end of the accounting period and of the profit or loss of the company for that period.

2.4 RIGHTS OF THE AUDITOR

The rights or powers given to auditors by legislation are designed to ensure that they are able to fulfil their duties and responsibilities to the members. These rights are fundamental to their independence.

In many countries, the typical statutory rights of the auditor are as follows:

(a) The right of access at all times to the books, records, documents and accounts of the company.

The auditor must obviously exercise this right with discretion so as not to disrupt unnecessarily the company's operations. Equally, if the client refuses access to the records, the auditor would never seek access to them forcibly, or even through the courts. The auditor would instead consider either resigning or modifying the auditor's report.

Auditors have to report to members if in their view proper accounting records have not been maintained and this could not be done without the right of access to such records.

(b) The right to require from the officers (principally directors) of the company such information and explanations as the auditors think necessary for the performance of their duties.

The auditors must report to members if they have not received the explanations or information required. It follows that they must be given the right to require such information and explanations.

An officer intentionally making a false statement to the auditors, knowing it to be false, may be committing a criminal offence.

(c) The right to:

   (i)   receive all notices relating to any shareholder meeting of the company

   (ii)   attend any shareholder meeting

   (iii)   be heard at any shareholder meeting on any part of the business which concerns them as auditor.

It is obviously important for the proper discharge of their duties that the auditor should be aware at first hand of what happens at meetings. Their right to speak at a meeting does *NOT*, if exercised, relieve them of their duty to make a comprehensive auditor's report to the members at the end of the audit process.

(d) The right to be sent by the company a copy of a notice of intention to propose their removal or replacement and the right to make written representations.

(e) The right to require the directors to requisition an extraordinary general meeting on their resignation and to attend and be heard at that and any other meeting which concerns them.

ACTIVITY 1

State what the auditors' overall duty to the members is and describe two specific duties and two rights generally provided to the auditor under statute to enable them to perform this duty.

For a suggested answer, see the 'Answers' section at the end of the book.

3 ENGAGEMENT CONSIDERATIONS

3.1 FACTORS TO CONSIDER BEFORE ACCEPTING AN AUDIT

Before an audit engagement can be accepted, an auditor must consider various factors which will affect the decision on whether or not to carry out the audit.

Those factors include:

(a) Ensuring that the potential client will agree to certain conditions such as allowing the auditor access to all the information that will be required for the auditor and that the directors will produce the financial statements in accordance with the Financial Reporting Standards used in that particular country

(b) Asking the potential client for permission to contact the previous auditor. The new audit will ask for information relevant to the decision whether or not to accept the appointment

(c) Ensuring there are no threats to the auditor's independence and objectivity

(d) Making an assessment of management's integrity

(e) Complying with any money laundering regulations (client due diligence)

(f) Ensuring the audit firm has the resources to carry out the engagement

(g) Assessing any risks at the potential client like poor internal control systems

(h) Discussing the fee and ensuring this is sufficient to perform the required work

(i) Ensuring the audit firm has the necessary skills to carry out the audit, and

(j) Whether the audit firm wants to be associated with the client (the client may have a poor reputation)

If any of the factors cannot be satisfied then the audit firm will not accept the new engagement.

3.2 ENGAGEMENT LETTERS

If the factors above are satisfied, then the audit firm will issue an engagement letter to the new client. This letter forms the contract between the audit firm and the audit client.

The main purposes of an engagement letter are to:

- minimise the risk of misunderstanding between the auditor and the client
- confirm acceptance of the engagement
- set out the terms and conditions of the engagement.

The letter is sent prior to the audit commencing. It will be reviewed each year although it does not have to be sent again unless there are significant changes in the audit or changes in client management.

Many audit firms do re-issue the engagement letter each year anyway as a method of reminding the client's management of the purpose of the audit.

Typical contents of an engagement letter include:

- the objective and scope of the audit
- the responsibilities of the auditor
- the responsibilities of management
- identification of the applicable financial reporting framework
- the expected form and content of the auditor's report.

CONCLUSION

Legislation will often set out a framework to regulate the appointment, removal, resignation and retirement of auditors. In many instances, safeguards are in place which are designed to ensure that, as far as possible, auditor independence is preserved.

Legislation will also impose a series of duties on the auditor which should be adhered to by anyone accepting an audit appointment. In order to put the auditor in a position to be able to perform these duties effectively, the legislation will back up the auditor by means of a powerful series of statutory rights or powers.

By covering the first three chapters of this text you have now studied the overall professional and statutory framework within which auditors operate.

KEY TERMS

Duties of the auditor – That which law requires the auditor to do.

Rights of the auditor – The powers given to the auditor by law.

SELF TEST QUESTIONS

		Paragraph
1	What are the typical statutory duties of the auditor?	2.2
2	What are the principal rights of an auditor?	2.4

EXAM-STYLE QUESTION 1

THE GROWFAST COMPANY

The Growfast Company was formed on 1 August 20X0 in order to manufacture minicomputers. The directors are unsure as to their responsibilities, and the nature of their relationship with the external auditors. The audit partner has asked you to visit the client and explain to the directors the more fundamental aspects of the accountability.

You are required to explain to the directors of Growfast:

(a) why there is a need for an audit **(5 marks)**

(b) the responsibilities of the directors in relation to the accounting function of the company. **(5 marks)**

(Total: 10 marks)

For a suggested answer, see the 'Answers' section at the end of the book.

Chapter 4

AUDITING CONCEPTS: TRUE AND FAIR, MATERIALITY

INTRODUCTION

The concept of divorce of ownership from control (introduced in Chapter 1) is seen to be a specific application of a general principle which has a wide range of applications – agency theory. This chapter takes as its starting point agency theory in the context of auditing and then introduces the role of the auditor's report as a means of the auditor communicating with company shareholders. Central to any discussion of the auditor's report is an exploration of two familiar and important but rather judgemental concepts – true and fair view and materiality.

This chapter covers syllabus areas A (1) and B (1).

CONTENTS

1. The auditor's report as a means of communication
2. True and fair
3. Materiality
4. Professional scepticism and professional judgement

LEARNING OUTCOMES

At the end of this chapter, you should be able to:

- appreciate the purpose and principal contents of the auditor's report
- understand the meaning of the true and fair view/present fairly concept
- appreciate the meaning of the concept of materiality and the role which it plays in the audit process
- understand the concept of reasonable assurance
- understand the concepts of professional scepticism and professional judgement and how and when they should be exercised during an audit.

1 THE AUDITOR'S REPORT AS A MEANS OF COMMUNICATION

1.1 THE EXTERNAL AUDITOR'S REPORT

The external auditor's report is the primary method of communication between the auditor and the shareholders of the company whose financial statements have been subject to audit. The auditor's report is typically the only output the shareholders see as the result of what is often a lengthy (and expensive) audit process. The auditor's report is therefore seen to be a very important communication document.

Not only is the auditor's report usually the only means of communication between the auditor and the shareholders, it is also a very condensed form of communication, usually covering no more than a single page, but it carries a very important message from the auditor. The structure, content and wording of the report is therefore seen to be very important, to ensure that the correct meaning of the auditor's opinion is communicated to the readers of the report as clearly as possible in such a concise form.

In order to help with this process the auditor's report has become a standardised document. The detailed content and format of the auditor's report is dealt with more fully in a later chapter.

1.2 THE STANDARD UNMODIFIED AUDITOR'S REPORT

When the auditor has completed the detailed audit work they will form and report an opinion on whether the financial statements that have been subject to audit present a true and fair view.

We shall assume for the purpose of this chapter that the auditor can conclude that a true and fair view is presented (the implications for the auditor's report where the auditor cannot come to this conclusion are dealt with in a later chapter). In this case the auditor can issue an **unmodified** auditor's report and opinion, so called because the wording is unaltered from the standard wording presented in ISA 700 *Forming an Opinion and Reporting on Financial Statements*.

The standard format and wording of the opinion from ISA 700 is presented below:

Unmodified auditor's report opinion

In our opinion the financial statements give a true and fair view of (or 'present fairly') the financial position of ABC Company as at December 31, 20X1, and of its financial performance and its cash flows for the year then ended in accordance with International Financial Reporting Standards.

ACTIVITY 1

Why not obtain a set of published financial statements of a company and review its contents? (The accounts of many larger companies can be usually be viewed or downloaded from the company website.) Compare it with the example auditor's report reproduced below (as introduced in Chapter 1 of this publication).

You should specifically examine the auditor's report to familiarise yourself with the layout and wording used. Bear in mind that individual auditors may vary the wording from that used in the example report below and specific legal requirements to which the company is subject may also require different wording to be used, but the basic form and content should be very similar.

INDEPENDENT AUDITOR'S REPORT TO...................[appropriate addressee]

Opinion

We have audited the financial statements of ABC Company (the Company), which comprise the statement of financial position as at December 31, 20X1, and the statement of comprehensive income, statement of changes in equity and statement of cash flows for the year then ended, and notes to the financial statements, including a summary of significant accounting policies.

In our opinion, the accompanying financial statements present fairly, in all material respects, (*or give a true and fair view of*) the financial position of the Company as at December 31, 20X1, and (*of*) its financial performance and its cash flows for the year then ended in accordance with International Financial Reporting Standards (IFRSs).

Basis for Opinion

We conducted our audit in accordance with International Standards on Auditing (ISAs). Our responsibilities under those standards are further described in the Auditor's Responsibilities for the Audit of the Financial Statements section of our report. We are independent of the Company in accordance with the International Ethics Standards Board for Accountants' Code of Ethics for Professional Accountants (IESBA Code) together with the ethical requirements that are relevant to our audit of the financial statements in [jurisdiction], and have fulfilled our other ethical responsibilities in accordance with these requirements and the IESBA Code. We believe that the audit evidence we have obtained is sufficient and appropriate to provide a basis for our opinion.

Key Audit Matters

Key audit matters are those matters that, in our professional judgment, were of most significance in our audit of the financial statements of the current period. These matters were addressed in the context of our audit of the financial statements as a whole, and in forming our opinion thereon, and we do not provide a separate opinion on these matters.

[Description of each key audit matter in accordance with ISA 701]

Responsibilities of Management and Those Charged with Governance for the Financial Statements

Management is responsible for the preparation and fair presentation of these financial statements in accordance with IFRSs, and for such internal control as management determines is necessary to enable the preparation of financial statements that are free from material misstatement, whether due to fraud or error.

In preparing the financial statements, management is responsible for assessing the Company's ability to continue as a going concern, disclosing, as applicable, matters related to going concern and using the going concern basis of accounting unless management either intends to liquidate the Company or to cease operations, or has no realistic alternative but to do so.

Those charged with governance are responsible for overseeing the Company's financial reporting process.

Auditor's Responsibilities for the Audit of the Financial Statements

Our objectives are to obtain reasonable assurance about whether the financial statements as a whole are free from material misstatement, whether due to fraud or error, and to issue an auditor's report that includes our opinion. Reasonable assurance is a high level of assurance, but is not a guarantee that an audit conducted in accordance with ISAs will always detect a material misstatement when it exists. Misstatements can arise from fraud or error and are considered material if, individually or in the aggregate, they could reasonably be expected to influence the economic decisions of users taken on the basis of these financial statements.

[Auditor's signature]

[Date of the auditor's report]

[Auditor's address]

There is no feedback to this activity.

2 TRUE AND FAIR

Perhaps the most significant phrase in the auditor's report is the reference to true and fair view (an alternative wording is that the financial statements are 'fairly presented.' Both phrases have identical meanings).

It is clearly very important that both auditors and users of the report sound appreciation of the meaning. Unfortunately, the precise definition has never been formally agreed.

Everyday meanings of the word true include: factually correct, not false, and accurate. Unfortunately it is not possible to confirm if the financial statements as a whole are factually accurate. The two key reasons are: that the auditor cannot investigate every single transaction and balance and, for that reason, must adopt a sample testing basis; and that certain components of the financial statements cannot be measured with certainty. The latter point refers mainly to the existence of estimates and judgements in the financial statements, for example; the useful economic life of an asset or a provision for future, uncertain costs.

Everyday meanings of the term fair include: *reasonable, unbiased, impartial, and equitable.* Again, as the auditor performs testing on a sample basis, it would be impossible to conclude that the financial statements are entirely free of management bias. It is also important to remember that the estimates made by the business are made by internal managers, all of whom have a self-interest in the profitability of the business (bonuses!).

The concept of 'true and fair' is dynamic and subject to change over time. What is regarded as 'true and fair' will be a matter of judgement for individual auditors and will be subject to a number of factors, such as:

- Statutory requirements for the preparation and presentation of financial statements – what does the law require to be included in annual financial statements, and how should it be presented?

- Which accounting framework is being applied? For example, financial statements may be prepared by applying International Financial Reporting Standards (IFRS) in full, or by applying the equivalent UK accounting and reporting standards – each framework will have its own specific requirements as to what may be required for financial statements to present a 'true and fair' view.

- The law, along with accounting and reporting standards, may change over time. For example, the 2006 Companies Act changed or updated some of the accounting requirements contained in the 1985 Companies Act.

- Judgement may need to be exercised when applying the requirements of individual financial reporting standards when preparing the annual financial statements which are then subject to audit.

    For example, IAS 16 *Property, Plant and Equipment* requires that non-current assets with a finite useful life are depreciated over their expected useful life to the business. The expected useful life of, say, a delivery van is likely to depend upon a number of factors such as annual mileage, servicing and maintenance policy, how well (or otherwise) it is driven – this is also likely to vary between different companies.

    One company may depreciate a delivery van on a straight-line basis over an estimated useful life of four years. Another company may depreciate an identical van over eight years depending upon its estimate of estimated useful life to that business. Both companies are applying the requirements of IAS 16 *Property, Plant and Equipment* in a manner which is relevant and appropriate to their circumstances.

    The important point here is that it is possible for different companies to apply the principles or requirements of financial reporting standards in a way that is relevant to each company, but which is not too prescriptive for rigid in the manner of application. The auditor must be similarly alert to evaluate the appropriateness of application of a reporting standard when conducting the audit of a set of financial statements and the particular business and operational features of a company.

It is also important to remember that the concept of 'true and fair' applies to narrative, as well as quantitative, disclosures. Therefore, the auditor should examine and evaluate these disclosures as part of the work to determine whether the financial statements show a true and fair view.

Therefore truth and fairness cannot be measured in absolute terms by an auditor. Instead auditors offer **reasonable assurance** based upon obtaining sufficient appropriate evidence to satisfy the requirements of the audit and International Standards of Auditing.

2.1 REASONABLE ASSURANCE

ISA 200 *Overall Objectives of the Independent Audit and the Conduct of an Audit in Accordance with International Standards on Auditing* examines the concept of reasonable assurance. It is explained that it means that a high, but not absolute, level of assurance is being given. An auditor cannot give absolute assurance because there will always be inherent limitations in an audit that affect the auditor's ability to detect material misstatements, such as:

- the use of testing and sampling during the audit. This is due to the need for the audit to be conducted within reasonable time and at reasonable cost.

- the inherent limitations of internal control (for example, the possibility of management override)

- the possibility of misrepresentation for fraudulent purposes

- the fact that evidence is often persuasive and not conclusive

- the financial statements include subjective estimates and other judgmental matters.

Thus, while an unmodified auditor's report is not a guarantee that the financial statements are free of material misstatement, it does offer a high degree of assurance from an independent professionally qualified accountant, so adds to the perceived reliability of the financial statements. The level of assurance offered and the process adopted by the auditor must be stated in the auditor's report so that the users do not misunderstand the level of assurance being offered to them.

ACTIVITY 2

Summarise in your own words what is meant by true and fair.

For a suggested answer, see the 'Answers' section at the end of the book.

3 MATERIALITY

3.1 THE CONCEPT

We have already stressed the important role played in accounting and auditing by skill and judgement. This results in the fact that many accounting areas are open to a high degree of subjectivity.

The auditor's report makes reference to the true and fair concept – it does not state that the financial statements are correct. Of course, financial statements are rarely, if ever, entirely correct – they will always contain estimates and other items which are based on judgement.

The practice has developed to reflect this situation whereby we do not aim to produce accounting information which is absolutely correct. This information is seen to be acceptable if it is *substantially* correct – or, in more technical terms, if it is not subject to any material error or misstatement which would distort the true and fair view.

The concept of materiality is fundamental to the presentation and classification of data in accounts.

However, in common with the true and fair concept, materiality is not easily defined and, again is often based on the judgement of the auditor. Guidance is given to the auditor by ISA 320 *Materiality in Planning and Performing an Audit*.

Materiality has been defined by the IASB in its *Framework for the Preparation and Presentation of Financial Statements* in the following terms:

Information is material if omitting, misstating or obscuring it could reasonably be expected to influence decisions that the primary users of general purpose financial statements make on the basis of those financial statements, which provide financial information about a specific reporting entity.

Materiality depends on the size of the item or error judged in the particular circumstances of its omission, misstatement or obscurement. Thus, materiality provides a threshold or cut-off point rather than being a primary qualitative characteristic which information must have if it is to be useful.

- Note that this definition relates materiality to the impact of an accounting item on the reader or user of the financial statements. A common-sense way of assessing the materiality of an item, error, omission or obscurement is to put yourself in the position of the reader and attempt to judge what impact, if any, the item would have on the picture which the financial statements present to you. The auditor also needs to consider the materiality of cumulative errors, omissions and obscurements found as they may not be material in isolation, but may be material cumulatively.

ACTIVITY 3

You are considering buying all the share capital of The Opportunity Company for a total of $10 million.

You have examined the draft financial statements which show net assets amounting to $9m.

You then discover two errors in those draft financial statements.

Error 1 – Inventories are overstated by $3m.

Error 2 – Accrued liabilities are understated by $0.1m.

Explain the likely materiality of each of these errors, based only on the information provided in the activity.

For a suggested answer, see the 'Answers' section at the end of the book.

3.2 ASSESSING MATERIALITY

The activity above based an assessment of materiality on a quantitative test or benchmark – the size of the errors involved. In that activity we related materiality to a statement of financial position measure – net assets. This is not the only possible quantitative approach to an assessment of materiality. Other possibilities would include relating errors, omissions or obscurements to quantitative benchmarks as follows:

- Revenue: ½% – 1%
- Profit before tax: 5% – 10%
- Gross assets: 1% – 2%

As a very general guide, many auditors would take the view that an error, omission or obscurement of less than 5% of profit before tax is not material, whilst an error of more than 10% of profit before tax is material – there may well be scope for significant judgement between these two percentages.

In addition to this numerical or benchmark approach to materiality, the point is often made that there are likely to be qualitative aspects to be recognised in assessing the impact of an item on the financial statements – these should also be built into the auditor's judgement of materiality.

Note that, as materiality is a matter of professional judgement, different audit firms may adopt different approaches to determining benchmark or 'rule of thumb' guides to assessing materiality. It is also likely that any individual audit firm may vary the benchmark guides depending upon the perception of audit risk associated with each individual audit assignment.

These qualitative factors are:

1 Nature of the item involved

Many items in financial statements are by their nature subject to a high degree of subjectivity, such as depreciation rates applied to non-current assets. In respect of these items the auditor will have to accept a reasonable margin of error.

By contrast, other items leave very little scope for judgement, such as share capital or related party transactions – on these types of items the auditor will typically take a tighter view on the question of materiality. It seems likely that auditors will typically expect this type of item to be correct. Where there are any items that **have** to be correct in the financial statements e.g. to comply with legislation, then even if the difference is very small it will be considered to be material.

2 Impact of the item involved

This principle relates back to the definition of materiality – the impact of the item on the view presented to the reader by the financial statements. The suggestion is that errors which may not be great in numerical terms may have a major impact on the picture presented by the financial statements.

Consider the following situation:

The draft financial statements of a company show a small pre-tax profit. The auditor discovers an inventory error which, if corrected would have the impact of changing the draft profit into a pre-tax loss. The error may not be material on normal numerical tests of materiality, but many auditors would see the impact of the item (turning a profit into a loss) as being material and would expect an adjustment to be made.

3 Recurring/non-recurring error

Recurring errors must be investigated no matter how small the percentage is as they imply that there is a problem with the accounting system.

4 Conceptual error

Typically, a conceptual error is one where the amount is incorrectly treated even though the amount is correct. For example, a non-current asset purchased has been written off to profit or loss in entirety in the year of purchase rather than being depreciated over its economic useful life. This would clearly affect the reported profit for the year in question and would therefore be material.

NB: Materiality requires the exercise of professional judgement and consideration of the unique circumstances of the entity.

ACTIVITY 4

What are the three main factors that an auditor will consider when assessing whether or not an item is material?

For a suggested answer, see the 'Answers' section at the end of the book.

3.3 THE ROLE OF MATERIALITY IN AUDITING

The detail of how the auditor uses the materiality concept in carrying out an audit will be dealt with in later chapters.

By way of a brief introduction, you will see that the materiality concept can be useful to the auditor in each of three main stages of the audit process:

- **Planning the audit** – in deciding where audit attention will be focused the auditor will plan to spend more audit time on areas which are material and on areas where material errors might arise.

- **Carrying out the audit work** – auditors will focus more attention on material transactions and account balances.

- **Reaching an appropriate audit opinion** – auditors will need to assess the impact of any errors, omissions or obscurements discovered on the truth and fairness of the financial statements in order to issue an appropriate audit opinion.

- ISA 320 *Materiality in planning and performing an audit* includes a concept of 'performance materiality.' This states that the auditor should set overall materiality for the financial statements as a whole. In addition, the auditor should establish an amount at less than overall materiality, referred to as 'performance materiality', when designing the nature, timing and extent of further audit procedures. The aim is to reduce the risk that misstatements in aggregate could exceed the total for materiality for the financial statements as a whole.

Definition **Performance materiality** is the amount set by auditors at below overall materiality to reduce to an appropriately low level the probability that the aggregate of uncorrected and undetected misstatements exceeds overall materiality.

4 PROFESSIONAL SCEPTICISM AND PROFESSIONAL JUDGEMENT

4.1 THE CONCEPT OF PROFESSIONAL SCEPTICISM

Professional scepticism is an attitude that includes a questioning mind, being alert to conditions which may indicate possible misstatement due to error or fraud, and a critical assessment of audit evidence.

4.2 HOW PROFESSIONAL SCEPTICISM SHOULD BE EXERCISED DURING AN AUDIT

ISA 200 *Overall Objectives of the Independent Auditor and the Conduct of an Audit in Accordance with International Standards on Auditing* states that auditors must plan and perform an audit with an attitude of professional scepticism, recognising that circumstances may exist that cause the financial statements to be materially misstated.

This requires the auditor to be alert to:

- audit evidence that contradicts other audit evidence obtained
- information that brings into question the reliability of documents and responses to inquiries to be used as audit evidence
- conditions that may indicate possible fraud
- circumstances that suggest the need for audit procedures in addition to those required by ISAs.

Professional scepticism needs to be maintained throughout the audit to reduce the risks of overlooking unusual transactions, over-generalising when drawing conclusions, and using inappropriate assumptions in determining the nature, timing and extent of audit procedures and evaluating the results of them.

Professional scepticism is also necessary to the critical assessment of audit evidence. This includes questioning contradictory audit evidence and the reliability of documents and responses from management and those charged with governance.

4.3 THE CONCEPT OF PROFESSIONAL JUDGEMENT

Professional judgement is the application of relevant training, knowledge and experience in making informed decisions about the courses of action that are appropriate in the circumstances of the audit engagement.

4.4 HOW PROFESSIONAL JUDGEMENT SHOULD BE APPLIED DURING AN AUDIT

ISA 200 *Overall Objectives of the Independent Auditor and the Conduct of an Audit in Accordance with International Standards on Auditing* also requires the auditor to exercise professional judgement in planning and performing an audit of financial statements.

Professional judgement is required in the following areas:

- Materiality and audit risk

- Nature, timing and extent of audit procedures

- Evaluation of whether sufficient appropriate audit evidence has been obtained

- Evaluating management's judgements in applying the applicable financial reporting framework

- Drawing conclusions based on the audit evidence obtained.

CONCLUSION

Agency theory can be seen to apply to auditing in the context of both directors and auditors acting as agents of shareholders. In all agency relationships there is a possibility of conflicts of interest arising which need to be monitored and controlled effectively.

Auditors, in their role as agents, communicate to the shareholders via the auditor's report on the truth and fairness of the financial statements. In reaching a conclusion on true and fair the auditor will need to exercise judgement. One significant aspect requiring audit judgement is the question of materiality – the impact that errors, omissions or obscurements may have on the picture presented to the reader by the financial statements.

An important theme running through much of this chapter is the significance of the exercise of judgement in auditing.

KEY TERMS

Auditor's report – A means of written, formal communication between auditor and shareholders in which the auditor expresses an opinion on the truth and fairness of the financial statements under audit.

Unmodified auditor's report – An auditor's report in which the auditor states that the financial statements do, in his opinion, present a true and fair view.

Materiality – A matter is material if its omission, misstatement or obscurement would reasonably influence the decisions of a user of the financial statements.

Reasonable assurance – The auditor gives 'reasonable assurance' that the financial statements are free from material misstatement.

Professional scepticism – Professional scepticism is an attitude that includes a questioning mind, being alert to conditions which may indicate possible misstatement due to fraud or error, and a critical assessment of audit evidence.

Professional judgement – Professional judgement is the application of relevant training, knowledge and experience in making informed decisions about the courses of action that are appropriate in the circumstances of the audit engagement.

FAU: FOUNDATIONS IN AUDIT

SELF TEST QUESTIONS

		Paragraph
1	What meanings could be attached to the words true and fair?	2
2	Explain the concept of materiality.	3
3	What factors should be considered in assessing whether an item is material?	3

PRACTICE QUESTION

CONCEPT OF MATERIALITY

What do you understand by the concept of materiality in relation to an audit? **(10 marks)**

For a suggested answer, see the 'Answers' section at the end of the book.

Chapter 5

AUDIT RISK AND PLANNING

INTRODUCTION

We are now about to embark on the practical auditing aspects – the work which an auditor will carry out in order to be in a position to establish whether the financial statements of the client present a true and fair view.

The first stage of the audit process is planning. In any context, a plan is something that should help the planner to achieve their objectives. The objective of an audit is to form an opinion on the truth and fairness of the financial statements. In order to achieve this objective effectively and efficiently the auditor will need to develop a plan of attack. This will, in simple terms involve answering three key questions – the 3Ws:

- When do we do the work – the timing of the audit?
- Who does the work – staffing the audit?
- What audit work do we do – the audit techniques which we need to apply and the areas of the financial statements to which we give most emphasis?

This chapter also covers the purpose and scope of an internal audit function, as well as the factors that the external auditor should consider when evaluating the work of internal auditors.

In order to design an effective audit plan the audit team must perform a thorough risk assessment. There are many elements of risk assessment but the overriding principle is to reduce the risk of giving an inappropriate audit opinion. This involves identifying where the risks of material misstatement lie and focussing audit efforts specifically on those areas. This chapter covers syllabus area B and A (6).

CONTENTS

1. Audit planning – an overview
2. Audit risk assessment
3. Audit planning – the role of materiality
4. Internal audit
5. Audit planning based upon risk assessment
6. Audit planning – staffing
7. Audit planning – developing the audit programmes
8. Audit evidence – a brief introduction
9. Recording the audit – audit working papers
10. Controlling the audit – quality control and review procedures

FAU: FOUNDATIONS IN AUDIT

LEARNING OUTCOMES

At the end of this chapter, you should be able to:

- Define audit risk and explain the risk-based approach to auditing

- Identify and explain the need for planning and the contents of overall audit strategy and plans

- Explain the purpose and scope of an internal audit function

- Identify the factors that external auditors should consider when evaluating the work of internal auditors

- Describe planning issues such as staffing

- Explain the use of analytical procedures

- Describe the reasons for maintaining audit documentation and the quality control procedures that should exist over the review of that documentation.

1 AUDIT PLANNING – AN OVERVIEW

1.1 THE PURPOSES OF AUDIT PLANNING

ISA 300 *Planning an Audit of Financial Statements* states that auditors should plan the audit work so as to perform the audit in an effective manner.

The ISA clearly distinguishes between:

- the overall audit strategy - this sets the scope, timing and direction of the audit and guides the development of the audit plan;

and

- the audit plan – this includes a description of the nature, timing and extent of planned risk assessment procedures and further audit procedures at the assertion level. It also includes other planned audit procedures that are required to be carried out so that the engagement complies with ISAs.

The **audit strategy** sets out in general terms how the audit is to be conducted and sets the scope, timing and direction of the audit. The **audit strategy** then guides the development of the **audit plan**, which contains the detailed responses to the auditor's risk assessment.

The purposes of planning are:

(a) to ensure that appropriate attention is paid to each area of the audit. This involves, for example, ensuring that adequate time is devoted to the audit of more complex, higher risk areas and more material areas (perhaps stocks in a manufacturing company). Equally, it would normally be appropriate to spend less audit time on more straightforward, lower risk and less material areas (perhaps petty cash balances)

(b) to ensure that potential problem areas are identified at the start of the audit, such as weaknesses in the controls operating in a particular area, which might lead to material misstatements in that area of the financial statements

(c) to identify any staff training needs specific to the audit, or where particular expertise may be required

(d) to ensure that the audit review and control process is performed on time, at the correct stages in the audit, and is effective.

Planning also assists in the proper allocation of work to the audit team, and the co-ordination of work done by other auditors and experts where these are to be used – it therefore helps the audit to be performed more efficiently. Planning will assist the direction and supervision of team members during the audit process.

As a starting point to the planning process, the auditor should identify and evaluate risks associated with an audit assignment. When this has been done, the auditor is then able to develop the overall audit strategy, followed by the detailed audit plan.

1.2 THE AUDIT STRATEGY

The audit strategy sets the scope, timing and direction of the audit. It allows the auditor to determine the following:

- the resources to deploy for specific audit areas (e.g. experience level, external experts)
- the amount of resources to allocate (e.g. number of team members)
- when the resources are to be deployed; and
- how the resources are managed, directed and supervised, including the timings of meetings, debriefs and reviews.

In determining the audit strategy the auditor should:

(i) Identify the characteristics of the engagement.

This includes consideration of: the financial reporting framework applied by the client; specific industry requirements (e.g. charities, financial services); the locations of the client, particularly if overseas; and the need for specialised knowledge.

(ii) Ascertain the reporting objectives to plan the timing of the audit and the nature of communications.

This includes: the need for and timing of client visits (interim, inventory count, final); expected communications and meetings with the client; communication requirements within the team.

(iii) Consider the significant factors that will direct the team's efforts.

This includes: materiality; risk; industry/economic changes; and changes at the client.

(iv) Consider the results of preliminary engagement activities.

This includes the results of prior year audits, interim audits and inventory counts.

(v) Ascertain the nature, timing and extent of resources necessary to perform the engagement.

This includes the need for particular expertise, experience, training requirements and available budgets.

1.3 THE AUDIT PLAN

Once the audit strategy has been established, the next stage is to develop a specific, detailed plan to address how the various matters identified in the overall strategy will be applied.

The audit plan is much more detailed than the overall strategy because it includes details of the nature, timing and extent of the specific audit procedures to be performed. Planning these procedures depends, largely, on the outcomes of the risk assessment process, which is discussed elsewhere in this chapter.

The audit plan should include specific descriptions of:

- the nature, timing and extent of risk assessment procedures
- the nature, timing and extent of further audit procedures, including:
  - what audit procedures are to be carried out
  - who should do them
  - how much work should be done (sample sizes, etc.)
  - when the work should be done (interim vs. final).
- any other procedures necessary to conform to ISAs.

2 AUDIT RISK ASSESSMENT

2.1 DEFINING AUDIT RISK

Unfortunately, the word risk has a number of different, but related meanings. The common thread underlying the various uses of the word risk is the concept of uncertainty – a risky situation is one where we cannot be sure of the outcome.

Definition **Audit risk** is the risk that the auditor expresses an inappropriate audit opinion when the financial statements are materially misstated. Audit risk is a function of the risks of material misstatement and detection risk.

At the planning stage of the audit the auditor determines the extent and nature of the audit work to be performed. Clearly, the greater the degree of audit risk attached to an assignment, the more audit work should be built into the audit plan. This in turn is likely to affect the time spent on the audit and the level of experience of audit staff required on the audit – the audit fee will therefore also be affected.

Similarly, the auditor may take the view that some areas of an audit are more risky than others – perhaps warranty provisions are seen to be a high risk area, but share capital is a low risk area. Similar considerations on timing and staffing will be built into the audit plan on an area by area basis.

2.2 RISK-BASED AUDIT APPROACH

ISA 315 (Revised 2019) *Identifying and Assessing the Risks of Material Misstatement* requires that the auditor adopts a risk-based approach to planning and performing the audit.

It enables auditors to assess the overall level of audit risk relating to a specific client, along with the audit risk attached to each element or component of the financial statements of a client. Consequently, more audit time and resource will be applied to those parts of the audit assignment which are considered to be of higher risk. The result of this approach is that overall audit risk should be reduced to an acceptable level. There now follows an explanation of how auditors can use the audit risk concept in the planning process.

Auditors will typically set an overall level of audit risk which they find acceptable in respect of the audit client concerned. Let us assume that this risk level is set at 5%. This means that the auditor is willing to accept a 5% chance that he may reach a wrong conclusion on the financial statements under audit.

If the auditor is willing to accept a 5% chance of getting it wrong, we can also say the auditor wants to be 95% confident of getting it right.

This risk level (or confidence level) will be based on the information which the auditor has collected as part of the audit planning process. In particular it will reflect the auditor's past experience of the client and assessment of the strengths of the controls operating in the client's accounting systems. A 5% audit risk level is typical in modern auditing.

Total audit risk is made up of three elements:

- inherent risk (or IR)
- control risk (or CR)

These two together are sometimes referred to as client or entity risk – they result from the characteristics of the enterprise under audit.

- detection risk (or DR)

These three risks together give total audit risk.

Each of the major components of audit risk are dealt with in detail below.

2.3 INHERENT RISK, CONTROL RISK AND DETECTION RISK

(a) Inherent risk

Definition The susceptibility of an assertion about a class of transaction, account balance or disclosure to a misstatement that could be material, either individually or when aggregated with other misstatements, before consideration of any related controls.

This risk element results from the nature of the enterprise under review, the industry in which it operates and the makeup of the items appearing in its financial statements.

The auditors must use their professional judgement and all available knowledge to assess inherent risk. If inherent risk is deemed to be high, the risk of material misstatement in an account balance or class of transactions is also high, and vice versa.

Inventory, for example is often more inherently risky than cash as there is greater scope for manipulation and error. A business in the construction industry or the fashion industry is more risky than a food retailer as it is more volatile.

FAU: FOUNDATIONS IN AUDIT

(b) Control risk

Definition The risk that a misstatement that could occur in an assertion about a class of transaction, account balance or disclosure and that could be material, either individually or when aggregated with other misstatements, will not be prevented, or detected and corrected, on a timely basis by the entity's internal control.

If control risk is deemed to be high, the risk of material misstatement in an account balance or class of transactions is also high, and vice versa.

This risk will be affected by such factors as the control environment including, for example, the integrity of the staff operating the system, the extent of supervisory controls, and the strength of controls in particular account areas. Our study of control systems and their impact on the audit is dealt with in the next two chapters.

(c) Detection risk

Definition The risk that the procedures performed by the auditor to reduce audit risk to an acceptably low level will not detect a misstatement that exists and that could be material, either individually or when aggregated with other misstatements.

This is the only component of overall audit risk which is under the control of the auditor. The lower the auditor wishes detection risk to be, the higher the amount of detailed audit testing which must be performed. One way of managing the level of detection risk (and hence the overall level of audit risk) is by changing the number of transactions which are subject to audit (the sample size concept).

A larger sample size will reduce the level of detection risk. In principle if the auditor accurately examines ALL transactions, detection risk is reduced to zero!

Now that we understand what audit risk is, we can move on to deal with how audit risk is identified and evaluated.

2.4 UNDERSTANDING THE ENTITY

In order to assess risk ISA 315 (Revised 2019) *Identifying and Assessing the Risks of Material Misstatement* states that the auditor must obtain an understanding of the client entity, its environment and the applicable financial reporting framework. The following are factors that the auditor should specifically gain an understanding of:

- The entity's organisational structure, ownership and governance, and its business model, including the extent to which the business model integrates the use of IT

- Industry, regulatory and other external factors

- The measures used, internally and externally, to assess the entity's financial performance

- The applicable financial reporting framework, and the entity's accounting policies and the reasons for any changes thereto

- How inherent risk factors affect susceptibility of assertions to misstatement and the degree to which they do so, in the preparation of the financial statements in accordance with the applicable financial reporting framework.

The auditor shall also evaluate whether the entity's accounting policies are appropriate and consistent with the applicable financial reporting framework.

There are a number of sources of information that the auditor can use to gain their understanding. However, ISA 315 (Revised 2019) specifically requires the auditor to perform the following procedures:

- Enquiries of management and others within the entity (e.g. about changes in staffing, company structure, products, competition)

- Analytical procedures

- Observation (e.g. of systems and controls) and

- Inspection (e.g. of key documents such as board minutes, legal correspondence, trade journals, management accounts, forecasts etc.)

As part of understanding the entity, the auditor should gain an understanding of the laws and regulations that may affect a client. This is important as, if a client has not complied with relevant laws and regulations, it may be liable to fines and restrictions in business activities which may have an impact upon the preparation and audit of the financial statements.

The auditor may use automated tools and techniques:

- to understand flows of transactions and processing as part of the auditor's procedures to understand the information system.

- to obtain direct access to, or a digital download from, the databases in the entity's information system that store accounting records of transactions which can be used by the auditor to confirm the understanding obtained about how transactions flow through the information system.

ISA 315 (Revised 2019) sets out the risk assessment procedures that provide a foundation for an audit of financial statements. The revised ISA establishes more robust requirements and detailed guidance to enhance audit quality.

The changes bring the standard up to date with developments in the profession and the business world and are made with the public interest as the main emphasis. The standard has been modernised to:

- Meet evolving business needs, including information technology, and how auditors use automated tools and techniques, including data analytics, to perform audit procedures.

- Enhance the auditor's required understanding of the entity's use of information technology relevant to financial reporting.

- Improve the standard's applicability to entities across a wide spectrum of circumstances and complexities.

- Emphasise the importance of exercising professional scepticism throughout the risk identification and assessment process.

Example risk assessment procedures

It is impossible to prepare a comprehensive list of risk assessment procedures that need to be carried out. The procedures need to be prepared in light of the unique circumstances of the client. However, examples include:

Enquiries of management:

- Have any share issues occurred during the year?
- Has the company invested in any new capital assets during the year?
- Have any new competitors or products entered the market?
- How does the company manage exposure to exchange rate risk?
- Have there been any changes in senior management during the year?

Observe:

- The application of controls over the counting of inventory during the year.
- The performance of year-end reconciliations (bank, supplier statement) to ensure they are performed regularly.
- Month-end adjustments/reconciliations being performed during an interim visit to ensure controls are applied throughout the year.

Inspect:

- Organisation charts to identify changes in key staff.
- Examples of controls operating throughout the year, e.g. evidence of review of month end reconciliations, evidence of review of aged receivables on a monthly basis.
- HR records/payroll records to identify movements in staff.
- News/media reports to identify any significant issues, such as potential legal action.
- Board minutes for significant events or transactions during the year that may create a risk of misstatement.

2.5 ANALYTICAL PROCEDURES

ISA 520 *Analytical procedures* requires that analytical review procedures are used at both the planning stage and final review stage of an audit. Analytical procedures can be defined as the evaluation of financial information by studying the relationships between both financial data and non-financial data. Such procedures can be used at many stages in the audit process. Here we are considering their use at the planning stage of the audit.

Analytical procedures include comparison of financial information with prior periods, budgets and forecasts and similar industries. They also include consideration of predictable relationships such as the relationship of purchases to sales, and payroll costs to the number of employees.

ISA 520 states that analytical procedures are mandatory at the planning stage and are performed for the following reasons:

- to assist the auditor in understanding the business and how it operates
- to identify any changes in the business over time, and the impact on operations
- to identify potential risk areas, and plan relevant procedures to address these areas.

As the final accounts will not be ready at this stage, the auditor will make use of interim, estimated or budgeted financial statements, and also the previous year's set of accounts. When performing this work, the auditor will examine both financial data and non-financial data, such as production volumes, sales volumes and the number of employees.

Prior to commencing the analytical review the auditor would have considered what results should be expected from performing the analytical review. These expectations would be formed following client management meetings to identify business changes, and also on the auditors' existing knowledge of the client. For example, the knowledge that the client has increased its production capacity may lead to an expectation that turnover will have increased. On the other hand, the knowledge that the industry in general has suffered a downturn in demand may lead the auditors to expect turnover to have decreased. They will then compare the actual results with those expected and look for reasons for any significant variations. Unexplained variations may indicate a misstatement in the figures in that area, which would lead the auditor to plan the audit work to devote more time and resources to those areas.

2.6 FACTORS AFFECTING THE USEFULNESS OF ANALYTICAL PROCEDURES

When intending to apply analytical procedures, auditors should consider:

(a) The plausibility and predictability of relationships identified for comparison and evaluation. For example there is usually a strong relationship between sales and commissions for example which should give the auditor a firm basis for evaluation of the relationship in the financial statements.

(b) The objectives of the analytical procedures and the extent to which the information on which they are based is reliable.

(c) The degree to which available information can be analysed – generally the more analysis available, the better. For example, it would be appropriate in the audit of a retail chain to apply analytical review procedures to individual outlets because in the total figures the trends and fluctuations of some outlets may be hidden by those of others. Note that the use by the client of computer systems may help the auditor in this respect – more analysis of information is likely to be available.

(d) The availability of both financial and non-financial information. If auditors are using financial information they may already have tested its validity. They must take care in using non-financial information, for example sales volume rather than sales value as this may have been prepared by management and may not be objective.

(e) The relevance of the information, for example whether budgets reflect expectations, or goals to be achieved.

(f) The comparability of information.

(g) The auditors' knowledge of the business.

Analytical procedures should be cost-effective and the results will be more credible if other audit work supports those conclusions. You should note that auditors will rarely, if ever, use these procedures as the sole basis for their conclusions. Analytical procedures are seen to generate supplementary evidence which (hopefully) supports other evidence derived from more specific and detailed audit testing procedures.

In some enterprises, where accounting ratios and trends remain constant, analytical review is an efficient test. In a rapidly growing company exhibiting variable trends it may well be a complete waste of time! As ever the auditor must choose the most cost effective selection of audit procedures.

FAU: FOUNDATIONS IN AUDIT

2.7 CARRYING OUT ANALYTICAL PROCEDURES

Analytical review procedures range from simple comparisons (e.g. current period amounts or ratios with earlier years' figures) to more sophisticated methods using computer audit software and advanced statistical techniques.

Note the wide ranging nature of analytical review procedures. Essentially analytical review involves comparison. The auditor should ensure that the various items making up the financial statements are consistent with:

(a) Each other (for example, the relationship between receivables and revenues, or between current assets and current liabilities).

(b) Known events (for example, the likely effects of government changing tax rates).

(c) The auditor's knowledge of the business (for example, if the product mix has changed, or new products have been introduced).

The auditor should ask the following key questions:

(a) What data, ratios and statistics exist which are of significance and relevance for the business? With a large organisation the auditor would also want to consider what analytical review techniques would be appropriate for the different sections of the business.

(b) With what should they compare e.g. similar companies, industry statistics etc.?

The possible approaches may be summarised as follows:

Types of data, ratios, etc.	Comparison with
Financial data (e.g. items in financial statements, management accounts, budgets, account balances)	(i) Corresponding period (ii) Budgets and forecasts
Non-financial data (e.g. production and employment statistics)	(i) Entries in accounting records (ii) Other financial data (e.g. an increase in the number of employees should result in an increase in payroll costs) (iii) Preceding period

Ratios and percentages, developed from data e.g.
    receivables collection period
    payables payment period
    inventory holding period
    current ratio
    quick ratio
    gearing ratio
    return on capital employed
    gross profit margins
	(i) Preceding period
	(ii) Budgets and forecasts
	(iii) Industry statistics

The approach to analytical procedures

The procedures remain the same whatever the stage of the audit. A series of steps are identified which are summarised and commented on below.

(a) Obtain an understanding of the business.

(b) Identify relevant and credible relationships.

For example, the gross profit percentage expresses the relationship between gross profit and sales revenues. In many businesses this ratio may fluctuate widely and may be of little use to the auditor, but for companies in the retail industry for example this ratio would generally remain constant.

(c) Establish the validity of any data to be used.

The auditor may decide to use his client's constant gross profit percentage in his analytical review techniques. Before doing this the auditor should confirm the validity of this figure and the data from which it is calculated.

(d) Predict a likely expected value – what would we expect the gross profit percentage to be in the current circumstances?

The auditors must take all of their knowledge of the business into account in making this prediction. For example, they may know of a factor in this particular accounting period affecting the gross profit percentage and they should adjust their calculations accordingly.

The auditor should therefore allow for the effect of such factors as:

(i) general inflation (as measured by the Retail Price Index)

(ii) specific price changes (goods and services used by the enterprise)

(iii) seasonal factors

(iv) industrial disputes, including those affecting key suppliers

(v) changes in the level of business activity in the economy as a whole

(vi) technological changes making products or services obsolete

(vii) changes in management policy e.g. expanding or contracting operations (this should be apparent from a review of management or directors' minutes).

(e) Compare predictions with actual and consider the implications of any variances.

Remember that there are two points to look out for:

(i) the changes that do occur but which differ significantly from those expected

(ii) the changes that would normally be expected to occur but which fail to do so.

The auditor should investigate both categories fully.

(f) Seek explanations for the above and corroborate those explanations. It is important that the auditor does not jump to conclusions here and assume that figures which differ from what the auditor expected are necessarily wrong! Always bear in mind that analytical procedures raise questions for the auditor (why does the gross profit figure not appear to make sense?) It is then up to the auditor to carry out additional audit procedures to find an answer!

The auditor should never just take management's word for why a change has happened or failed to happen – audit evidence should be sought to support the explanation! In practice auditors are trained to take the view that analytical procedures raise questions – only further audit testing can produce answers to those questions.

ACTIVITY 1

Analytical review procedures are used by the auditor for a number of purposes. Describe briefly the nature of these procedures during the audit and the circumstances in which they will be used by the auditor.

For a suggested answer, see the 'Answers' section at the end of the book.

2.8 RESPONSE TO RISK ASSESSMENT

Risk analysis is an important stage of the audit. In conducting a thorough assessment of risk auditors will be able to:

- Identify areas of the financial statements where misstatements are likely to occur early in the audit.
- Plan procedures that address the significant risk areas identified.
- Carry out an efficient, focussed and effective audit.
- Minimise the risk of issuing an inappropriate audit opinion to an acceptable level.
- Reduce the risk of reputational and punitive damage.

However, whilst the assessment of risk is important the critical factor for the auditor is their response to identified risks. This is covered in ISA 330 *the Auditor's Responses to Assessed Risks*. The key objective though is to reduce audit risk, and this can be achieved by manipulating detection risk, as follows:

- allocating complex or risky areas of the engagement to suitably experienced and competent staff
- placing more, or fewer, reliance on the results of systems and controls testing
- altering the volume of substantive procedures performed after the year-end
- altering the volume of balances tested by changing sample sizes
- performing more, or fewer, substantive analytical procedures as opposed to other, more detailed ones
- consulting external experts on technically complex or contentious matters
- changing the timing and frequency of review procedures, including using additional partners to review work, and
- developing expectations that can be used when performing substantive analytical procedures.

ACTIVITY 2

What are the main areas of a client's business that the auditor would consider when evaluating the risk level of that business?

For a suggested answer, see the 'Answers' section at the end of the book.

3 AUDIT PLANNING – THE ROLE OF MATERIALITY

3.1 CONCEPT OF MATERIALITY

The concept of materiality was examined in an earlier chapter. It was concluded that an item is material if its omission or misstatement could influence the decisions of users of the financial statements. The auditor's requirement to consider materiality is explained in ISA 320 *Materiality in Planning and Performing an Audit*.

It was also stated earlier that one aspect of assessing materiality is a quantitative element – broadly, bigger errors are more likely to have a material impact than smaller errors.

The auditor in planning the audit therefore needs to establish materiality levels – the size of error discovered during the conduct of the audit which may be considered to be material.

It is unlikely that an individual transaction will be identified that has been materially misstated. It is more common for a number of smaller misstatements to have a collective or cumulative effect that leads to a material misstatement in the financial statements. This may occur, for example, if a number of similar transactions have all been wrongly accounted for – the collective or cumulative impact of several smaller misstatements is more likely to have a material impact upon whether the financial statements show a true and fair view.

ISA 320 *Materiality in Planning and Performing an Audit* therefore distinguishes between overall materiality and performance materiality.

- Overall materiality is judged or determined by the auditor to be the amount of any misstatement that changes the view presented by the financial statements – i.e. they no longer show a true and fair view. This is normally quantified in financial terms based upon benchmarks as a percentage of revenue, profit before tax and/or total assets.

- Performance materiality is set at a lower level than overall materiality for the purposes of planning and performing audit work. Consequently, this approach is more likely to identify not only an individual transaction that has been materially misstated but also identify situations where a number of transactions have been misstated (none of which are material on an individual basis) but which cumulatively result in a material misstatement in the financial statements.

For example, if overall materially has been set by the auditor at $50,000, performance materiality may be set at, say, $45,000. This means that audit work will be planned and performed to give a reasonable expectation that misstatements of $45,000 will be identified during the audit. If one misstatement of $45,000 is identified, the auditor may reasonably conclude that there has been no material misstatement which will affect the financial statements. However, if two misstatements of, say $47,000, are identified, cumulatively that will be a misstatement of $94,000 which would be regarded as having a material impact upon whether the financial statements show a true and fair view.

Therefore, the lower the materiality level set, this will lead to a larger sample size for audit testing, which will consequently lead to a reduction in the overall level of audit risk.

3.2 THE LINK BETWEEN MATERIALITY AND RISK

An overall materiality level for the audit is set based on the evaluation of client risk, but this may be adjusted for specific areas of the audit in response to the risk assessment of that particular audit area. Typically, for a high risk area of the audit – perhaps inventory – the materiality level for that area is set well below the overall materiality level.

The lower the materiality level that the auditor sets the larger the sample size – the auditor will increase the sample size in order to increase confidence that all material errors are identified. A small sample in high risk areas may leave a significant number of material errors undetected!

4 INTERNAL AUDIT

4.1 INTRODUCTION

The auditor can place reliance on the work carried out by the client's internal audit function when forming an opinion on the financial statements. The auditor, however, still has sole responsibility for forming the opinion on the financial statements.

Companies must create a strong system of internal control in order to fulfil their responsibilities. However, it is not sufficient to simply have mechanisms in place to manage a business. The effectiveness of these mechanisms must be regularly evaluated. All systems need some form of monitoring and feedback. This is the role of internal audit.

Having an internal audit function is generally considered to be best practice, but is not required by law.

4.2 THE DIFFERENCE BETWEEN INTERNAL AND EXTERNAL AUDITORS

	External audit	Internal audit
Objective	Express an opinion on the truth and fairness of the financial statements in a written report.	Improve the company's operations by reviewing the efficiency and effectiveness of internal controls.
Reporting	Reports to shareholders.	Reports to management or those charged with governance.
Availability of report	Publicly available.	Not publicly available. Usually only seen by management or those charged with governance.
Scope of work	Verifying the truth and fairness of the financial statements.	Wide in scope and dependent on management's requirements.

Appointment and removal	By the shareholders of the company.	By the audit committee or board of directors.
Relationship with company	Must be independent of the company.	May be employees (which limits independence) or an outsourced function (which enhances independence).

4.3 THE ROLE OF THE INTERNAL AUDIT FUNCTION

The role of internal audit can vary depending on the requirements of the business.

Key activities of the internal audit function

- Assessing whether the company is demonstrating best practice in corporate governance.
- Evaluating the company's risk identification and management processes.
- Testing the effectiveness of internal controls.
- Assessing the reliability of financial and operating information.
- Assessing the economy, efficiency and effectiveness of operating activities (value for money).
- Assessing compliance with laws and regulations.
- Providing recommendations on the prevention and detection of fraud.

Most of these activities can be seen as helping management comply with corporate governance requirements.

Additional roles

In addition to the above, internal audit will carry out ad hoc assignments, as required by management. For example:

- Fraud investigations – this may involve detecting fraud, identifying the perpetrator of a fraud and quantifying the loss to the company as a result of a fraud.

- IT systems reviews – performing a review of the computer environment and controls.

- Mystery shopper visits – for retail and service companies the internal audit staff can pose as customers to ensure that customer service is at the required level.

- Contract audits – making sure that where material or long term contracts are entered into by the organisation, the contract is written to protect the organisation appropriately and contractual terms are being adhered to by the supplier in line with the service level agreement.

- Asset verification – such as performing cash counts and physical inspection of non-current assets to verify existence.

- Providing direct assistance to the external auditor – internal audit staff can help the external auditor with their procedures under their supervision, in accordance with ISA 610 *Using the Work of Internal Auditors*.

4.4 FACTORS TO BE CONSIDERED BY THE EXTERNAL AUDITORS WHEN EVALUATING THE INTERNAL AUDIT FUNCTION

As the external auditor needs to understand and document client systems in order to assess control risk, they may be able to place reliance upon the work performed by the internal audit function.

The external auditor will take the following factors into account when making their assessment of the internal audit function:

- **Objectivity** – the external auditor will consider the status of the internal audit function within the entity, who they report to, whether they have any conflicting responsibilities or restrictions placed on their function. They will also consider to what extent management acts on internal audit recommendations.

- **Competence** – the external auditor will consider whether internal auditors have adequate resources, technical training and proficiency, and whether internal auditors possess the required knowledge of financial reporting. Consideration will also be given to whether the internal auditors are members of professional bodies.

- **Systematic and disciplined approach** – the external auditor will consider whether internal audit is properly planned, supervised, reviewed and documented, whether the function has appropriate quality control procedures, audit manuals, work programmes and documentation.

If any one of the above factors is lacking, the external audit should not use the work of the internal audit function.

4.5 FACTORS TO BE CONSIDERED BY THE EXTERNAL AUDITORS WHEN EVALUATING THE WORK OF INTERNAL AUDITORS

ISA 610 identifies the factors that the external auditor should consider before placing reliance on the work done by the internal auditors. The external auditor will reperform some of the work carried out by the internal auditors as part of their assessment.

Specific assessment	Conclude
Assess the specific work that may be relied upon: - Whether the work was properly planned, performed, supervised, reviewed and documented - Whether there is sufficient appropriate evidence to support the auditor's conclusions - Whether the conclusions reached are appropriate.	The external auditor should: - Test the work of internal audit, and may observe their procedures, in order to conclude on the adequacy of their work for the purpose of the external audit - Extend their own procedures if they conclude the internal audit work is not adequate.

ACTIVITY 3

You are currently involved in planning the audit of Button Co. At the beginning of the year that you are auditing, the company set up an internal audit department. From your initial discussions with the client, you have established that the internal auditors have undertaken a number of assignments across the company, and have fed back to the board on their findings.

What factors should you take into account when considering whether you can rely on the work undertaken by the internal audit staff?

For a suggested answer, see the 'Answers' section at the end of the book.

5 AUDIT PLANNING BASED UPON RISK ASSESSMENT

The result of the risk assessment is that the auditor is now able to decide upon the audit strategy and develop a detailed audit plan. This will be documented in the audit planning memorandum which forms part of the audit working papers. As part of the process to formalise and document the planning process, the auditor will undertake a range of procedures, some of which are listed below.

5.1 TYPICAL PLANNING PROCEDURES

Whilst there are a wide range of procedures used in practice, common methods include:

(a) Consider the background of the client's business.

(b) Review the previous year's working papers for an existing client or request access to working papers of the previous auditor (if any) in the case of a new client. The purpose of this procedure is to identify any high risk audit areas so that appropriate audit emphasis can be applied in the current audit.

(c) Consider any relevant changes in legislation or accounting practice that may have an impact on the audit.

(d) Review any management or interim accounts which the client may have prepared for internal use during the period under review. This will give the auditor an insight into the client's performance and help to identify possible problems during the accounting period to date.

(e) Meet senior management to discuss problems that they have encountered during the year, and to ascertain the present position of, and expectations of the business in the foreseeable future. It is useful if this meeting involves a wide range of client managers – operational managers, directors as well as financial staff.

(f) Consider the timing of the various stages to be performed in the audit. This is important in the context of meeting any deadlines which may apply. It also helps with manpower planning and staffing of the audit. It is also relevant to consider the timing of computer-assisted audit techniques that may be used – these techniques will be discussed in a later chapter.

(g) Consider and agree the work to be done by the client's staff to provide assistance to the auditor. This may improve the efficiency of the audit (and may therefore reduce the audit fee!). Often it is possible for client staff to carry out routine tasks on behalf of the auditor, such as the preparation of account analysis schedules. The auditor will, of course, need to check the completeness and accuracy of the information prepared by the client if it is to be relied upon for audit purposes.

(h) Consider arranging independent expert help e.g. when the nature of inventory is specialised.

(i) Determine the number of audit staff needed and the level of experience that they should possess. The auditor will also need to plan the amount of time required from each member of the audit team – and when that time is required.

(j) Discuss the general approach to the audit, and any possible problems and high risk areas with the audit team.

(k) Prepare a time budget for the audit. This will then be used as the basis for the preparation of a fee estimate for the audit to be presented to the client.

(l) Inform the client of the projected dates when the auditors will attend and perform their tasks.

ACTIVITY 4

Prepare a list of the sources of evidence available to the auditor when obtaining knowledge of the business at the planning stage of the audit.

For a suggested answer, see the 'Answers' section at the end of the book.

5.2 THE PLANNING MEMORANDUM

The audit plan should be documented in an audit planning memorandum which forms part of the audit working papers.

Clients may operate in a dynamic, changing environment. If significant business changes take place during the course of the audit, or if changes become necessary to the way the audit is conducted, such changes should be documented in the audit planning memorandum, together with the reasons for those changes.

The work of planning is therefore a continuous process throughout the audit. Many auditing firms have formalised the planning process by using a standard Audit Planning Memorandum. In addition to the key areas already mentioned above, the memorandum is used to record:

- evidence of initial decisions as to which audit procedures are relevant

- any amendments to those procedures which arise as the audit work progresses.

The following is an example of a fictitious planning memorandum for the audit of a company called Peppers Ltd.

HASTINGS & WARWICK

Client: Peppers Ltd   Prepared by: K.E.D.   Date: 5.6.X6

Period: Y/e 31 July 20X6   Reviewed by: Date:

Audit plan

1	Terms of engagement including reports required and client expectations	Normal Companies Act audit; we write up nominal ledger and prepare draft statutory accounts from client records.
2	The company and its business	New company set up in 20X1 to retail PCs and related software packages – provides some consultancy services. Financed mainly by proprietors and overdraft until $100,000 new capital injected by Capital Venture Ltd in January 20X6. Turnover about $1,200,000 ($650,000 last year).
3	Special audit problems	Possible obsolete inventory due to changes in technology; NX50 software may be unsalable. Billing of sales is likely to give rise to errors – new systems are invoiced in advance of delivery; consultancy work is billed retrospectively and there is little by way of 'work in progress' records.
4	Results of analytical procedures	Client produces management accounts comprising sales analysis and cash flows (not reproduced); these are in line with the forecasts done in the report to Capital Venture Ltd.
5	Evaluation of audit risk	In view of the rapid growth of the business, the importance placed on the accounts by Capital Venture Ltd and the problems in recording sales, this audit should be treated as higher than normal risk. No reliance can be placed on the accounting systems nor on any analytical procedures.

6	Preliminary estimate of materiality	$7,000 based on estimate of turnover of $1.2m and likely profit of around $120,000–$250,000.
7	Audit approach	No attempt to rely on internal controls or analytical procedures. The following specific procedures should be carried out: • Reconcile purchases and sales of computer systems and check that cut off is correct, bearing in mind that it is the company's practice to invoice before delivery. • Review consultants' diaries for the last 3 months to check that all assignments are included in WIP or billings. • For other procedures and objectives, see the audit programme which has already been prepared (not reproduced).
8	Other matters	The company moved to new premises in April; we need to take particular care that improvements are treated as tax efficiently as possible.
9	Budget and fee	Budget $15,500, excluding sales tax.
10	Timetable and staffing	G. Smith and J. Taylor to complete by 2.10.X6.

Audit plan approved

Manager   Date

_____

Partner

_____

_____   _____

ACTIVITY 5

(a) What are the objectives and purposes of audit planning?

(b) Outline six typical planning procedures.

For a suggested answer, see the 'Answers' section at the end of the book.

6 AUDIT PLANNING – STAFFING

6.1 INTRODUCTION

In the introduction to this chapter we pointed out that much of the audit planning process revolves around the 3Ws.

- **What** audit work do we do? Most of the contents of the chapter so far have dealt with this aspect of planning.

- **When** do we do the work? Timing has been referred to where relevant in our coverage so far.

- **Who** does the audit work? This is the staffing issue which we deal with next.

6.2 PLANNING THE STAFFING OF THE AUDIT

We noted earlier in the chapter that planning procedures include the appropriate staffing of the audit.

Planning should cover such points as:

- number of staff required

- level of expertise required; and whether external professional assistance will be necessary

- length of time each member of staff will be needed

- exact timing of their work.

To assist in the allocation of staff to each stage of the audit, larger firms will designate job titles to each member of the audit team. An example of the roles involved in an audit team is given below:

Job title	Job description as regards the audit
Partner	Agree fees with client.
	Review audit working papers.
	Sign auditor's report (after approval of accounts by directors).

Job title	Job description as regards the audit
Manager	Set broad time limits to job.
	Assign staff to job.
	Agree detailed timetable with supervisor or senior.
	Review staff requirements and timetable at various stages.
	Review audit in detail at end of interim and final audits.
Supervisor (or junior manager)	Take charge of large jobs e.g. a large group of companies, where each company or division is audited by a senior.
Senior	Take charge of the audit.
	Agree audit timetable with client, and manager or supervisor.
	Decide on detailed audit work.
	Compile audit working papers.
Clerks, semi-seniors and juniors	Perform detailed audit work assigned by seniors.

A key principle of audit planning involves ensuring that the audit work is allocated to a member of staff who has the skill and experience to perform that work to an acceptable standard. The more complex, higher risk areas of the audit should not be allocated to new or inexperienced members of the firm.

A system for appropriate training of employees and for a systematic review of their work by a more senior member of the audit team is also important to the success of the audit. These aspects are dealt with under the 'controlling the audit' heading below.

ACTIVITY 6

State what the audit partner's typical responsibilities will be in respect of each audit assignment.

For a suggested answer, see the 'Answers' section at the end of the book.

6.3 BRIEFING MEETINGS

It is usual to hold an audit briefing meeting (or audit planning meeting) before the detailed audit work begins. This meeting is typically held on the first day of the interim audit, and gives the audit manager and partner the opportunity to explain the audit approach to the assembled entire audit team.

The manager will typically describe the client to the audit team members, explain the audit methodology expected to be used (i.e. systems testing or substantive testing), highlight any problems experienced in previous years, and give the auditors an opportunity to raise initial queries they may have concerning the engagement.

Such a meeting will prevent time being wasted at the start of the audit by individual auditors not knowing what they are supposed to be doing, so should increase the efficiency of the audit process.

7 AUDIT PLANNING – DEVELOPING THE AUDIT PROGRAMMES

7.1 THE ROLE OF THE AUDIT PROGRAMME

We have already referred to the fact that the audit plan sets out the planned risk assessment procedures and planned further audit procedures intended to be carried out during the audit engagement. The plan will not go into detail on precisely what audit work is to be carried out, which member of the audit team is responsible for that work, when it should be done and (often) how long that piece of audit work is expected to take. This level of detail will be found in the audit programme for each area which adds flesh to the general skeleton of the audit set out in the audit planning memorandum.

Definition The **audit programme** records the audit testing to be performed. It specifies the nature and extent of the checking, and the members of staff who have carried out the work and the date on which the work was performed. It also contains evidence of review of work i.e. by whom and the date.

It is vital that the work programmes (particularly the nature, timing and extent of further audit procedures) are designed based as a response to the assessed risks of material misstatement, in accordance with the principles of ISA 330 *The Auditor's Responses to Assessed Risks*. In very basic terms, the auditor must perform a more thorough audit where assessed risk is high. This can be achieved by performing more substantive tests.

The audit programme serves as:

(a) a set of instructions to the audit team

(b) a means of controlling and recording the proper execution of the work

(c) a record of the audit procedures to be adopted, the audit objectives, timing, sample size and basis of selection of the sample for each area.

The audit programme is an important part of the auditor's working papers and records a significant part of the audit evidence required to justify the audit opinion.

Audit programmes should be considered as the minimum amount of testing that is required to be performed. Auditors should be flexible in their approach so that if unexpected results are obtained they are able to design further tests to satisfy their objectives.

An extract from an audit programme is shown below. Again, it is not necessary to learn the detail of the contents of this – be aware of the general structure and presentation of the document.

7.2 EXAMPLE OF PART OF A WAGES AND SALARIES AUDIT PROGRAMME

AUDIT PROGRAMME	Prepared by:
AUDIT AREA: Wages and Salaries	Date:
Client:	Reviewed by:
Period:	Date:

(a) **Tests of control**

Control objectives

To establish that:

(i) the computation of wages and salaries is only in respect of the client's employees and at authorised rates of pay

(ii) wages and salaries are in accordance with records of work performed, e.g. time, output, commissions on sales

(iii) payrolls are calculated accurately

(iv) payments are only made to the correct employees

(v) payroll deductions are correctly accounted for and paid to the appropriate third parties

(vi) all transactions related to wages and salaries are accurately entered in the accounting records.

7.3 AMENDMENTS TO THE PLANNED AUDIT WORK

It is important that a clear record of any changes to the audit plan is maintained to support and justify the overall strategy adopted for the audit.

ISA 300 *Planning an audit of financial statements* states that 'the overall audit strategy and the audit plan should be updated and changed as necessary during the course of the audit'.

7.4 STANDARDISED AUDIT PROGRAMMES AND PROFESSIONAL JUDGEMENT

Definition A **standardised audit programme** is a pre-prepared listing of objectives and tests which is used on any audit.

Standardised audit programmes are common in practice and are often drawn from a database of procedures in large firms. They are generally used in those audit areas which are common to all audits – perhaps areas such as sales, purchases and payroll.

Their advantages are that they streamline work and act as a checklist to ensure that all important areas are considered. They improve the efficiency of the audit and facilitate delegation and control.

However they have a disadvantage in that, if used slavishly, they may stifle professional judgement. Auditors need to use professional judgement in their work as all audits will be different and therefore tests need to be designed for the different circumstances found in each audit.

A middle way is used by some firms who, in their audit manual, will suggest the items to be included in an audit programme rather than requiring a standard form to be filled in.

8 AUDIT EVIDENCE – A BRIEF INTRODUCTION

This study text deals with the topic of audit evidence in great depth later. Good knowledge of the area is fundamental to your ability to handle practical audit tasks in the examination for this paper. At this stage, we are going to limit ourselves to a general introduction to the topic, partly to establish a useful link with the area of audit working papers which is the subject matter of the next section of this chapter.

Consider the audit evidence process as shown in the diagram below.

An overview – the audit evidence process

Commentary

As we know the auditor has a legal duty to express an opinion on the truth and fairness of the financial statements.

This opinion – the conclusion reached at the end of the audit process – must be supported by audit evidence – this is any piece of verifiable information which assists the auditor to reach a conclusion on the financial statements.

The auditor will generate this audit evidence by carrying out audit tests – pieces of work designed by the auditor to generate relevant and reliable audit evidence.

All the above must be properly recorded and documented in audit files and audit working papers – see the next section.

9 RECORDING THE AUDIT – AUDIT WORKING PAPERS

9.1 INTRODUCTION

Working papers record all of the work performed by the auditor and the evidence obtained during the audit work. The working papers are usually divided between two categories of files:

(a) current file

(b) permanent file.

The current file will contain the work performed for the current period, whereas the permanent file will contain that information which is more static and/or is of relevance to every year's audit of that client. The permanent file is also useful to provide new or junior auditors with background details about the client's business and systems prior to commencement of the audit.

Typical contents of a permanent file and current file are shown later in this chapter. These do not need to be memorised, but it is important to understand the type of information held on each of the files.

ISA 230 *Audit Documentation* covers this area and states that the auditor should document matters which are important in providing audit evidence to support the auditor's opinion and evidence that the audit was carried out in accordance with ISAs.

9.2 RECORDING THE AUDIT PROCESS

Definition **Working papers** (also called **audit documentation**) are the record of the planning, performance, supervision and review of an audit as well as of the evidence obtained to support the auditor's report.

Auditors are required to record **all** matters which are important in supporting the audit opinion and in particular their reasoning on all significant matters that require the exercise of judgement. It is in areas such as these that the auditors may subsequently be questioned by the client or possibly by the courts if legal claims are filed against the auditor; it is important for the auditors to be able to show the evidence on which they reached their conclusion.

Working papers serve a number of purposes, including:

- Assisting the engagement team to plan and perform the audit.

- Assisting members of the engagement team responsible for supervision to direct and supervise the audit work, and to discharge their responsibilities in accordance with quality control requirements.

- Enabling the engagement team to be accountable for its work.

- Retaining a record of matters of continuing significance to future audits.

- Enabling the conduct of quality control reviews and inspections.

- Enabling the conduct of external inspections in accordance with applicable legal, regulatory or other requirements.

The characteristics of a good set of audit working papers are often described as follows:

- Working papers should provide an experienced auditor with no previous connection with the audit in question with an understanding of the work performed and the basis of decisions taken.

- Working papers are confidential and should not be made available to third parties without client consent. During the audit the auditor must ensure that all papers are securely maintained. Extracts from the papers can be made available to the client entirely at the discretion of the auditor; however, the auditor's working papers are not a substitute for proper accounting records!

9.3 STANDARDISATION OF AUDIT WORKING PAPERS

This book has already introduced the fact that auditors will often use standardised, pre-prepared documents of various types (checklists, questionnaires and audit programmes for example). These can be seen as examples of standardisation of audit working papers.

Standardisation of working papers offers several advantages.

(a) It improves the efficiency of the preparation and review of working papers.

(b) It facilitates the delegation of work.

(c) It helps to maintain quality control.

(d) It is useful for routine documentation such as checklists for ensuring compliance with applicable accounting standards.

However, a certain amount of flexibility is essential, and it is important that the auditor should always remember the need to exercise professional judgement. It is never appropriate to follow mechanically a standard approach without evaluation of whether or not it is appropriate based upon the circumstances of each individual client. One of the major criticisms of the use of standardised working papers is that they may stifle the initiative of the audit team.

9.4 GUIDELINES ON COMPLETION OF AUDIT WORKING PAPERS

The following general guidelines should be followed in the preparation of working papers.

(a) Permanent ink should be used. Alternatively, working papers may be prepared electronically – e.g. on word processing or spreadsheet packages, with adequate backup.

(b) Descriptions and explanations should be given of audit symbols used (these are often referred to as tick marks).

(c) All working papers must be neat and tidy so that they clearly, concisely and logically show the schedules, results of tests, etc. They should each be headed with:

   (i) client's name and file number

   (ii) period end

(iii) subject of working paper

(iv) reference of working paper within current or permanent file (see below)

(v) initials of preparer and date of preparation

(vi) initials of reviewer and date of review.

All working papers which record audit programmes should contain a summary of the results of the test and a conclusion (or opinion) on its outcome, including evaluation of any errors or exceptions identified during the performance of the work. These conclusions on each section of the audit work will build up to the overall, final audit opinion.

Schedules supporting a figure in the statement of financial position or statement of profit or loss should:

(a) consist of a summarised schedule (a lead schedule) showing the make-up of the final figure, and be supported by backing schedules showing the make-up of those figures on the lead schedule

(b) have extensive cross-referencing between the backing schedules, lead schedules and the accounts themselves to facilitate explanation of any figure in the accounts or working paper

(c) give comparative figures for the previous year so that the auditors can review and explain movement/differences between the years

(d) fully reflect any final adjustments that are made to the accounts

(e) show the tests carried out to verify the figures on the schedules.

The client may already have prepared a schedule which the auditors require for their audit. In order to save audit time and costs, arrangements should be made for copies to be available to the auditors (who should satisfy themselves as to their reliability). If the client does not, but could, prepare schedules, they should be encouraged to do so. This point was referred to earlier in this chapter as a standard audit planning procedure.

In addition, all records of matters raised by the auditors during the audit must be documented together with the reply received to the query and the manner in which the query has been resolved for audit purposes.

We are now going to show you examples of the material that might typically be found in a permanent and current audit file. Again, do not attempt to learn this – use it as a means of becoming familiar in general terms with the purpose and contents of the two types of audit file.

9.5 TYPICAL PERMANENT AUDIT FILE CONTENTS

Typical information on a permanent audit file includes:

- Names of management, those charged with governance, shareholders
- Systems information
- Background to the industry and the client's business
- Title deeds
- Directors' service agreements
- Copies of contract and agreements.

9.6 TYPICAL CURRENT AUDIT FILE'S CONTENTS

The audit work for a specific period is kept on a current audit file.

Typically, there are at least three sections, as follows:

- Planning
- Performance
- Completion.

Planning

The main element of this section is likely to be the Audit Planning Memorandum. This document is the written audit plan and will be read by all members of the audit team before work starts. Its contents are likely to include:

- background information about the client, including recent performance
- changes since last year's audit (for recurring clients)
- key accounting policies
- important laws and regulations affecting the company
- client's trail balance (or draft financial statements)
- preliminary analytical procedures
- key audit risks
- overall audit strategy
- materiality assessment
- timetable of procedures
- deadlines
- staffing and a budget (hours to be worked x charge out rates)
- locations to be visited.

Performance

Working papers are likely to consist of:

- lead schedule – showing total figures, which agree to the financial statements
- back up schedules – breakdowns of totals into relevant sub-totals
- audit work programme detailing:
    - the objectives being tested
    - work completed
    - how samples were selected
    - conclusions drawn
    - who did the work
    - date the work was completed
    - who reviewed it.

Completion

The completion (also known as review) stage of an audit has a number of standard components:

- going concern review
- subsequent events review
- final analytical procedures
- accounting standards (disclosure) checklist
- written representation from management
- summary of adjustments made since trial balance produced
- summary of unadjusted misstatements
- draft final financial statements
- draft report to those charged with governance and management letter.

9.7 CONFIDENTIALITY, SAFE CUSTODY AND OWNERSHIP

Auditors should adopt appropriate procedures for maintaining the confidentiality and safe custody of their working papers.

There is no specific legislation in existence providing guidance to the auditor on the period of retention of audit working papers; this is a matter of judgement. The auditor should follow ethical guidance in this matter which states a minimum period of six years. They may release parts of (or entire) working papers to the client, as long as such disclosure does not undermine the independence or validity of the audit process.

It is fundamental that information is not made available to third parties without the permission of the client; this is examined in the later chapter on 'auditor's liability'.

Note also that the audit working papers are the property of the auditor, not the client.

9.8 INFORMATION TECHNOLOGY AND DOCUMENTATION

Nowadays, auditors tend to use specialist audit software and the majority of their working papers are electronic. This use of information technology in the documentation of audit work has improved efficiency of audits.

It is essential, however, that this information is kept confidential and as a result, audit firms have to ensure they have appropriate procedures in place, such as; firewalls, back-up procedures and virus protection software.

ACTIVITY 7

You are an assistant auditor working for a medium-sized accountancy and auditing practice. The audit senior for whom you are currently working has given you a number of working papers to file (as shown below). How would you split them between the current audit file and the permanent audit file?

(a) Memorandum and Articles of Association

(b) Audit programme for receivables

(c) Details of accounting policies

(d) Ratio analysis (comparing current year's sales to competitors' sales)

(e) Bank account details – bank name, branch and account number

(f) Organisation charts

(g) Extracts from minutes of meetings of the board of directors

(h) Report to management

(i) Product pricing policy

Indicate in which of the two audit files each of the above should appear.

For a suggested answer, see the 'Answers' section at the end of the book.

10 CONTROLLING THE AUDIT – QUALITY CONTROL AND REVIEW PROCEDURES

10.1 INTRODUCTION

It is important that auditors perform a high quality audit for a number of reasons. A reputation for high quality work is likely to attract additional clients and therefore help the practice to grow and develop. In addition, if the audit work performed is of a high quality, there will be a lower chance of the auditors facing negligence claims which can be costly and damage the reputation of the firm, or, worse still, cause the firm to go out of existence. Further, if individual auditors or firms are performing sub-standard audit work the general reputation and image of the profession as a whole is at risk. Quality control and review procedures are therefore seen to be an essential part of modern auditing and a requirement of International Standard of Quality Control 1 and ISA 220 *Quality Control for an Audit of Financial Statements*.

A detailed knowledge of quality control procedures is not required. An overview of the quality control aspects of the audit is included for completeness of understanding.

10.2 ASPECTS OF QUALITY CONTROL

The quality control process can operate in a number of ways in an audit practice, as detailed below. You will note that a number of these have already been dealt with in this book.

Acceptance and continuation of audit engagements

As we have already seen, before accepting a new audit engagement the firm should ensure that it is competent to undertake the work. It should consider carefully whether there are threats to its independence and objectivity and, if so, whether adequate safeguards can be established. The firm should also assess the integrity of the owners, directors and management of the entity. Finally, it should comply with the ethical requirements of the professional accountancy bodies in relation to changes in appointment.

Resources

The firm should have sufficient audit engagement partners and audit staff with the competencies necessary to meet the needs of the audit.

Assignment of personnel to audit engagements

An audit engagement partner should be appointed to each audit engagement undertaken by a firm, to take responsibility for the engagement on behalf of the firm and the firm should assign audit staff with the competencies necessary to perform the audit work expected of them to individual audit engagements.

Training of audit staff

We saw in an earlier chapter that membership via qualification with a Recognised Qualifying Body (RQB) is a pre-requisite of membership of a Recognised Supervisory Body (RSB) and hence entitlement to audit under the UK Companies Act 2006. Training requirements include the setting of examinations and practical training. The practical training does not stop when an auditor has qualified. The practical training continues through the requirement to undertake **continuing professional development** (CPD). Since January 2005 CPD has been compulsory for all ACCA members.

Large firms typically run internal training courses to satisfy the CPD requirement; smaller firms are often members of a training consortium which provides equivalent courses.

At a less formal level, the use of staff library resources, access to technical websites and subscriptions to technical journals all help audit staff to keep up to date with modern auditing practices and should therefore be in place in all auditing firms.

Consultation

The firm should have procedures to facilitate consultation and to ensure that sufficient resources are available to enable appropriate consultation to take place in relation to difficult or contentious matters. The results of any consultation that are relevant to audit conclusions should be documented in the audit working papers. Examples might include procedures under which technical experts (on areas such as taxation, computer systems or specialised types of industries) are available within the firm to advise operational auditors when the occasion arises.

Engagement partner

The firm should designate a specific partner to take responsibility for each individual audit engagement. The engagement partner should be responsible for ensuring that adequate arrangements are in place to safeguard their objectivity and the firm's independence. The engagement partner should also ensure that audit work is directed, supervised and reviewed in a manner that provides reasonable assurance that the work has been performed competently.

10.3 REVIEW PROCEDURES

Audit review is an important part of the audit process and involves the audit work being subject to a second look by a more experienced auditor. The objective of the review is to ensure that sufficient appropriate audit evidence has been documented to justify the conclusions drawn. A number of types of audit review are now widely used. These are discussed below.

(a) **'Hot' review**

A 'hot' review is a review carried out during an audit assignment before the auditor's report is signed. For example, the working papers produced by a member of the audit staff should be checked by a more experienced member of the staff soon after they are prepared. Such a review is evidenced by the reviewer initialling and dating that particular working paper.

At the end of the audit, but before the auditor's report is signed, the manager or partner should review the entire audit file and the final accounts.

(b) **Post-audit review** ('cold' review)

A 'cold' review is a review carried out after the auditor's report has been signed. Some firms use a small group of experienced employees to form a review team or department. This team has the job of reviewing in detail a regular sample of the work performed by an audit group and ensuring that the audit has been conducted in accordance with the firm's standard procedures.

(c) **Peer review**

Another example of a cold review is a peer review in which one firm of auditors reviews the working practices of another firm and reports to the partners of the investigated firm on the ways in which their procedures might be improved.

ACTIVITY 8

What aspects should a firm's quality control procedures cover?

For a suggested answer, see the 'Answers' section at the end of the book.

CONCLUSION

Auditors must plan the audit to ensure that the audit is effectively performed. They should consider the nature and extent of the work required, and this will be documented in the audit planning memorandum. The work performed is dependent primarily on the risk and materiality levels which the auditors will evaluate at the planning stage. Following completion of the overall audit plan the auditors will prepare audit programmes containing the detailed tests to be performed to achieve the audit objectives.

Working papers are important as they record the various elements of audit evidence obtained and used as the basis for reaching the audit opinion.

Quality control of the audit is required at all stages and includes a review of the audit work after it has been completed.

A lengthy but important chapter in the context of what is to follow!

FAU: FOUNDATIONS IN AUDIT

KEY TERMS

Audit strategy – this sets the scope, timing and direction of the audit and guides the development of the audit plan

Audit plan – this includes a description of the nature, timing and extent of planned risk assessment procedures and further audit procedures at the assertion level. It also includes other planned audit procedures that are required to be carried out so that the engagement complies with ISAs.

Analytical procedures – study of relationships among both financial and non-financial data including comparison of financial information with prior periods, budgets and forecasts and similar industries.

Audit risk – this is the risk that the auditor expresses an inappropriate audit opinion when the financial statements are materially misstated. Audit risk is a function of the risks of material misstatement and detection risk.

Inherent risk – the susceptibility of an assertion about a class of transaction, account balance or disclosure to a misstatement that could be material, either individually or when aggregated with other misstatements, before consideration of any related controls.

Control risk – the risk that a misstatement that could occur in an assertion about a class of transaction, account balance or disclosure and that could be material, either individually or when aggregated with other misstatements, will not be prevented, or detected and corrected, on a timely basis by the entity's internal control.

Detection risk – the risk that the procedures performed by the auditor to reduce audit risk to an acceptably low level will not detect a misstatement that exists and that could be material, either individually or when aggregated with other misstatements.

Misstatement – the difference between the amount, classification, presentation or disclosure of an item in the financial statements and the amount, classification, presentation or disclosure that is required for the item to be in accordance with the applicable financial reporting framework (i.e. applicable legal and accounting requirements). A misstatement may be a matter of fact, or a matter of judgement. A misstatement may be either not material or material – the latter will affect the view presented by the financial statements. The auditor should therefore plan and perform his work so that the risk of not detecting a material misstatement is reduced to an acceptable level.

Risk of material misstatement – the risk that the financial statements as prepared by the directors contain a material misstatement. This risk will vary for each company depending upon a range of factors such as the reliability of the accounting systems and procedures and consists of two components – inherent risk and control risk.

Audit programme – a document which records the audit testing to be performed. It specifies the nature and extent of the checking, and the members of staff who have carried out the work and the date on which the work was performed. It also contains evidence of review of work i.e. by whom and the date.

Standardised audit programme – a pre-prepared listing of objectives and tests which is usable on all audits.

Audit evidence – any piece of verifiable information which assists the auditor to reach a conclusion on the financial statements.

Audit test – work designed by the auditor to generate relevant and reliable audit evidence.

Current file – a file of working papers containing the work performed for the current period's audit.

Permanent file – a file which contains information which is of relevance to every year's audit.

Hot review – the working papers produced by a member of the audit staff are checked by a more experienced member of the staff before the auditor's report is signed.

Post-audit review ('cold' review) – a review carried out after the auditor's report has been signed.

Audit review department – a group of experienced employees forming a review team. This team has the job of reviewing in detail the work performed by an audit group and ensuring that the audit has been conducted in accordance with the firm's standard procedures.

Peer review – a system where one firm of auditors reviews the working practices of another firm and reports to the partners of the investigated firm on the ways in which their procedures might be improved.

Internal audit – An independent, objective assurance and consulting activity designed to add value and improve an organisation's operations.

SELF-TEST QUESTIONS

		Paragraph
1	What are the primary purposes of planning the audit?	1.1
2	What techniques are used in analytical procedures?	2.5
3	What are the definitions of inherent risk, control risk and detection risk?	2.3
4	What are the different job titles of staff who may be included in the audit?	6.2
5	What is the purpose of the audit programme?	7.1
6	What are the reasons for preparing working papers?	9.1
7	What are the typical contents of a permanent audit file and a current audit file?	9.5

FAU: FOUNDATIONS IN AUDIT

PRACTICE QUESTION

KOALA LIMITED

Koala Limited is a medium-sized company, manufacturer and wholesaler of soft toys with a small factory in Basingstoke, a travelling sales force of six representatives and an accounts department consisting of a qualified chief accountant (Miss Jones) and two accounts clerks.

You were the manager in charge of the audit last year and have recently carried out your preliminary planning for this year's audit (to 30 September 20X7). From discussions with Miss Jones you have discovered that on her appointment in late 20X6 new systems were introduced and you expect to be able to rely from 1 January on the internal controls of the new system in all areas. Previously you were unable to rely on internal control over purchases, wages or salesmen's expenses, and carried out very extensive detailed testing in these areas.

You are required to draft a memorandum setting out the intended means of approaching the audit, to ensure attention is devoted to all critical aspects and to assist in direction and control of the audit.

(15 marks)

For a suggested answer, see the 'Answers' section at the end of the book.

Chapter 6

INTERNAL CONTROLS

INTRODUCTION

In the previous chapter we outlined the risk-based approach to auditing which focuses on the key areas of risk within a client's business.

Part of this approach requires the auditor to understand the internal controls that operate within an organisation as a basis for risk assessment to determine the overall audit strategy and the detailed audit plan. The auditor can then identify deficiencies in the system of internal control which are likely to be a source of risk of possible misstatement in the financial statements and can then adopt a suitable audit approach to manage that risk.

This approach focuses the audit work on the accounting systems, which produce the figures, not on the figures themselves. The thinking is if:

1   the controls in the system are sound in principle, and
2   the controls in the system are operating effectively, then

the figures produced by the system are likely to be true and fair.

It is important that both of these factors are in place – a sound accounting system is of no value to the auditor if the client staff involved with the system are not operating it effectively.

This chapter deals with item 1 above – the work the auditor carries out on the accounting systems. The following chapter deals with item 2 – how the auditor will assess whether the systems in place are operating satisfactorily.

If the auditor is happy with both aspects, a systems-based audit will be performed with a limited amount of testing of transactions and balances. If there are major problems with either of the two aspects, the auditor will carry out extended testing of transactions and balances only.

This chapter covers syllabus areas C (1), C (2) and C (3).

CONTENTS

1   Internal control

2   Ascertaining and understanding the system

3   Documenting the system

4   Evaluating the system of internal control

5   Inherent limitations of internal control

FAU: FOUNDATIONS IN AUDIT

LEARNING OUTCOMES

At the end of this chapter, you should be able to:

- understand the concept of internal control and its significance in the systems audit approach

- identify the types of internal controls that may exist in an accounting system

- appreciate and apply the methods used to ascertain and document the systems of internal control

- understand and apply the techniques available for the evaluation of internal controls

- appreciate that systems of internal control should never be relied upon entirely by auditors.

1 INTERNAL CONTROL

ISA 315 (Revised 2019) *Identifying and Assessing the Risks of Material Misstatement* requires that auditors need to understand an entity's internal controls. In particular, it identifies five components of a system of internal control and we will consider each in turn.

1.1 DEFINITION OF INTERNAL CONTROL

Definition   **Internal control** is the process designed and effected by management and others to provide reasonable assurance about the achievement of the entity's objectives with regard to reliability of financial reporting, effectiveness and efficiency of operations and compliance with applicable laws and regulations.

Internal control is achieved by management establishing an effective **system of internal control**.

Definition   **The system of internal control** comprises the **control environment** and **control activities (i.e. policies and procedures)**. It includes all the policies and procedures adopted by the directors and management of an entity to assist in their objective of achieving, as far as practicable, the orderly and efficient conduct of the business, including adherence to internal policies, the safeguarding of assets, the prevention and detection of fraud and error, the accuracy and completeness of the accounting records, and the timely preparation of reliable financial information.

You will note from this definition that there are two elements that combine together to produce the overall system of internal control of an enterprise – the control environment and the control activities.

Whilst it is traditional to identify the system of internal control as comprising the control environment and control activities, in fact ISA 315 (Revised 2019) *Identifying and Assessing the Risks of Material Misstatement* identifies five separate components of internal control as follows:

1 The control environment

This is a broad concept which refers to the overall attitude, awareness and actions of management regarding internal controls and their importance. In short, it is management's overall attitude to the significance of internal control within the organisation.

It is reflected in, for example, management style, the corporate culture, values, philosophy and operating style, the organisational structure, personnel policies and procedures.

Personnel policies and procedures, for example, would include those covering recruitment, retention and dismissal. The organisational structure should have clear lines of reporting responsibility and the maintenance of an internal audit function and audit committee demonstrates a commitment to high level controls.

For example, employees should clearly understand what is required of them as part of their work responsibilities and also understand the consequences of not complying with company policies and practices, such as misuse of company internet or email facilities.

The use of management accounts for the purposes of variance analysis is also a high level control.

The control environment provides a background to detailed control activities. It does not of itself, of course, ensure the effectiveness of the system of internal control as a whole.

2 The entity's risk assessment process

This is the entity's process for identifying business risks relevant to financial reporting objectives and deciding about actions to address those risks. Auditors are interested in business risks because certain issues which may affect the business may also be a risk to the financial statements being misstated. For example, economic downturn puts pressure on the entity to meet the expectations of finance providers and consequently management may be tempted to manipulate the financial statements.

A further example would be the situation whereby an entity was under financial pressure and failed to comply with all relevant laws and regulations, such as health and safety regulations as a way of cutting costs. This would put the entity at risk of fines and other penalties (not to mention loss of reputation) which may then require provisions to be included in the financial statements.

If an entity has strong procedures to identify and manage the business risks that it faces, the risk of material misstatement will be lower.

3 The information system and communication

This includes the financial reporting system and consists of the procedures established to initiate record, process and report entity transactions and to maintain accountability for the related assets, liabilities and equity.

Examples of parts of the information system include daybooks and ledgers to record transactions, together with registers to record non-current assets, shareholders etc.

ISA 315 (Revised 2019) requires the auditor to understand how the entity communicates significant matters that support the preparation of the financial statements and related reporting responsibilities in the information system and other components of the system of internal control:

- Between people within the entity, including how financial reporting roles and responsibilities are communicated;
- Between management and those charged with governance; and
- With external parties, such as those with regulatory authorities.

4 Control activities

These are more detailed day to day operating policies and procedures established to achieve the entity's specific objectives. Objectives in an accounting context would include the proper authorisation, timely and accurate recording of transactions in the correct period, the safeguarding of assets and ensuring the existence of assets recorded. They include particular procedures to prevent, detect and correct errors. They differ from entity to entity and are affected by the size of the entity and the activities in which it is involved. We will look at these in greater detail later in this chapter.

Many of the internal control activities, which would be relevant to the larger enterprise, are not practical, appropriate or necessary in the small enterprise. Managements of small enterprises have less need to rely on formal internal controls, because of their personal contact with, or involvement in, the operation of the enterprise itself.

Examples of control activities include the following:

- authorisation procedures e.g. to pay supplies only when goods and services have been received.
- physical controls to restrict access to permitted areas only. This may be achieved by the use of employee electronic swipe cards or photographic identity cards which must be shown to gain access to the premises.
- regular bank reconciliations.

5 The entity's process to monitor the system of internal control

An entity should review its overall control system to ensure it still meets its objectives and operates efficiently and effectively. Auditors are required by ISAs to identify control deficiencies observed throughout the audit but it remains the company's responsibility to monitor the effectiveness of its own internal controls.

Monitoring may be performed either as a separate evaluation exercise, or on an on-going basis. In the case of the former, this could be an investigation as to how controls have been circumvented by employees to manipulate the accounting records. In the case of the latter, this could be an on-going review to monitor internet and email usage by employees to ensure that such usage complies with company policies and practices.

1.2 THE BENEFITS OF INTERNAL CONTROL FOR THE ENTERPRISE

We can identify the following principal benefits, which may arise for an enterprise from a sound system of internal control.

(a) Assurance that all transactions are completely and accurately processed.

(b) Confidence that only authorised transactions take place.

(c) Assurance that adequate documentation supporting transactions is created and retained.

INTERNAL CONTROLS : CHAPTER 6

(d) Assurance that the company's assets and liabilities are correctly stated, in order for them to make informed decisions on the operation of the business.

(e) Minimisation of the risk of fraud and misappropriation of assets.

1.3 THE BENEFITS OF INTERNAL CONTROL TO THE AUDITOR

If a sound system of internal control exists the auditor will be able to rely on those controls and reduce his audit testing accordingly whilst still being able to provide an audit opinion on the financial statements.

1.4 THE AUDITOR'S WORK ON INTERNAL CONTROL

ISA 315 (Revised 2019) emphasises the importance of internal control to the auditor. Auditors should obtain an understanding of the accounting and system of internal control sufficient to plan the audit and develop an effective audit approach. Auditors should also use professional judgement to assess the components of audit risk and to design audit procedures to ensure it is reduced to an acceptably low level.

At an early stage in their work auditors will have to decide the extent to which they wish to place reliance on the internal controls of the enterprise. As the audit proceeds, that decision will be kept under review and, depending on the results of their examination, they may decide to place more or less reliance on these controls.

We can summarise the work which the auditor will need to do on the systems of internal control as follows.

Step	Commentary	Reference
Ascertain the systems and controls operating in each transaction cycle	Find out how the client processes transactions and what controls are in place. The major transaction cycles in a business are: revenues, purchases, payroll, payments, receipts.	Section 2 in this chapter
Record those systems and controls	The systems are documented in the audit working papers – typically, the permanent file.	Section 3 in this chapter
Confirm that the records are correct	It is important that the auditor's record of the accounting system should be correct and up to date, otherwise a wrong evaluation may result.	Section 3 in this chapter
Evaluate and conclude on the effectiveness of the systems of control	The auditor assesses whether the systems and controls in place are likely to produce true and fair figures.	Section 4 in this chapter

Controls are inadequate	Controls are adequate		
Do not rely on the controls	Test the controls	Perform test of controls to establish whether the controls in the system, are actually working.	Chapter 7
		Perform a verification audit.	Chapter 7

1.5 CATEGORIES OF INTERNAL CONTROLS

The term 'internal control' encompasses all five components of internal control identified by ISA 315 (Revised 2019) (see section 1.1 above). Thus an internal control could be an effective element of the control environment, an effective risk assessment process carried out by the entity, etc.

Internal controls are often split into the following categories:

Control activities

Generally, control activities that may be relevant to an audit may be categorised as policies and procedures that pertain to the following:

- Authorisation and approvals – an authorisation affirms that a transaction is valid and typically takes the form of an approval by a higher level of management or of verification and a determination if the transaction is valid.

    An example of an authorisation and approval control is a supervisor approving an expense report after reviewing whether the expenses seem reasonable and within policy.

    An example of an automated approval is when an invoice unit cost is automatically compared with the related purchase order unit cost within a pre-established tolerance level. Invoices within the tolerance level are automatically approved for payment. Those invoices outside the tolerance level are flagged for additional investigation.

- Reconciliations – controls that compare two or more data elements. If differences are identified, action is taken to bring the data into agreement. Reconciliations generally address the completeness or accuracy of processing transactions.

- Verifications – controls that compare two or more items with each other or compare an item with a policy, and will likely involve a follow-up action when the two items do not match or the item is not consistent with policy. Verfications generally address the completeness, accuracy or validity of processing transactions.

- Physical or logical controls – controls that encompass the physical security of assets such as secured facilities over access to assets and records, banking cash immediately, authorisation for access to computer programs and data files, electronic tagging of inventory and portable non-current assets.

- Segregation of duties – assigning different people the responsibilities of authorising transactions, recording transactions, and maintaining custody of assets. Segregation of duties is intended to reduce the opportunities to allow any person to be in a position to both perpetrate and conceal errors or fraud in the normal course of the person's duties.

    Possible application:

    Consider an inventory purchasing system in a manufacturing company:

Stage	Documentation	Responsibility
Initiation	Stores requisition	Stores keeper
Authorisation	Purchase order	Purchasing officer
Custody	Goods received note	Receiving officer
Recording	Invoice	Accounts dept

- Certain control activities may depend on the existence of appropriate higher level policies established by management or those charged with governance. For example, authorisation controls may be delegated under established guidelines, such as investment criteria set by those charged with governance. Alternatively, non-routine transactions such as major acquisitions or divestments may require specific high level approval, including in some cases that of shareholders.

Monitoring of controls

As discussed above, an important management responsibility is to establish and maintain internal control on an ongoing basis. Management's monitoring of controls includes considering whether they are operating as intended and that they are modified as appropriate for changes in conditions.

Monitoring of controls may include activities such as management's review as to whether bank reconciliations are being performed on a timely basis, internal auditors' evaluation of sales personnel's compliance with the entity's policies on terms of sales contracts, and a legal department's oversight of compliance with the entity's ethical or business practice policies.

1.6 AN APPLICATION – DIRECT CONTROLS IN A PAYABLES/ PURCHASING SYSTEM

It is a useful exercise for you to consider the major transaction cycles referred to above and identify the principal controls which you would expect to find in a typical system.

A suggestion is presented below for a purchases system.

1. Use of pre-numbered and properly authorised purchase requisitions to instigate all procurement.

2. Strict controls over custody of purchase orders to prevent inappropriate use.

3. Use of pre-numbered and properly authorised purchase orders by a competent purchasing department and check to ensure that purchases are within approved budgets.

4. Accreditation procedure for approval of company's suppliers.

5. Checking of incoming goods for quality and quantity.

6. Raising of appropriate paperwork to record receipt of goods.

7. Detailed procedures to safeguard the company's interest in dealing with damaged or short deliveries.

8. Purchase invoices to be matched and checked with purchase orders and goods received notes. Prices and calculations to be checked before processing.

9. Proper approval of purchase invoices by predetermined signatory prior to processing of invoice.

10. Controls and checks over the accurate posting of invoices to the payables ledger.

11. Regular reconciliation of supplier statements with payables ledger balances, ideally prior to payment of cheques.

12 Careful control over custody, raising and approval of cheques for suppliers.

13 Appropriate goods returned procedures to ensure that their receipt is recorded, that they are checked to confirm whether they can be returned to stock or should be worked on to rectify any problem and that the supplier account is properly updated.

Note that the key controls as noted above also indicate how an effective segregation of duties can be incorporated into a control system. In a large organisation, each task may be performed by staff in a different department. This may not be possible in a smaller organisation, but it may still be possible to incorporate elements of segregation of duties. In particular, no individual should be responsible for recording consecutive stages of a transaction process. For example, the person who raises a requisition for materials required should not be the same person who approves the purchase order.

ACTIVITY 1

Think about the accounting systems in operation at your place of employment and consider what internal controls exist and whether or not these work effectively.

There is no feedback to this activity.

2 ASCERTAINING AND UNDERSTANDING THE SYSTEM

2.1 ASCERTAINING THE ACCOUNTING SYSTEM

As we have seen before auditors are required to obtain and document an understanding of the accounting system and control environment sufficient to determine their audit approach, whether that be a systems based approach, or a substantive/verification approach. It also helps with the assessment of inherent and control risk as part of the audit planning process.

The first step in this process is to ascertain the accounting system – i.e. find out what the accounting system is for a particular transaction cycle.

A number of methods are available to the auditor for the purpose of ascertaining the client's accounting systems. These are summarised below, and then each method is dealt with in more detail.

Methods of ascertaining accounting systems

1 Examine previous audit work

2 Review client's systems documentation

3 Interview client's staff

4 Trace transactions

5 Examine client's documents

6 Observe client's procedures

2.2 METHODS OF ASCERTAINING THE SYSTEM

1 Examining previous audit work

In any situation except the first audit, the audit files should contain a record of the system as it operated at the last audit date. Unless there have been major changes (this possibility should always be considered), this will only require updating. But note that a detailed systems investigation will be required at the first audit of a new client.

2 Review of client's systems documentation

Some clients, especially large clients, will have manuals of accounting procedures. These will provide a valuable source of information. The auditor should be careful that such documentation is up to date, and should always confirm such information.

3 Interviews with client's staff

The auditor may find it appropriate to use discussions with client staff who operate the system as a means of establishing how the system operates. Again it is very important to confirm such information.

4 Tracing transactions (walk-through tests)

In order to follow a particular sequence relating to a single transaction, it may be best to follow through a few typical transactions. This technique (often known as **walk-through tests**) is also often used to confirm the auditor's understanding of a particular process which has already been documented following interviews with client staff for example.

5 Examining client's documents

A review of a sample of a client's transaction documents (for example, purchase orders and purchase invoices) may be taken as a source of information on how the system in that area of the business operates. It provides evidence of information collected by the client at different stages in the system operation.

6 Observation of client's procedures

It will often be useful to watch the client carrying out procedures such as wages pay-out and opening of the post as it provides visual evidence of controls in operation. The auditor should be aware that as the staff knows they are being observed they may be inclined to perform a process in line with documented procedures rather than as they usually do it.

Once the auditor has obtained information about how the systems operate and has an understanding of the system he needs to confirm his understanding and ensure that his understanding and documentation of the system is correct. This simply involves taking a small number of transactions through the system from source to destination (often known as 'from cradle to grave'). Such tests are particularly useful where the auditor is relying on the client's documentation of the system.

3 DOCUMENTING THE SYSTEM

3.1 INTRODUCTION

Documenting the system is an extremely important stage in the audit; ISA 300 *Planning an audit of financial statements* states that in planning the audit, auditors should obtain and **document** an understanding of the accounting system and control environment sufficient to determine their audit approach.

The various methods of recording the system may be summarised as follows:

1   Narrative notes

2   Organisation charts

3   Internal control questionnaires (ICQs) and Internal control evaluation questionnaires (ICEQs)

4   Flowcharts

These are examined in more detail below.

3.2 METHODS OF RECORDING THE SYSTEM

1   **Narrative notes**

This is a simple and apparently convenient way of describing systems. Having ascertained the system, the auditor draws up a narrative description of it for the audit files. An example might be:

'Sales invoices are prepared by ....They are checked by ....and then passed to ...... for recording in the customer's account in the receivables ledger etc.'

However, this method suffers from several disadvantages of a practical nature:

(i)   It is long-winded; systems notes can take up a disproportionate amount of space.

(ii) Notes may be difficult to interpret and review.

(iii) It is time consuming to incorporate system changes into the notes and omissions may occur.

(iv) It may be difficult to see if part of the system has been missed out altogether.

(v)   Deficiencies in the controls in the system may not be immediately apparent.

This method is suitable for very small simple systems where relatively few transactions are involved. It is more often used in conjunction with other methods rather than being used in isolation.

2 Organisation charts

The organisation chart provides a convenient way of describing the relationships between individuals in an organisation. However it does not specify the precise **duties** of the individuals concerned and it only describes the **formal** relationships between them. In practice, **informal** relationships may have important implications for the auditor. An example of an organisation chart is set out below:

ORGANISATION CHART

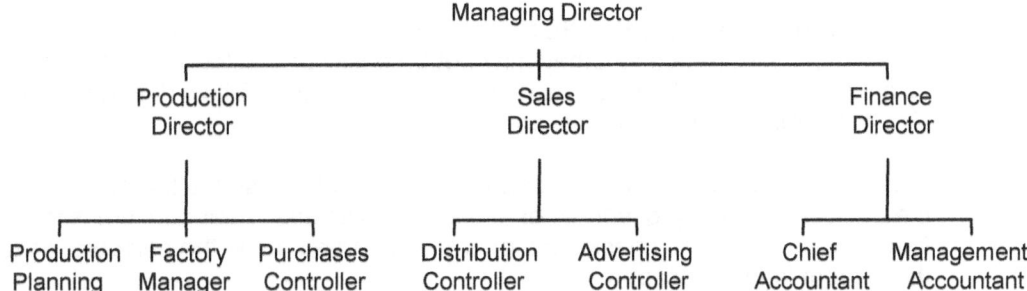

The information gained from the organisation chart will only provide limited information and usually will be supplemented by more detailed information contained in narrative or flowchart form.

3 Internal control questionnaires (ICQs)

ICQs are usually regarded as documents for *evaluating* rather than *recording*. However the various questions making up the ICQs can be constructed in such a way as to require answers in the form of descriptive notes on the system. In this way they can fulfil both functions. ICQs are considered in more detail later.

Internal control evaluation questionnaires (ICEs)

ICEs ask what controls the client uses to mitigate a specific risk rather than asking whether a specific control is in place. ICQs and ICEs are considered in more detail later.

4 Flowcharts

This is becoming an increasingly widely used technique for recording accounting systems in audit files.

A flowchart is a diagrammatical representation of an accounting system. A good flowchart will be supplemented with narrative, which helps with the understanding of the system.

Flowcharts have the following advantages:

(i) They portray the flow of documents through the system and enable the auditor to relate those movements with procedures and checks carried out as part of that system.

(ii) They show the movement of documents in such a way that, when properly prepared, the sources and destinations of all documents will be clear.

(iii) They help to highlight deficiencies in the control of the business.

(iv) They enable audit tests to be clearly related to deficiencies in the accounting system.

(v) They can be used to clearly highlight controls in the system.

Standard symbols are used to represent documents, operations and checks carried out. Flow lines are used to join up the symbols and represent the movement of documents. Dotted lines are used to represent the flow of information between documents.

One possible disadvantage is that if standard conventions and notation have not been adopted in their preparation, they may not be easily understood. A further possible disadvantage is that they may be complex and difficult to follow depending upon the size and structure of an organisation.

Manual systems flowcharts – as opposed to computer systems flowcharts – deal with the clerical (manual) procedures of accounting systems. Their concern is to chart the flow of documents and checks and operations carried out in the particular section of the system being described.

In this paper you will not be asked to draw flowcharts from scratch. However, you may be asked to interpret flowcharts and draw conclusions about the effectiveness of the system from them. For this to be achieved you must first understand how flowcharts are constructed. This is our next topic.

ACTIVITY 2

List four ways in which an auditor might record his client's system, and briefly summarise the advantages and limitations for each one.

For a suggested answer, see the 'Answers' section at the end of the book.

3.3 MANUAL SYSTEMS FLOWCHARTS

Principles

To enable internal controls to be evaluated flowcharts *must* highlight the following:

(a) the sequence of operations happening to each document (e.g. authorisation, checking, matching, filing)

(b) the segregation of staff duties and who is responsible for each operation.

There are a number of systems of flowcharting in operation. The following system is used widely by members of the accountancy and auditing profession. Students who work for a practising firm which uses some other method are strongly advised to concentrate on their firm's system if they are familiar with their own firm's approach – it will be acceptable for your work in this paper.

The following pages explain some of the key points in preparing such flowcharts and contain an example of such a chart. Remember that you only need to be able to understand and interpret the chart, rather than to be able to prepare it!

Symbols used in manual systems flowcharts

Standard symbols used are as follows:

Symbol	Meaning
☐	A document
Stacked documents (1,2,3,4)	A multi-part set of documents
☐ with N	Pre-numbered document
Rectangle with vertical line	A book of account
X	An operation performed on a document
◇	A check performed on a document
▽	Filing a book or document
⟶	Document flow
---▶	Information flow
○	Connector with another page/flowline

Use of the major symbols

1 **The document symbol**

Each document in the flowchart should have a vertical flowline. Such vertical flowlines represent a movement in time within a particular department. When the document is moved to another department, this movement in position will be represented by a horizontal line – departments are therefore listed across the page.

Example 1

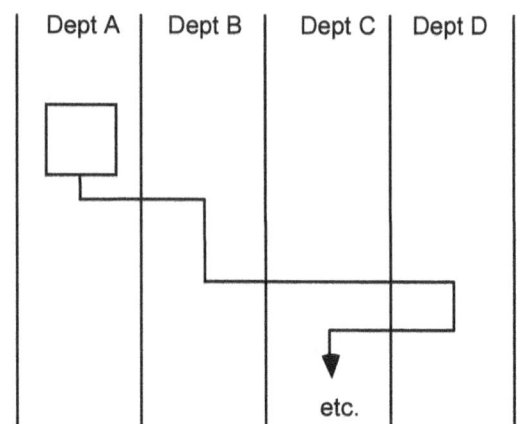

Here the document is originated in Dept A. It is moved to Dept B, then Dept C.

Note that only vertical and horizontal lines are used, never diagonal lines.

2 **The operation symbol**

Various operations will be performed on a document. It will, for instance, be prepared, added up, used to prepare other documents, etc. Any operation, other than a check function, is represented by the cross symbol. Each operation symbol should be supported by a brief narrative explaining the nature of the operation. The flowchart should also disclose the type of document concerned.

Example 2

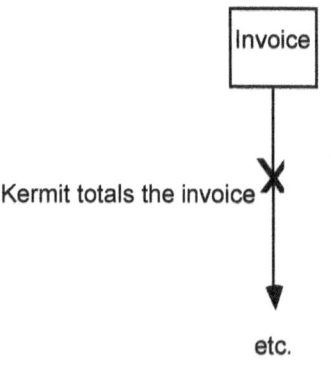

Note that the operation symbol is positioned on a vertical flowline. It should never appear on a horizontal flowline since that would suggest in this case that Kermit totals the invoice while it is moving from one department to another.

3 The information flow symbol

Example 3

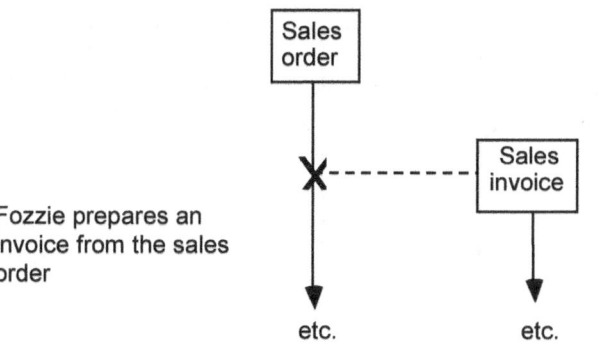

Fozzie prepares an invoice from the sales order

Here one document is prepared from another. The movement of information to the sales invoice is shown by a dotted line. Such information flowlines are always horizontal, never vertical. Note that flowlines then continue for both the order and the invoice.

Example 4

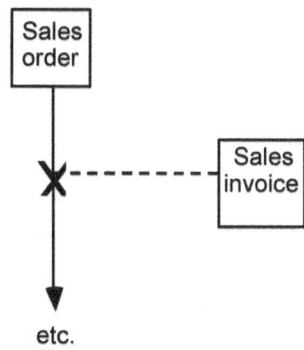

This example is wrong because:

(a) no narrative exists to explain the nature of the operation; and

(b) the sales invoice has no flowline, it disappears into thin air.

4 The check symbol

Example 5

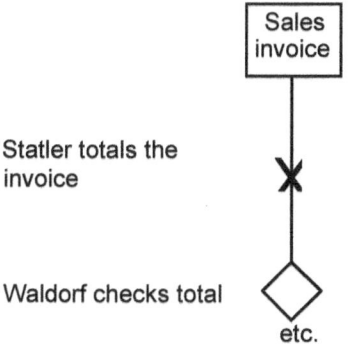

Statler totals the invoice

Waldorf checks total

This example shows a simple check on a single document. Such a symbol highlights the controls within an accounting system. Narrative is needed to explain fully the nature of the check.

Example 6

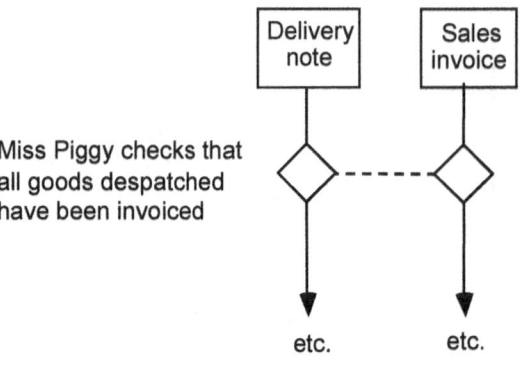

Miss Piggy checks that all goods despatched have been invoiced

This shows a check between two documents. Note the use of the information flowline again and that both the delivery note and the sales invoice continue with vertical flowlines of their own.

The filing symbol

Once documents have been processed they will often be filed away. Such files are either permanent or temporary. The two sorts of file are denoted by the same symbol but the temporary files are marked with a letter 'T'. It will often be useful to indicate the order of filing either numerically, alphabetically or in chronological order. This can be done by marking the symbol with the letter N, A, or D.

Example 7

Filed awaiting delivery of goods.

Checked weekly to latest deliveries by Zoot

When goods are received purchase order initialled by Scooter

Note that with the temporary filing symbol the flowline of the document must continue. With the permanent filing symbol the flowline stops since the document has reached its ultimate destination.

The book of account symbol

The flowchart should use the 'book' symbol to show the book which is already in existence. It should also show the book being refiled once the posting is completed.

Example 8

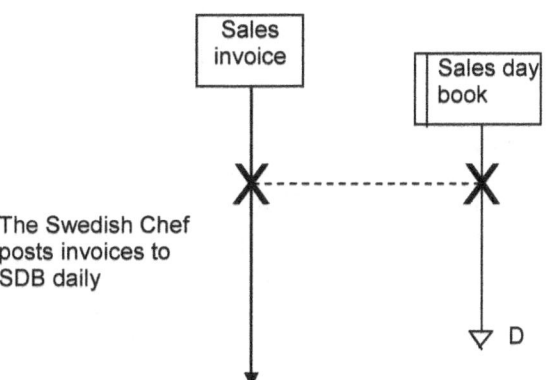

The Swedish Chef posts invoices to SDB daily

Note that the same flowline principles apply to books as to documents. A vertical flowline is needed which ends with the refiling of the sales day book which will be kept chronologically.

Depicting multi-part sets of documents

Example 9

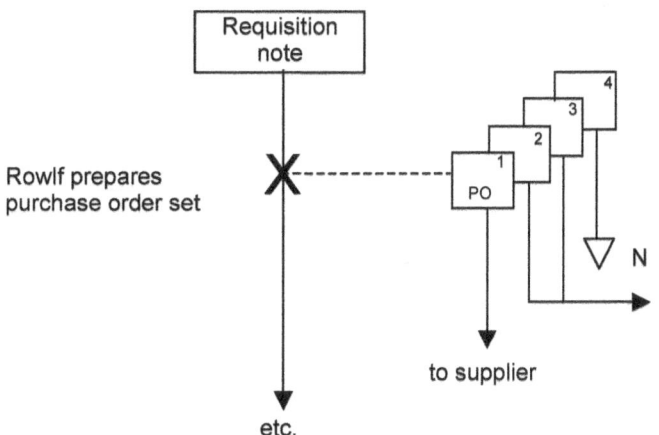

Rowlf prepares purchase order set

Note that each part of the set must have a flowline emanating from it. In this example. PO1 is sent to the supplier, PO2 and PO3 together go off to another department and PO4 is filed numerically.

Example of flowchart

PIGS IN SPACE COMPANY: Purchases system ordering and receiving

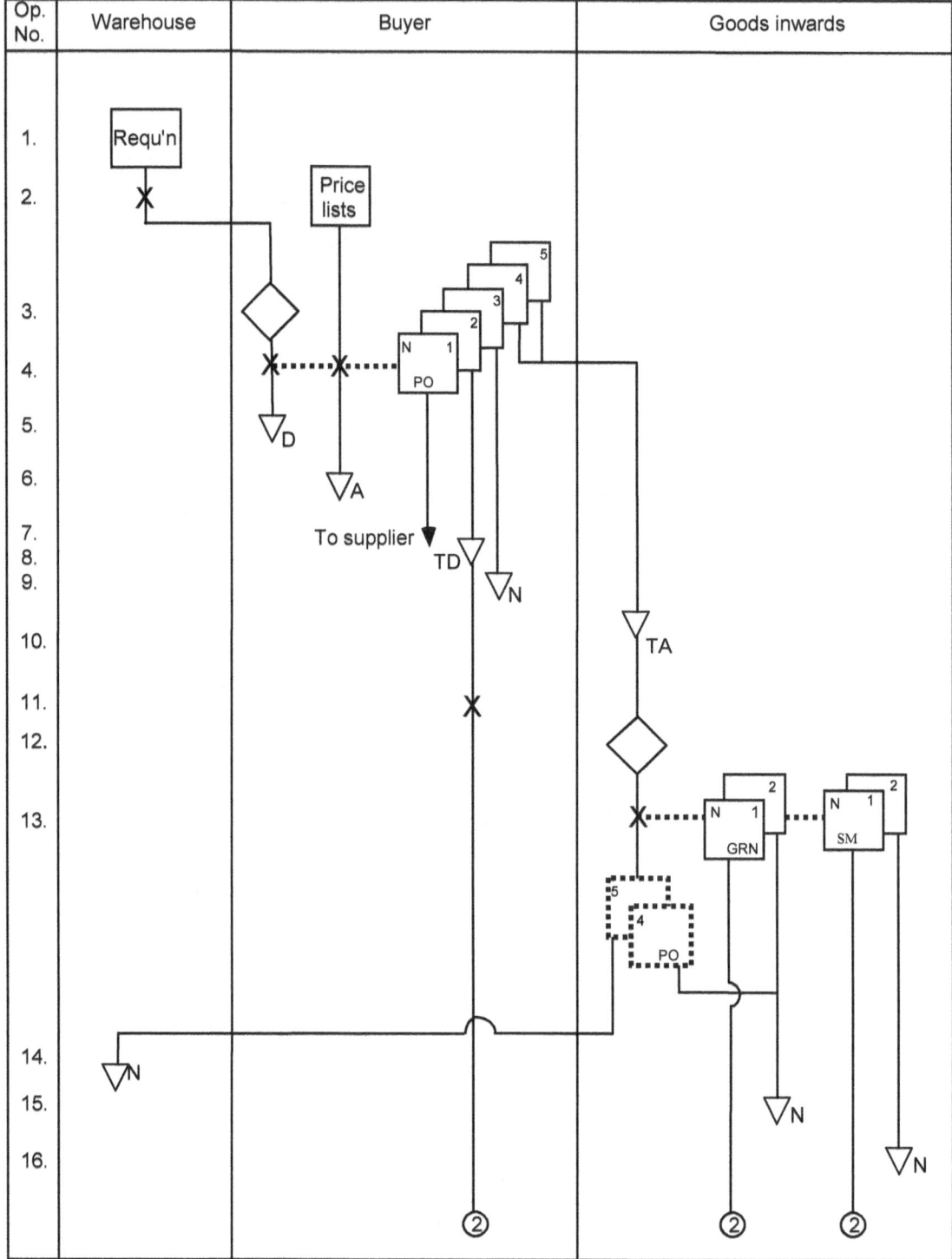

Narrative to the above flowchart

1. Requisition note raised when goods are at a pre-set re-order level. Order quantity is pre-determined by use of a copy of the previous purchase order.

2. Signed by warehouse manager.

3. Buyer checks authorisation.

4	Purchase order set prepared.
8	PO2 filed temporarily to act as a check on overdue deliveries.
10	PO4 and PO5 are filed until goods are received.
11	Weekly check on overdue deliveries.
12	Goods checked to PO to ensure they are in agreement.
13	If not damaged, goods are accepted and a goods received note set is raised. Where quantity received is below order a shortage memo set is also raised and a note made on the purchase order.
14	PO5 is sent back to the warehouse to act as the next requisition note.

Commentary on the above flowchart

(a) All operations and checks are positioned on vertical lines within a particular department.

(b) Horizontal lines show the movement of a document between departments.

(c) In practice the flowchart would continue, dealing with the processing of the purchase invoice/credit note/day books/payables ledger/cash book etc. The flowlines at the bottom of the page would continue to page 2 of the flowchart.

(d) Note that the narrative to the flowchart does not deal with all of the operation numbers since some should be self-explanatory e.g. operation 9 represents the numerical filing of PO3 in the buying department.

4 EVALUATING THE SYSTEM OF INTERNAL CONTROL

4.1 INTRODUCTION

Having ascertained, confirmed and recorded the system, the auditor now needs to carry out a preliminary evaluation of the system in order to make a decision as to whether he will be able to rely on internal controls and adopt a systems audit approach. If he cannot rely on internal controls he will need to use a verification approach to the audit.

Note that the outcome of an evaluation of the system of internal control could be that there are deficiencies in that system. As well as having a direct impact upon the audit approach adopted, the auditor is required by ISA 265 *Communicating Deficiencies in Internal Control to Those Charged with Governance and Management* to communicate promptly with the client to advise them of any significant deficiencies in the system of internal control identified during the course of their work. As a matter of good practice, auditors will normally explain the implications of such deficiencies and make appropriate recommendations to eliminate or mitigate those deficiencies.

Two main approaches have been developed by auditors to assist in this evaluation process: internal control questionnaires (ICQs) and internal control evaluation questionnaires (ICEQs).

4.2 INTERNAL CONTROL QUESTIONNAIRES (ICQS)

(a) **Introduction**

In the large company audit, it is usual for auditors to seek to place reliance on internal controls so that they may limit their testing of transactions and balances. This is because the volume of transactions being processed can make transaction testing very time-consuming – and costly. The auditor will be interested in evaluating whether the system contains those direct accounting controls and whether these are working effectively so that he can form his audit opinion. A typical method of evaluating the quality of controls in an accounting system is by completion of an **internal control questionnaire**. Remember that the ICQ can be used to obtain information about how the system operates and the controls within it.

Definition An **ICQ** is a formal and usually standardised document which comprises a list of internal controls in existence and highlights any deficiencies.

Internal control questionnaires have a number of objectives:

(i) to **ascertain** a client's systems of accounting and internal control

(ii) to **evaluate** the control system thus recorded, and hence

(iii) to **identify** those controls which indicate strengths in the system upon which the auditor will seek to place reliance, and

(iv) to **identify** those areas where there are weak or no controls and which therefore must be subjected to more extensive substantive testing and reported in the Report to Management. This report is considered later.

One advantage of an ICQ is that it represents an attempt at a formalised, systematic, approach to the audit of large complex organisations.

However, use of ICQs may have the following drawbacks:

- ICQs can become too complex, lengthy and detailed for meaningful evaluation of accounting systems.

- There is a danger that ICQs can provoke too stylised an approach to an assignment, concentrating as they do *on the controls* themselves *rather than upon the fraud or irregularity that the controls are designed to prevent.*

It is possible that you may be expected to draft an ICQ in a particular area as part of your examination. In carrying out this task you should bear in mind the guidelines set out below.

(b) **Construction of an ICQ**

(i) It is good practice when designing ICQs to state, as a brief introduction:

(1) a list of control objectives which each sub-system under consideration should seek to achieve

(2) any business considerations specific to the enterprise under review which should be taken into account.

This provides information to the audit staff of key areas to be considered during the audit.

(ii) The questions in an ICQ should be designed to ascertain **whether the control objectives are being achieved** and should therefore cover such aspects as:

(1) instructions given to the client's staff in the performance of their duties

(2) authorisation procedures

(3) documents and procedures used to originate transactions

(4) recording procedures

(5) sequence of procedures

(6) custody procedures

(7) relative independence of the persons involved at each stage of a transaction (i.e. segregation of duties).

(iii) The questions should be framed such that a Yes/No answer is given, with a No answer usually indicating a control deficiency.

(iv) An ICQ should carry such basic information as:

(1) the name of the document (ICQ)

(2) the system to which it relates (e.g. purchasing cycle)

(3) the client to whom it relates

(4) the accounting period under review

(5) evidence of who has prepared and reviewed the document, and when

(6) the provision of columns for:

– Yes and No answers

– comments where neither Yes or No are applicable

– indicating the significance or otherwise of apparent deficiencies

– references to audit programmes

– references to Reports to management.

Example of part of an ICQ

INTERNAL CONTROL QUESTIONNAIRE Prepared by:

THE PURCHASING CYCLE Date:

CLIENT:

PERIOD: Reviewed by:

Date:

(a) Control objectives.

(b) 7Business considerations.

(c) The questionnaire.

(a) **Control objectives**

To ensure that:

(i) purchased goods/services are ordered under proper authorities and procedures

(ii) purchased goods/services are only ordered as necessary for the proper conduct of the business operations and are ordered from suitable suppliers

(iii) goods/services received are effectively inspected for quality, quantity and condition

(iv) invoices and related documentation are properly checked and approved as being valid before being entered as trade payables

(v) all valid transactions relating to trade payables (suppliers' invoices, credit notes and adjustments), and only those transactions, should be accurately recorded in the accounting records.

(b) **Business considerations**

	Key points	Effect on audit procedures and on financial statements
(i)	**Nature of the company's purchases**	Auditor must be aware of the varying nature of goods purchased.
(ii)	**The existence of a purchasing department**	As far as possible ordering should be centralised.
(iii)	**The company's purchasing policy**	The fixing of minimum/maximum inventory and re-order levels should ensure efficient control. However, buying in bulk, with resulting higher inventory levels, may be part of a company policy to reduce unit costs, in which case inventory obsolescence problems may arise.

INTERNAL CONTROLS : **CHAPTER 6**

(iv) **The selection of suppliers**   The purchasing department should maintain a suppliers' register to record past purchases, prices, satisfaction received etc. The constant seeking of alternative sources of supply at keener prices is an indication of efficient management.

(c) **Questionnaire**

		Yes	No	Comments	*References*
	Initiation and authorisation				
1	Are standard order forms (SOFs) issued showing names of suppliers, quantities ordered and prices?				
2	Are copies of SOFs retained on file in numerical sequence?				
3	Are orders appropriately authorised and do authority limits exist?				
4	Are the persons in 3 above independent of those who issue requisitions?				
5	Is a record kept of orders placed but not executed? If yes, specify type of record kept and filing sequence.				
	Custody				
6	Are goods from suppliers inspected on arrival as to quantity and quality?				
7	Is the receipt of supplies recorded (e.g. by Goods Received Notes)?				
8	Are these records prepared by a person independent of those responsible for: – ordering functions? – processing? – recording?				

KAPLAN PUBLISHING

		Yes	No	Comments	*References*
	Recording				
9	Are all invoices received				
	– compared with copy orders?				
	– compared with goods received notes?				
	– checked for prices?				
	– checked for calculations, extensions and additions?				
10	Are the functions in 9 above performed by a person independent of those responsible for:				
	– ordering?				
	– receipt, control and custody of goods?				
11	Are payables ledger personnel independent of those responsible for:				
	– approving invoices and credit notes?				
	– cheque payments?				
12	Is the person maintaining the control account independent of payables ledger personnel?				

ACTIVITY 3

You are performing the audit at a client's firm. One of the junior auditors sees you completing an ICQ and asks you what it is used for.

Explain to him what an ICQ is, and its main objectives.

For a suggested answer, see the 'Answers' section at the end of the book.

4.3 INTERNAL CONTROL EVALUATION QUESTIONNAIRES (ICEQS)

To overcome these possible shortcomings identified in the previous section relating to ICQs, many auditing practices have amended their approach to internal control evaluation by the adoption of a different type of document, *Internal Control Evaluation Questionnaires* (ICEQs).

The ICEQ is designed to determine if desirable internal controls are present, using direct control questions to ascertain where specific frauds or errors are possible. It is normally employed where systems information has *already* been recorded (usually in the form of flowcharts).

Note that virtually all the rules applicable to the construction of an ICQ apply to the construction of an ICEQ. In fact the format itself is very similar – as may be seen from the example below. The structure of the questions, however, differentiates between the two techniques.

Key questions are asked in an ICEQ, the answers to which prompt further supplementary questions. Reference is made to a supporting flowchart which is the means of ascertaining the existing systems. Normally, the questions are framed in such a way as to obtain a consistent response to all questions – a positive answer identifies a control and a negative response highlights the absence or non-operation of a control.

It has the advantage that the ICEQ document is shorter and less complex, but it may require more skill and judgement on the part of the auditor to prepare and then evaluate the completed document.

Example of part of an ICEQ adopted by a practising firm

INTERNAL CONTROL EVALUATION		Prepared by:
QUESTIONNAIRE		Date:
PURCHASES – PAYABLES – PAYMENTS		
CLIENT:		
		Reviewed by:
PERIOD:		Date:
(a)	Control objectives.	
(b)	Business considerations.	
(c)	The checklist.	
(a)	**Control objectives**	
	As ICQ	
(b)	**Business considerations**	
	As ICQ	
(c)	**The checklist**	

| | | Comments | Reference |

1 Purchases

1.1 Can goods be purchased without authority?

(a) purchase requisitions and order approvals?

(b) limit of buyers' authority to order; are there stepped authorisation levels?

(c) purchasing segregated from receiving, accounts payable and inventory records?

(d) unissued orders safeguarded against loss?

1.2 Can liabilities be incurred although goods not received?

(a) is the receipt of goods segregated from purchasing, accounts payable and inventory records?

(b) are all goods passed directly to stores?

(c) GRNs or equivalent prepared independently?

(d) adequate comparison with order, claims for short shipment, etc?

(e) invoices, GRNs, direct to accounts payable not purchasing?

(f) invoices checked to order and GRNs, prices checked?

(g) check of extensions, additions, discounts?

(h) documents cancelled to prevent re-use?

(i) unmatched documents investigated regularly?

(j) freight checked, bills matched to consignments?

(k) purchase returns and allowances controlled – follow-up?

(l) forward purchases controlled?

INTERNAL CONTROLS : **CHAPTER 6**

                                          Comments   Reference

1.3 Can cut-off errors occur?

(a) time lapse from receipt of goods to invoice processing?

(b) valuation of unmatched GRNs?

(c) adequate control and recording of receipts?

1.4 Can invoices be wrongly allocated?

(a) general ledger analysis?

(b) analysis independently checked?

(c) staff purchases controlled?

(d) independent and regular review?

1.5 Can liabilities be recorded for goods or services not ordered?

(a) goods received without authority?

2 Payables

2.1 Can liabilities be incurred but not recorded?

(a) payables balances agreed periodically?

(b) supplier's statements independently reconciled on a regular basis e.g. monthly?

(c) invoice register?

(d) forward contracts?

(e) order backlog follow-up?

(f) debit balances controlled?

3	**Payments**

Comments   Reference

3.1 Can payments be made if not properly supported?

(a) discounts taken?

(b) control over invoices before validating complete?

(c) cheque signatories independent of purchasing, receiving, accounts payable and cheque preparation?

(d) signatories examine supporting documentation prior to payment and ensure completeness has been checked?

(e) control over signature plates or pre-signed cheques?

(f) control where one signature?

(g) frequency with which cheques mailed?

(h) independent regular bank reconciliation, and review of the reconciliation by an independent person?

(i) cheques crossed *account payee only*, continuity accounted for, control over unused cheques?

(j) bank transfers controlled – standing orders, direct debits?

(k) issue of bearer or 'cash' cheques?

(l) advances and loans controlled?

(m) bank transfer payments, traders credits?

3.2 Can payments for non-routine purchases be made if not authorised or properly supported?

(a) services, expense accounts, taxation payments in advance, staff purchases and goods on consignment?

(b) use of company credit and debit cards controlled?

                                                            Comments   Reference

   3.3 **Can non-current assets be acquired or removed without proper authorisation and recording?**

- (a) approved work orders for non-current assets and major repairs at the correct level of authority?

- (b) approval of cost over-runs by an appropriate person?

- (c) reporting of scrapping or disposals?

- (d) detailed non-current asset register, regular physical inspection and review of values?

- (e) periodic insurance appraisals, adequate coverage?

- (f) control over loose tools?

ACTIVITY 4

Explain the difference between an ICQ and an ICEQ (sometimes just called ICE), giving examples of the types of questions that each may contain in relation to a purchases system.

For a suggested answer, see the 'Answers' section at the end of the book.

5 INHERENT LIMITATIONS OF INTERNAL CONTROL

It is possible to reduce the volume of transaction testing required in conducting an audit if the internal controls are sound and are operating effectively, but it is not likely that an auditor will be able to rely on internal controls entirely. This is because all control systems have inherent limitations such as:

- (a) the need to balance the cost of the control with its benefits

- (b) the fact that internal controls are usually applied to regular, recurring transactions, not one-off year-end adjustments or unusual transactions, which are often large and subject to error

- (c) the potential for human error

- (d) the possibility of fraudulent collusion (two or more persons operating together) to 'get round' controls that segregate duties

    For example, the supervisor responsible for checking and authorising overtime claims could collude with employees, to enable excess overtime payments to be claimed.

(e) the abuse of authority and override of controls by senior managers or the owners of the business

Abuse of authority might involve ordering personal goods through the firm. It is very easy for directors and managers of organisations of any size to instruct staff to bypass normal procedures such as the requirement for authorisation for payments.

(f) the obsolescence of controls which have not changed to reflect changes in the business activities or organisation.

In practice, the training of auditors always involves a warning never to rely on internal controls entirely, no matter how effective they may appear to be. Hence some verification of transactions is always carried out as part of the auditor's work. Auditors should always be aware of the possibility of fraud and error, and if they find something unusual during their audit testing, which may not form part of that piece of work, they should always investigate further.

CONCLUSION

It is the responsibility of management to ensure the establishment and operation of a sound system of internal control and the auditor must ascertain, record, confirm and evaluate the system as part of the audit work. There are many types of control that could be introduced but the costs of additional controls must be weighed against the expected benefits.

The auditor can evaluate the system of internal control using either an Internal Control Questionnaire (ICQ) or an Internal Control Evaluation Questionnaire (ICEQ). An ICQ lists the controls that might exist and highlights any potential gaps. However ICQs can become very lengthy and can be completed in a 'tick the box' mentality rather than concentrating on possible irregularities that might occur if controls are not effective. Consequently ICEQs have been developed – these contain fewer questions but may need to be completed by more experienced auditors if appropriate conclusions are to be drawn.

If the auditor's evaluation of the controls indicates that they are adequate to generate figures which will be true and fair, the next step for the auditor is to test those controls to establish whether they are actually working as laid down on paper – this is examined in the next chapter.

KEY TERMS

System of internal control – The system of internal control comprises the control environment and control activities. It includes all the policies and procedures adopted by the directors and management of an entity to assist in their objective of achieving, as far as practicable, the orderly and efficient conduct of the business, including adherence to internal policies, the safeguarding of assets, the prevention and detection of fraud and error, the accuracy and completeness of the accounting records, and the timely preparation of reliable financial information.

Control environment – The overall attitude, awareness and actions of management regarding internal controls and their importance.

Control activities – These are all policies and procedures designed to endure that management directives are carried out throughout the organisation.

Segregation of duties – An appropriate division of responsibilities to reduce the opportunity for fraud and manipulation.

Walk-through test – The process whereby the auditor traces transactions through the stages in an accounting system as a means of confirming that the auditor has a correct record and understanding of the system in operation.

Internal control questionnaire (ICQ) – A formal document which comprises a list of internal controls in existence and highlights any deficiencies.

Internal control evaluation questionnaire (ICEQ) – A form designed to determine if desirable internal controls are present, using direct control questions to ascertain where specific frauds or errors are possible.

SELF TEST QUESTIONS

		Paragraph
1	What is the definition of a system of internal control?	1.1
2	Name five categories of internal controls.	1.4
3	What methods can be used to ascertain a client's accounting system?	2.1
4	What are walk-through tests?	2.2
5	What methods can be used to record a client's accounting system?	3.1
6	What are the objectives of ICQs?	4.2
7	What is the purpose of ICEQs?	4.3

FAU: FOUNDATIONS IN AUDIT

PRACTICE QUESTION 1

INTERNAL CONTROLS

You have read that 'If the auditor wishes to place reliance on any internal controls, he should ascertain and evaluate those controls and perform tests on their operation'.

Required:

(a) What are the major objectives of a system of internal control? **(7 marks)**

(b) Explain briefly the major categories of internal control. **(8 marks)**

(Total: 15 marks)

For a suggested answer, see the 'Answers' section at the end of the book.

PRACTICE QUESTION 2

WAGES AND SALARIES

In relation to wages and salaries, state five objectives that an effective system of internal control should achieve. **(10 marks)**

For a suggested answer, see the 'Answers' section at the end of the book.

PRACTICE QUESTION 3

SALES AND RECEIVABLES

In relation to sales and receivables, state five objectives that an effective system of internal control should achieve. **(10 marks)**

For a suggested answer, see the 'Answers' section at the end of the book.

Chapter 7

THE AUDIT EVIDENCE PROCESS: TESTS OF CONTROL

INTRODUCTION

We saw in the previous chapter how the auditor can identify the controls within a client's accounting system. Before the auditor can adopt a systems audit approach (i.e. rely on those controls to produce true and fair figures) they must satisfy themselves that the controls are actually operating effectively.

The auditor needs to generate evidence (documented in the audit files) which will allow a conclusion to be reached on this. Audit evidence, as we have already mentioned, is generated by the auditor performing a series of audit tests. We referred to walk-through tests in an earlier chapter; these are principally used by the auditor to establish whether he has a correct record and understanding of the client's accounting system.

- Audit tests are of two main types, each playing a different role in the audit process.

- Tests of control – to establish whether the controls in the accounting systems are operating effectively and can be relied upon – these are dealt with in this chapter.

- Substantive tests – to establish whether transactions and balances are correctly recorded – these are dealt with in later chapters.

This chapter will identify the main tests of control which will be applied to each of a client's accounting systems (or transaction cycles). However, before we can cover tests of control in detail we need to introduce the concept of audit evidence in general and this will be covered in the first part of the chapter.

This chapter covers syllabus C (3), D (1).

FAU: FOUNDATIONS IN AUDIT

CONTENTS

1. A reminder – the concept of audit evidence
2. The characteristics of good audit evidence
3. Audit testing procedures
4. Testing the sales system
5. Testing the purchases system
6. Testing the wages and salaries system
7. Testing other systems

LEARNING OUTCOMES

At the end of this chapter, you should be able to:

- appreciate the concept of audit evidence and the characteristics of good audit evidence

- understand the range of testing procedures available as a means of generating audit evidence

- identify the control objectives relevant to each of the major systems of a typical enterprise

- identify the control activities (policies and procedures) required to achieve these objectives

- design appropriate tests of control for each of the major accounting systems of a typical enterprise.

1 A REMINDER – THE CONCEPT OF AUDIT EVIDENCE

Audit evidence, as we have seen, can be defined in simple terms as any piece of information which assists the auditor to reach a conclusion on the truth and fairness of the financial statements.

Audit evidence might therefore include such items as:

- Documents such as purchase orders, invoices, receipts, employee time sheets, customer orders, letters, bank statements, contracts and other legal documents

- Entries in accounting records

- Answers from management to questions raised by the auditor

- Information from external parties who enter into transactions with the entity, such as customers and suppliers, the bank, solicitors, government agencies (the tax authorities, for example)

- Computations produced by the client or by the auditor himself, for example, depreciation calculations, computations of accruals and prepayments

- Information gained from the auditor's observations. An example would be the auditor attending and observing the client's inventory count.

The auditor will draw on a range of these sources of evidence, the choice, to an extent, will be determined by the type of evidence that is available. However, the auditor also needs to consider the quality of the evidence used. A basic principle of auditing is to ensure that the highest quality evidence available is used to support the audit conclusion. Guidelines on the quality of audit evidence have been provided by the auditing profession.

2 THE CHARACTERISTICS OF GOOD AUDIT EVIDENCE

2.1 INTRODUCTION

ISA 500 *Audit Evidence* requires that auditors obtain **sufficient appropriate audit evidence** to be able to draw reasonable conclusions on which to base the audit opinion.

Sufficient relates to the **quantity** of evidence, **appropriate** relates to the **quality or reliability and relevance** of evidence.

Notice that the words 'sufficient' and 'appropriate' are relative not absolute terms – the auditor will need to use judgement when collecting audit evidence, as in many areas of audit work. Key questions for the auditor to consider therefore will be:

- Do I have enough evidence to reach a conclusion on this audit area?

- Is the evidence that I have reliable enough to allow me to reach a conclusion on this area of the audit?

2.2 SUFFICIENT, APPROPRIATE EVIDENCE

The auditor's judgement as to what amounts to sufficient appropriate evidence is influenced by such factors as:

(a) The assessment of audit risk involved. As a general guideline, the higher the audit risk, the more cautious the auditor will be in arriving at a conclusion. This suggests that a relatively large amount of high quality and highly relevant evidence will be looked for in this situation.

(b) The nature of the accounting and systems of internal control. Proof of effective systems and strong controls is, in its own right, a form of audit evidence. The auditor may be happy to add to this a relatively small amount of additional evidence.

(c) The materiality of the item. More material items will typically require more and higher quality audit evidence.

(d) The auditor's knowledge and experience of the business. If the auditor is new to the client or industry, more additional evidence may be required than if the auditor has significant experience of the client.

(e) The findings of audit procedures. If audit procedures indicate problems that may bring into question the truth and fairness of the financial statements, additional evidence will need to be generated in order to enable the auditor to reach a valid conclusion on the area.

(f) The source and reliability of the information. Often, auditors will strike a balance between sufficient and appropriate. The more appropriate (relevant and reliable) the evidence is, the smaller the amount the auditor may accept in order to reach a conclusion.

(g) Size of the organisation – a small entity is less likely to have as tight controls as a large organisation; often one person will be responsible for a number of activities or procedures. This would affect the auditor's assessment of the reliability of evidence produced by the client.

In assessing the **reliability** of audit evidence, the auditor can be guided by the following general principles:

- Evidence is more reliable when it is obtained from independent sources outside the entity.

- Evidence that is generated internally is more reliable when the related controls imposed by the entity are effective.

- Evidence obtained directly by the auditor is more reliable than evidence obtained indirectly or by inference (for example, the auditor would prefer to actually observe the application of a control than to enquire about how it is applied).

- Written evidence is more reliable than verbal evidence.

- Evidence provided by original documents is more reliable than using photocopies or faxes of documents.

When using documents as a source of audit evidence, the auditor should always try to use original documents rather than photocopies or faxes of documents.

ACTIVITY 1

Describe the reliability of a number of items of audit evidence relating to non-current assets. These items are:

- an invoice from a supplier of an item of plant to the client

- a calculation of the depreciation for the year prepared by the auditor

- a verbal statement from the managing director of the client that the market value of the company's factory premises amounts to $20 million.

For a suggested answer, see the 'Answers' section at the end of the book.

3 AUDIT TESTING PROCEDURES

As we know, audit tests are procedures carried out by the auditor in order to generate audit evidence.

There are a number of audit testing procedures that may be available to the auditor. Which procedures are actually used will depend on the area that is being audited, and the evidence available to the auditor.

Whenever you are asked to design or carry out **any** audit tests, the procedures listed below should be considered in order to identify what may be appropriate in the circumstances which you are dealing with:

Inspection

This covers the physical review or examination of records, documents and tangible assets. An example in a test of controls is examining purchase invoices for evidence of authorisation by a responsible person. Documents may be inspected for evidence of checking (e.g. confirmation of prices charged by suppliers on purchase invoices) or confirmation that goods have been received (e.g. a properly completed and signed goods received note). Physical inspection of inventory and property, plant and equipment will confirm their existence and also their condition would also be a useful source of audit evidence. However, note that physical examination of an asset does not confirm ownership and it may not provide conclusive evidence of valuation.

Observation

This technique involves looking at a process or procedure being performed. An example is the distribution of wage packets to see that internal control procedures are adhered to or the observation by auditors of inventory being counted in accordance with inventory counting instructions.

Inquiry

Seeking relevant information from knowledgeable persons inside or outside the enterprise.

An example in tests of control is asking management for an explanation of the entity's policy for vetting credit customers. The reliability of this technique depends on the qualification and integrity of the source. This would then be verified by reviewing documents completed during the vetting process for evidence of completion of the process.

External confirmation

External confirmation (a specific type of inquiry) concerns obtaining a representation directly from a third party. For example, the auditor may seek direct confirmation of receivables balances by writing to the customers.

Recalculation

Inspecting the arithmetical accuracy of records or performing independent calculations (e.g. checking the addition of the trial balance or recalculating depreciation charges).

Reperformance

Reperformance is the auditor carrying out procedures or activities that were originally performed as part of the entity's system of internal control, for example reperforming the aging of receivables balances in an aged debt analysis.

FAU: FOUNDATIONS IN AUDIT

Analytical procedures

As described earlier in connection with audit planning. You should note that these procedures are mainly used in substantive testing rather than as a test of controls.

3.1 THE DIFFERENCE BETWEEN TESTS OF CONTROL AND SUBSTANTIVE TESTS

The focus of a test of control is not the monetary amount of a transaction. A test of control provides evidence of whether a control procedure has operated effectively. For example, inspecting an invoice for evidence of authorisation. It is irrelevant whether the invoice is for $100 or $1000 as it the control being tested, not the amount. Therefore, it could be said that a test of control provides indirect evidence over the financial statements. The auditor makes the assumption that if controls are working effectively there is less risk of material misstatement in the financial statements. However, the test of control itself does not test the figure within the financial statements, this is the purpose of a substantive procedure.

ACTIVITY 2

Your firm has just taken on a new client X Company. You have been assigned to the audit of the sales system. You are currently drawing up the relevant audit programme for approval by the audit manager.

List and describe two tests of control you would perform to check that X Company had been reconciling the receivables ledger and receivables ledger control account on a monthly basis.

For a suggested answer, see the 'Answers' section at the end of the book.

Each major accounting system should have *control objectives* and *control policies and procedures*. The auditor will then perform tests of control to ensure the controls are working.

- **Control objectives** – what objectives are the internal controls seeking to achieve?

- **Control activities** – the policies and procedures that should be in place to ensure the control objectives are achieved.

- **Tests of control** – audit work performed to generate evidence as to whether the controls are operating.

An important principle of auditing needs to be mentioned in respect of tests of control. If an auditor discovers that a control is not operating in respect of a particular transaction, this event is known as an exception. The materiality concept does not apply to exceptions discovered in tests of controls.

For example, it is just as significant if an auditor discovers that a purchase invoice with a value of $2 has not been authorised for payment as if the invoice had a value of $2 million. The auditor should not ignore exceptions where only small amounts are involved. it is the control that is being tested, not the transaction! He would need to assess why the control did not work in that instance and therefore whether he needs to extend his testing.

4 TESTING THE SALES SYSTEM

4.1 CONTROL OBJECTIVES FOR SALES AND RECEIVABLES

For many businesses, sales are made on credit and so objectives for the sales cycle includes control over receivable balances as well.

The control objectives are as follows.

To ensure that:

(a) customers' orders are authorised, controlled and recorded in order to execute them promptly.

(b) goods shipped and work completed are controlled so that invoices are issued and revenue recorded for all sales.

(c) goods returned and claims by customers (for example, in respect of damaged goods) are controlled in order to determine the liability for goods returned and claims received.

(d) invoices and credits are appropriately inspected for accuracy and are authorised before being entered in the receivables' records.

(e) only authorised receivables' transactions are entered in the accounting records.

(f) there are activities to make sure that sales invoices are subsequently paid by customers and that doubtful amounts are identified in order to determine any provisions or write offs required.

4.2 CONTROL ACTIVITIES OVER SALES AND RECEIVABLES

There are a large number of controls that may be required in the sales cycle due to the importance of this area in any business and the possible opportunities that exist for diverting sales and cash receipts away from the business.

Typical control activities at key stages of the sales cycle are:

(a) **Orders**

   (i) Existing customers should be allocated a credit limit and it should be checked whether this limit has been exceeded when a new order is accepted. If so, the matter should be referred to credit control.

   (ii) Any new customer should be referred to the credit control department before the order is accepted.

   (iii) All orders received should be recorded on pre-numbered sales order documents so that a check can be made that all orders have been dealt with – a completeness check.

   (iv) All orders should be authorised before any goods are despatched.

   (v) The sales order document should be used to produce a despatch note for the goods outwards department. No goods may be despatched without a despatch note.

(b) **Despatch**

- (i) Despatch notes should be pre-numbered and a register kept of them to enable them to be matched to sales invoices and customer orders.

- (ii) Despatch notes should be authorised before goods leave the entity.

- (iii) Regular reviews should be carried out to ensure that all despatches have been invoiced.

(c) **Invoicing and credit notes**

- (i) Sales invoices should be authorised by a responsible official and matched with the authorised order and despatch note.

- (ii) All invoices and credit notes should be entered in daybook records, the receivables ledger, and receivables ledger control account. Batch totals should be maintained for this purpose.

- (iii) Sales invoices and credit notes should be checked for prices, casts and calculations by a person other than the one preparing the invoice.

- (iv) All invoices and credit notes should be serially pre-numbered and regular sequence checks should be carried out.

- (v) Credit notes should be authorised by someone unconnected with despatch or receivables ledger functions.

- (vi) Copies of cancelled invoices should be retained.

- (vii) Any cancellation of an invoice should lead to a cancellation of the related despatch note.

- (viii) Cancelled (and free of charge) invoices should be signed by a responsible official.

- (ix) Each invoice should distinguish between different types of sales and, if relevant, different rates of sales tax. Any coding of invoices should be periodically checked independently.

(d) **Returns**

- (i) Any goods returned by the customer should be checked for obvious damage and, when accepted, a document should be raised.

- (ii) All goods returned should be used to prepare appropriate credit notes.

(e) **Receivables**

- (i) A receivables ledger control account should be prepared regularly and checked to individual receivables ledger balances by an independent official.

- (ii) Receivables ledger personnel should be independent of despatch and cash receipt functions.

- (iii) Statements should be sent regularly to customers.

(iv) Formal control activities should exist for following up overdue debts which should be highlighted either by the preparation of an aged list of balances or by the preparation of regular customer statements.

(v) Letters should be sent to customers for collection of overdue debts. A policy should be in place for the institution of legal proceedings where appropriate.

(f) **Irrecoverable debts**

(i) The authority to write off an irrecoverable debt should be in writing and at the correct level of seniority. Appropriate adjustments should be made to the receivables ledger and the control account.

(ii) The use of court action or the writing-off of an irrecoverable debt should be authorised by an official independent of the cash receipt function.

4.3 TESTS OF CONTROL

Tests of control should be designed to check that the control activities are being applied and that objectives are being achieved. Tests may be appropriate under the following broad headings.

(a) Carry out sequence test checks on invoices, credit notes, despatch notes and orders. Ensure that all items are included and that there are no omissions or duplications.

(b) Inspect evidence for authorisation of:

- acceptance of the order (the creditworthiness check)
- despatch of goods
- raising of the invoice or credit note
- pricing and discounts
- write-off of irrecoverable debts.

Inspect to ensure that the relevant signature exists and that the control has been applied.

(c) Review the arithmetical accuracy of:

- invoices, including pricing and sales tax calculations
- credit notes.

This is often done by means of a 'grid stamp' containing several signatures on the face of the document. Ensure that the control has been applied by checking the accuracy of such invoices and credit notes.

(d) Observe the process whereby despatch notes and goods returned notes are matched with invoices and credit notes.

(e) Inspect control account reconciliations have been performed regularly and reviewed.

In all cases, tests should be performed on a *sample* basis. Relevant aspects of sampling are dealt with in a later chapter.

ACTIVITY 3

You have been asked by your audit manager to design an audit programme comprising tests of control to ensure that the sales system's control activities are being adhered to. Assume that the control activities used are those that would typically be found in any sales system. Outline the contents of the audit programme that you would produce.

For a suggested answer, see the 'Answers' section at the end of the book.

5 TESTING THE PURCHASES SYSTEM

5.1 CONTROL OBJECTIVES FOR PURCHASES AND PAYABLES

Purchases are often made on credit and so the purchases cycle includes payables. You also need to bear in mind that 'purchases' has a wide meaning in terms of the purchases cycle as purchases will include not only inventory items but also all types of expense and the purchase of non-current assets.

The control objectives are as follows.

To ensure that:

(a) purchased goods/services are ordered under proper authority and using proper policies and procedures

(b) purchased goods/services are only ordered as necessary for the proper conduct of the business operations and are ordered from suitable, approved suppliers

(c) goods/services received are inspected for quality, quantity and description

(d) invoices and related documentation are properly checked and approved as being valid before being entered as trade payables

(e) all valid transactions relating to payables (suppliers' invoices, credit notes and adjustments), and only those transactions, should be accurately recorded in the accounting records.

5.2 CONTROL ACTIVITIES OVER PURCHASES AND PAYABLES

As with the sales system, there are a large number of controls that may be required in the purchases cycle due to the importance of this area in any business and once again, the following list is classified by type of control.

(a) **Orders**

(i) Requisition notes for purchases should be authorised at the correct level of seniority.

(ii) All orders should be authorised by a responsible official whose authority limits should be pre-defined.

(iii) Major items e.g. capital expenditure, should be authorised at an appropriate level, possibly by the Board of Directors.

(iv) All orders should be recorded on official documents showing suppliers' names, quantities ordered and price.

(v) Copies of orders should be retained as a method of following up late deliveries by suppliers.

(vi) Re-order levels and quantities should be pre-set and preferably recorded in advance on the requisition note.

(b) **Receipt of goods**

(i) Goods inwards areas should be identified to deal with the receipt of all goods.

(ii) All goods should be checked for quantity, quality and description. Goods received notes should be raised for all goods accepted. The GRN should be signed by a responsible official.

(iii) GRNs should be checked against purchase orders and policies and procedures should exist to notify the supplier of under or over-deliveries. GRNs should be sequentially numbered and inspected periodically for completeness.

(c) **Invoicing and returns**

(i) Purchase invoices received should be stamped with an approval grid and given a unique serial number to ensure purchase invoices do not go astray.

(ii) Purchase invoices should be matched with goods received notes and purchase orders and should not be processed until this is done.

(iii) The invoice should be checked against the order and the GRN, and casts and extensions should also be reviewed.

(iv) The invoices should be signed as approved for payment by a responsible official independent of the ordering and receipt of goods functions.

(v) Invoice sequential numbers should be checked against purchase day book details.

(vi) Input sales tax should be recorded separately from the expense element of the invoice total.

(vii) Invoices should be properly allocated to the general ledger accounts, perhaps by allocating expenditure codes. Samples of coding should be inspected independently by a senior member of staff.

(viii) Batch controls should be maintained over the posting of invoices to the purchases day book, general ledger and payables ledger.

(ix) A record of goods returned should be kept and checked to the credit notes received from suppliers.

(d) **Payables ledger and suppliers**

(i) A payables ledger control account should be maintained and regularly checked against balances in the payables ledger by an independent official.

(ii) Payables ledger records should be kept by persons independent of the receiving of goods, invoice authorisation and payment routines.

(iii) Statements from suppliers should be checked against the ledger account.

5.3 TESTS OF CONTROL

As already noted, tests of control should be drawn up so as to check that control activities are being applied and to achieve control objectives. One suggested way to design tests of control for a particular situation is to list the documents in a transaction cycle and generate appropriate tests of control for each document. We shall illustrate this approach here in connection with the purchases cycle. (Note that a similar technique could be applied to other transaction cycles!)

Purchase Order
(i) Inspect for evidence of a sequence check.
(ii) Inspect for evidence of approval by appropriate responsible individual.
(iii) Observe adherence to authority limits and

Goods Received Note
Inspect for evidence of a sequence check. Also, observe a check of quality of goods and evidence of the goods received note being matched to the purchase order.

Observe physical controls over stores.

Goods Returned Note
Inspect for evidence of a sequentially numbered returns notes for all rejected/ returned items.

Purchase Invoice
(i) Inspect for evidence of sequence check.
(ii) Inspect for evidence of matching purchase invoices with goods received notes and purchase orders.
(iii) Inspect for evidence of checking casts, extensions and tax treatment.
(iv) Inspect for evidence of comparison of invoice details to goods received note.
(v) Observe approval of purchase invoice for further processing.

Credit Note
Inspect for evidence of matching credit notes to goods returned notes.

Payables ledger
Inspect for evidence of authorisation of adjustments to payables ledger.

Payables ledger control
(i) Inspect for evidence of review of reconciliation of payables ledger listing.
(ii) Inspect for evidence of authorisation of adjustments to payables ledger control account.

ACTIVITY 4

One of your audit firm's clients has asked you for advice on what control activities should be implemented in their company's purchases system. Write the client a letter stating the key control areas within the purchases cycle and specify **in detail** the control activities required over invoicing.

For a suggested answer, see the 'Answers' section at the end of the book.

6 TESTING THE WAGES AND SALARIES SYSTEM

6.1 CONTROL OBJECTIVES – WAGES AND SALARIES

The control objectives are as follows.

To ensure that:

(a) payment of wages and salaries are made only in respect of the client's authorised employees.

(b) payment are made at authorised rates of pay.

(c) wages and salaries payments are in accordance with records of work performed, e.g. time, output, commissions on sales, or in line with agreed annual salary payments.

(d) payroll and payroll deductions, e.g. income tax, social security contributions and pension contributions, are calculated accurately.

(e) payment is made to the correct employees.

(f) liabilities to the tax authorities for tax and social security contributions are properly recorded.

(g) all voluntary deductions are authorised by the employee in writing.

6.2 CONTROL ACTIVITIES – WAGES AND SALARIES

(a) **Approval and control of documents**

   (i) There should be written authorisation by the correct personnel to employ or dismiss any employee.

   (ii) Changes in rates of pay should be authorised in writing by an official outside the wages department.

   (iii) Overtime worked should be authorised in advance by a manager/supervisor.

   (iv) An independent official should review the payroll and sign it.

   (v) The wages cheque should be signed by two signatories and agreed with the signed payroll.

(vi) Where weekly pay relates to hours at work, clock cards should be used. There should be supervision of the cards and the timing devices, particularly when employees are clocking-on or off.

(vii) Where a piece work system operates, payment should only be made for work of an appropriate quality which has been inspected and approved.

(viii) Personnel records should be kept independently of the payroll department for each employee giving details of engagement, retirement, dismissal or resignation, rates of pay, holidays, maternity, paternity, sickness etc., with a specimen signature of the employee.

(ix) A wages supervisor should be appointed who could perform some of the authorisation duties listed above.

(b) **Arithmetical accuracy**

(i) Where appropriate, payroll should be prepared from clock cards, job cards, etc. and a sample checked for accuracy against current rates of pay.

(ii) Payroll details should be inspected for the accurate calculation of deductions (both statutory and voluntary) e.g. tax, social security, pensions, trade union subscriptions, etc.

(c) **Control accounts**

(i) Control accounts should be maintained in respect of each of the deductions showing amounts paid periodically to the tax authorities, trade unions, etc.

(ii) Overall analytical checks should be carried out to highlight major discrepancies e.g. check against budgets, changes in amounts paid over a period of time, check against personnel records.

(iii) Management should exercise overall review and control.

(d) **Access to assets and records**

Ideally, payment should be made by cheque or by direct transfer into the individual employee bank account. If payment is made in cash, the following control activities should be in place:

(i) Employees should sign for their wages and provide evidence of who they are.

(ii) No employee should be allowed to take the wages of another employee.

(iii) When wages are claimed late, the employee should sign for the wage packet and the release of the packet should be authorised.

(iv) The system should preferably allow the wages to be checked by the employee before the packet is opened, by using specially designed wage packets.

(v) The wages department should preferably be a separate department with their personnel not involved with receipts or payments functions.

(vi) The duties of the wages staff should preferably be rotated during the year, and ensure that no employee is responsible for all the functions in respect of any particular department.

(vii) The employee making up the pay packets should not be the employee who prepares the payroll. Ideally two persons would be responsible for preparing the pay packets.

(viii) A surprise attendance at the pay-out should be made periodically by an independent official.

(ix) Unclaimed wages should be recorded in a register and held by someone outside the wages department until claimed or until a predefined period after which the money should be rebanked. An official should investigate the reason for unclaimed wages as soon as possible.

ACTIVITY 5

Summarise the main controls that you would expect to find in a payroll system involving the payment of monthly salaries by direct transfer into employee bank accounts.

For a suggested answer, see the 'Answers' section at the end of the book.

6.3 TESTS OF CONTROLS – WAGES AND SALARIES

A suggested programme of tests of control is set out below. This would, of course, be modified to suit the particular circumstances of the client.

(a) Test a sample of time sheets, clock cards or other records, for evidence approval by responsible official. Pay particular attention to the approval of overtime where relevant.

(b) Test for evidence of authorisation by a responsible official (e.g. signature) of payments for casual labour.

(c) Observe wages distribution for adherence to established policies e.g. individual employees are properly identified and sign for their wages packet etc.

(d) Test for evidence of authorisation by a responsible official for payroll amendments by reference to personnel records.

(e) Test controls over payroll amendments, ensuring that standard, pre-numbered, forms are used and are fully completed, with evidence of review and authorisation.

(f) Review payroll calculations for evidence of checking (e.g. a signature of the financial controller).

(g) Examine payrolls for evidence of approval by a responsible official.

(h) Inspect payrolls and other documentation for evidence of independent checks of payrolls (e.g. working papers prepared by internal audit).

(i) Inspect payroll reconciliations to confirm that they are carried out regularly and that there is evidence of review by a responsible official.

(j) Examine procedure for payroll expense variances and review any exception reports produced for evidence of subsequent review and action.

(k) Test controls over unclaimed wages to ensure the unclaimed wages are recorded and are stored in a safe place.

7 TESTING OTHER SYSTEMS

7.1 INTRODUCTION

The type and range of other systems that the auditor may encounter will depend upon the nature of the business but, as a general rule, most other systems you may encounter will be concerned with the safe custody of an asset of the business. Thus there will be a system for inventory in a manufacturing entity and a system for non-current assets in many businesses. There will also be a system in place for bank and cash. Some businesses may have significant investments and thus will have a system to maintain control of this type of asset.

In this section, we will consider control systems for non-current assets and inventory as well as bank and cash.

7.2 INVENTORY

You will be aware that there is a close link between inventory on the one hand and sales and purchases on the other hand. In light of this, you will not be surprised that many of the points in this section have already been dealt with in covering sales and purchases above – they are repeated here briefly to give you the overall picture. The auditor's work in relation to inventory is considered in more detail in a later chapter.

Control objectives

Although inventory records may vary considerably from client to client, the control objectives are generally the same in all cases, namely:

(i) That all purchases of inventory are properly authorised and recorded

(ii) That all goods are securely maintained in suitable locations; this is especially important for perishable or high value items

(iii) Inventory records are up to date and accurately maintained and are supported by regular physical inventory counts

(iv) All goods despatched are recorded and authorised at the appropriate level of seniority

(v) Adequate steps should be taken to identify all inventory for which write-downs may be required on the grounds that their net realisable value is below cost

(vi) Inventory levels should be controlled so that materials are available when required but that inventory is not unnecessarily large.

Control activities over inventory

(i) **Approval and control of documents**

- Issues from inventories should be made only on properly authorised requisitions.

- Reviews of damaged, obsolete and slow moving inventory should be carried out. Any write-offs should be authorised.

(ii) **Arithmetical accuracy**

- All receipts and issues should be recorded on inventory cards, cross-referenced to the appropriate GRN or requisition document.

- The costing department should allocate direct and overhead costs to the value of work-in-progress according to the stage of completion reached.

- To do this standard costs are normally used. Such standards must be regularly reviewed to ensure that they relate to actual costs being incurred.

- If the value of work-in-progress is directly comparable with the number of units produced, checks should periodically be made of actual units against work-in-progress records.

(iii) **Control accounts**

- Total inventory records may be maintained and integrated with the main accounting system; if so they should be reconciled to detailed inventory records and discrepancies investigated.

(iv) **Comparison of assets to records**

- Inventory levels should be periodically checked against the records by a person independent of the stores personnel, and material differences investigated.

- Where continuous inventory records are not kept adequately a full inventory count should be held at least once a year.

- Maximum and minimum inventory levels should be pre-determined and regularly reviewed for adequacy.

- Re-order quantities should be pre-determined and regularly reviewed for adequacy.

(v) **Access to assets and records**

- Separate centres should be identified at which goods are held.

- Deliveries of goods from suppliers should pass through a goods inwards section to the stores. All goods should pass through stores and hence be recorded and checked as received.

- Inventories should be held in their locations so that they are safe from damage or theft.

- All inventory lines should be identified and held together e.g. in bins which are marked with all relevant information as to size, grade, origin, title for identification.

- Access to the stores should be restricted.

Tests of controls

(i) Observe physical security of inventories and environment in which they are held e.g. controlled access to factory, CCTV etc.

(ii) Observe procedures for recording of inventory movements in and out of inventory ensuring segregation of duties in respect of goods in/out and the posting of the movements.

(iii) Inspect for evidence of authorisation for adjustments to inventory records.

(iv) Inspect for evidence of authorisation for write-off or scrapping of inventories.

(v) Inspect for evidence of controls over recording of movements of inventory belonging to third parties.

(vi) Inspect for evidence of authorisation of inventory movements i.e. the use made of authorised goods received and despatch notes.

(vii) Inspect for evidence of preparation and review of reconciliations of inventory counts to inventory records (this gives overall comfort on the adequacy of controls over the recording of inventory).

(viii) Inspect for evidence of sequence checks upon despatch and goods received notes for completeness.

(ix) Observe adequacy of inventory counting procedures and attend the count to ensure that all relevant policies and procedures are complied with.

7.3 NON-CURRENT ASSETS

Control objectives

The control objectives are to ensure that:

(i) non-current assets are correctly recorded, adequately secured and properly maintained

(ii) acquisitions and disposals of non-current assets are properly authorised

(iii) acquisitions and disposals of non-current assets are for the most favourable price possible

(iv) non-current assets are properly recorded, appropriately depreciated and written down where necessary.

Control activities over non-current assets

(i) Annual capital expenditure budgets should be prepared by someone directly responsible to the board of directors.

(ii) Such budgets should, if acceptable, be agreed by the board and minuted.

(iii) Applications for authority to incur capital expenditure should be submitted to the board for approval and should contain reasons for the expenditure, estimated cost, and any non-current assets replaced.

(iv) A document should show what is to be acquired and be signed as authorised by the board or an authorised official.

(v) Non-current assets manufactured or constructed by the entity itself should be separately identifiable in the entity's costing records and should reflect direct costs plus relevant overhead but not include any profit. This might apply where, for example, a building entity constructs its own office block.

(vi) Disposal of non-current assets should be authorised at the appropriate level of seniority and any proceeds from sale should be related to the authority.

(vii) A register of non-current assets should be maintained for each major group of assets. The register may be sub-divided to deal with each class or type of non-current asset, such as motor plant and equipment and office equipment. The register should contain the following details:

- the individual sequential register/serial number of the asset

- the date of purchase and capitalised cost

- the location of the asset – this is particularly important in larger mufti-site organisations

- the depreciation method and rate to apply to the asset

- the annual depreciation charge and net carrying value at each year end

- if an asset is for the use of an individual employee (e.g. motor vehicle or laptop), the name and location of the individual

- the date of disposal and disposal proceeds when this occurs.

(viii) Identify each item within that group and contain details of cost and depreciation. Each asset should be uniquely numbered and this number recorded on the asset itself.

(ix) A physical inspection of non-current assets should be carried out periodically and checked to the non-current asset register. Any discrepancies should be noted and investigated.

(x) Assets should be properly maintained and adequately insured.

(xi) Depreciation rates should be authorised and a written statement of policy produced.

(xii) Depreciation should be reviewed annually to assess the need for changes in the light of profits or losses on disposal, new technology, etc.

(xiii) The calculation of depreciation should be reviewed for accuracy.

(xiv) Non-current assets should be reviewed for the need for any write-down.

(xv) Where portable assets exist e.g. laptops, these should be appropriately controlled and signed in and out of the entity premises.

Tests of controls

(i) Inspect for evidence of authorisation of purchase to board minutes, capital expenditure budgets and capital expenditure form.

(ii) Inspect for evidence of authorisation for disposals of significant assets to board minutes.

(iii) Confirm existence of non-current asset register which adequately identifies assets and comments on their current condition. Inspect for evidence that the register is periodically reconciled with the general ledger.

(iv) Inspect for evidence of periodic reconciliation of register to physical identification and existence of assets.

(v) Inspect for evidence of authorisation of depreciation rates, and particularly any change in rates used.

(vi) Review client working papers for evidence that the client checks or re-performs depreciation calculations.

ACTIVITY 6

You have recommended that one of your clients should set up a non-current asset register to ensure proper and effective control over their non-current assets. They have asked you to provide them with additional information to assist them in implementing this recommendation.

(a) State what typical information should be recorded in the register.

(b) List typical control activities that should be performed using the register to ensure that proper control is maintained over the non-current assets.

For a suggested answer, see the 'Answers' section at the end of the book.

7.4 BANK AND CASH

Your studies of the sales, purchases and the wages and salaries systems earlier in this chapter has indicated some of the typical processes involved in cash payments and receipts. There will however be controls over and above those already discussed, due to cash being a significant asset for many businesses and it is also at a higher risk of potential misappropriation.

Control objectives

The control objectives over bank and cash are generally the same in all cases, namely:

(i) That payments are only made in respect of valid business expenses. The business does not want to be operating inefficiently by making unnecessary payments

(ii) All receipts and payments are recorded accurately and promptly. Management will find it difficult to run the business without up-to-date information about the cash position

(iii) Risk of misappropriation of cash from the business is minimised

Control activities over bank and cash

(i) **Request and authorisation**

- The cheque signatory is a senior member of staff, independent of the day-to-day recording of business transactions.

- Cheques are only signed after appropriate supporting evidence has been submitted.

- Cheques in respect of large amounts require a second signatory.

(ii) **Payments, receipts and recording**

- The initial recording of receipts is carried out by two independent members of staff. This should largely prevent the possible misappropriation of receipts of accidental non-recording.

- Stamping of posting forms once all the figures have been posted to the relevant main ledger accounts. This helps to ensure completeness of information.

- The performance and review of monthly bank reconciliations.

Note that this section assumes payment is by cheque. If settlement is by other means, such as bank transfer, then similar authorisation controls should apply over the payment method used.

Tests of controls

(i) Observe the mail opening process to ensure that one person is opening the post and another person is recording the cash received in the cash log (segregation of duties).

(ii) Enquire of management where the cash receipts not banked are stored. Inspect the location to ensure the cash is suitably secure.

(iii) Compare bank statements with the cash received log to confirm amounts are banked promptly.

(iv) Enquire of staff as to who performs the bank reconciliation and confirm the person is suitably responsible.

(v) Review the file of bank reconciliations for evidence of regular performance and review by senior finance team member.

(vi) Observe the process for recording cash received into the relevant ledgers – ensure that the cashier updates the cash book from the cash received log and a member of the sales ledger team updates the sales ledger (segregation of duties).

(vii) Inspect for evidence of a second signatory on cheques to be paid out for large amounts.

CONCLUSION

The previous chapter dealt with the auditor's work in connection with ascertaining, confirming, recording and evaluating the client's accounting systems. A positive outcome of this aspect of the audit means that the auditor can consider the use of a systems audit approach – provided there is also a positive outcome to the aspect of the audit covered in this chapter – the testing of controls to establish whether they are working effectively. So, by this stage, the auditor will know whether a systems approach is to be used – focusing on the accounting systems supplemented by a reduced amount of substantive testing, or a verification approach with extensive substantive testing.

This should indicate to you the significance of the material covered in this and the preceding chapter – it affects the entire direction which the audit takes.

Tasks expected of you often focus on the area of control systems and tests of controls. Main areas covered in the chapter and the most likely areas for examination purposes are: sales, purchases and payroll.

KEY TERMS

Audit evidence – Information which assists the auditor to reach a conclusion on the truth and fairness of the financial statements.

Sufficient audit evidence – The quantity of audit evidence necessary to support a conclusion.

Appropriate audit evidence – Reliable and relevant audit evidence.

Control objectives – Objectives that internal control should set out to achieve in a given area.

Control activities – The policies and procedures that should be in place to ensure the control objectives are achieved.

Tests of control – Audit work performed to generate evidence as to whether the controls are operating satisfactorily.

SELF TEST QUESTIONS

		Paragraph
1	What are the characteristics of good audit evidence?	2.1
2	What guidelines are available to the auditor to assess the reliability of audit evidence?	2.2
3	List the five standard auditing testing procedures.	3
4	Explain the role of materiality in tests of control.	3
5	What are the control objectives for the return of goods by a customer?	4.1
6	What are the control objectives for the purchase of goods by the business?	5.1
7	What are the control objectives for the payroll?	6.1
8	What are the control objectives for inventories?	7.2
9	What are the control objectives for non-current assets?	7.3
10	What are the control objectives for bank and cash?	7.4

THE AUDIT EVIDENCE PROCESS: TESTS OF CONTROL : **CHAPTER 7**

PRACTICE QUESTION 1

STICKY BAR CHOCOLATES – 1

Sticky Bar Chocolates is a company which employs 46 sales representatives in the country of Auditoria, each with a defined geographical area to cover. Each rep is supplied with a new car, changed every three years. At the end of each week, each rep submits a claim on a pre-printed form for expenses with supporting vouchers. Expenditure is on petrol, repairs and servicing of the car, hotels, lunches and entertaining. Each claim is scrutinised by Mr Jones who is deputy chief accountant. He verifies that the claims are supported by vouchers. He clears any inconsistencies with the rep concerned and makes out cheques for signature by two directors of the company. The authorised expense form should accompany the cheque for signature. The total amount paid out by the company in the year to 30 April 20X7 was $320,000. The company made a profit in that year of $1.5 million.

(a) Discuss the shortcomings of this system and suggest ways of improving the system.
(6 marks)

(b) Describe tests of control and list the tests of control that the auditor would perform on this system. **(4 marks)**

(Total: 10 marks)

For a suggested answer, see the 'Answers' section at the end of the book.

PRACTICE QUESTION 2

STICKY BAR CHOCOLATES – 2

Sticky Bar Chocolates is a company which employs 46 sales representatives in the country of Auditoria, each with a defined geographical area to cover. Each rep is supplied with a new car, changed every three years. At the end of each week, each rep submits a claim on a pre-printed form for expenses with supporting vouchers. Expenditure is on petrol, repairs and servicing of the car, hotels, lunches and entertaining. Each claim is scrutinised by Mr Jones who is deputy chief accountant. He verifies that the claims are supported by vouchers. He clears any inconsistencies with the rep concerned and makes out cheques for signature by two directors of the company. The total amount paid out by the company in the year to 30 April 20X7 was $320,000. The company made a profit in that year of $1.5 million.

(a) Describe substantive procedures and tabulate the substantive procedures that the auditor would perform on the item 'sales representatives' expenses'. **(5 marks)**

(b) During the audit, the auditor discovered that the sales representative in one area was submitting false claims for entertaining customers. What further action should the auditor take? **(5 marks)**

(Total: 10 marks)

For a suggested answer, see the 'Answers' section at the end of the book.

FAU: FOUNDATIONS IN AUDIT

EXAM-STYLE QUESTION 1

HOWDEN – 1

Howden is a large manufacturing company which has grown considerably in recent years. Following your audit of the company for the year ended 31 May 20X7 you issued a memorandum on internal control in which you brought certain deficiencies in internal control to the attention of management. The chief accountant of Howden agrees that the company has grown too large for the systems of internal control that have been in force for some years and has asked your advice on the sort of control you would wish to see in force in a purchases and trade payables system.

Required:

(a) Inform the chief accountant of the basic division of duties which you would expect to find in any system of internal control, giving your reasoning. **(5 marks)**

(b) Advise him of the main internal control features you would expect to find in the buying function of the purchases and trade payables system of Howden. **(5 marks)**

(Total: 10 marks)

For a suggested answer, see the 'Answers' section at the end of the book.

EXAM-STYLE QUESTION 2

HOWDEN – 2

Howden is a large manufacturing company which has grown considerably in recent years. Following your audit of the company for the year ended 31 May 20X7 you issued a memorandum on internal control in which you brought certain deficiencies in internal control to the attention of management. The chief accountant of Howden agrees that the company has grown too large for the systems of internal control that have been in force for some years and has asked your advice on the sort of control you would wish to see in force in a purchases and trade payables system.

Required:

Advise the chief accountant of the main internal control features you would expect to find in the following functions of the purchases and trade payables system of Howden:

(a) receipt of goods **(5 marks)**

(b) accounting for purchases **(5 marks)**

(c) payment of outstanding balances. **(5 marks)**

(Total: 15 marks)

For a suggested answer, see the 'Answers' section at the end of the book.

EXAM-STYLE QUESTION 3

THE QUICKSAND COMPANY

Mr A Black has recently acquired the controlling interest in Quicksand, who are importers of sportswear. In his review of the organisational structure of the company Mr Black became aware of weaknesses in the procedures for the signing of cheques and the operations of the petty cash system. Mr Black engages you as the company's auditors and requests that you review the controls over cheque payments and petty cash. He does not wish to be a cheque signatory himself because he feels that such a procedure is an inefficient use of his time. In addition to Mr Black, who is the managing director, the company employs 20 personnel including four other directors, and approximately 300 cheques are drawn each month. Further the petty cash account normally has a working balance of about $600, and $300 is expended from the fund each month. Mr Black has again indicated that he is unwilling to participate in any internal control activities which would ensure the efficient operation of the petty cash fund.

Required:

(a) Prepare a letter to Mr Black containing your recommendations for good internal control procedures for petty cash. **(9 marks)**

(Marks will be awarded for the style and layout of the answer.)

(b) Discuss the audit implications, if any, of the unwillingness of Mr Black to participate in the cheque signing procedures and petty cash function. **(6 marks)**

(Total: 15 marks)

For a suggested answer, see the 'Answers' section at the end of the book.

Chapter 8
SAMPLING

INTRODUCTION

Before dealing with the techniques of substantive testing in detail, it is appropriate to cover the topic of sampling as it is applied in auditing. Sampling, in simple terms, means that audit tests are applied only to some, not all, of the items under audit.

You are only required to deal with the basics of sampling. Sampling, particularly statistical sampling can use extremely complex mathematics in a real auditing environment. Whilst we shall deal with the topic of statistical sampling in this chapter, the maths which we shall cover will be kept to an absolute minimum.

You should note that the vast majority of audit testing operates on a sample basis. This reduces the work load on the auditor, and therefore reduces the cost of the audit to the client. In addition, it would be impossible to complete many audits of large enterprises, where strict deadlines have to be met, if the auditor were to examine every item making up the figures in the financial statements. However, he must ensure that his sampling is accurately performed in order to satisfy the audit objectives and give him sufficient basis for his audit opinion.

This chapter covers syllabus area D (4).

CONTENTS

1   An introduction to audit sampling

2   Constructing audit samples

3   Statistical and non-statistical sampling compared

LEARNING OUTCOMES

At the end of this chapter, you should be able to:

- understand the nature of audit sampling and its uses in performing an audit assignment

- appreciate the main differences between statistical and non-statistical sampling techniques

- appreciate and apply the principles involved in constructing a sample and interpreting the results obtained

- demonstrate an understanding of the basic principles of statistical sampling.

FAU: FOUNDATIONS IN AUDIT

1 AN INTRODUCTION TO AUDIT SAMPLING

1.1 DEFINITION OF AUDIT SAMPLING

Definition   ISA 530 *Audit Sampling* **defines audit sampling** as the application of audit procedures to less than 100% of the items within a population of audit relevance such that all sampling units have a chance of selection in order to provide the auditor with a reasonable basis on which to draw conclusions about the entire population.

An analysis of this definition brings out a number of points important to your understanding of sampling in general, and specifically sampling as applied to auditing.

- If an auditor applies testing procedures to anything less than 100% of the items under audit, then sampling procedures are being used. So, if an auditor applies tests of control to 9,999 of 10,000 sales invoices, the auditor is using a sample. (The 10,000 sales invoices here are known as the **population** under audit).

- The auditor is not concerned with the result of the sample as such. The auditor is using the sample as a means to an end – that end being a conclusion on the population as a whole.

- Having established this point, it is then clear that one of the major requirements of sampling procedures is that the sample selected for testing purposes should faithfully reflect the population on which the auditor is seeking a conclusion – the sample should be representative of the population in order for the auditor to make valid conclusions about the population as a whole.

1.2 WHY USE SAMPLING IN AUDITING?

Sampling is normally appropriate for areas in which there are a high number of similar transactions e.g. credit sales for the period. It may not be cost effective to test all transactions and the auditor will therefore use sampling. Even if the costs were ignored, full testing would not necessarily achieve the specified audit objectives for that area e.g. full testing on sales invoices for example would not verify that all sales are recorded (i.e. it may not demonstrate completeness – there may be sales made which have not been invoiced), nor would it deal with human error on the part of the auditor.

The use of sampling in conjunction with properly thought out objectives and properly constructed tests allows more valid conclusions to be reached than the (now outdated) traditional system of testing 'as many transactions as possible' in the time available.

The ISA makes a very important point that summarises the use of sampling and states that when using either statistical or non-statistical methods, auditors should design and select an audit sample, perform audit procedures thereon and evaluate sample results so as to obtain appropriate audit evidence.

Cases where sampling is **not** appropriate include the following situations.

- The auditor is 'on enquiry' as a result of previous information. The auditor's suspicions have been raised and therefore a greater degree of caution will need to be exercised in carrying out the audit work. This may involve applying audit tests to the entire population in these circumstances.

- Populations are too small for valid conclusions to be drawn and, in any event, it is quicker to test all transactions rather than spend time constructing a sample.

- All the transactions in a particular area are material and should therefore be subject to examination by the auditor.

- The data may be material by nature, such as directors' emoluments which require precise disclosure in the financial statements, regardless of their size.

- The audit area does not consist of items of the same kind i.e. there is a non-homogeneous population. In this situation, it would be difficult, if not impossible, to construct a representative sample.

1.3 SAMPLING RISK

Definition The risk that the auditor draws a different conclusion from the results of a sample than that which would have been drawn had the entire population been examined.

It may happen that the results of audit tests applied to all the items in a sample do not reveal errors – but some of the items not included in the sample MAY include errors or misstatement. In this situation, a conclusion based on the sample would differ from a conclusion drawn for the entire population – sampling risk is at play here.

Auditors are faced with sampling risk in both tests of control and substantive procedures as follows:

(i) **Tests of controls**

- the risk of placing a higher than necessary assessment on control risk because the error in the sample is greater than the error in the population as a whole.

OR

- the risk of placing a lower than required assessment on control risk because the error in the sample is less than the error in the population as a whole.

(ii) **Substantive procedures**

- the risk of concluding that a recorded account balance or class of transactions is materially misstated when it is not because the error in the sample is greater than the error in the population as a whole.

OR

- the risk of concluding that a recorded account balance or class of transactions is acceptable when it is materially misstated because the error in the sample is less than the error in the population as a whole.

The auditor should use a rational basis for planning, selecting and testing the sample and for evaluating the results (see below) so that there is a reasonable level of assurance that the sample is representative of the population, and that sampling risk is reduced to an acceptable level.

ACTIVITY 1

State the components of audit risk and identify which of the elements of risk will include sampling risk.

For a suggested answer, see the 'Answers' section at the end of the book.

1.4 STATISTICAL AND NON-STATISTICAL SAMPLING

Statistical sampling involves the use of mathematical procedures, such as probability theory to draw conclusions on the population. Non-statistical techniques rely on the auditors' judgement to draw conclusions. Non-statistical sampling is sometimes referred to as **judgemental sampling**. Firms in practice use a combination of both, but it must be noted that auditors do not eliminate the need for the use of judgement when using statistical techniques as judgement is still needed in setting materiality levels for example. This idea will be dealt with later in this chapter.

2 CONSTRUCTING AUDIT SAMPLES

2.1 AUDIT SAMPLING – THE STAGES INVOLVED IN THE PROCESS

The steps involved in sampling can be summarised as follows:

- sample design
- selection of the sample
- evaluation of the sample results.

Each of these is now dealt with in more detail.

2.2 SAMPLE DESIGN

When designing an audit sample, auditors should consider:

- the specific audit objectives
- the population from which they wish to sample
- determining the sample size
- sample selection methods.

Audit objectives

Objectives will relate to tests of control or substantive procedures – whichever is appropriate to the audit work currently being performed.

Let us assume here that the auditor has set the following specific objective for a test of controls relating to a sales system:

Auditors want to be 90% confident that 95% (+/– 3%) of credit notes have been authorised in accordance with company procedures.

This objective contains:

1 **A confidence level**

   This is the degree of certainty that the auditor wants to obtain from the tests – here, 90% confidence.

2 **A precision limit**

   These are the parameters set within which the auditor is prepared to work – here 95% +/– 3% i.e. between 92% and 98%.

These factors will influence the sample size used by the auditor.

Population

Definition The **population** is any group of items sharing a common characteristic.

Examples are all receivables at a reporting date or all the goods and services purchased in a year. The essential feature of a population is that it must be homogeneous, i.e. it is composed of similar or uniform parts. Suppose that the population consists of all wage calculations for a year, but the auditors know that the wages supervisor changed half way through the year. They may judge that the possibility of error is greater after the change than before. Hence there are really two populations. The sampling plan for each population will be different.

If the auditor is concerned that the non-homogeneous characteristics of the population may make sampling difficult or impossible to apply, one solution which may be adopted is **stratification**. This involves breaking a larger non-homogeneous population into a number of layers or **strata** – mini populations which do show homogeneous characteristics.

In the example mentioned above, the auditors may take the wages transactions processed by the original supervisor as one population, and those processed under the new supervisor as a second, separate population.

Stratification by value or size of item in the population is a commonly used technique.

Sample size

When determining the sample size, auditors should consider

- sampling risk

- the errors that would be acceptable before a true and fair view is threatened (tolerable or acceptable misstatement)

- the extent to which they expect to find errors (expected error).

The appendices to ISA 530 *Audit Sampling* include commentary on the influence various factors may have on sample size for both tests of control and also tests of transactions. Some relevant factors are as follows:

Factors influencing sample size for tests of controls	
Factor	Effect on sample size
Sampling risk	• The greater the reliance upon the results of tests of controls using audit sampling, the lower the sampling risk that an auditor will be willing to accept, which will result in a larger sample size. • The lower the assessment of control risk, the more likely that an auditor will place reliance.
Tolerable misstatement	• The higher the tolerable misstatement, the smaller will be the sample size will be. • The lower the tolerable misstatement, the larger the sample size will be.
Expected error	• If errors are expected, a larger sample size is normally required to gain confirmation that the actual error rate is less than the tolerable misstatement rate.
Number of items in population	• Unless the population is small, this factor has negligible effect on sample size.

Factors influencing sample size for substantive tests	
Factor	**Effect on sample size**
Inherent risk	• The higher the assessment of inherent risk, the more audit evidence is required to, and a greater sample size is likely to be required.
Control risk	• The higher the assessment of control risk is likely to mean that more reliance is placed upon substantive tests. This will particularly be the case if control risk is assessed as too high to place any reliance upon tests of controls.
Detection risk	• The lower the sampling risk that an auditor is willing to accept, the larger will be the sample size required to generate sufficient audit evidence.
Tolerable misstatement	• The higher the monetary value of the tolerable misstatement an auditor is willing to accept, the smaller will be the sample size.
Expected error	• If errors are expected, the larger will be the sample size required to gain evidence that the actual error rate is less than the tolerable misstatement rate.
Population value	• The less material the monetary value of the population, the smaller the sample size required is likely to be.
Number of items in population	• Unless the population is small, this factor has negligible effect on sample size.
Stratification of one large population into several smaller populations	• This may lead to several smaller samples which, collectively, would be less than a sample based upon one large population.

(a) **Sampling risk**

The impact of sampling risk on the sample size can be summarised as follows:

- in areas where the auditor is looking for a high degree of assurance from the audit work (areas where inherent risk and control risk are high), the auditor will be looking to minimise detection risk, which, as we saw in an earlier activity, includes sampling risk. This will suggest **a large sample size**.

    HIGH RISK AREA ⟶ LARGE SAMPLE SIZE

- In areas where the auditor is willing to accept a lesser degree of assurance (areas of low inherent and control risk), the auditor will be able to accept a higher degree of detection risk. This will suggest **a smaller sample size**.

    LOW RISK AREA ⟶ SMALLER SAMPLE SIZE

(b) **Tolerable (or acceptable) misstatement**

Definition   **Tolerable misstatement** is a monetary amount set by the auditor in respect of which the auditor seeks to obtain an appropriate level of assurance that the monetary amount set by the auditor is not exceeded by the actual misstatement in the population.

This means that, in the case of tests of control, the auditors will accept a certain number of instances of a failure to apply a control procedure and still conclude that the procedure is operating properly.

Tolerable misstatement is considered during the planning stage and, for substantive procedures, is related to the auditor's judgement about materiality.

SMALL TOLERABLE MISSTATEMENT ⟶ LARGE SAMPLE SIZE

LARGE TOLERABLE MISSTATEMENT ⟶ SMALL SAMPLE SIZE

(c) **Expected error**

Definition   **Expected error** is the actual level of error that the auditor anticipates exists in the population.

The auditor's assessment of expected error is often based on past experience – the errors discovered in previous years' audits, together with such factors as known problems or changes in circumstances which have taken place during the current period.

SMALL EXPECTED ERROR ⟶ SMALL SAMPLE SIZE

LARGE EXPECTED ERROR ⟶ LARGE SAMPLE SIZE

2.3 SAMPLE SELECTION

The ISA states that the auditors should select sample items in such a way that the sample can be expected to be representative of the population in respect of the characteristics being tested.

It then goes on to say that for a sample to be representative of the population all the items in the population are required to have an equal or known probability of being selected.

It is vital that the sample should be representative if the auditor is to be in a position to draw a conclusion on the population based on the results of the sample.

A number of sample selection methods are available to the auditor.

(a) **Random selection**

Definition   **Simple random sampling** is a method of selection in which every item in a population has the same statistical probability of being selected as every other item.

The sample will therefore be representative of the population as a whole. This often involves selecting by use of random numbers, either by the use of computer programs which generate random numbers or of random number tables. An acceptable alternative to random selection is haphazard selection (see below).

(b) **Value weighted selection**

Definition   **Value weighted selection** is a sampling method which uses the currency unit value (for example, the $) rather than the items as the sampling population.

For example, one dollar is selected out of the first two thousand and thereafter each two thousandth dollar is selected. Since an individual currency unit cannot be examined, the item which includes that dollar is selected for examination. The advantage of value weighted selection is that high-value items have a greater chance of being selected and audit effort is directed to them. Since each currency unit, and thus each item, has a chance of being selected this method achieves a representative sample.

This should not be confused with 100% examination of items above a certain value, in which items below that value stand no chance of being selected and thus the result cannot be representative. The chance of each item being selected is proportional to the value of that item and in effect a perfectly stratified sample is selected.

The most common form of value weighted selection used in practice is **monetary unit sampling (MUS)** which is examined later in this chapter as an example of a statistical sampling method. Such techniques are useful where the objective of the test is to test for overstatement, but not for understatement. Items materially understated have less chance of being selected using this method.

(c) **Systematic selection**

Definition   **Systematic sample selection** method is where the auditor calculates a uniform sampling interval by dividing the population size by the sample size.

For example, if a population to be sampled is 600 items and the sample size is 50 the sampling interval will be 12. One of the first 12 items will be selected as the starting point and thereafter every twelfth item will be selected. In determining the starting point each of the first 12 items (in this example) should have a chance of being selected. The starting point may be selected haphazardly or randomly.

Systematic selection is particularly useful when sampling from non-monetary populations, for example despatch notes.

One problem with systematic selection is that it may not achieve a representative sample where the population is arranged in a fixed pattern. For example, if every 50th item in a population has a particular characteristic (say it arises from the Bristol branch) then systematic selection may result in a sample containing a greater or smaller proportion of items with that characteristic than exist in the population as a whole.

(d) **Block sampling**

Definition **Block sampling** is a method in which a number of adjacent transactions or items will be selected, e.g. all sales invoices in a particular week, or all receivables with a name beginning with a particular letter.

There are two main disadvantages of this approach:

1 The block selected may not show characteristics that are representative of the population as a whole. Although of course this is an inherent problem in any form of sample selection it is more apparent in block sampling where all testing is concentrated in a small part of the population.

2 In order to minimise costs, it is probable that only relatively few blocks of items may be selected. This is particularly the case where the sampling unit is a period of time rather than individual items. For example, if transactions are being selected for vouching it may seem to be practicable only to select a few days' transactions out of the whole year. A sample with only a few blocks is then unlikely to be adequate to reach a reasonable conclusion.

Nevertheless block sampling can result in significant cost savings in audit time, and there are some occasions where practical considerations may require the use of block sampling, for example when visiting a branch.

(e) **Judgemental/haphazard selection**

Definition This is a selection process in which the auditor attempts to give all items in a population a chance of being selected by choosing items according to judgement.

The auditor should avoid conscious bias and predictability in selecting items. For example, a tendency to favour items that appear to be 'easy', i.e. items that do not have crossings out and corrections around them or are simply easily located, should be avoided. Also bias should not be introduced by only examining items from current periods or by selecting items consciously because of their size or because they appear unusual. Haphazard selection is acceptable as an alternative to random selection providing the tendency to bias is resisted. Haphazard selection is not appropriate when using statistical sampling methods.

2.4 EVALUATION OF TEST RESULTS

Having carried out, on each sample item, those audit procedures which are appropriate to the particular audit objective, auditors should:

(a) analyse any errors detected in the sample, and

(b) draw inferences for the population as a whole.

The vital point, you will recall, is that the auditor is attempting to draw a valid conclusion on the **population** as a whole from the results of the **audit tests performed on the sample**.

(a) **Analysis of errors in the sample**

In analysing the errors detected in the sample, the auditors first need to determine whether an item in question is in fact an error.

In designing the sample, the auditors define those conditions which constitute an error by reference to the audit objectives. For example, in a substantive procedure relating to the recording of trade receivables, a misposting between customer accounts does not affect the total receivables figure. Therefore, it may be inappropriate to consider this an error in evaluating the sample results of this particular procedure, even though it may have an effect on other areas of the audit such as the assessment of bad and doubtful debts.

Errors identified in the tests need to be extrapolated to the population as a whole.

For example, out of a population with a money value of $10,000, errors of $42 are discovered in a sample with a total value of $2,500. The following projection could be performed:

$$\text{Total errors in the population} = \frac{\$42}{\$2,500} \times \$10,000 = \$168.$$

(b) **Draw inferences for the population as a whole**

If this is less than the tolerable misstatement the auditor will have obtained sufficient evidence that the population is fairly stated. If tolerable misstatement is exceeded the auditor may perform additional procedures, and perhaps finally suggest adjustments to the financial statements.

ACTIVITY 2

A new audit junior has started working for your firm and has asked you to explain some sampling terms to him, and to inform him why auditors use sampling.

Required:

Define the following:

(a) tolerable misstatement

(b) expected misstatement

(c) confidence level

(d) precision limit

and give a brief explanation as to why auditors use sampling techniques.

For a suggested answer, see the 'Answers' section at the end of the book.

3 STATISTICAL AND NON-STATISTICAL SAMPLING COMPARED

3.1 INTRODUCTION

You do not need an in depth knowledge of statistical sampling techniques. This section expands on the brief explanations given earlier in the chapter. Your objective here should be to gain a general framework of understanding, without going into too much detail.

Let us start by reminding you of the two types of sampling techniques.

(a) **Statistical sampling**

Definition **Statistical sampling** is a technique using probability theory and random selection to determine the sample size, evaluate quantitatively the sample results, and measure the sampling risk.

(b) **Non-statistical sampling**

Definition **Non-statistical sampling** (sometimes known as judgement sampling) is a technique which does not rely on probability theory and requires more subjectivity in making sampling decisions.

3.2 COMPARISON OF THE TWO METHODS

It is important to note the following features between the two techniques:

- Statistical sampling is more expensive, as appropriate technical procedures need to be developed and staff must be trained in the use of those procedures.

- Statistical sampling keeps sample sizes as small as possible whilst still achieving the objectives of the sampling exercise, whereas non-statistical methods can result in large samples.

- There is less scope for bias with statistical techniques and the auditor can draw detailed and mathematically valid conclusions about the nature of the population.

3.3 CONDITIONS NECESSARY FOR THE USE OF STATISTICAL SAMPLING

If statistical sampling is to be used, the following conditions need to be present:

(a) The population to be tested must be homogeneous. This is necessary if the statistical theory is to be valid.

(b) The population must be reasonably large, otherwise the benefits of the technique will not be achieved. Statistical techniques need to be adjusted to work on small populations.

(c) Expectation of error must be low – in other words control risk must already have been assessed by the auditor as low or medium. (High control risk results in impractically large sample sizes under many statistical sampling techniques).

(d) The items in the population must be easily identifiable once selected, so that checking of the items chosen is easily carried out. This means in practice that items such as invoices must be pre-numbered and filed in sequence.

An illustration will clarify the procedure.

3.4 A SIMPLE ILLUSTRATION OF STATISTICAL SAMPLING

(a) **The test**

An auditor wishes to test a population of 100,000 purchase invoices using statistical sampling.

The following data has been determined by the auditor:

Confidence level	90%
Precision	± 1.5%
Expected error rate	2%

In other words, at the conclusion of the test the auditor wants to be able to state:

'I am 90% confident that the error rate in the whole population lies between 0.5% and 3.5% (2% plus or minus 1.5%).'

Statistical tables give a sample size in this case of 235 – do not worry about where this comes from!

(b) **The sample and its results**

- 235 invoices will be selected at random and tested.

- If in fact the error rate encountered does not exceed 2%, the conclusion stated above may be drawn.

- If the error rate exceeds 2%, it is not possible to apply the same confidence and precision level to the error rate actually discovered. This is because the higher the error rate assumed in the calculation, the larger the sample to be checked becomes.

- If a 3% error rate were encountered the auditor would need to check (per statistical tables) 348 invoices. It would therefore be necessary to select and check a further 113 items (348 minus 235) if the auditor is to be able to conclude with 90% confidence that the error rate in the total population is 3% plus or minus 1.5%.

Conclusion The auditor must be careful when selecting the sampling method to be used to ensure the audit objective is achieved. Statistical sampling is more complex, but there is less scope for bias and it is more defensible as an audit technique (the auditors can explain exactly why they chose the items that they did).

ACTIVITY 3

Explain the main differences between statistical sampling and non-statistical sampling.

For a suggested answer, see the 'Answers' section at the end of the book.

3.5 AN OUTLINE OF STATISTICAL SAMPLING TECHNIQUES

A number of statistical sampling techniques are available to auditors. This section gives a brief outline of three main techniques and their uses in auditing.

The three techniques considered here are:

- attribute sampling
- variables sampling
- monetary unit sampling.

Attribute sampling

Definition **Attribute sampling** provides results based on two possible values (i.e. correct, not correct).

As a consequence of this basic characteristic, attribute sampling is generally used in tests of control where the objective of a test is non-monetary in nature i.e. *does a control operate or not*. Each deviation from a prescribed control procedure is therefore given an equal weight in the evaluation of results.

The major advantage of attribute sampling is that the mathematical theory on which it is based is relatively straightforward. In an audit context it is therefore reasonably simple to use and a low cost technique.

However, the correct/not correct nature of questions dealt with by attribute sampling means that it cannot be used where the auditor is interested in tests of monetary amounts i.e. substantive audit procedures.

Variables sampling

Definition **Variables sampling** is concerned with items that can take a value within a continuous range of possible values and is used to provide conclusions as to the monetary value of a population. It can test either whether a certain statement is true or false or give an estimate of the true value of a population.

This definition means that variables sampling could be used where, for example the auditor is looking to be, say, 95% confident that the true value of the trade receivables lies between $59.6m and $60.4m and the best estimate is $60m. It is therefore ideally suited to substantive testing where the auditor is typically interested in money values.

However the calculations involved are lengthy and can typically only be performed easily by computer applications. As a consequence the use of pure variables sampling methods is not wide spread in auditing practices. Fortunately, a useful compromise technique **monetary unit sampling** has been developed to do the same job as variables sampling but in a much more straightforward way.

Monetary unit sampling (MUS)

Definition This technique combines the relative simplicity of the maths used in attribute sampling with some of the power of variables sampling, so it can be used to deal with money values and is therefore widely used by auditors in carrying out substantive testing.

The key principle underlying MUS techniques is that monetary items of differing amounts are viewed as being made up of a number of monetary units all of the same size. So, a sales invoice for $10,000 is viewed as comprising 10,000 $1 units of sales; a purchase invoice for $5,000 is viewed as 5,000 $1 units of purchases. It is this technique which simplifies the maths used by MUS.

The sample selected by the auditor under MUS is not viewed as a sample of, say, sales invoices – it is seen as a sample made up of a number of $1 units of sales.

Concepts of confidence level, tolerable misstatement and acceptable misstatement, as referred to earlier in this chapter, are used to determine a sample size, based on statistical probability tables.

Monetary unit sampling was developed from attribute sampling for use by auditors. It is one of the principal statistical sampling techniques in use within the audit profession and requires estimation of confidence levels and precision limits.

CONCLUSION

Sampling is a necessary and useful means of forming conclusions on audit evidence. The main benefit of sampling is that it allows the audit to be completed more efficiently from the point of view of both auditor and the client. The main problem with sampling is sampling risk – the possibility that the conclusion reached from the sample may not be valid for the population as a whole.

The sampling process involves sample design, selection of the sample and evaluation of the sample results to enable the auditor to draw conclusions about the population as a whole.

Sampling may either be by statistical or non-statistical methods. Statistical methods are based on probability theory – an outline knowledge is required but you will not be expected to go into great detail.

KEY TERMS

Audit sampling – The application of audit procedures to less than 100% of the items within an account balance or class of transactions to enable auditors to obtain and evaluate evidence about some characteristic of the items selected in order to form or assist in forming a conclusion concerning the population.

Sampling risk – The risk that the auditor draws a different conclusion from the results of a sample than that which would have been drawn had the entire population been examined.

Statistical sampling – The use of mathematical procedures, such as probability theory to draw conclusions on the population.

Non-statistical sampling – A technique which does not rely on probability theory and requires more subjectivity in making sampling decisions.

Confidence level – This is the degree of certainty that the auditor wants to obtain from the tests.

Tolerable misstatement – A monetary amount set by the auditor to obtain an appropriate level of assurance.

Stratification – This involves breaking a larger non-homogeneous population into a number of layers or strata which show homogeneous characteristics.

Random sample selection – Simple random sampling is a method of selection in which every item in a population has the same statistical probability of being selected as every other item.

Attribute sampling – A statistical sampling method which provides results based on two possible outcomes (i.e. correct, not correct).

Variables sampling – A statistical sampling technique concerned with sampling units which can take a value within a continuous range of possible values and is used to provide conclusions as to the monetary value of a population.

Monetary Unit Sampling – A statistical sampling technique which combines the simplicity of the maths used in attribute sampling with some of the power of variables sampling, so it can be used to deal with money values. It is widely used by auditors in carrying out substantive testing.

SELF TEST QUESTIONS

		Paragraph
1	What is the definition of audit sampling?	1.1
2	What is sampling risk?	1.3
3	What are the three steps in constructing an audit sample?	2.1
4	What is the meaning of population in the context of audit sampling?	2.2
5	When determining the sample size, the auditors should consider which three factors?	2.2
6	What is tolerable misstatement?	2.2
7	What two things should the auditor do in the evaluation of test results?	2.4
8	What conditions are necessary for the use of statistical sampling?	3.3

PRACTICE QUESTION

(a) What are the main advantages that can be derived by an auditor from the successful employment of statistical sampling techniques, as opposed to non-statistical sampling? Would you conclude that statistical sampling should be preferred?

(9 marks)

(b) Under what conditions is statistical sampling likely to prove most successful in an audit? **(6 marks)**

(Total: 15 marks)

For a suggested answer, see the 'Answers' section at the end of the book.

Chapter 9

AUDIT VERIFICATION WORK 1 – GENERAL PRINCIPLES

INTRODUCTION

We are now moving on to deal with the substantive testing, or verification, aspect of the audit. In recent chapters we have been following through the early steps in the time structure of an audit:

- planning, recording, controlling the audit
- evaluation of internal controls
- testing the controls
- the use of sampling techniques.

By this stage, the auditor will have made a decision on the general approach to be taken to the audit work. If the control systems are operating satisfactorily the amount of verification work will be reduced. If the controls are weak or are not operating effectively, a high level of verification work will be performed. It is this verification work that we are dealing with in this and the next few chapters.

This audit work involves the auditor gathering evidence which will lead to a conclusion as to whether transactions and balances reflected in the client's financial statements are properly stated – true and fair.

Assessors in auditing topics will always set out to test your knowledge and abilities in this area – it is fundamental to your studies.

This chapter deals with a number of general audit verification principles. The next chapters deal with specific statement of financial position and statement of profit or loss and other comprehensive income items.

This chapter covers syllabus areas D (1), D (2) and D (3).

FAU: FOUNDATIONS IN AUDIT

CONTENTS

1. Audit verification techniques
2. Review of financial statements
3. Accounting estimates

LEARNING OUTCOMES

At the end of this chapter, you should be able to:

- understand the general principles involved in verifying items that appear in a client's financial statements

- appreciate the nature and content of financial statements and be aware of the principles underlying their preparation

- understand the particular audit verification problems that arise in connection with accounting estimates.

1 AUDIT VERIFICATION TECHNIQUES

1.1 INTRODUCTION

At the verification stage of the audit, the auditor is typically presented with a set of draft financial statements prepared by the client. The role of the auditor is to generate evidence to allow a conclusion to be reached as to whether the information contained in those financial statements, and the way the information is presented and disclosed, give a true and fair view.

We know already that part of the audit evidence is generated by the auditor performing audit tests. Here, in verification work, the auditor will use substantive testing procedures, designed to give evidence relating to the figures in the financial statements. However, the testing procedures available to the auditor here are the same as those we saw earlier. As a reminder, audit-testing procedures available to the auditor are:

Inspection

This covers the physical review or examination of records, documents and tangible assets. An example in substantive testing is examining purchase invoices to ensure that they have been properly recorded and analysed in the financial statements.

Observation

This procedure is mainly applicable to tests of control, but may also be used in substantive testing, such as the auditor observing the client's inventory count to gain evidence that the inventory figure in the financial statements had been arrived at accurately.

Enquiry

This involves seeking relevant information from knowledgeable persons inside or outside the enterprise.

An example in substantive testing is asking management for an explanation as to why a receivable balance has, or has not, been treated as an irrecoverable debt.

External confirmation

External confirmation (a specific type of enquiry) concerns obtaining a representation directly from a third party. For example, the auditor may seek direct confirmation of receivables balances by writing to the debtors. Guidance is provided in ISA 505 *External Confirmations*, to assist the auditor with the design of confirmation procedures to ensure that the evidence obtained is both sufficient and appropriate.

Recalculation

Checking the arithmetical accuracy of records or performing independent calculations, for example computing or re-computing the depreciation expense for the year.

Reperformance

Reperformance is the auditor carrying out procedures or controls that were originally performed as part of the entity's internal control system, for example reperforming the ageing of receivables balances in an aged debt analysis.

Analytical procedures

You should note that these procedures are mainly used in substantive testing rather than as a test of controls. They may help the auditor to understand relationships between figures in the financial statements. This is sometimes referred to as the business approach to auditing.

1.2 CHOICE OF VERIFICATION TECHNIQUES

There are no specific rules that exist as to the type(s) of techniques that the auditor should use in a given set of circumstances.

This is principally a matter of audit judgement and the nature of the audit objective(s). The auditor has to look at each individual item in its own right, identify the audit objective(s) for that particular item and then decide the most reliable audit evidence available. The circumstances and evidence available will affect the type of technique(s) he uses.

1.3 AUDIT OBJECTIVES AND FINANCIAL STATEMENT ASSERTIONS

As just stated the type(s) of technique(s) used depend on the audit objectives that the auditor is seeking to achieve.

The general objective to be achieved by audit verification work is to establish whether the financial statements present a true and fair view.

We can identify a number of more detailed objectives which underlie this overall objective. These more detailed objectives allow the auditor to design a series of substantive tests on each audit area (inventory, receivables, etc.) which will build up the overall bank of evidence necessary to support the overall audit opinion.

In carrying out substantive audit tests (verification work), the auditor will be looking for evidence on statement of profit or loss items, statement of financial position items and general presentation and disclosure:

(a) Assertions about classes of transactions and events and related disclosures:

   (i) **Occurrence** – transactions and events that have been recorded or disclosed, have occurred and such transactions and events pertain to the entity

   (ii) **Completeness** – all transactions and events that should have been recorded have been recorded, and all related disclosures that should have been included in the financial statements have been included

   (iii) **Accuracy** – amounts and other data relating to recorded transactions and events have been recorded appropriately, and related disclosures have been appropriately measured and described

   (iv) **Cut-off** – transactions and events have been recorded in the correct accounting period

   (v) **Classification** – transactions and events have been recorded in the proper accounts

   (vi) **Presentation** – transactions and events are appropriately aggregated or disaggregated and clearly described, and related disclosures are relevant and understandable in the context of the requirements of the applicable financial reporting framework.

(b) Assertions about account balances and related disclosures:

   (i) **Existence** – assets, liabilities and equity interests exist

   (ii) **Rights and obligations** – the entity has the rights to assets, and liabilities are the obligations of the entity

   (iii) **Completeness** – all assets, liabilities and equity interests that should have been recorded have been recorded and all related disclosures that should have been included in the financial statements have been included

   (iv) **Accuracy, valuation and allocation** – assets, liabilities and equity interests have been included in the financial statements at appropriate amounts and any resulting valuation or allocation adjustments are appropriately recorded, and related disclosures have been appropriately measured and described

   (v) **Classification** – assets, liabilities and equity interests have been recorded in the proper accounts

   (vi) **Presentation** – assets, liabilities and equity interests are appropriately aggregated or disaggregated and clearly described, and related disclosures are relevant and understandable in the context of the requirements of the applicable financial reporting framework.

The above objectives link into a concept known as the financial statement assertions. These are the representations of the directors that are embodied in the financial statements. The concept takes the view that, by approving the draft financial statements and presenting them to the auditors for audit, the directors are making a number of promises, or assertions. The role of substantive testing is to verify these assertions.

The key assertions made by the financial statements and the related objectives of the substantive testing set out above can be summarised as follows:

ASSERTION	TESTING OBJECTIVE
Assets shown include all rights under the control of the enterprise	Completeness
Transactions arising during the period are reflected in the period's financial statements	Occurrence
The assets and liabilities are recorded at the correct value	Valuation
Assets and liabilities included in the statement of financial position actually exist	Existence
The organisation has legal right to the assets	Rights and obligations
A transaction or event has been recorded appropriately	Accuracy
All transactions and events have been recorded in the correct accounting period	Cut-off

ACTIVITY 1

You are about to commence the audit of a client who has a large number of non-current assets. You are aware that one of the audit objectives in this area is 'to ensure that all assets stated in the statement of financial position actually exist'.

What audit verification technique(s) would you use to satisfy this objective?

For a suggested answer, see the 'Answers' section at the end of the book.

ACTIVITY 2

As part of the planning process for the audit of a client, you have been asked to perform the following audit procedures relating to inventory:

1   Select from items in the warehouse and trace their inclusion in the inventory count sheets,

2   Select from items in the inventory count sheets and trace their identification in the warehouse.

3   Inspect items of inventory for evidence of obsolescence or damage.

4   Attend inventory counts at the premises of third parties who hold inventory on behalf of your client.

Which of the financial statement assertions are being tested by each of these audit procedures?

For a suggested answer, see the 'Answers' section at the end of the book.

FAU: FOUNDATIONS IN AUDIT

ACTIVITY 3

You are about to commence the audit of a client who has significant liabilities. As part of the audit work, you will perform the following audit procedures:

1. Inspect the bank confirmation letter for details of loan accounts held, together with terms of repayment.

2. Obtain a selection of supplier statements and reconcile these to the payables ledger balances, investigating and reconciling items.

3. Ensure that trade payables and accruals are included as current liabilities in the statement of financial position.

4. Review the list of trade payables and accruals in comparison with previous year(s) and investigate any significant differences for possible omission of liabilities.

Which audit assertion(s) are being tested by each of these audit procedures?

For a suggested answer, see the 'Answers' section at the end of the book.

ACTIVITY 4

As part of the audit of a client company, you have been asked to perform some audit work in relation to prepayments.

Required:

State and explain **THREE** of the audit assertions relevant to the audit of prepayments.

For a suggested answer, see the 'Answers' section at the end of the book.

ACTIVITY 5

As part of the audit of a client company, you have been asked to perform some audit work in relation to vehicle running costs.

Required:

State and explain **THREE** of the audit assertions relevant to the audit of vehicle running costs.

For a suggested answer, see the 'Answers' section at the end of the book.

2 REVIEW OF FINANCIAL STATEMENTS

2.1 CONTENT OF FINANCIAL STATEMENTS

It is important that you are clear as to exactly what the financial statements consist of under modern accounting practice.

They comprise the following:

(a) the primary statements:

   (i) statement of financial position

   (ii) statement of profit or loss and other comprehensive income

   (iii) statement of changes in equity

   (iv) statement of cash flows.

(b) the notes to the accounts, including a statement of significant accounting policies.

It is also traditional for the annual report document to include further reports (which are not part of the financial statements) such as:

(c) the directors' report

(d) the chairman's report

(e) the auditor's report (where the accounts have been audited).

The main principles underlying the preparation and presentation of company financial statements are now set out by the International Accounting Standards Board's (IASB) document the *Conceptual Framework*.

The major points from this document are summarised below:

1   **The elements of financial statements**

   The starting point here is definitions of assets and liabilities. The other elements are then defined in terms of these.

   Assets are rights or other access to future economic benefits controlled by an entity as a result of past transactions or events.

   Liabilities are obligations of an entity to transfer economic benefits as a result of past transactions or events.

   Owners' equity is arrived at by deducting liabilities from assets (capital = assets – liabilities).

   Gains and losses are determined in terms of increases and decreases in owners' equity.

2 Recognition in financial statements

Recognition essentially means the process of recording an item in the accounts. The principles here address such questions as when is it acceptable to recognise (record) an asset or liability and when should assets and liabilities be de-recognised (no longer recorded in financial statements). The main points to note are:

- Assets and liabilities should be recognised when there is evidence of their existence AND they can be reliably measured.

- They should be derecognised when the rights (assets) or obligations (liabilities) no longer exist.

2.2 THE TIMING OF AUDIT PROCEDURES

Whereas tests of control can be, (and often are with large organisations), performed by the auditor before the client's year end – at the so called interim audit stage – substantive audit procedures and verification work will be performed primarily at or very soon after the client's year end, as these procedures normally rely on the availability of draft financial statements.

Verification of the individual assets and liabilities by the auditor extends into the period after the reporting date (i.e. the period between the yearend date and the date of approval of the financial statements). The auditors will use this to their advantage when seeking to verify amounts stated for contingent liabilities, and for events after the reporting period (these are explained in a later chapter).

3 ACCOUNTING ESTIMATES

Definition An **accounting estimate** is defined as 'a monetary amount for which the measurement, in accordance with the requirements of the applicable financial reporting framework, is subject to estimation uncertainty'.

3.1 INTRODUCTION

This area is governed by ISA 540 *Auditing Accounting Estimates and Related Disclosures*.

The auditors should ensure that where management have made estimates in the preparation of the financial statements – and this will, in effect, always be the case for certain items – they obtain sufficient, appropriate audit evidence to support that figure.

Examples of typical circumstances where estimates are made are as follows:

(a) allowances to reduce inventories and receivables to their estimated realisable value

(b) provisions for depreciation and deferred tax

(c) accrued revenue

(d) provisions for losses on legal disputes and other contingent liabilities.

Areas such as those described above are inherently more risky than non-judgmental items and control risk is usually higher as these are non-routine transactions.

In principle, the auditor should pay special attention to such items and would perform the following steps:

(a) review and test the process used by management to develop the estimate

(b) use an independent estimate (generated by the auditor) to compare with management's estimate; if necessary the auditor should consider using an independent expert

(c) review subsequent events.

The auditor will normally test the calculations of the estimate, assess the assumptions made (e.g. the court is 90% likely to find in our favour), compare estimates with those made in previous periods and ensure that the estimate is in accordance with the auditor's knowledge of the business and the other audit evidence obtained.

It is important to recognise that it is the directors and management who are responsible for making accounting estimates, not the auditors. The auditors will need to pay attention to this area, especially where the amounts are material, as there is a higher risk of misstatement. This is a complex area, and the auditor is more likely to need to exercise judgement in such situations as evidence available to support the estimate is not always conclusive.

The auditor must separately assess inherent risk and control risk when assessing the risk of material misstatement relating to accounting estimates. When assessing inherent risk the auditor should consider:

(a) the degree to which the estimate is subject to estimation uncertainty

(b) the degree of complexity and subjectivity involved in the method, assumptions and data used to make the estimate

(c) the degree of complexity and subjectivity used in the selection of management's estimate.

3.2 AUDIT PROCEDURES ON ACCOUNTING ESTIMATES

The auditor should obtain sufficient, appropriate audit evidence as to whether an accounting estimate is reasonable in the circumstances and, when required, is appropriately disclosed.

It is important that the auditors gain an understanding of the procedures used by management when making estimates. If there is no objective data available to enable the auditors to assess the estimate, then they should consider the implications for their report.

Specific procedures that should be performed are as follows:

(a) **Review and test the process used**

The auditor should:

(i) evaluate the data used, and consider the assumptions on which the estimates are based (are they realistic and reasonable?)

(ii) test the calculations used in the estimate

(iii) compare estimates made in prior periods with actual results of those periods (this will give comfort on how much reliance can be placed on management's procedures). This is a useful area for the application of analytical procedures

(iv) consider the review and approval procedures used by management

(v) test the operating effectiveness of controls over how management made the accounting estimate, together with appropriate substantive procedures.

(b) **Use of an independent estimate**

The auditors should either estimate the figure themselves or if appropriate obtain a third party estimate. If they obtain a third party estimate then they should evaluate the data, consider the assumptions, and test the procedures used, in order to verify its accuracy. This independent estimate should then be compared with that of management and any differences investigated.

(c) **Review of subsequent events**

The auditors should review transactions after the period end which relate to the estimates made; these may remove the need to use estimates.

3.3 EVALUATION OF AUDIT RESULTS

ISA 540 requires that auditors should make a final assessment of the reasonableness of the accounting estimate based on their knowledge of the business and whether the estimate is consistent with other audit evidence obtained during the audit.

Auditors should consider any differences identified between the accounting estimate and the results of their work. The materiality of the difference will affect their actions:

(a) if the difference is small then it is unlikely that adjustment will be required

(b) if the cumulative effect of all estimates or any one estimate is material then adjustment should be required

(c) if the directors refuse to make any required adjustment, then the auditors should consider the implications for their report.

ACTIVITY 6

Explain what is meant by an accounting estimate, and give three examples.

For a suggested answer, see the 'Answers' section at the end of the book.

Conclusion The use of accounting estimates is a subjective area; however, the auditor should still seek to obtain sufficient, appropriate audit evidence to verify its reasonableness and accuracy.

CONCLUSION

This chapter has introduced you to the application of standard audit testing procedures to carry out substantive testing as used at the final stage of the audit. These procedures are used by the auditor to generate evidence that will enable the auditor to reach a conclusion on whether the financial statement assertions are satisfied.

In carrying out these procedures the auditor should be aware of the theoretical framework within which financial statements are prepared (the IASB's *Framework*) and the particular audit problems resulting from accounting estimates.

We are now ready to move on to look at the application of these testing procedures to major areas of the financial statements.

KEY TERMS

Financial statement assertions – Financial statements under audit embody assertions by the directors which the auditor seeks to verify.

Assets – Rights or other access to future economic benefits controlled by an entity as a result of past transactions or events.

Liabilities – Obligations of an entity to transfer economic benefits as a result of past transactions or events.

Owners' equity – The excess of assets over liabilities.

Gains and losses – Increases and decreases in owners' equity.

Accounting estimate – A monetary amount for which the measurement, in accordance with the requirements of the applicable financial reporting framework, is subject to estimation uncertainty.

SELF TEST QUESTIONS

		Paragraph
1	What are the verification techniques used by the auditor?	1.1
2	What are the financial statement assertions?	1.3
3	What are the primary financial statements?	2.1
4	What is the definition of an asset and liability given in the IASB's Framework?	2.1
5	How does the auditor verify accounting estimates?	3.2

FAU: FOUNDATIONS IN AUDIT

EXAM-STYLE QUESTION 1

Your firm has just employed five new junior auditors who have no auditing experience.

As a senior auditor, you have been asked to provide some of their training to supplement their formal studies. One of the audit partners has asked you to include in the training programme a module dealing with general principles of audit verification work.

Required:

(a) Explain what is meant by the audit of the financial statements. **(5 marks)**

(b) Explain what is meant by the financial statement assertions, and briefly explain each of the assertions. **(10 marks)**

(Total: 15 marks)

For a suggested answer, see the 'Answers' section at the end of the book.

EXAM-STYLE QUESTION 2

Your firm has just employed five new junior auditors who have no auditing experience.

As a senior auditor, you have been asked to provide some of their training to supplement their formal studies. One of the audit partners has asked you to include in the training programme a module dealing with general principles of audit verification work.

Required:

Explain who is responsible for making accounting estimates, and give five examples of accounting estimates which may be encountered during a typical audit assignment.

(Total: 10 marks)

For a suggested answer, see the 'Answers' section at the end of the book.

EXAM-STYLE QUESTION 3

Your firm is preparing for the audit of a client that has a significant number of tangible non-current assets. As part of the audit planning process, you are involved in drafting audit programmes for review and approval by partners prior to audit.

Required:

Prepare a schedule which identifies, for each of the following financial statement assertions, two appropriate procedures to obtain relevant audit evidence.

(a) Valuation **(5 marks)**

(b) Existence **(5 marks)**

(c) Completeness **(5 marks)**

(Total: 15 marks)

For a suggested answer, see the 'Answers' section at the end of the book.

Chapter 10

AUDIT VERIFICATION WORK 2 – INVENTORY

INTRODUCTION

This is the first of several chapters dealing with the detailed verification work i.e. substantive testing procedures, which the auditor will perform on the items appearing in the draft financial statements of a client.

The chapters will draw on the general verification principles dealt with in Chapter 9. The concepts of audit risk and materiality are also relevant to these audit areas and could usefully be revised at this stage.

Inventory, dealt with in this chapter, is perhaps the area in a typical statement of financial position, which has historically given auditors more problems than any other. Many of the leading negligence cases involving auditors revolved around the approach taken to the audit of inventory. The implication is that inventory is often a high-risk area, requiring careful audit planning and often a high degree of judgement in carrying out audit procedures.

This chapter covers syllabus areas D (3).

CONTENTS

1   Inventory: financial statements and audit implications

2   The auditor's work on the inventory count

3   The auditor's work on inventory valuation

4   Problem areas in the audit of inventory

LEARNING OUTCOMES

At the end of this chapter, you should be able to:

- appreciate that inventory and related areas is one of the more important elements appearing in the financial statements for many enterprises

- understand and apply audit procedures relating to verifying both physical inventory quantities and the valuation placed on inventory

- appreciate the major problem areas relating to inventory which may require particular audit attention.

1 INVENTORY: FINANCIAL STATEMENTS AND AUDIT IMPLICATIONS

1.1 THE IMPORTANCE OF INVENTORY AND WORK-IN-PROGRESS

Definition The term **inventory** includes raw materials, bought in parts, work-in-progress (manufactured goods in an incomplete state) and finished goods.

Inventory can be inherently risky, due to the nature of the balance itself, if it quickly becomes obsolete as it may not be valued appropriately at the lower of cost and NRV as required by accounting standards.

This asset is very important from the audit viewpoint for the following reasons:

(a) Misstatement of inventory balances has a direct effect on reported profit of two accounting periods – closing inventory of one year is, of course, opening inventory of the next year. As a result of the subjective nature of many aspects of the inventory figure in the financial statements it is the easiest asset for management to manipulate.

(b) Inventory can be very difficult for an auditor to verify.

- There may be thousands of different lines of inventory – a typical large supermarket carries approximately 40,000 different product lines and, of course, large quantities of each and in lots of different locations.

- There may be some inventory items of a very specialist nature – pharmaceutical or engineering companies may present this type of problem to the auditor.

(c) The quantities of inventory held at a given moment may be difficult to establish. It may not be possible to cease inventory movements during the inventory count with the effect that accurate inventory quantities may be hard to establish.

(d) Valuation may be difficult especially with specialist inventory and obsolete inventory. As a consequence net realisable values may be hard to establish. The amount of overheads that can be attributed to inventory may be subjective in nature.

(e) Inventory losses from pilferage, wastage etc. may be difficult to control.

The key audit assertions relating to inventory that the auditor will focus upon are as follows:

- **Existence** – does the inventory exist, and how can this be confirmed? This will often be confirmed by attending an inventory count. In addition, the auditor may seek confirmation of the quantity and existence of inventory held by a third party on behalf of a client by obtaining written certification from the third party.

- **Rights and obligations** – how does the auditor confirm ownership of inventory, together with any associated obligations or claims? The auditor should ensure that any items of inventory held on behalf of third parties is segregated and excluded from the count and valuation. Terms of business from suppliers may identify any obligations associated with goods received until thy have been paid for.

- **Completeness** – how does the auditor obtain confirmation of the completeness of inventory records? One test would be to select physical items from the warehouse or stockroom and trace their inclusion in the inventory count sheets.

- **Valuation** – how does the auditor obtain conformation of the valuation of items of inventory? The auditor should ensure that any old or obsolete items of inventory are documented on the inventory count sheets so that they can be written down to an appropriate valuation. The cost of items of inventory may be confirmed by reference to recent purchase invoices.

1.2 INVENTORY VALUATION

For financial reporting purposes, IAS 2 *Inventories* requires individual inventories to be measured at the lower of cost and net realisable value.

You should be familiar with this from your financial accounting studies.

Definition   **Cost** is expenditure which has been incurred, in the normal course of business, in bringing the product or service to its present location and condition (including appropriate costs of conversion). Conversion costs include direct costs such as labour which relates to WIP and finished goods and production overheads.

A major aspect of the auditor's work on inventory is, as we shall see later, verification of the valuation placed on inventory. In order to carry out this aspect of the audit verification work, the auditor must be fully aware of the inventory valuation principle shown above.

The key points to recall here are:

- Cost is based on activities conducted in the ordinary course of business. Abnormal costs, such as costs resulting from excessively high or low activity levels, should not therefore be included in the cost of inventory.

- Cost should only be included if it is incurred in bringing the item to its present location and condition. Post production costs are therefore not to be included in the cost of inventory, but production overheads should be included if they fit into the definition given above.

Inventory valuation methods such as FIFO (First In First Out or average cost, are acceptable provided the value approximates to the actual value of the actual inventory on hand at the reporting date. LIFO is unlikely to satisfy this test and is therefore unlikely to be acceptable.

Definition   **Net realisable value** is estimated or actual selling price (net of trade discounts but before settlement discounts) less further costs to completion and further costs of marketing, selling or distribution.

1.3 INVENTORY QUANTITIES

In addition to valuing the inventory correctly, it is clearly important that the company can determine accurately the physical quantity of inventory on hand at any point in time. Many companies will maintain accounting records of inventory but, from the audit point of view, the inventory records substantiated by physical inventory counts are important as inventory records by themselves are notoriously unreliable.

In accordance with ISA 501 *Audit Evidence – Specific Considerations for Selected Items*, if inventory is material to the financial statements the auditor should:

- Attend the physical inventory count
- Evaluate management's counting instructions and procedures
- Observe the performance of the count procedures
- Inspect the inventory (confirms existence and valuation due to condition); and
- Perform test counts.

2 THE AUDITOR'S WORK ON THE INVENTORY COUNT

2.1 AVAILABLE INVENTORY COUNTING METHODS

The two principal methods of systems of inventory counting available to clients are continuous and periodic.

- Under a **continuous** system (also called a **perpetual** system), some items of inventory are counted say every week or every month through the accounting period.
- Under a system of **periodic** inventory counting, all inventory is counted at the same time, typically at the reporting date.

It is clearly important that the auditor should be aware of which system is in operation by the client in order that suitable audit arrangements can be made.

2.2 CONTINUOUS INVENTORY COUNTING

Where suitable accounting records of inventory are maintained, it is often backed up by a programme of continuous inventory counting as part of general inventory control procedures. In a continuous inventory count system, inventory is counted on a regular on-going basis throughout the accounting period.

If such a programme of continuous inventory counting is in operation by a client, the auditor should ensure that:

(a) Each item of inventory is physically inspected and counted at least once a year, and more frequently in the case of items liable to loss etc.

(b) Inventory records are kept up to date.

(c) The records are amended as a result of physical counting, and that there are appropriate reports and investigation procedures for discrepancies.

(d) Two people carry out each count, and there is a rotation of pairing of the checkers.

Providing the continuous inventory count procedures in place by a client are acceptable and deemed to be reliable by the auditor, auditors may use the information provided for audit purposes, even though this system means that all the inventory on hand at the reporting date was not counted at that date.

There are several advantages to be gained from a well organised system of continuous inventory checking.

(a) Disruption caused by the inventory count is minimised – each inventory count takes a shorter period of time to complete.

(b) More regular inventory counting will allow for earlier identification of errors and obsolete inventory.

(c) Increased discipline is imposed over storekeepers caused by the surprise elements of random checks. This should result in a higher level of control being exercised over inventory.

2.3 PERIODIC INVENTORY COUNTING

Under this system, inventory is counted only once in each accounting period.

The count will usually be undertaken at or near the financial year end. If undertaken shortly before or after the financial year end, the time gap between the physical count and financial year end should be kept to a minimum, so as to minimise the risk of inaccuracies arising in the final inventory figure.

ACTIVITY 1

A potential client has approached your firm as he is setting up a new company selling computer stationery. He has asked for advice on inventory counting methods and informs you that he has heard of periodic and continuous inventory counting, but doesn't understand what these terms mean.

Explain the difference between these two methods.

For a suggested answer, see the 'Answers' section at the end of the book.

2.4 ORGANISATION OF INVENTORY COUNTS

Regardless of the inventory counting system in operation – continuous or periodic – it is vitally important both for financial reporting purposes, and for audit purposes, that the count is carried out accurately.

It is the responsibility of management (not the auditor) to establish appropriate procedures to be followed by staff in organising and conducting the inventory count.

However, the auditor should carefully review the inventory count arrangements that a client has in place.

Clear procedures should be drawn up by the client well in advance of the inventory count taking place. These instructions should be made available to client staff who are going to be involved in the count so that they have a chance to review them, become familiar with their contents and clarify any areas of doubt or uncertainty.

In addition, the auditor should review a copy of the procedures before the inventory count is held by the client. In reviewing the procedures, the auditor is assessing their adequacy – will the client's procedures, if carried out effectively, ensure that a full and accurate count is taken, which can then be used as the basis for the quantity of inventory on hand at the yearend to be reflected in the financial statements? If the auditor identifies any weaknesses in the procedures he should discuss these with the client with the aim of the procedures being amended. Set out below are the main features that should appear in inventory count instructions.

FAU: FOUNDATIONS IN AUDIT

1 **The organisation of the inventory**

(a) The inventory area is in a well organised, tidy condition in order to make the counting process as efficient as possible.

(b) Goods are clearly described and suitably labelled.

(c) Goods are protected against deterioration and misappropriation (restriction of access to stores).

(d) Goods held for third parties (i.e. goods not belonging to the company), and slow-moving, obsolete inventory, etc. are identified and separated.

(e) There is an adequate plan of the area to be covered, which should be tidy.

2 **Carrying out the inventory count**

(a) The procedures to be followed by each relevant department, branch, etc. should be clear and appropriate to each area of the business.

(b) Competent supervisors should be appointed for each inventory area, with teams (pairs) of technically competent counters allocated to the supervisors. One person for each team should be responsible for counting, the other for recording and checking the count. The storekeepers should not be responsible for counting unless their work is independently checked (segregation of duties!)

(c) Inventory should be suitably marked to indicate that it has been counted e.g. chalk mark, docket/ticket, etc.

(d) A standardised pre-numbered form should be used for recording the inventory count, the issue and return of which should be controlled so that all inventory counted and areas are accounted for, and that proper accounting records are kept.

(e) Movement of inventory during the inventory count should be prevented or closely controlled.

(f) Comparisons should be made as soon as practicable after the inventory count with the continuous inventory records so that any discrepancies may be investigated and the records adjusted where appropriate.

2.5 THE AUDITOR'S ATTENDANCE AT THE INVENTORY COUNT

ISA 501 *Audit Evidence – Additional Considerations for Selected Items* requires the auditor to attend the client's inventory count if inventory is material to the financial statements and if the auditor is to rely on the inventory count as a source of evidence as to the physical quantities of inventory on hand. It follows from this that:

- if inventory is not material, or

- if the accounting record rather than the inventory count is used as the source of inventory quantities

then the auditor is not expected to attend the count. These exceptions are not encountered on a regular basis in practice.

The auditor's role

The auditor will usually attend the client's inventory count, *the purpose of attending being to assess the effectiveness of the client's inventory counting procedures*. Attendance at inventory counts is primarily a test of controls, not a substantive procedure. It is not the auditor's responsibility to count inventory, but the client's. The auditor will perform test counts but these tiny samples are not intended to be representative of the populations they are drawn from.

We can analyse the role of the auditor in connection with the inventory count under three headings:

- before the inventory count
- during the inventory count
- after the inventory count.

Before the inventory count

The auditor should perform the following procedures:

(a) Review prior year's working papers, familiarise himself with the nature, volume and location of inventory. The controlling and recording procedures over inventory should also be considered.

(b) Identify problem areas in relation to the system of internal control and decide whether reliance can be placed on internal auditors (if available).

(c) If inventory held by third parties is material, or the third party is insufficiently independent or reliable, then arrange an inventory count attendance at the third party's premises, otherwise, arrange third party confirmation by way of letter to the auditor.

(d) If the nature of the inventory is specialised then the auditor will need to arrange expert help or to review the client's own arrangements for identifying and valuing the inventory.

(e) Examine the client's inventory counting instructions, as explained above: If found to be inadequate, the matter should be discussed with the client with a view to improving them prior to the inventory count.

During the inventory count

The main task here is to ensure that the client's staff are carrying out their duties effectively. Here, the auditor is using the audit testing procedure of observation.

In addition to observing the inventory count process being carried out, the auditor should also:

(a) Make two-way test counts from factory floor to inventory sheets, and from inventory sheets to factory floor. These are checked with the figures counted by the client and discrepancies investigated. The test counts are used for follow up audit work later. This tests completeness and existence.

(b) Make notes of items counted, damaged inventory, where inventory appears to be obsolete and instances where the inventory count procedures are not being followed.

(c) Examine and test control over the inventory sheets. The client should keep an inventory sheet register.

(d) Examine cut-off procedures.

(e) Pay particular attention to goods held on behalf of third parties (for example, goods on consignment) and how these are segregated and recorded.

(f) Reach and record a conclusion as to whether or not the inventory count was satisfactory, and hence provides reliable evidence supporting the final inventory figure.

If the auditor in attendance at the inventory count does *not* feel that the procedures are being carried out adequately, he must bring this to management's attention immediately and seek to rectify the position as it may not be possible to obtain the relevant evidence at a later date.

After the inventory count

The auditor should perform the following procedures after the inventory count:

- Verify that the cut off details obtained at the inventory count are accounted for in the correct period.

- Review the final inventory sheets and follow up test counts to the final statements of inventory. This test is designed to ensure that inventory quantities that actually existed at the date of the count are reflected in the final financial statements.

- Ensure that continuous inventory records (if applicable) are adjusted or reconciled to the physical count.

The cut-off concept

As financial statements are drawn up at a specific point in time, it is important that the right transactions are fully recorded in the right period. This is a simple but useful way of looking at cut off.

For example, if sales are recorded as a transaction of the current period by recognising a year end receivable, the corresponding cost of sales entry must also be made in the current period and the item must not be included in yearend inventory. This is an example of **sales cut off**.

Similarly, if goods are received during the current period and recorded in closing inventory, at the year end, the payable for the item must also be recorded. This is an example of **purchases cut off**.

Tests the auditor would carry out to ensure correct cut-off include the following.

(a) During inventory count attendance, note the serial numbers of the last sales invoice, despatch note and goods received note generated before the inventory count.

(b) After the inventory count, check the year-end despatch notes to sales invoices and the sales daybook and vice versa to ensure that despatches and the related invoice both fall before the year end.

(c) Similarly for purchases, ensure year-end goods receipts notes and related purchase invoices are correctly treated in the current period.

(d) Take a sample of goods received and goods despatched just after the year end and ensure that the related inventory was not included in the count in the case of goods received, and that it was included, in the case of goods despatched.

ACTIVITY 2

Explain the main reasons why the auditors attend the inventory count and state what action they would take if they identified that the client's laid down inventory count procedures were not being followed.

For a suggested answer, see the 'Answers' section at the end of the book.

3 THE AUDITOR'S WORK ON INVENTORY VALUATION

The main objective of the auditor attending the inventory count is to obtain evidence relating to the existence and condition of inventory. Attendance will provide some evidence relating to the valuation of inventory – for example, the auditor should record details of inventory showing signs of obsolescence – but much more work will be required before the auditor can reach an overall conclusion on inventory valuation. Attendance at the inventory count will also provide some assurance over the completeness of the inventory figure included in the financial statements as physical items can be selected from the warehouse and then traced to the inventory count sheets.

The auditors need to perform additional valuation tests. The audit work which the auditor will need to perform in respect of the valuation of inventory will depend on the type of inventory items under review.

Raw materials and consumable supplies

As these items of inventory are in their raw state (no work has yet been done on them by the client), the principal element of cost to consider is their purchase price from the material supplier. In addition there may be incidental costs such as delivery charges to consider.

Typical audit procedures applied to the verification of these inventory items will be as follows:

(a) Ascertain what elements of cost are included e.g. carriage in, duties, etc.

(b) Ascertain the method of valuing inventory issues.

(c) If standard costs are used, enquire into how and when standards were set, how these compare with actual costs and how variances are treated.

(d) Compare costs used with purchase invoices received, before the inventory count.

(e) Compare quantities with inventory records with a particular aim of finding items which have been in inventory for an unduly long period. Discuss these items with a responsible official in order to find out when they might be used, if at all, in order to ascertain a reasonable net realisable value. Consider the need for any write down of the value of these items of inventory.

(f) Follow up valuation of all damaged or obsolete inventory noted during observance of physical inventory count with a view to establishing a net realisable value and again consider any write down which may be necessary.

Work-in-progress (i.e. part completed goods)

The range of costs to consider here will include cost of materials, labour costs and production overheads. The client will have already calculated the element of these individual costs that need to be included in this type of inventory.

Typical audit procedures applied to the verification of these inventory items will be as follows:

(a) Ascertain what elements of cost are included. If overheads are included, ascertain the basis on which they are calculated and how they are apportioned to the work in progress, and review this basis with the available costing and financial information. If labour is included, check the calculations to costing and payroll records.

(b) Ascertain how the state of completion of the work in progress is measured and if estimates are made, on what basis they are made.

(c) Inspect materials costs to ensure that they exclude any abnormal wastage factors – abnormal costs should not be included.

(d) Inspect overheads balances to ensure that any additions include only normal expenses based on normal production capacity and that any costs arising from under-utilisation of production facilities, excessive waste or exceptional circumstances (i.e. abnormal costs again) are not carried forward in the inventory valuation.

(e) Enquire into any old, obsolete or damaged items and ensure that these are valued at a reasonable estimated net realisable value. Check this with previous or subsequent sales of similar items.

Finished goods and goods for resale

Note that if these items have been manufactured or processed by the client, the cost will consist of the same elements as were identified in work in progress above. If the items were brought in by the client in their completed state, cost of the inventory will comprise the purchase price from the supplier.

Typical audit procedures applied to the verification of these inventory items will be as follows:

(a) Enquire into what costs are included, how these have been established and ensure that any overhead element included is based on normal costs and is reasonable in relation to the information disclosed by the draft accounts. If labour is included, check the calculations to costing and payroll records.

(b) Agree the final cost with the client's official sales prices, bearing in mind any trade discounts which are normally granted off the list prices. This enables the auditor to ensure that inventories are valued at net realisable value if this is less than cost. For any such items, also check to identify if the relevant partly processed inventories and raw materials have also been written down.

(c) Compare inventory valuation with after date sales prices on goods sold to ensure that inventory will be valued at the lower of cost and net realisable value.

(d) Follow up any items which inventory records show are more than, say, six months in inventory. Enquire into reasons for this and ascertain possible realisable value of such items. This may indicate that the items are obsolete. The auditor would need to consider the nature of the item and length of average holding for such items.

(e) Follow up any inventories which at the time of observance of physical inventory count were noted as being damaged or obsolete.

(e) Discuss with sales manager any possible policy of selling off certain lines at less than usual selling prices e.g. 'loss leaders' due to competition, substitute products on the market etc.

(g) Follow up valuation of all 'seconds' items and ensure that they are valued at a reasonable estimated net realisable value if less than cost.

4 PROBLEM AREAS IN THE AUDIT OF INVENTORY

4.1 INTRODUCTION

Certain practical matters which may cause difficulty in some audits are explained briefly below. Where relevant, the auditor should take them into consideration when verifying inventory.

4.2 OVERHEADS

Definition **Overheads** are expenses incurred in the manufacture of goods and include items like factory property taxes and lighting and heating.

Production overheads should normally be included in the cost of goods being produced, based on the normal activity level of the company. An estimate of overheads to be incurred at this level of activity will need to be calculated, and allocated to the goods produced based on this activity level. If the company produces less goods than expected, then the unabsorbed overheads should be written off as an expense and not included in the inventory valuation.

In addition, most costing systems base overhead allocations on budgeted figures. These are obviously pre-determined figures, calculated before the actual overhead costs for the period are known and before the actual level of production is known. Activity levels in excess of that expected may require a reapportionment of overheads. If this is not done, it may result in an excessive amount of overhead being included in inventory valuation.

4.3 CHOICE OF OVERHEAD ALLOCATION METHOD

There are many different ways of including overheads into the cost of inventory. Each company must make its own decision about which method to use. The method must give a close approximation to the actual cost of overheads incurred in making the inventory.

The auditor will need to apply judgement in order to evaluate the appropriateness of the method used by the client.

4.4 NET REALISABLE VALUE

Definition **Net realisable value** is the actual or estimated selling price less all further costs to completion and all costs to be incurred in marketing, selling and distribution.

As you are already aware, inventory should be valued at the lower of cost and net realisable value.

It is not always easy to arrive at a figure for net realisable value. This is often another area where estimates will be used and where the auditor will need to assess the reasonableness of those estimates. A wide variety of sources of information may be available in order to assess net realisable value. These include:

- selling prices realised after the year end
- price lists.

Where net realisable value is found to be less than cost, the individual inventory lines affected should be revalued at the (lower) net realisable value. The only exception to this rule is for raw materials and components to be used in manufacture. These items may have their own net realisable value being less than cost. However, these items are not normally sold in their raw state. Because of this, no reduction in value is needed if it can be shown that the product made from these items can still be sold at above its cost.

There are a number of situations where net realisable value may be less than cost. These can be a helpful guide for auditors. The situations identified include:

(a) increased costs of manufacture

(b) reduced selling prices of products

(c) deterioration of inventory (particularly food stuffs)

(d) obsolescence of products (perhaps due to technological changes)

(e) deliberate selling at loss (supermarket 'loss leaders')

(f) buying and production errors.

ACTIVITY 3

Briefly explain how overheads should be allocated to inventory.

For a suggested answer, see the 'Answers' section at the end of the book.

CONCLUSION

Inventory is a material asset in the financial statements of many enterprises which is relatively easily manipulated. Auditors will often treat inventory as a relatively high risk area. This together with its materiality impact, means that auditors will devote a significant amount of audit time to inventory.

There are two main areas to consider:

- Audit evidence in relation to the existence and condition of inventory is derived primarily from the auditor's attendance at inventory counts. Attendance at the inventory count will also provide some assurance over the completeness of the inventory figure included in the financial statements as physical items can be selected from the warehouse and then traced to the inventory count sheets.

- Evidence is also required on the valuation of inventory – the lower of cost (including relevant labour and overhead) and net realisable value.

KEY TERMS

Inventory – Raw materials, bought in parts, work-in-progress (manufactured goods in an incomplete state) and finished goods.

Cost of inventory – Expenditure which has been incurred, in the normal course of business, in bringing the product or service to its present location and condition (including appropriate costs of conversion). Conversion costs include direct costs such as labour, which relates to WIP and finished goods, and production overheads.

Net realisable value – Estimated or actual selling price (net of trade discounts but before settlement discounts) less further costs to completion and further costs of marketing, selling or distribution.

Continuous inventory count system – Some items of inventory are counted every week or every month throughout the accounting period. **Note:** This may also be referred to as a 'perpetual system'.

Periodic inventory count system – All inventory is counted at the same time, typically at the reporting date.

Cut-off – Refers to the principle that requires transactions to be fully recorded in the appropriate accounting period.

SELF TEST QUESTIONS

		Paragraph
1	What are the two methods of the timing of inventory counts?	2.1
2	What is the purpose of the auditor's attendance at the inventory count?	2.5
3	What procedures are necessary for the auditor to check the valuation of raw material inventory?	3
4	In what situations may NRV be less than cost?	4.4

EXAM-STYLE QUESTION 1

NERO SCRAP AND HAULAGE COMPANY

You are the auditor of Nero Scrap and Haulage, carrying out the audit of the accounts for the year ending 30 June 20X7. The company owns 30 lorries and a large yard. Ferrous scrap is collected from numerous metal-working firms in the area, stored in the yard until it can be compressed with the company's scrap pressing machine. The scrap is then taken by lorry to a steel works, 100 miles away. The lorries are then used to take new steel sheets from the steel works to steel wholesalers.

(a) You have been sent the company's instructions to its employees on the assessment of inventory quantities.

State what you would expect to see in these instructions in respect of unpressed inventory in the yard. **(4 marks)**

(b) Scrap prices vary greatly from day to day. State how the inventory should be valued. **(2 marks)**

(c) List the steps you could take to verify that correct valuation of the inventory of scrap had been made. **(4 marks)**

(Total: 10 marks)

For a suggested answer, see the 'Answers' section at the end of the book.

EXAM-STYLE QUESTION 2

NERO SCRAP AND HAULAGE COMPANY

You are the auditor of Nero Scrap and Haulage, carrying out the audit of the accounts for the year ending 30 June 20X7. The company owns 30 lorries and a large yard. Ferrous scrap is collected from numerous metal-working firms in the area, stored in the yard until it can be compressed with the company's scrap pressing machine. The scrap is then taken by lorry to a steel works, 100 miles away. The lorries are then used to take new steel sheets from the steel works to steel wholesalers.

(a) While engaged on the audit, the new transport manager brings you a plain envelope containing four $5 notes and tells you that it had just been received from the company's lorry tyre suppliers with a message that it was last month's commission to the previous transport manager.

Discuss the audit implications of this discovery. **(6 marks)**

(b) The company carries the sheets on behalf of the steel wholesalers and charges haulage. Draft an audit programme for the audit of haulage charges made to the steel wholesalers customers. Specific tests of control should be included. The company's records are maintained manually. **(9 marks)**

(Total: 15 marks)

For a suggested answer, see the 'Answers' section at the end of the book.

EXAM-STYLE QUESTION 3

CAMRY PRODUCTS

In connection with your examination of the financial statements of Camry Products for the year ended 31 March 20X7, you are reviewing the plans for a physical inventory count at the company's warehouse on 31 March 20X7. The company assembles domestic appliances, and inventories of finished appliances, unassembled parts and sundry inventory are stored in the warehouse which is adjacent to the company's assembly plant. The plant will continue to produce goods during the inventory count until 5 pm on 31 March 20X7. On 30 March 20X7, the warehouse staff will deliver the estimated quantities of unassembled parts and sundry inventory which will be required for production for 31 March 20X7; however, emergency requisitions by the factory will be filled on 31 March. During the inventory count, the warehouse staff will continue to receive parts and sundry inventory, and to despatch finished appliances. Appliances which are completed on 31 March 20X7 will remain in the assembly plant until after the physical inventory count has been completed.

You are required to list the principal procedures which the auditor should carry out when planning attendance at a company's inventory count. **(Total: 10 marks)**

For a suggested answer, see the 'Answers' section at the end of the book.

EXAM-STYLE QUESTION 4

CAMRY PRODUCTS

In connection with your examination of the financial statements of Camry Products for the year ended 31 March 20X7, you are reviewing the plans for a physical inventory count at the company's warehouse on 31 March 20X7. The company assembles domestic appliances, and inventories of finished appliances, unassembled parts and sundry inventory are stored in the warehouse which is adjacent to the company's assembly plant. The plant will continue to produce goods during the inventory count until 5 pm on 31 March 20X7. On 30 March 20X7, the warehouse staff will deliver the estimated quantities of unassembled parts and sundry inventory which will be required for production for 31 March 20X7; however, emergency requisitions by the factory will be filled on 31 March. During the inventory count, the warehouse staff will continue to receive parts and sundry inventory, and to despatch finished appliances. Appliances which are completed on 31 March 20X7 will remain in the assembly plant until after the physical inventory count has been completed.

You are required to:

(a) describe the procedures which Camry Products should establish in order to ensure that all inventory items are counted and that no item of inventory is counted twice.
(10 marks)

(b) describe the audit procedures you would carry out at the time of the inventory count in order to ensure that inventory cut-off is correct. **(5 marks)**

(Total: 15 marks)

For a suggested answer, see the 'Answers' section at the end of the book.

Chapter 11

AUDIT VERIFICATION WORK 3 – NON-CURRENT ASSETS

INTRODUCTION

This chapter examines the audit verification procedures relating to all non-current assets. As you will probably be aware from your financial reporting studies, this includes three main categories of assets:

- tangible non-current assets
- intangible non-current assets (not examinable)
- non-current asset investments (not examinable).

These assets will often be a material item in a client's statement of financial position, particularly in the case of a manufacturing company and represent another area where auditor judgement will be required – notably in the area of depreciation.

This chapter covers syllabus areas D (2) and D (3).

CONTENTS

1 Non-current assets: an introduction

2 Verification procedures: tangible non-current assets

3 Using the work of an auditor's expert

LEARNING OUTCOMES

At the end of this chapter, you should be able to:

- apply basic accounting principles to a wide range of non-current assets
- understand and apply audit verification techniques to
    - tangible non-current assets.

1 NON-CURRENT ASSETS: AN INTRODUCTION

1.1 DEFINITION

Non-current assets are those assets which are held for continuing use in the business and are not intended for resale.

Non-current assets can be analysed as follows:

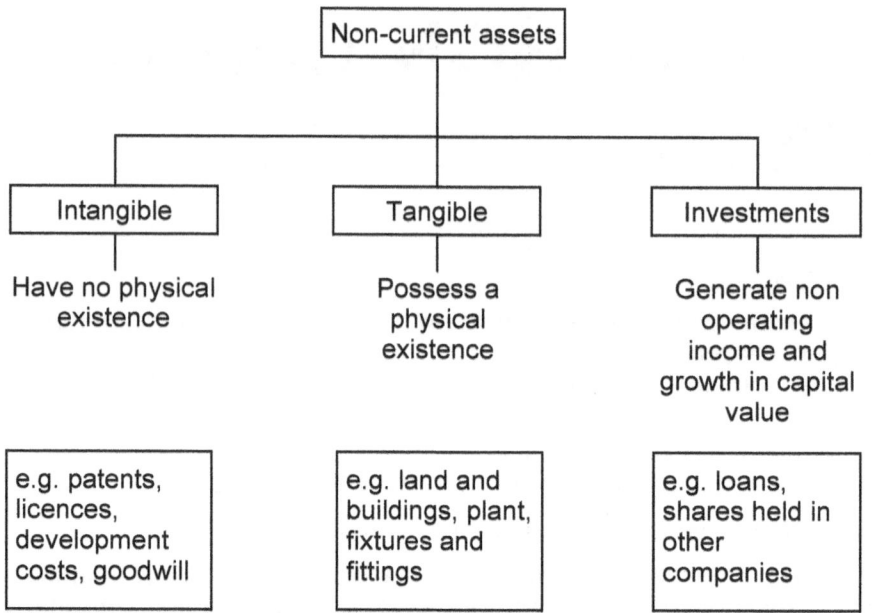

Any assets not intended for continuing use are treated as current assets regardless of when they will be realised.

You should note that audit work applicable to intangible non-current assets and investments are not examined in this paper.

1.2 NON-CURRENT ASSETS – MAJOR DISCLOSURE REQUIREMENTS

In general, a schedule of non-current assets (property, plant and equipment, PPE) is required in published financial statements. This general rule applies to all three categories of non-current assets. An example is shown here relating to tangible non-current assets – similar schedules would also be published in respect of intangible non-current assets and non-current asset investments.

Information requirements for tangible assets (PPE)

	Land and buildings	Plant and machinery	Fixtures, fittings, tools and equipment	Payments on account and assets in course of construction	Total
Cost or valuation	$	$	$	$	$
At beginning of year	X	X	X	X	X
Additions	X	X	X	X	X
Disposals	(X)	(X)	(X)	(X)	(X)
At end of year	X	X	X	X	X
Accumulated depreciation					
At beginning of year	X	X	X	X	X
Disposals	(X)	(X)	(X)	(X)	(X)
Provisions for the year	X	X	X	X	X
At end of year	X	X	X	X	X
Carrying amount:					
At end of year	X	X	X	X	X
At beginning of year	X	X	X	X	X

The carrying amount of land and buildings comprises:

	20X3 $	20X2 $
Freehold property	X	X
Long leaseholds	X	X
Short leaseholds	X	X
	X	X

Where tangible assets are included at a valuation the notes must disclose:

(a) the years in which the valuation took place, and for each year, the value of those assets

(b) for any valuation during the year the names of the valuers, or their qualifications, and the bases of valuation adopted.

It is also necessary to disclose:

(a) the accounting policies as regards to depreciation and to account for any impairment in the value of assets

(b) the carrying value of plant and machinery and fixtures and fittings that are held under finance leases (see below). Leased assets should be split between short leases and long leases.

Short leases are leases that have less than 50 years to run at the reporting date. All other leases are long leases.

The above movement schedule, as it is often called, is useful as an introduction to the audit work on non-current assets. It highlights some of the key areas where the auditor will focus attention, for example, additions and disposals.

1.3 COST OR VALUATION

Companies can usually choose to include tangible non-current assets in the statement of financial position at either cost or valuation. The most frequently encountered category of asset that is stated at valuation rather than cost is land and buildings.

The following points should be noted:

(a) The basis used i.e. cost or valuation, must be disclosed in the accounts.

(b) If the assets are revalued the surplus on revaluation should be disclosed as other comprehensive income and credited direct to a revaluation reserve as it is an unrealised gain. Disclosure takes place in the other comprehensive income section of the statement of comprehensive income.

(c) Revaluation of non-current assets is not normally compulsory unless there has been an impairment (fall) in value in which case the asset must be written down in the statement of financial position. Usually the debit is made in the statement of profit or loss, but it can be taken to revaluation reserve in certain circumstances.

(d) Depreciation of revalued assets should be based on the revalued amount and current estimates of useful life.

1.4 DEPRECIATION

Depreciation is a subjective area; it is important that the auditor considers the requirements of IAS 16 *Property, Plant and Equipment* in respect of the appropriate accounting principles and the disclosure requirements.

Important points which should be noted in respect of depreciation are as follows:

(a) Assessment of depreciation, and its allocation to accounting periods, involves the consideration of three factors:

(i) cost (or valuation when an asset has been revalued in the financial statements)

(ii) the nature of the asset and the length of its expected useful life to the business having due regard to the incidence of obsolescence

(iii) estimated residual value of the asset at the end of its useful life in the business of the enterprise.

(b) If the asset's estimated useful life has been revised, the remaining carrying value should be charged over the new estimated life.

(c) Profit/loss on disposal should be disclosed, if material.

(d) All assets with a finite economic life must be depreciated, even if market value exceeds carrying value.

(e) Freehold land need not normally be depreciated – it has an infinite economic life.

(f) Buildings on freehold land should be depreciated – they have a finite life.

(g) The method by which depreciation is calculated for each category of assets should be disclosed in the accounts together with the effective useful lives assumed.

1.5 NON-DEPRECIATION OF NON-CURRENT ASSETS

You should note that some companies do not depreciate certain properties such as hotels and supermarkets on the grounds that the asset is constantly maintained to a high standard and that the residual value will always be higher than cost and that the property has an indefinite useful life (e.g. a well-kept 500-year-old pub).

This argument, although not frequently encountered, can be acceptable providing that refurbishment costs are charged as an expense in lieu of depreciation.

Also, investment properties, i.e. land and buildings which are held for rental and investment purposes, rather than held as operating assets of the enterprise, need not be subject to depreciation. These assets can instead be revalued to their market value on an annual basis.

1.6 INTERNAL CONTROL OVER NON-CURRENT ASSETS

This is a revision of previous chapters on controls. It is the responsibility of the directors to establish a system of internal control over non-current assets with the following objectives:

(i) non-current assets are correctly recorded, adequately secured and properly maintained

(ii) acquisitions and disposals of non-current assets are properly authorised

(iii) acquisitions and disposals of non-current assets are for the most favourable price possible

(iv) non-current assets are properly recorded, appropriately depreciated, and written down where necessary.

You should note that a key feature of controls systems over non-current assets is the existence of a non-current asset register, containing full details of each individual asset under the control of the company. If the auditor wishes to rely on the asset register, then it should be tested by the auditor just as in any other situation of carrying out tests of controls.

FAU: FOUNDATIONS IN AUDIT

ACTIVITY 1

Given the above control objectives, what types of controls would you expect to find in a non-current asset system?

For a suggested answer, see the 'Answers' section at the end of the book.

2 VERIFICATION PROCEDURES: TANGIBLE NON-CURRENT ASSETS

2.1 VERIFICATION PROCEDURES

Remember that verification procedures are designed to support the key financial statement assertions of:

(a) Completeness

(b) Rights and obligations (i.e. ownership)

(c) Accuracy, valuation and allocation

(d) Existence

(e) Occurrence

(f) Classification

(g) Presentation

There follows a summary of the principal verification techniques which will be used to generate evidence on these assertions. The techniques shown below are related to each major category of tangible non-current assets, but you should note that there are common themes, that apply to all of the categories. The assertions to which each procedure relates are also identified. You should focus upon the assertions (a) – (d) inclusive for your study of this chapter.

2.2 THE NON-CURRENT ASSET REGISTER

Remember that the non-current asset register is very useful to the auditor during the course of the audit.

For example, samples of non-current assets may be selected from the register to confirm the existence of non-current assets. Also, assets may be traced from physical asset back to the register to test completeness.

The register may be maintained in a manual format or it may be a computerised register. Whichever format is used, it should be sufficient to enable identification of individual non-current assets owned and used by an entity.

ACTIVITY 2

You have been asked to set up a non-current asset register for an entity which is subject to audit. List the details or headings that you would include in such a register.

For a suggested answer, see the 'Answers' section at the end of the book.

2.3 FREEHOLD AND LEASEHOLD LAND AND BUILDINGS

(a) Examine a sample of title deeds, land registry certificates, conveyancing documentation from solicitors, and leases. Pay particular attention to any 'encumbrances' i.e. mortgages or other securities held over assets *(existence, rights and obligations, classification)*.

(b) Review a sample of entries in the non-current asset register and trace back to source documentation to ensure properly stated at cost *(valuation and allocation)*.

(c) Review company policies for depreciation and ensure appropriate in the light of the useful life of the building (commonly over 50 years) and ensure that land is not depreciated *(valuation and allocation)*.

(d) Review a sample of calculations of depreciation and ensure accurate and in line with company policy – note that freehold land should not normally be subject to depreciation *(valuation and allocation)*.

(e) Inspect assets and establish the need for any write-down for impairments in value. Discuss with directors *(valuation)*.

(f) If freehold or leasehold assets are let to third parties, inspect tenancy agreements, and perform analytical procedures on rental income. Note that this procedure is an example of a useful general auditing technique allowing the auditor to relate together statements of financial position and comprehensive income items – if there is an asset in the statement of financial position, is there any related profit impact of the assets? *(completeness of income)*.

(g) Inspect freehold land and building valuations to ensure that they are stated in accordance with the relevant regulations (usually cost or valuation less accumulated depreciation) *(valuation)*.

(h) Inspect disclosure of assets held under leases to ensure that they are appropriately disclosed as long-term or short-term *(valuation)*.

(i) Physically inspect a sample of assets *(existence)*.

(j) Reconcile the non-current asset register to the general ledger *(valuation)*.

2.4 PLANT, MACHINERY, FIXTURES AND FITTINGS AND MOTOR VEHICLES

(a) Examine a sample of invoices, contracts, finance leases or other evidence of title to assets including vehicle registration documents *(existence, rights and obligations)*.

(b) Review company policies for depreciation and ensure appropriate in the light of the useful life of the assets *(valuation)*.

(c) Review a sample of calculations of depreciation and ensure accurate and in line with company policy *(valuation)*.

(d) Inspect assets and establish the need for any write-down for impairments in value. Discuss with directors *(valuation)*.

(e) Inspect sales tax calculation to ensure that is appropriately capitalised where it is not recoverable *(valuation)*.

(f) Review asset disclosures to ensure that they are stated in accordance with legislation and that the carrying value of assets held under finance leases is disclosed separately *(rights and obligations)*.

(g) Physically inspect a sample of assets *(existence)*.

(h) Verify that the cost and accumulated depreciation of asset disposals has been removed *(valuation)*.

(i) Recalculate profit/ loss on disposal of assets *(accuracy)*.

2.5 ASSETS IN THE COURSE OF CONSTRUCTION

Such assets are built by the company for itself and can include plant and machinery as well as buildings. The tests are as above except that there are no title deeds or documents of title to examine. Instead the auditor may perform the following tests on the company's own records.

(a) Observe the company's system for allocating costs to the asset to ensure that it is appropriate. Some tests of control may be necessary here. Such costs include raw materials, goods taken from trading inventory, costs of labour and sometimes interest costs.

(b) Review costs to ensure that those that are included relate to the project by taking a sample of costs included and tracing back to costings and source documentation.

The danger is always that costs that should be expensed and so reduce profits, are in actual fact being capitalised in the statement of financial position, thus turning losses into assets!

ACTIVITY 3

You have been asked by the audit manager to draft an audit programme to test the **valuation** of tangible non-current assets for a new client which owns a fleet of 30 motor vehicles for its sales force and various fixtures and fittings. Present your answer in the format of a standard audit programme.

For a suggested answer, see the 'Answers' section at the end of the book.

3 USING THE WORK OF AN AUDITOR'S EXPERT

3.1 THE NEED TO CONSULT OTHERS

An auditor does not need to be an expert in all aspects of their clients' business activities. Where an auditor lacks specific knowledge or expertise, they should seek the assistance of an expert. Examples of when this may be necessary include:

- Property valuation

- Specialist inventory, such as livestock or jewellery.

ISA 620 *Using the Work of an Auditor's Expert* requires the auditor to obtain sufficient and appropriate evidence that the work of the expert s adequate for the purpose of the audit. The auditor should therefore be satisfied regarding the independence, objectivity and competence of the expert used. This may include reviewing the experience, membership of an appropriate professional body and professional reputation of the expert prior to their appointment.

3.2 MATTERS TO BE AGREED

Having confirmed the suitability of the expert to be used (perhaps using a qualified chartered surveyor to value freehold land and buildings), the auditor should then confirm the terms of the work to be performed by the expert, and include matters such as:

- The nature and scope of the work

- The respective roles and responsibilities of the auditor and of the expert

- The nature, timing and extent of work required

- The need for the expert to respect confidentiality of the auditor and clients business affairs.

3.3 CONSEQUENCES OF USING AN EXPERT

The auditor is solely responsible for the opinion expressed on the truth and fairness of the financial statements in the auditor's report. Therefore, like any other form of audit evidence, the auditor should document and evaluate the work of the expert to determine to what extent it can be regarded as reliable.

This will include obtaining and reviewing a written report from the expert and making any further enquiries considered necessary to substantiate or corroborate the work of the expert.

CONCLUSION

This chapter has dealt with the principal audit verification techniques applicable to the main category of non-current assets covered by the syllabus – tangible non-current assets.

As with all verification work, the audit work can be structured around the financial statement assertions – completeness, occurrence, valuation, existence, rights and obligations, measurement, presentation and disclosure. You will have noted that there is lot of regulation of the accounting treatment of non-current assets – these requirements need to be fully reflected in the audit verification work.

KEY TERMS

Non-current assets – Assets that are held for continuing use in the business and are not intended for resale.

Tangible non-current assets – Non-current assets which have a physical existence.

SELF TEST QUESTIONS

		Paragraph
1	State four examples of tangible non-current assets.	1.1
2	What tangible non-current assets are often not stated at cost less depreciation?	1.3
3	How is ownership verified for freehold land and buildings?	2.2

EXAM-STYLE QUESTION 1

ENGINEERING COMPANY

You are part of an audit team engaged upon the audit of an engineering company which has a substantial number of items of plant and machinery in its books.

(a) How would you establish that the non-current assets which had been purchased during the year had been properly authorised by the directors? **(5 marks)**

(b) What is a non-current asset register? Why is it necessary for the company to maintain such a register and what use would you make of it in the course of your audit? **(5 marks)**

(Total: 10 marks)

For a suggested answer, see the 'Answers' section at the end of the book.

EXAM-STYLE QUESTION 2

ENGINEERING COMPANY

You are part of an audit team engaged upon the audit of an engineering company which has a substantial number of items of plant and machinery in its books.

(a) State the procedures you would expect to be in operation concerning the scrapping of plant and machinery. **(5 marks)**

(b) Explain how depreciation rates should be authorised and state how you would satisfy yourself that these rates were adequate. **(5 marks)**

(c) The company does not wish to charge depreciation on assets which are not in use. On what basis would you decide whether or not this decision was satisfactory? **(5 marks)**

(Total: 15 marks)

For a suggested answer, see the 'Answers' section at the end of the book.

Chapter 12

AUDIT VERIFICATION WORK 4 – RECEIVABLES AND CASH AND BANK

INTRODUCTION

Chapter 11 dealt with audit verification procedures relating to inventory – often a high risk and material area of the audit. This chapter deals with verification procedures for the remaining principal current assets of an enterprise – receivables and cash and bank balances.

You should be familiar by now with the standard financial statement assertions and with the related objectives of audit verification work. The main emphasis of this chapter is to demonstrate how these principles can be applied to receivables and cash balances. You should also be aware of the main problem areas relating to these key audit areas i.e. irrecoverable/doubtful debts, misappropriation of funds for cash and bank balances.

This chapter covers syllabus areas D (2) and D (3).

CONTENTS

1. The audit of receivables balances – general principles
2. Direct circularisation procedures
3. The audit of bank and cash balances

LEARNING OUTCOMES

At the end of this chapter, you should be able to:

- understand and apply audit verification procedures to receivables balances
- design, perform and evaluate the results of a receivables circularisation
- understand and apply audit verification procedures to bank and cash balances
- draft the main contents of a bank confirmation letter.

1 THE AUDIT OF RECEIVABLES BALANCES – GENERAL PRINCIPLES

1.1 INTERNAL CONTROL OVER SALES AND RECEIVABLES

As a brief reminder of previous chapters you should remind yourself of the main points relating to internal controls over receivables. Note that there are very close links with the sales accounting system here.

As covered in an earlier chapter, the objectives of internal controls in this area include ensuring that:

(a) Customers' orders should be authorised, controlled and recorded in order to execute them promptly.

(b) Goods shipped and work completed should be controlled to ensure that the invoices are issued and revenue recorded for all sales.

(c) Goods returned and claims by customers (for example, in respect of damaged goods) should be controlled in order to determine the liability for goods returned and claims received.

(d) Invoices and credits should be appropriately checked for accuracy and should be authorised before being entered in the receivables' records.

(e) Only authorised customers' transactions should be accurately entered in the accounting records.

(f) There should be procedures to ensure that sales invoices are subsequently paid by customers and that doubtful amounts are identified in order to determine any provisions or write offs required.

In addition internal controls over receivables should ensure that the possibility of any falsification of the receivables' accounts is eliminated. Segregation of duties is an important part of the controls. So, for example, the cashier should not have access to the receivables ledger, and the receivables ledger clerk should not have access to cash received. Thus, the possibility of **teeming and lading** (i.e. the offsetting of one customer's cash received against another customer's account to cover up a misappropriation of the first customer's cash received) could only be brought about by collusion. Collusion, you will remember, is an inherent limitation of any system of internal control.

1.2 THE AUDIT OF RECEIVABLES – GENERAL APPROACH

In order to verify the figure in the financial statements for receivables the auditor would perform a number of substantive procedures as outlined below.

Control account

The auditor should obtain a list of the receivables balances in the receivables ledger from the client and agree the total with the control account. This acts as a check on the completeness and accuracy of the listing of receivables' balances which will be extensively used in the following detailed audit verification work.

Year end receivables account balances

(i) Obtain an aged receivables listing and discuss any significantly overdue balances with management to identify action to be taken, and whether or not the debts are likely to be paid (this will assist the auditor in verifying the reasonableness of the allowance for doubtful debts).

(ii) Inspect the authorisation for debts written off as irrecoverable and review external correspondence relating to these debts.

(iii) Review with the payables ledger balances for customers who are also suppliers and to whom the client owes money. Contra entries should be made to net off the two amounts to avoid overstating both assets and liabilities.

(iv) Inspect the balances to ensure that they are made up of specific invoices relating to recent transactions and enquire into any balances which appear to be in dispute, or old.

(v) Carry out direct confirmation of receivables balances by writing to customers. This is known as circularisation and will be considered further in the next section.

(vi) Review the individual accounts of major customers and those that appear unusual either by nature, composition or size of the balances or the transactions therein.

(vii) Review and test the year end cut-off procedures for sales, as dealt with in a previous chapter.

Analytical procedures

The auditor would typically perform the following analytical procedures in respect of receivables:

(i) A comparison of receivables collection period ratio $\left(\dfrac{\text{receivables}}{\text{sales}}\right) \times 365$ with budget and/or prior years. He may also compare this to similar companies in the industry. Separate computations may be appropriate to take into account different classes of business, varying credit terms and other factors.

(ii) A comparison of the proportion of the debts in different age bands to prior years. This information should be available directly from the client.

A high or increasing incidence of old debts may indicate either poor or deteriorating economic conditions or credit control. In such instances the work on doubtful debts and any year end doubtful debt allowance will become critical.

Irrecoverable debts

This is one of the more subjective areas involved in the audit of receivables balances.

Audit procedures to establish appropriate allowances for doubtful debts include consideration of:

(i) the company's previous irrecoverable debt experiences

(ii) evidence from the receivables' circularisation

(iii) aged analysis of receivables

(iv) events after the reporting period (see below and later chapters).

In the light of this information the auditor will have to consider whether the allowance made by management in the accounts is adequate.

Both specific and general allowances may be made. Specific allowances are made for those debts which are known to be doubtful. General allowances (usually a percentage of total receivables) must be based on past experience in accordance with the requirement of IAS 39.

Returns inwards and credit notes

There should be strict internal controls over returns inwards and credit notes issued, to prevent the fraudulent cancellation of a company debt, or to 'hide' irrecoverable debts.

From an audit point of view the major problem is likely to be the issue of a substantial volume of credit notes after the year end to cancel false sales made before the year end. This is known as 'window dressing' – recording a sale and the resulting receivable in the current period and then issuing a credit note to reverse the transaction in the following period (it could be seen as another example of a cut off problem). For this reason, both the system, and any events after the reporting period, should be carefully examined to detect any possible misstatement of annual profits resulting from this procedure.

Prepayments

These are often disclosed in the financial statements under the general heading of receivables and similar audit considerations apply. However, prepayments are typically immaterial in amount and in this connection may attract relatively little audit attention. On the other hand, this is an area where subjective accounting estimate will often be required. Analytical procedures – comparing one period with another and seeking an explanation for major differences – are often extensively used in this area. If major differences are identified then the auditor would investigate further.

Prepayments are commonly made for rent, gas, electricity and telephone standing charges and other items where the expenditure has been paid for in the current period, but relates to the next period.

Audit evidence may include:

(i)   considering the client's own system (if any) for accounting for prepayments

(ii) obtaining a schedule of prepayments, ensuring that it is cast correctly and comparing it with prior year prepayments and performing other analytical procedures

(iii) test checking a sample of prepayments for correct calculation, referring to supporting documentation.

ACTIVITY 1

Explain what analytical procedures the auditor might perform in respect of **trade receivables** and the reasons for this.

For a suggested answer, see the 'Answers' section at the end of the book.

2 DIRECT CIRCULARISATION PROCEDURES

2.1 INTRODUCTION

Circularisation is one of the most effective methods for confirming the existence of receivables balances, with guidance being given by ISA 505 *External Confirmations*. The auditor communicates directly with the customers of the client to seek direct confirmation of the amounts outstanding.

Replies to the circularisation will generally be considered to constitute reliable evidence – they arise outside the client under audit and they are in a written form.

The auditor must ask the client's permission before writing to the customers, but, if the quality of the evidence is to be preserved, it is important that the process is under the auditor's control. So for example the replies should be sent direct to the auditors, not to the client to preserve their integrity as an item of audit evidence.

The circularisation of receivables satisfies a number of objectives:

(a) Reliable evidence is provided as to whether receivables are overstated – customers can usually be relied on to complain if the balance they are supposed to owe is too large.

(b) Evidence, albeit weaker, is provided as to whether receivables are understated – customers are less likely to complain if the balance is too small.

(c) Indirect evidence is generated of the accuracy of the sales figures.

(d) Evidence of the functioning of internal controls is generated – accurate receivables balances result from effective control procedures.

(e) Evidence is provided of the efficiency of the cut-off procedures if carried out at the year end.

(f) Evidence of the collectability of debts is generated. If a customer maintains that the client's balance on their account is overstated, this may represent a receivable recorded by the client which requires to be written off or provided for.

Evidence is also obtained as to irregularities such as **teeming and lading** and **window dressing** which are referred to above. It does not however give evidence as to *recoverability*. A customer may agree that he *owes* us a lot of money; this does not guarantee that he will *pay* us!

2.2 TIMING AND FORM OF CIRCULARISATION

Ideally the circularisation should be carried out at the year end, as this provides direct evidence of figures in the statement of financial position. In practice, pressures to complete the audit by a deadline may mean that the circularisation is carried out one or two months before the year end, and balances are then 'rolled forward' to the year end.

In the latter case movements on the control accounts should be reviewed in the period between the circularisation and the year end for reasonableness.

There are two types of circularisation:

(a) *positive* – customer are asked to confirm to the auditor direct if they **agree or disagree** with the balance

(b) *negative* – customer only asked to respond if they **disagree.** This method may be appropriate where there are a large number of small balances, and where the system is well controlled.

Positive circularisations are now generally used as these provide better quality evidence. A non-reply to a negative circularisation request will be taken by the auditor indicating agreement – but in fact the letter may never have been received by the customer or the customer may have taken a decision simply not to reply.

The circularisation letter or form is usually accompanied by a copy of the customers' ledger account in the client's books; this makes it easier for the *customer* to reconcile differences between their records and the client's records.

Examples of letters used in the two types of methods are shown later in this chapter.

2.3 CONTROL OF CIRCULARISATION

As stated earlier it is important that in all cases the circularisation must be controlled by the auditor if the reliability of the audit evidence generated is to be preserved and maximised. This control by the auditor should be reflected at all the key stages in the circularisation process, as indicated below:

Selection

Customers to be circularised should be selected by the auditor from a receivables ledger listing which agrees to the general ledger control account. The auditor is primarily concerned with the possible overstatement of receivables. When we come to look at payables, where we are primarily concerned with understatement, we will see that we will not necessarily select our sample from the year-end list of payables.

Particular attention should be given to:

(i) old unpaid accounts

(ii) accounts written off during the period under review

(iii) accounts with credit balances

(iv) accounts with large balances.

The following should not be overlooked:

(i) accounts with nil balances

(ii) accounts which have been paid by the date of the examination.

If a client is unwilling to circularise a particular balance because, for example, there are delicate negotiations in progress, the auditor should establish that the reason is a genuine one (and not an attempt to 'cover up' a problem balance), and then perform alternative procedures such as those noted below.

Despatch of letters

The letters should be reviewed for accuracy by the auditor once they have been prepared and should be kept under the control of the auditor until they are posted. In checking the letter, particular attention should be paid to the client's address and to the account balance circularised.

The auditor's working papers should contain a **control schedule** recording all relevant details of the circularisation.

Response

Responses should be sent directly to the auditor. The auditor should compare the replies against his schedule. A reminder should be sent if no replies are received.

2.4 REPLIES AND NON-REPLIES

The audit work on the response to the circularisation will typically involve the following:

REPLIES RECEIVED

Agreed replies

If the reply agrees with the balance circularised, the auditor should inspect the letter to ensure that it has been signed and dated by a responsible official of the company and that the reply gives no cause for suspicion on the part of the auditor – for example there is no evidence that the person signing the reply is not independent of the client. If the auditor is happy with these points, the reply is filed in the current audit file.

Disagreed but reconciled

If the reply indicates that the customer disagrees with the balance circularised, the auditor (or the client on behalf of the auditor) should attempt to reconcile the two balances. Reconciling items may often be simple timing differences such as goods or cash in transit or credit notes not yet recorded. Replies involving these types of difference should be relatively easy to reconcile. Once the auditor is happy with the reconciling items, these can be filed and, in effect, can be treated as agreed replies.

Disagreed – not reconciled

Alternatively, disagreement of balances may result from more serious problems, indicating errors in the client's receivables balances or possibly weaknesses in the accounting and control systems. Examples of these items might be sales invoices posted twice, cash received not recorded or disputes relating to prices charged or the availability of settlement discounts. These replies should be reviewed carefully by the auditor and discussed with client management – they may indicate that receivables are overstated in the draft financial statements.

NON-REPLIES

The auditor must not ignore receivables included in the circularisation from which no reply is received. The audit work involved should be as follows:

- Firstly, every attempt should be made to obtain a reply – second and third letters could be sent, faxes, emails and telephone calls could be used, or the auditor could ask the client to contact the customer and request a reply. However, auditors must recognise that some companies have a policy of just not replying to audit circularisation requests!

- If a reply is still not obtained, the auditor will need to take other steps to verify the balance in question.

- The best evidence of the validity of a receivable is the customer paying the debt due – in the case of a non-reply, therefore, the first route that the auditor will take is to look for subsequent cash – cash received by the client after the circularisation date. Ideally, the cash remittances should have been accompanied by remittance advices which enable the auditor to match the cash received with invoices outstanding at the date of the circularisation.

- In the absence of subsequent cash the auditor will need to perform what are usually known as alternative procedures. This involves the auditor analysing the balance on the customer account at the date of the circularisation and examining all the documents that support that balance. So, for every invoice outstanding, the auditor should ideally examine:

    – a signed customer order

    – a signed delivery note

    – an invoice issued by the client.

    Any amounts included in the balance circularised for which this evidence is not available should be treated as doubtful debts for the purposes of the figures in the financial statements i.e. an asset balance whose existence is in question.

2.5 EVALUATION OF THE RESULTS OF THE CIRCULARISATION

After the completion of the circularisation it will form a key part of the evidence in relation to the receivables figure.

The auditor will summarise the results of the circularisation in the current audit file and will need to evaluate the results in terms of:

(a) percentage response

(b) number of disagreements

(c) outcome of follow-up of disagreements

(d) the materiality of the amounts involved.

The evaluation will as usual require the application of the auditor's judgement to the information and, if the receivables circularised were based on statistical sampling techniques, mathematical analysis of the results will be required.

2.6 EXAMPLES OF REQUESTS FOR THIRD PARTY CONFIRMATION

(a) **Positive method**

Swallow Company
Bird Estate
Highcity
Beds

30 April 20XX
Hugh Allen Company
Brow Estate
Lowtown
Beds

Dear Sirs

CONFIRMATION OF INDEBTEDNESS

1. In accordance with the request of our auditors, ABC & Co, we shall be obliged if you will confirm directly to them your indebtedness to us at 31 March 20.. which, according to our records, amounted to $1,457.67, as shown by the enclosed statement.

2. If you are in agreement with the balance shown, please sign this letter in the space provided below and return it intact DIRECTLY TO OUR AUDITORS in the enclosed reply paid envelope.

3. If you disagree with the balance, please notify our auditors, giving full details of the difference.

PLEASE NOTE THAT THIS IS NOT A REQUEST FOR PAYMENT.

We thank you for your co-operation in the above matter.

Yours faithfully

Swallow Company

Reply to: ABC & Co
Certified Accountants
2 Low Close
Downtown
Beds

The balance shown above is correct/incorrect*

Signature: Position:

Date:

Details of difference:

(If relevant)

*Please delete as appropriate.

(b) **Negative method**

> Dear Sirs
>
> *CONFIRMATION OF INDEBTEDNESS*
>
> (Paragraph 1 per positive method)
>
> (Paragraph 2 omitted)
>
> If you disagree with the balance, please inform our AUDITORS DIRECTLY, giving full details of the difference by completing the form below . . . .
>
> Yours faithfully
> etc.
>
> The balance shown above is incorrect.
>
> Signature: Position:
>
> Date:
>
> Details of difference:

ACTIVITY 2

You are about to commence planning the audit of Ramus who have a large number of trade receivables; the receivables figure is also material in the context of the financial statements. The audit senior has asked you to draft a list of the substantive tests for inclusion in the receivables audit programme to verify the value attributed to the trade receivables.

Required:

List the substantive tests required to verify the values attributed to trade receivables in the financial statements of Ramus. *You are not required to draft the audit programme itself.*

For a suggested answer, see the 'Answers' section at the end of the book.

3 THE AUDIT OF BANK AND CASH BALANCES

3.1 INTRODUCTION

Because of their liquidity, these assets represent the most vulnerable of all the company's assets. On the other hand, they are amongst the most easily verified, because they are objective in nature and they lend themselves to being confirmed directly by third parties or by physical counts.

3.2 INTERNAL CONTROLS OVER BANK AND CASH

Due to the vulnerability of liquid assets, internal controls are usually very tight in order to eliminate (or minimise) the possibility of fraud. The objectives of cash internal controls are as follows.

(a) All sums are received and subsequently accounted for.

(b) Only authorised and valid payments should be made.

(c) All receipts and payments are promptly and accurately recorded.

3.3 VERIFICATION – BANK ACCOUNTS

There are two aspects to the verification work on a client's bank balances:

- Direct confirmation from the bank or other financial institution, of the account balance. This gives the auditor written external evidence from a very reliable source.

- Examination of the bank reconciliation.

Each of these is now dealt with in more detail.

3.4 DIRECT BANK CONFIRMATION

This is achieved via a **bank confirmation letter** (also known as a bank certificate).

Definition A **bank certificate** is a standard request letter sent by the auditor to the bank requesting details of the client's financial arrangements managed by the bank.

The auditor should obtain a bank certificate as part of any audit. A standard request letter has been agreed with the clearing banks; this is shown below, together with the standard procedure followed by auditors.

Standard procedure

(a) The standard letter should be sent in duplicate on each occasion by the auditors on their own note paper to the manager of each bank branch with which it is known that the client holds an account or has dealt with since the end of the previous accounting period.

(b) Auditors should ensure that the bank receives the client's authority to permit disclosure. The clearing banks state that this authority must be evidenced by either:

   (i) the client's countersignature to the auditor's standard letter; or

   (ii) a specific authority contained in an accompanying letter; or

   (iii) a reference in the standard letter to a standing written authority given on a specified earlier date, which remains in force.

(c) Wherever possible, the letter should reach the branch manager at least two weeks in advance of the date of the client's financial year end. Special arrangements should be made with the bank if, because of time constraints, a reply is needed within a few days.

(d) In reviewing the bank's reply it is important for auditors to check that the bank has answered all questions in full.

FAU: FOUNDATIONS IN AUDIT

Example of a standard letter

Standard letter of request for bank report for audit purposes

(a) The form of this letter should **not** be amended by the auditor

(b) Sufficient space should be left for the bank's replies (two thirds of each page is recommended).

The Manager,

...................................(Bank)

...................................(Branch)

Dear Sir,

....(Name of customer)

Standard request for bank report for audit purposes

For the year ended ....

In accordance with your above-named customer's instructions given:

(i) hereon

(ii) in the attached authority

(iii) in the authority dated .... already held by you

} Delete as appropriate

please send to us, as auditors of your customer for the purpose of our business, without entering into any contractual relationship with us, the following information relating to their affairs at your branch as at the close of business on .... and, in the case of items (b), (d) and (j) during the period since .... For each item, please state any factors which may limit the completeness of your reply; if there is nothing to report, state 'none'.

We enclose an additional copy of this letter, and it would be particularly helpful if your reply could be given on the copy letter in the space provided (supported by an additional schedule stamped and signed by the bank where space is insufficient). If you find it necessary to provide the information in another form, please return the copy letter with your reply.

It is understood that any replies given are in strict confidence.

Information requested   *Reply*

Bank accounts

Please give:

(a) Full titles of all accounts, whether in sterling or in any other currency, together with the account numbers and balances thereon, including NIL balances:

   (i) where your customer's name is the sole name in the title

   (ii) where your customer's name is joined with that of other parties

   (iii) where the account is in a trade name.

Information requested *Reply*

Notes:

(i) Where the account is subject to any restriction (e.g. a garnishee order or arrestment), this information should be stated.

(ii) Where the authority upon which you are providing this information does not cover any accounts held jointly with other parties, please refer to your customer in order to obtain the requisite authority of the other parties. If this authority is not forthcoming, please indicate.

(b) Full titles and dates of closure of all accounts during the period.

(c) The separate amounts accrued but not charged or credited to the above date, of:

    (i) provisional charges (including commitment fees), and

    (ii) interest.

(d) The amount of interest charged during the period if not specified separately in the bank statement.

(e) Particulars (i.e. date, type of document and accounts covered) of any written acknowledgement of set-off, either by specific letter of set-off, or incorporated in some other document or security.

(f) Details of:

    (i) overdrafts and loans repayable on demand, specifying dates of review and agreed facilities

    (ii) other loans specifying dates of review and repayment

    (iii) other facilities.

Customer's assets held as security

(g) Please give details of any such assets whether or not formally charged to the bank.

If formally charged, give details of the security including the date and type of charge. If a security is limited in amount or to a specific borrowing, or if there is to your knowledge a prior, equal or subordinate charge, please indicate.

If informally charged, indicate nature of security interest therein claimed by the bank.

Whether or not a formal charge has been taken, give particulars of any undertaking given to the bank relating to any assets.

Information requested	Reply

Customer's other assets held

(h) Please give full details of the customer's other assets held, including share certificates, documents of title, deed boxes and any other items listed in your registers maintained for the purpose of recording assets held.

Contingent liabilities

(i) All contingent liabilities, viz:
- (i) total of bills discounted for your customer, with recourse
- (ii) date, name of beneficiary, amount and brief description of any guarantees, bonds or indemnities given to you by the customer for the benefit of third parties
- (iii) date, name of beneficiary, amount and brief description of any guarantees, bonds or indemnities given by you, on your customer's behalf, stating where there is recourse to your customer and/or to its parent or any other company within the group
- (iv) total of acceptances
- (v) total sterling equivalent of outstanding forward foreign exchange contracts
- (vi) total of outstanding liabilities under documentary credits
- (vii) others – please give details.

Other information

(j) Please give a list of other banks, or branches of your bank, or associated companies where you are aware that a relationship has been established during the period.

Yours faithfully

....
Disclosure authorised
For and on behalf of

....
(Name of customer)

....

....

....
(Signed in accordance with the mandate for the conduct of the customer's bank account.)

....
(Official stamp of bank)

....
(Authorised signatory)

....
(Position)

....
(Date)

ACTIVITY 3

State the main categories of information requested from the bank by the auditor in the bank confirmation letter.

For a suggested answer, see the 'Answers' section at the end of the book.

3.5 AUDIT REVIEW OF THE BANK RECONCILIATION

You should be very familiar with the bank reconciliation process from your basic accountancy studies. The auditor needs to inspect the reconciliation between the cash book figure (which appears in the financial statements) and the bank statement figure (which has been directly confirmed by the bank). This stage is of great importance to the auditor.

The reconciliation should establish that:

(i) any differences between the bank and the client's records can be specifically identified

(ii) the differences are differences of timing which should clear in the period after the reporting date

(iii) previous differences have all been cleared

(iv) any differences other than timing differences (e.g. errors or omissions by the bank or the client) are advised to the bank or adjusted in the client's accounting records.

Audit procedures on the reconciliation

Reconciliations usually start with the balance per the cash book and reconcile this to the balance per the bank statement, although the reverse is also acceptable.

A simple example might show:

Bank reconciliation as at 31 July 20X4

	$
Balance per cash book	12,345.22
Add Unpresented cheques	223.46
Less Outstanding lodgements	(16.34)
Difference	1.34
Balance per bank statement	12,553.68

Reconciling items are usually due to timing delays. '*Unpresented cheques*' are those which have been sent to suppliers but not yet banked. '*Outstanding lodgements*' are cheques received by the company and paid into the bank, but not yet credited by the bank i.e. there is usually a delay of two to three days for the cheques to be cleared.

All unpresented cheques and outstanding lodgements should be inspected to ensure that they do 'clear' shortly after the period end by reviewing bank statements just after the period end. Any old items should be considered carefully. If a cheque has not been presented to the bank after 6 months, it may be that the supplier has lost it or has gone out of business. In any case the cheque will be 'out of date' and the bank will not honour it even if it is presented. The auditor should consider the need for the payable to be reinstated and a new cheque issued, or the need for the cheque to be written back as income.

Differences, even small differences **must** be investigated as they may represent large errors in both directions that net each other off.

If there are known errors or omissions affecting the cash book, the normal procedure is to adjust the cash book for these items and then reconcile the adjusted cash book figure with the bank statement figure. For example:

	$
Draft balance per cash book as at 31 July 20X3	12,153.32
Add sundry receipts per bank statement not in cash book	123.45
Less direct debits per bank statement not in cash book	(21.55)
Add error in addition of cash book	90.00
Adjusted balance per cash book as at 31 July 20X3	12,345.22

Again, all of the adjusting items need to be checked to their source. As these are cash book errors and the cash book forms part of the double entry system, there is likely to be a double entry effect of these adjustments which the auditor should establish has been correctly dealt with.

Reconciliations are normally performed on a monthly basis and should show evidence of review i.e. who reviewed it and on what date. The auditor should check that they are cast correctly.

3.6 VERIFICATION – CASH BALANCES

Liquid assets are the most vulnerable of a company's assets because of their nature. However, they are generally the easiest for the auditor to verify as they can be confirmed directly by third parties or by physical counts.

Control procedures over cash (as opposed to bank) balances were considered in an earlier chapter – they could now usefully be revised.

The amount of audit verification work that the auditor will carry out on cash balances will be very much dependent on their materiality. If, for example, the only cash balance held in a large company is a small imprest petty cash float where controls are strong, the auditor may carry out no substantive work at all.

However, in situations where cash balances are more material, standard audit procedures would include:

- attendance at a cash count at the reporting date or performing a surprise cash count in the presence of the client. If the auditor counts the cash himself he should do so in the presence of two or more officers of the company and obtain a signed receipt when the cash is handed back to the client
- if cash is held at more than one location, all cash at all locations should be counted simultaneously
- the auditor should agree the cash balance with the figure in the accounting records and check the validity of any reconciling items.

CONCLUSION

Receivables are often a major asset of an organisation and therefore may require significant audit attention.

The principal audit verification procedure involves the circularisation of a sample of receivables which generates high quality, written, external evidence for the auditor. The auditor usually uses positive confirmation and should control the circularisation and carefully analyse the replies received.

Bank balances are readily verifiable with a third party, i.e. the bank, through the use of bank confirmation letters. These should be in a standard format and used by the auditor in accordance with a standard procedure agreed with the banking industry. The bank letter can also be used to ask other questions such as bank guarantees. The other major aspect of the auditor's work on bank balances is a careful examination of the bank reconciliations completed by the client.

The amount of audit work on cash balances will depend on the materiality of the amounts involved – it will revolve primarily around the auditor attendance at cash counts.

KEY TERMS

Receivables' circularisation – The audit procedure whereby letters are sent to a sample of credit customers of the client who owe money, replies to which give external written evidence for audit verification purposes.

Positive circularisation – The customer is asked to reply to the auditor whether they agree with the account balance given or not.

Negative circularisation – The customer is asked to reply to the auditor only if they disagree with the balance given.

Alternative procedures – The technique whereby auditors attempt to prove the validity of a receivables balance where the customer does not reply to a circularisation request by inspection of the documentation underlying each item comprising the account balance.

Bank certificate/bank confirmation letter – A standard request letter sent by the auditor to the bank requesting details of the client's financial arrangements managed by the bank.

SELF TEST QUESTIONS

Paragraph

1	What substantive tests should the auditor perform in the audit of year end receivables balances?	1.2
2	How can analytical procedures assist in the audit of receivables?	1.2
3	What are the two types of receivables' circularisation?	2.2
4	How should an auditor evaluate the results of a receivables' circularisation?	2.5
5	What are the two aspects of verification of cash and bank balances?	3.3
6	What will the bank require from the client when it receives a letter from the auditor?	3.4

FAU: FOUNDATIONS IN AUDIT

PRACTICE QUESTION 1

ASKWITH

A senior audit clerk is briefing an experienced junior auditor who is about to commence the audit of the receivables of Askwith. The receivables ledger, says the senior clerk, is maintained by the client on a computer. Sales invoice and credit note data are fed to the computer via 12 terminals in regional offices. All cash entries, journal entries relating to irrecoverable debts and other adjustments, and any other special entries are input via two terminals located at the client's head office. The computer produces, as a monthly routine, an aged receivables' schedule containing on average 3,000 live balances. Your task, as the junior auditor, is to verify the accuracy of the aged receivables' schedule including arranging for circulars to be sent to a representative sample of receivables.

Required:

(a) Draft a suitable letter to be used to circularise receivables. **(3 marks)**

(b) State the steps to be taken by the auditor where no reply is received to the initial circularisation of receivables and explain what alternative procedures might be used to verify the balances. **(6 marks)**

(c) Explain the significance of cut-off tests relating to trade receivables and suggest THREE appropriate detailed tests. **(6 marks)**

(Total: 15 marks)

For a suggested answer, see the 'Answers' section at the end of the book.

PRACTICE QUESTION 2

DEFAULTERS

You are currently carrying out the interim audit of Defaulters. The audit senior has asked you to carry out the cash audit, and as a part of your work you are about to review the bank reconciliation statement of the company. The cash book showed a debit balance of $37,802 as at 31 May 20X1 which included the previous week's receipts of cash which had not yet been paid into the bank. A receipt of $200 on the bank statement has not yet been entered into the cash book, and the balance per the bank statement was $31,100. You have found that the unpresented cheques were as follows:

Cheque number	Amount ($)	Date
134	232	1.3.X1
183	300	2.4.X1
284	506	12.4.X1
861	380	31.5.X1
862	412	31.5.X1
863	290	31.5.X1

AUDIT VERIFICATION WORK 4 – RECEIVABLES AND CASH AND BANK : CHAPTER 12

The cashier has informed you that the receipts not yet deposited with the bank were $7,588 and has given you the following bank reconciliation statement:

		$	$
Balance per cash book 31 May 20X1		37,802	
Add: Unpresented cheque	861	380	
	862	412	
	863	290	
			1,082
			38,884
Less: Undeposited receipts		7,588	
Petty cash balance		196	
			(7,784)
Balance per bank 31 May 20X1			31,100
Deduct unrecorded credit			(200)
Actual cash 31 May 20X1			30,900

You ascertain that the chief accountant had reviewed the cash transactions during the month of May and were satisfied that the cash book balance of $37,802 was, in fact, correct but was not responsible for preparing the bank reconciliation statement. You have not as yet verified the petty cash system which is maintained on an imprest.

Required:

(a) Prepare an audit schedule showing the amount of cash which the cashier may have misappropriated from the company listing the audit work which would be carried out in order to verify this amount. **(12 marks)**

(b) Explain how the cashier had attempted to conceal the possible theft of cash from the company. **(4 marks)**

(c) Describe two weaknesses in internal control which have contributed to the theft of cash by the cashier. **(4 marks)**

(d) Explain the action the auditor should take when he suspects the existence of possible improprieties. **(5 marks)**

(Total: 25 marks)

For a suggested answer, see the 'Answers' section at the end of the book.

Chapter 13

AUDIT VERIFICATION WORK 5 – LIABILITIES

INTRODUCTION

The previous chapters dealt with the audit procedures used to verify assets. We now turn our attention to the verification of the major categories of payables which may appear in a client's financial statements.

The usual testing procedures can be used to cover the financial statement assertions. Any deliberate misstatement of payables is likely to understate the figures as this will present a better picture of financial performance and position. Much of the audit evidence relating to payables therefore focuses on completeness – the auditor will want to ensure that all payables, which exist, are recorded in the financial statements.

For this reason many auditors find reaching a conclusion on payables more difficult than reaching a conclusion on assets balances. In the case of assets, you are starting from a figure given by the client and setting out to verify that the assets representing that figure exist. In the case of payables the auditor is looking for items that are not there – the auditor is principally searching for unrecorded amounts.

This chapter covers syllabus areas D (2) and D (3).

CONTENTS

1. An introduction to liabilities: the audit approach
2. The audit of provisions
3. The audit of contingent liabilities
4. Sources of audit evidence

LEARNING OUTCOMES

At the end of this chapter, you should be able to:

- understand the audit approach to payables
- apply that approach to trade payables, accruals and provisions

1 AN INTRODUCTION TO LIABILITIES: THE AUDIT APPROACH

1.1 CLASSIFICATION

Liabilities can be classified as follows:

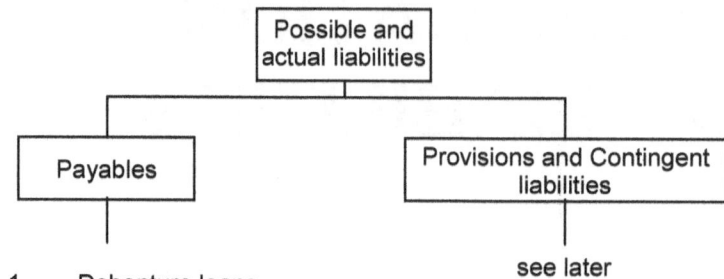

1. Debenture loans
2. Bank loans and overdrafts
3. Payments received on account
4. Trade payables
5. Bills of exchange payable
6. Other payables including taxation and social security

Amounts falling due within one year **(current liabilities)** must be shown separately in the financial statements from amounts falling due after more than one year **(non-current liabilities)** for each item.

1.2 TRADE PAYABLES

Of the various categories in the above listing, the item requiring most work under the general heading of liabilities will be trade payables. Many companies will have a large number of trade payables accounts – the audit approach to this will therefore usually involve sampling.

The other items are likely to be checked in detail, where material. Some of the items are not included below, as they are outside the scope of the syllabus. The items that are relevant are as follows.

1.3 INTERNAL CONTROLS OVER PURCHASES AND TRADE PAYABLES

As outlined in previous chapters internal controls over trade payables are designed to ensure that:

(a) purchased goods/services are ordered under proper authorities and procedures

(b) purchased goods/services are only ordered as necessary for the proper conduct of the business operations and are ordered from suitable suppliers

(c) goods/services received are effectively inspected for quality, quantity, description and condition

(d) invoices and related documentation are properly checked and approved as being valid before being recorded as trade payables

(e) all valid transactions relating to trade payables (suppliers' invoices, credit notes and adjustments), and only those transactions, should be accurately recorded in the accounting records.

1.4 TRADE PAYABLES – SUBSTANTIVE PROCEDURES

Always bear in mind that the audit emphasis here will be on **completeness** – have all payables that exist been fully recorded in the financial statements?

The main verification procedures are as follows:

(a) Obtain a schedule of the trade payables with appropriate age analysis and check this with the control account and the payables ledger.

(b) Debit and credit balances should be separated, debit balances being included in receivables.

(c) Review the individual accounts with the largest volume of transactions during the period (not necessarily the largest balances at the yearend).

(d) Review the year-end cut-off procedures for purchases.

The following should be considered during the tests of individual balances:

(i) Is the balance made up of specific items outstanding for a reasonable period?

(ii) Have all the items been authorised for payment?

(iii) Does the balance agree with the supplier's statements? A comparison is made between the amounts that the client believes they owe suppliers and the amounts showing on the supplier statements (written, third party, external evidence). There may be differences/a need to investigate further in order to verify the amounts owed. Reasons include:

- A dispute between the client and the supplier.

- Cut off problems i.e. the client records the following year's payables in the current year or because goods returned to the supplier in the current year and not recorded in the current year.

- The client may have sent the money before the year end but the receipt was not recorded by the supplier until after the year end.

- Money received by the supplier may have been posted to the wrong account, leaving the client's balance still showing as outstanding, in error.

(iv) Consider the need to perform a payables circularisation. Because external evidence exists in the case of payables – in the form of supplier statements – auditors do not often undertake a payables circularisation. However, if controls are weak or supplier statements are unavailable or considered to be unreliable, a circularisation of a sample of payables balances may be appropriate, or requests may be made to specific suppliers.

(v) Review payments to payables just after the year end.

(e) Review the internal controls over the purchases system which ensure that all goods received are properly recognised as payables of the entity.

(f) Perform analytical procedures on payables, comparing age analysis with previous periods and payables payment period $\left(\frac{\text{payables}}{\text{cost of sales}}\right) \times 365$. This again may help the auditor to detect possible unrecorded liabilities – any major changes in the ratio over time should be investigated in the light of this possibility.

(g) A general review for unrecorded liabilities should be carried out. In addition to analytical procedures, the auditor's knowledge of the business can be very helpful here. For example, if the auditor knows that X is a major supplier of inventory items to the client, but the amount shown as owing to X at the reporting date is small, this would warrant some investigation by the auditor.

ACTIVITY 1

Trade payables usually form the major component of an entity's payables, and as such will therefore require a substantial amount of audit work.

Required:

(a) Explain why an entity should ensure that there is a satisfactory system of internal control over payables.

(b) State what the auditor should consider when testing individual balances.

For a suggested answer, see the 'Answers' section at the end of the book.

1.5 BANK OVERDRAFTS

Bank overdrafts are shown under liabilities even though there may be balances on other accounts which are shown as assets the only exception being if there is a legal right of set-off.

Verification of bank overdrafts is via the bank confirmation letter, as outlined in the previous chapter.

1.6 ACCRUALS

Accruals, like prepayments are commonly made for rent, gas, electricity, telephone and other items where the expenditure has been incurred in the current period but where no invoice has yet been received or paid. Therefore, the need to account for accruals arises as a result of receiving the goods or services before the year-end, and not receiving the invoice for inclusion in the Purchase Day Book until after the year-end. If accounting for accruals was not done, expenses and liabilities would be understated in the financial statements. Accruals are often immaterial and reliance is often placed on analytical procedures. Nevertheless, as year-end adjustments, there are rarely any controls over accruals and any errors are likely to be those of understatement.

One practical point to remember is that accruals are often required for utility type services such as fuel and power. As a further issue, if there are weaknesses in the control over the purchase or goods and/or services, it is likely to have an impact upon completeness and reliability of any amounts included for accruals in the financial statements. This is because there may be unrecorded purchases which have also not been accounted for as accruals.

Audit procedures, similar to those applied to prepayments, will include:

(i) Considering the client's own system (if any) for identifying and recording accruals.

(ii) Obtaining a schedule of accruals, ensuring that it is cast correctly. It should be compared with prior year accruals subject to other analytical procedures. Again, the auditor should use his knowledge of the business to identify possible unrecorded accrued payables. Areas that companies often miss in establishing year end accruals include employee and directors bonuses, sales staff commission and employee holiday pay.

(iii) Test checking a sample of accruals for correct calculation, referring to supporting invoices received in the next period.

(iv) Include confirmation of the completeness of accruals in the management representation letter. This is dealt with in further detail later.

1.7 LONG-TERM BANK LOANS

The audit procedures are the same as for a similar item under current liabilities. It should also be appreciated that if all or part of the bank loan has a due date of payment within one year of the reporting date, then that loan (or the part payable within one year) must be disclosed under current liabilities.

Particular points to note in respect of these items include:

- Evidence relating to bank loans can be obtained from the standard bank confirmation letter already dealt with.

- In addition to verifying the amount outstanding on the loan itself, the auditor should consider the adequacy of any accrual for unpaid interest.

1.8 DEBENTURE LOANS

Definition A **debenture loan** is a written acknowledgement by an entity, usually under seal, of a loan made to it, containing provisions as to payment of interest and repayment of capital.

(a) **Issue**

The auditor should refer to the client's memorandum and articles to ascertain the borrowing powers of the entity, since, although a trading entity has implied power to borrow up to any amount, it is possible that such power may be restricted by the memorandum or articles. Legal problems may arise if the entity exceeds its borrowing powers.

When a new issue of debentures takes place in the year it is necessary to disclose the class of debentures issued, the amount issued for each class and the consideration received. The auditor should ensure that the cash proceeds are received and properly recorded by the entity. Any discounts or costs of the issue should be properly recorded – this is outside the scope of this unit.

(b) **Redemption**

Debentures may be redeemable according to the terms of the issue, at specified dates, by annual or other drawings (a process for selecting which debentures are to be redeemed that year), or at the option of the entity, after due notice has been given of intention to repay. The auditor should examine the provisions of the debenture deed or the debenture bonds relating to the redemption, and ascertain that they are duly complied with.

The auditor's principal duties with regard to the redemption are to:

(i) examine the debenture deed as to the terms of the redemption, and note that these have been complied with

(ii) check the payment of cash to the debenture holders

(iii) inspect the cancelled bonds.

2 THE AUDIT OF PROVISIONS

2.1 DEFINITION

Definition A **provision** is a liability of uncertain timing and/or amount.

A provision may be regarded as an obligation arising from a past event or transaction on which it is probable that there will be an outflow of economic benefits, but the exact amount to settle the obligation and/or the timing of settlement cannot be determined.

As a provision meets the definition of a liability, it should be recognised and accounted for in the financial statements. Judgement may therefore be required to quantify a provision and also to estimate the timing of settlement, so that it can be correctly classified in the statement of financial position as either a current or non-current liability.

For a provision to be recognised in the financial statements in a given reporting period, three criteria must be satisfied:

(a) a present obligation arises from a past transaction or event

(b) it is probable that there will be an outflow of economic benefits (e.g. a cash payment will be required)

(c) the amount required to settle the obligation can be reliably estimated.

There are a number of situations when a provision may be required to be recognised in the financial statements, including the following examples:

(a) pending legal actions and associated costs, for example, if an employee is injured at work using machinery that had not been properly maintained by the business entity. It may also occur if a customer was injured as a result of buying and using a defective product sold by a business entity.

Note that, in the above situations, it is probable that there will be an outflow of economic benefits due either to the business entity not maintaining machinery properly, or because it sold a defective product.

(b) costs of employee redundancy or severance pay when a decision had been made before the reporting date to close down part of the entity's business activities.

(c) damages and costs relating to environmental damage caused by business activities during the reporting period, such emission of noxious gas or liquids into the environment in excess of legal limits.

One important point regarding provisions is that they must be quantified and accounted for if the recognition criteria have been met. It is not possible to exclude a provision from the financial statements when it is required on the grounds that it is difficult to quantify and/or difficult to estimate when it will be settled.

The auditor's judgement in this area may often be helped by advice from experts, typically lawyers.

Procedures used when auditing provisions

Auditors must plan and perform procedures to ensure accounting estimates and judgmental areas are reasonable. For example, if there is a provision for a legal claim the auditor should discuss with management the matter giving rise to the provision and obtain confirmation from the client's lawyers as to the possible outcome and probability of having to make a payment. The auditor will also review subsequent events as by the time the audit is taking place the matter may have been settled. A written representation will also be obtained from management as the matter is one of judgement and uncertainty.

As another example, if several member of the client staff were made redundant recently as a result of falling sales, a redundancy provision will be required for any staff not yet paid at the year-end. There is a risk of understated liabilities. The auditor could discuss with management the progress of the redundancy programme and review and recalculate the redundancy provision.

2.2 DISCLOSURE

Disclosure may be required of the information below for any provision recognised in the financial statements (this depends on relevant applicable legislation of the country). Typically disclosure is made of:

(a) the nature of the provision

(b) any uncertainties or assumptions relating to estimation of the provision, and

(c) the timing of when it is expected to be settled.

3 THE AUDIT OF CONTINGENT LIABILITIES

3.1 DEFINITION

Definition A **contingency** may be defined as a condition which exists at the reporting date where the ultimate outcome (gain or loss) will only be confirmed by the occurrence or non-occurrence of one or more uncertain future events. It may be a contingent liability or a contingent asset.

Definition A **contingent liability** is a possible obligation depending upon whether some uncertain future event occurs, or it is a present obligation arising from a past event, but the outflow of economic benefits is not probable or cannot be reliably estimated.

IAS 37 *Provisions, Contingent Liabilities and Contingent Assets,* requires that **probable losses** should be accrued (i.e. recognised as a liability), **possible losses** should be disclosed in notes to the financial statements. Losses that are assessed as **remote** are ignored.

It is, therefore, very important to consider whether a contingent liability should actually be recognised in the financial statements as a liability or merely disclosed as a note to the accounts. This is another example when judgement needs to be exercised when accounts are prepared and audited. It may be the case that management would prefer the **disclosure note** approach to dealing with a contingent liability, whereas the auditor may consider that it needs to be recognised as a liability in the statement of financial position if a true and fair view is to be presented.

Typical contingent liabilities include:

(a) guarantees given by the client in respect of loans to third parties e.g. to guarantee a subsidiary entity's overdraft. If the subsidiary fails to repay the overdraft the bank may enforce the guarantee against the client.

(b) damages and costs in respect of legal actions, where the outcome is not probable (otherwise it would be recognised as a provision – see earlier section), but perhaps where liability is in dispute or it is assessed to be less than probable.

(c) possible claims under guarantees or warranties arising out of past transactions.

As with accounting for a provision, the auditor's judgement in this area may often be helped by advice from experts, typically lawyers.

When considering contingent gains the following should be remembered. **Probable gains** should not be recognised but disclosed only in the notes to the financial statements. Contingent gains that are assessed as being only possible or remote should not be disclosed in the financial statements.

3.2 DISCLOSURE

Disclosure may be required of the information below for any contingent liability not *provided* for in the financial statements (this depends on relevant applicable legislation of the country). Typically disclosure is made of:

(a) the amount or estimated amount of that liability

(b) its legal nature

(c) whether any valuable security has been provided by the entity in connection with that liability and, if so, what.

4 SOURCES OF AUDIT EVIDENCE

We have already identified the practical issue that the auditor needs to search for the possibility of unrecorded liabilities. This aspect of the audit work is particularly relevant to the area of provisions and contingencies, as the client may have failed to recognise the existence of these items in the draft financial statements.

There are a range of sources of information available to the auditor which can be used in a search for provisions and contingencies. The principal sources are set out below:

(a) **Standard letter of request to the bank**

This is likely to provide the necessary evidence in respect of and guarantees. This letter was considered in an earlier chapter as the primary method of verifying bank balances, together with interest and charges incurred but not yet applied by the bank.

(b) **Pending legal matters**

Pending lawsuits and other actions against the entity often present problems to the auditors. In accordance with ISA 501 *Audit Evidence – Specific Considerations for Selected Items*, auditors should perform the following procedures:

(i) Enquiry of management (or others, such as in-house legal teams, internal auditors etc.

(ii) Reviewing minutes of meetings of those charged with governance

(iii) Inspection of correspondence between the entity and its external legal counsel; and

(iv) Inspecting legal expense accounts/ledgers.

The auditor would also request that management writes a written representation confirming that they have disclosed all relevant matters of a legal nature to the auditor. They may also consider it useful to obtain the client's consent to send a letter requesting confirmation of specific matters to the client's solicitor. An example of such a letter is shown below:

In connection with the presentation and audit of our accounts for the year ended . . . . . . the directors have made estimates of the ultimate amount (including costs) which might be incurred by the company, and which are regarded as material, in relation to the following matters on which you have been consulted. We should be obliged if you would confirm that in your opinion these estimates are reasonable.

Matter	*Estimated liability including costs*
Libel action against the company in connection with statements appearing in newspaper.	$25,000

Signed . . . .

Dated . . . .

etc.

(c) **Written representations**

This will be considered later as a form of audit evidence. As with all form of audit evidence, its reliability should be evaluated by the auditor. It also reminds the directors to acknowledge their responsibilities which will include the correct treatment of material provisions and contingencies.

The knowledge of provisions and contingent liabilities may very well be confined to management and is therefore a suitable matter for inclusion in such a letter. In addition it will remind the directors of their responsibility to disclose such matters to the auditor.

CONCLUSION

This chapter completes your work on substantive audit procedures. The main area to focus on is the audit of trade payables. Bear in mind that the auditor's main area of interest here is completeness – have all payables that exist been recorded? This can make the audit of payables a more challenging area than the audit of assets, particularly if those items are known only to the directors.

In addition, the audit of provisions and contingencies requires an assessment of whether an item meets the definition of a provision for recognition in the financial statements, or whether it is a contingent liability which requires only disclosure in the notes to the financial statements.

KEY TERMS

Debenture – A written acknowledgement by an entity of a loan made to it, containing provisions as to payment of interest and repayment of capital.

Contingency – A condition which exists at the reporting date where the ultimate outcome will only be confirmed by the occurrence or non-occurrence of one or more uncertain future events.

Provision – A liability of uncertain timing and/or amount.

SELF TEST QUESTIONS

		Paragraph
1	In presenting a statement of financial position, should bank overdrafts be netted off against bank balances?	1.5
2	Is it permitted to exclude recognition of a provision in the financial statements on the basis that it is difficult to quantify?	2.1
3	In what circumstances are contingent liabilities recorded in the financial statements?	3.1
4	Is it helpful to the auditor if there is a paragraph in the letter of representation from the directors to confirm the nature and extent of all material provisions and contingencies they are aware of?	4.1

PRACTICE QUESTION 1

You are working as an experienced junior on the audit of The Trendy Gear Company, a retail fashion company. The audit team has now completed the audit planning and are in the process of drafting detailed audit programmes for all stages of the audit work.

Your audit senior asks you to prepare the audit programme dealing with the purchases and trade payables areas of the audit. She reminds you the firm uses statistical sampling techniques on this client and adopts a policy of circularising payables on all audit engagements. She also mentions that sample sizes for the audit of trade payables are yet to be decided by the manager and partner.

Required:

As a preliminary step to preparing a formal audit programme, list the audit tests that should be applied to: purchases

You are **not** required to present your answer in the form of an audit programme.

You are expected to cover both tests of control and substantive tests. **(25 marks)**

For a suggested answer, see the 'Answers' section at the end of the book.

Chapter 14

COMPUTERS IN AUDIT

INTRODUCTION

This chapter deals with the use of computers in the audit process. There are two main aspects to their use by the auditor:

- The auditor can use computer systems to help with the planning and performance of the audit – this is a common feature of modern auditing.

- The client may well use computer-based systems for some or all of their processing. The auditor therefore needs to have an understanding of such systems and of the auditing techniques which can be applied to them.

This chapter deals with both of these aspects.

Of course, information processing technology can now be a very specialised and technically complex area.

This chapter covers all of the computerised aspects mentioned in the study guide, as well as syllabus areas C (3) and D (5).

CONTENTS

1 The use of computers in managing the audit

2 Special features of computer-based systems

3 Auditing in a computer environment

4 Internal control in computer-based systems

5 Reliance by auditors on internal controls

6 Automated tools and techniques

7 The internet

8 Appendix: some control terminology explained

FAU: FOUNDATIONS IN AUDIT

LEARNING OUTCOMES

At the end of this chapter, you should be able to:

- appreciate the scope for the use of computers by auditors in planning and performing the audit

- identify the impact on the audit process where the client uses computer-based accounting systems (which is most organisations)

- appreciate the additional control procedures which should be in place in connection with a computer-based accounting system

- understand and apply test of information processing controls, including the use of audit software, test data and other analytics tools.

- explain the advantages and disadvantages of the use of automated tools and techniques to the auditor.

- understand how the use of the internet has affected the auditor in assisting him with his audit work and the implications for the audit.

1 THE USE OF COMPUTERS IN MANAGING THE AUDIT

1.1 INTRODUCTION

Auditors are increasingly using specialised computer systems in planning and performing the audit. This is designed to make the auditing process more efficient and therefore more cost effective.

Typical applications which may be used are:

(a) **Flowcharting client's systems**

Specialist flowcharting software packages can assist the auditor in the production of clear, well presented flowcharts. Although the package cannot review the system for the auditor, they do produce legible output and can be easily updated when systems change, unlike manually produced flowcharts.

(b) **Evaluation of audit risk**

The auditors can input into the computer their assessment of the audit risk for the various transactions and balances in the client's systems, and the software may also provide guidance to the level of testing required via an expert systems shell.

(c) **Preparation of audit programmes**

Audit programmes can be input and easily updated on computers. Some firms may also have standard audit tests, for example, a summary of work to be performed when attending the inventory count. When the test is required, it is simply inserted into the relevant audit programme, which saves time, avoids duplication of effort and ensures consistency of audit approach.

(d) **Analytical procedures**

Standard templates can be set up on a spreadsheet package which will automatically calculate ratios and perform standard analysis from data input by the auditor. The auditor can input key details such as statement of financial position totals from the financial statements and other financial information. The spreadsheet may also perform comparisons with previous years to assist the auditor with the analytical procedures.

(e) **Preparation of audit working papers**

By using laptops the auditor can type up audit working papers immediately after the tests have been completed. These can then be emailed to the Head Office to facilitate timely review. The documents will be of a higher standard of legibility and the automated working papers can assist in ensuring that all the work is completed.

(f) **Audit review**

If the auditor and the reviewer are at different locations the auditor can email the files electronically to the reviewer, thus speeding up the review process.

(g) **Communication**

The large audit firms are worldwide operations. Use of electronic communications such as e-mail allows for transfer of audit files for peer reviews, sharing of audit information etc. which should improve the overall quality of audit work.

(h) **Control of the audit**

A spreadsheet package can easily be used for recording and managing time spent by each member of the audit team in conducting the audit, and therefore ensuring that the overall audit time budget is monitored.

1.2 SOFTWARE

(a) **Commercially available packages**

Most audit firms will purchase at least one word processing package and one spreadsheet package. These programs will then be used as outlined above to assist the auditors in their audit work. Flowcharting packages are also commercially available as are audit packages with standard documentation and tests.

(b) **Specialist programs written in-house**

Larger audit firms will employ computer programmers in-house to write specialist software for use only by that audit firm. Examples of this type of software include databases of standard audit tests that can be copied into audit programmes, and expert systems that will assist the auditor in the determination of audit risk and setting of testing levels.

FAU: FOUNDATIONS IN AUDIT

1.3 CONTROLS

The controls that must be exercised by the auditor when computers are used in audit work will include the following:

(a) **Backup of files**

Backup copies of all audit files kept on the computer should be made regularly (at least once per day). These backup copies should be kept in a separate location from the computer itself. If then the computer is lost or damaged, the copy files can be used to continue work on that client.

When an audit is finished, and the client's files are deleted from the hard disk at least two and preferably three backup copies should be made. This ensures that if one copy becomes corrupted or lost, then the files can be retrieved from the second copy of the files.

(b) **Security of files**

Audit information on clients can be very sensitive. Adequate procedures must be in force to ensure that only authorised audit staff can gain access to the audit information. All audit computers should therefore be protected by passwords, and disks with client data stored in safe locations e.g. a fire proof safe.

The auditor should ensure that at no time is the PC left unattended when outside the audit firm such that a risk of unauthorised access could arise.

Care must also be taken to ensure that computers holding client data are not stolen. If a computer is left at a client's premises overnight then it should either be locked in a safe, or securely chained and padlocked to a table. Preferably it would remain with the auditor at all times.

(c) **Adequacy of documentation**

There is a danger with computers that not all the data or reasoning used to reach a particular decision will be documented. This can arise due to lack of ability to use the system. Adequate documentation must therefore be kept, including print-outs of all major documents, for future reference, together with the reasons for the decisions made.

(d) **Testing of programs**

Before any program is used on audits, it should be tested to ensure that it is as far as possible error free. This is particularly true of programs written by the audit firm itself. The auditors could be particularly exposed in court if they made a wrong decision due to faulty or inadequately tested software.

You will see later in this chapter that auditors will expect their clients to have controls of this type in place in their computer systems. It would, of course, be extremely embarrassing if it were discovered that the auditor did not have adequate controls over their own computers.

ACTIVITY 1

Explain how the auditor can use computers to assist in the performance of audit work.

For a suggested answer, see the 'Answers' section at the end of the book.

The remainder of this chapter deals with the audit implications of the client using computer-based accounting systems, which is the majority of cases.

2 SPECIAL FEATURES OF COMPUTER-BASED SYSTEMS

There are a number of distinguishing features of computer-based systems which must be recognised and considered by the auditors.

(a) concentration of controls in the IT Department

(b) lack of primary records

(c) encoded data

(d) loss of audit trail

(e) data needed for audit purposes may be overwritten

(f) program controls may be important to ensure the completeness and accuracy of accounting records

(g) the need for specialist expertise

(h) availability of computer time.

Each of these is dealt with in more detail below.

Concentration of controls in the computer department

Historically the need to standardise procedures and control the computer resources of a business led to a concentration of controls in the computer department, staffed primarily by technical experts. It should be recognised that such a concentration, where it exists, represents a potential weakness. There is a danger of inadvertent or deliberate corruption of data by experts particularly where others in the organisation have little or no knowledge of the technical aspects of the system.

Most organisations have minimised this danger by adopting control procedures which apportion responsibilities within the computer department (segregation of duties again!) and allow other (user) departments to check the accuracy of processed data. The auditor's work, particularly at the planning stage, will involve identifying the extent of these controls. Clearly if such controls are concentrated in the computer department the adequate functioning of the department will be important to the audit.

The recent reduction in costs of computer hardware has led to the dispersal of both processing and controls in some systems and more companies are now using de-centralised systems with PCs, usually linked together via a network, spread throughout the organisation. This enables the users to be more closely involved with the data processing function but may lead to an absence of standardisation of procedures and controls and, to an extent, a lack of technical expertise. This potential problem is considered in more detail later.

Lack of primary records

In some computer-based accounting systems conventional day books will not be maintained. In others an originating document may not be created. In an on-line system for example (a system with a direct link between input and output devices) an operator may receive an order by telephone and use a terminal to key in the relevant data immediately. The system creates despatch and invoice documentation and updates inventory and customer files. The auditor would be unable to trace these transactions back to an originating document.

Such problems are relevant to both management and auditors and should be considered at the time the system is designed. It would be essential for computer generated reports to be provided and reviewed carefully by management.

Encoded data

There is always a danger of transposition errors arising at the encoding stage. The auditor's procedures should take into account the existence of checking procedures (e.g. check digits, data validation, confirmation by a second user) particularly on amendments to standing data items (for example, pay rates in a payroll system) and on the conversion from one system to another.

Loss of audit trail

This is seen to be a classic problem resulting from an audit client using a computer-based accounting system.

The majority of computer systems are usually designed to limit the volume of printed data as a matter of speed and efficiency. Control is implemented by exception reporting principles so that detailed print-outs of electronically stored data are not available. The auditor is therefore unable to trace an individual transaction through the system from originating document to financial statements (or vice-versa) in the traditional way. There is said to be a loss of (visible) audit trail.

The auditor must assess the implications of this at the planning stage. It may result in a need to use automated tools and techniques to obtain appropriate evidence that controls have functioned adequately.

Data needed for audit purposes may be overwritten

When data is stored electronically on tape or disk it may eventually be overwritten with new data. The auditors will need to plan audit testing to ensure that the appropriate data is available. They need to make frequent visits to the client's premises to ensure that they cover an adequate spread of transactions during the year or ensure that they are provided with back up data at the relevant points during the year.

Program controls may be important to ensure the completeness and accuracy of accounting records

As you know, it is a general principle of auditing that the auditor must test controls upon which they wish to rely. This means that they will need to test programmed controls. These are controls built into the computer program which operate automatically as the program is run. An example of a program control which you may be familiar with is the use of check digits.

To check the operation of these program controls, the auditor will have to check that the computer programs have sufficient in-built controls by using computer-assisted auditing techniques (see later in this chapter).

A further complication which often arises is that the program controls are regularly amended by the client. Old programs may be overwritten and may be unavailable at the accounting year end. The implication is that once again the auditors must be prepared to review and test controls regularly during the year so that they can obtain adequate evidence regarding the functioning of controls during the whole period.

The need for specialist expertise

As computers become extensively used, more powerful and more complex, auditors need to develop a greater degree of knowledge of computer systems so that they are capable of auditing more advanced systems used by their clients. However, it is no longer realistic to expect all staff to have a high level of technical competence to conduct all audits.

There is often a strong case for the employment of computer specialists. Survey data shows that there is a swing in internal audit departments toward using DP specialists rather than accountants for such audit work. This trend may spread to external audits as audit competence is put together on a team basis.

There is a major problem for external auditors in that employing and training special computer staff is expensive. This may be a particular problem for smaller practices that do not at present have an extensive portfolio of clients with complex computer-based accounting systems. The use, as and when required, of external experts may be a solution to this problem.

Availability of computer time

The use of computer-assisted auditing techniques often involves the use of the client's computer facilities. There may be a need to organise such facilities well ahead of the required dates. This is part of the audit planning process.

ACTIVITY 2

Explain the additional factors which need to be taken into consideration by the auditor when auditing computerised systems as opposed to manual systems.

For a suggested answer, see the 'Answers' section at the end of the book.

3 AUDITING IN A COMPUTER ENVIRONMENT

The key points concerned with auditing in a computer environment are as follows:

(a) The principles of auditing in a computer environment are the same as in other circumstances. ALL audits must be planned, recorded and controlled; all audits will involve an evaluation of accounting systems; all audits will entail a review and reporting procedure.

(b) Detailed practical guidance should be obtained by those who are unaccustomed to auditing in a computer environment. This will, of course, be less significant now than it was 20 years ago. Nowadays computers are an everyday fact of life, with all students being comfortable with using them, and nearly all businesses using computers to a greater or lesser degree.

(c) Emphasis must be laid on the knowledge and skills that an auditor will need when auditing in a computer environment. In particular, it is recommended that auditors should develop a basic understanding of the fundamentals of data processing, and attain a level of technical computer knowledge and skills commensurate with the particular circumstances of the audit.

(d) With the introduction of smaller computers, there is a greater likelihood of weak internal controls, and this will normally lead to greater emphasis being placed on substantive testing of transactions and balances, and on other procedures such as analytical review, rather than on tests of control.

(e) Where there is a computer-based accounting system, many of the auditor's procedures may still be carried out manually.

(f) There are two major types of controls over computer-based accounting systems ('general controls' and 'information processing controls'), and the two interrelate (this is discussed later in the chapter).

(g) Where third party service organisations (such as computer service bureaux or software houses) are used for the purpose of maintaining part or all of an enterprise's accounting records and procedures, the auditor may encounter practical obstacles, as the enterprise may be placing some reliance on the proper operation of internal controls exercised by the third party. It is recommended that, where the auditor finds it impracticable to obtain all the information and explanations that he requires from the enterprise itself, he should carry out other procedures. These may include taking steps he considers necessary to enable him to rely on the work performed by other auditors, or carrying out procedures at the premises of the third party. Guidance in this area is provided by ISA 402 *Audit Considerations Relating to Entities using Service Organisations,* but no detailed knowledge of this topic is required for this paper.

4 INTERNAL CONTROL IN COMPUTER-BASED SYSTEMS

Let us start with a very important principle.

The normal categories of control dealt with in an earlier chapter (authorisation, segregation, etc.) will apply in a computer-based system just as they will in a manual system.

In addition to these there will be controls over the computer system itself, because of the specific features (problems) of computer-based processing discussed above. These additional controls are the subject of this section – they are an extra layer of control on top of the normal control categories – they do not replace them.

The picture we have is therefore:

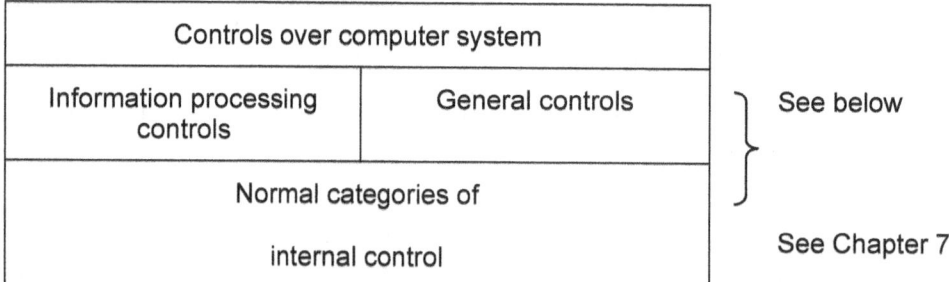

4.1 CLASSIFICATION OF CONTROLS OVER COMPUTER SYSTEMS

It is conventional to recognise only two types of controls:

(a) information processing controls

(b) general controls.

You should note that there is an Appendix towards the end of this chapter which explains some of the control terminology that you may not be familiar with. You should refer to this Appendix to clarify terms as necessary.

4.2 INFORMATION PROCESSING CONTROLS

Definition   **Information processing controls** are those controls which are specific to an individual application, and comprise input, processing, output and master file controls.

A computer application is a use to which the computer system is put – word processing, database, spreadsheet, receivables ledger system, payroll system etc. Note that as our definition tells us that information processing controls are specific to a particular application, it follows that they will be different (although often similar) in detail for each computer application. This point also applies in manual systems. The controls which apply in a payroll system will be different from those that apply in an inventory control system!

Information processing controls are likely to consist of both manually-performed and computer-performed controls.

The objective of information processing controls is to ensure the completeness and accuracy of all processing and the validity of the accounting entries made.

Practical examples of information processing controls include the following:

(a) **Batch total checks** to confirm the total value of items processed e.g. the total value of a batch of purchase invoices processed. This may, for example, consist of more than one total, such as totals for gross amount, sales tax and net amount.

(b) **Run to run controls** use the batch control information (such as batch number, batch totals etc.) to monitor a batch as it progresses from one computer programme procedure to another. For example, in the case of a (simplified) purchase order system, this may go through several programmes – data input, trade payables update, inventory update and output. After each run or stage of processing, batch control totals are recalculated and checked with the control totals from the data input run stage. Any errors or inconsistencies are highlighted and reported at the end of each run. Errors or discrepancies can then be followed up by an appropriate person and missing or amended data can then be input as appropriate.

(c) **Range checks** to confirm that quantities and/or values processed are within an acceptable range e.g. quantity sold per sales invoice must fall within the range 1 – 100 units. Such a check provides both a lower and upper limit to be checked. Any negative quantity or quantity in excess of 100 units would not be accepted, or can only be overridden by a suitably responsible person.

(d) **Limit checks** are similar to range checks, except that they include either an upper limit check or a lower limit check, but not both e.g. quantities of goods purchased must not be a negative quantity.

(e) **Hash totals** are derived from the non-financial data that is part of a batch being processed and they are used to confirm the completeness and validity of the batch items processed. For example, if the receivables ledger account numbers consist of six digits (e.g. 342719) then the account numbers may be totalled to provide the hash total. When the batch has been processed, the hash total is confirmed which helps to validate not only the number of sales invoices processed, but also the validity of the account numbers as, if a wrong account number is input and processed, the hash total will not agree.

(f) **Format or field checks** to confirm that all relevant data fields have been completed e.g. input or processing would not be allowed to continue if there was missing or incomplete data.

(g) **Check-digit verification checks** confirm the validity of account numbers e.g. receivables ledger account numbers have a prefix of 'SLA' and must include the digit '7' within the account number, whereas payables ledger account numbers have a prefix of 'PLA' and must include the digit '5' within the account number. Therefore processing of transactions to the receivables and payables ledgers as required would be prevented unless they had the correct prefix and also contained the essential check digit within the account number.

(h) **Exception checks** ensure that an exception report is produced to highlight or identify errors or unusual items input. This enables such items to be reviewed by an appropriate person so that corrective action can be taken as necessary. For example, the carry forward of a negative quantity for an item of inventory would be highlighted on an inventory usage summary.

(i) **External file labels** are visible and legible labels to enable a user to check that the correct disk or file has been selected for update etc. They will normally include a file title plus edition or volume number, together with date of origination.

(j) **Internal file labels** are magnetic records on a data disk or file which identify the data contained within that disk or file which the system software is able to identify.

The role of information processing controls can be shown by the following simple diagram representing a payroll system:

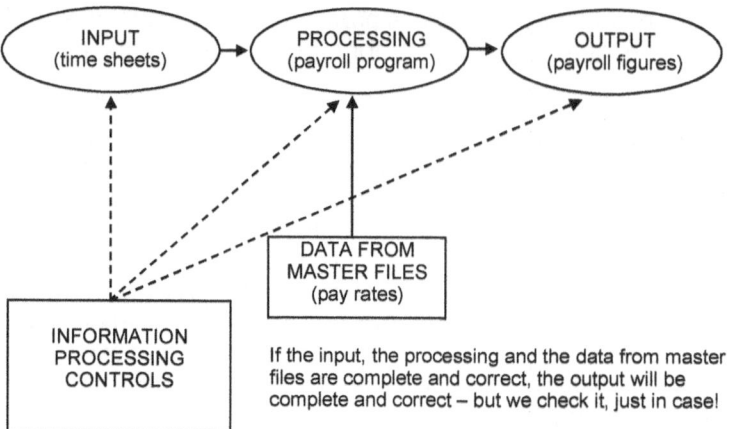

If the input, the processing and the data from master files are complete and correct, the output will be complete and correct – but we check it, just in case!

Based on the analysis above, information processing controls fall under the following six main headings each with its own **control objectives** for:

(a) **Completeness of input**

- To ensure that a document is raised for every transaction.
- To ensure that each document is input in timely fashion.

(b) **Accuracy of input**

- To ensure that all data is correctly input.

(c) **Authorisation of input**

- To ensure that each transaction is authorised.
- To ensure that the individual who authorised the transaction was empowered to do so.

(d) **Controls over processing (updating)**

- To ensure that all input data is accurately and completely processed on a timely basis.
- To ensure that the correct versions of master files and standing data files are used.
- To ensure that the processing of each transaction is accurate to produce accurately updated master files.

(e) **Control over output**

- To ensure that output is checked for completeness and accuracy.
- To ensure that output is properly distributed to the correct person and actioned.

(f) **Controls over master files**

- To ensure that all data held on master files is accurate and up-to-date.
- To ensure that any amendment to standing data is properly authorised.

Master files contain data of continuing or permanent importance to an entity. They usually relate to one functional area of activity e.g. the sales system, purchases system, payroll system etc.

For example, master files data relating to employees and payroll costs are likely to include the following:

- Employee number or reference
- Employee name
- Date of birth
- Address and telephone contact details
- Location or department
- Job title/grade
- Annual salary
- Other benefits e.g. pension scheme, bonus entitlement etc.
- Tax code or rate applicable
- Bank account details
- Start date and (when applicable) leaving date

This information is unlikely to change every month for each employee but is it vital that the information is up to date so that employees can be paid the correct amount at each pay date. If any item of information should change, for example an employee joins or leaves employment; amendments to the master file should be made promptly and accurately to ensure payroll costs are complete and accurate.

Controls relevant to maintenance and update of master files include:

- Restricted access to master files – perhaps by password access only to properly authorised employees.
- Properly authorised amendments by a responsible person. This will help to ensure that only valid amendments or updates are processed.
- There should be segregation of duties between authorisation of amendments and processing of those amendments.
- A sequential log should be maintained of access to master files, along with any amendments made, identifying the date, time and individual who has accessed the files.
- Records of amendments to master files should be reviewed regularly and checked by a responsible person to confirm their validity.

FAU: FOUNDATIONS IN AUDIT

- Controls over processing of amendments to master files such as record counts and control totals should be implemented.
- Periodic review of master files by an independent responsible person tracing back to authorised amendments and other authorised base documents to confirm validity of those files.

The standard **control techniques** for information processing controls under the six headings are shown below.

Principal control techniques: information processing controls

PROCESSING (d) above	OUTPUT (e) above	MASTERFILE (f) above
• Batch reconciliation	• Check batch control outputs to inputs	• Check amendments on a one to one basis
• Run to run totals to ensure no data lost between processing activities	• Summary of totals	• Periodic printout and checks
• Summary processing e.g. check total depreciation equal to summary of elements	• 'End of Report' message – there is no more output to come	• Record counts checked
• External file labels	• Checklist for distribution of output	• Independent control totals
• Internal file labels	• Follow up exception reports	

↑ ↑ ↑

INFORMATION PROCESSING CONTROLS

↓

INPUT

↓ ↓ ↓

COMPLETENESS (a) above	ACCURACY (b) above	AUTHORISATION (c) above
• One for one checks i.e. each input checked to output	• Check digits	• Manual authorisation
• Batch control totals	• Reasonableness checks to ensure data within certain ranges	• Clerical review of transactions
• Hash totals	• Existence checks e.g. to check that customer account exists	• One for one checking of amendments to standing data
• Document counts	• Manual controls e.g. batch controls and arithmetic checks	• Programmed checks on authorisation limits
• Sequence checks		
• Matching each master file record to a transaction record		

COMPUTERS IN AUDIT : CHAPTER 14

ACTIVITY 3

(a) State the data that you would expect to be maintained on master files relating to the management of sales made to credit customers.

(b) State the controls that you would expect to operate in relation to the maintenance and amendment of master files for sales to credit customers.

For a suggested answer, see the 'Answers' section at the end of the book.

4.3 GENERAL CONTROLS

Definition **General controls** relate to the environment within which systems are developed, maintained and operated. Such controls can be expected to apply to all applications.

The objective of such controls is to ensure the integrity of application development and implementation and to ensure that computer operations are properly administered to protect hardware, programs and data files.

It is conventional to envisage controls in the following areas and the control objectives for each are:

(a) **Controls over systems development (application development)**

- To ensure developments are fully authorised.
- To ensure proper standards are followed during development.
- To ensure changes are properly tested and documented.

(b) **Controls to prevent/detect errors during program execution**

- To ensure any errors arising are noted and resolved.

(c) **Controls to prevent/detect changes to data files**

- To ensure changes are authorised.
- To ensure changes are made accurately.

(d) **Controls to ensure continuity of operations**

- To ensure the system can continue to function in the event of disaster or breakdown.

(e) **Controls to ensure that systems software is properly installed and maintained**

- To ensure all access is authorised.
- To ensure only authorised amendments are made.

(f) **Controls to ensure that proper documentation is kept**

- To ensure that documentation is sufficient and of a satisfactory quality (standards should be set).
- To ensure that documentation is maintained up to date.

KAPLAN PUBLISHING

Control techniques for general controls

ERRORS DURING PROGRAM EXECUTION (b) above	CHANGES TO DATA FILES (c) above	CONTINUITY OF OPERATIONS (d) above
• Systems software should report errors e.g. wrong file, hardware malfunction • Detailed operations reported and checked to ensure completeness • Job scheduling	• Prior authorisation by nominated individuals • Password protection • Back up files • Record of amendments for subsequent checking • Physical protection of files	• Back up procedures • Standby arrangements • Testing back up procedures • Protection against fire and theft • Maintenance agreements • Insurance • Copies of files maintained in a secure location

↑↑↑

GENERAL CONTROLS

↓

SYSTEMS DEVELOPMENT

↓↓↓

APPLICATION DEVELOPMENT (a) above	PROGRAM CHANGES (a) above	INSTALLATION, MAINTENANCE & DOCUMENTATION (e) and (f) above
• Systems design standards • Programming standards • Testing procedures • Full documentation • Approval by users before implementation • Internal audit involvement • Segregation of duties between development and operations	• Supervision and training • Authorisation of changes • Documentation of changes • Password protection to prevent unauthorised access • Back up of programs • Physical protection of files • Rotation of duties • Thorough testing • Approval of changes	• Testing and documentation • Protection of systems software (read only) • Segregation of duties (programmers, operators, users) • Good quality documentation

It is probably worth a reminder at this stage that you are not required to be a computer expert – try to gain a general appreciation and understanding of the type of controls required, rather than attempting to learn every point of detail.

ACTIVITY 4

Explain the difference between information processing controls and general controls giving two examples of each type of control.

For a suggested answer, see the 'Answers' section at the end of the book.

5 RELIANCE BY AUDITORS ON INTERNAL CONTROLS

5.1 INTRODUCTION

Having considered in detail examples of both information processing controls and general controls, the question arises as to what extent the auditor should rely upon such controls.

As you know, auditing standards require the auditor to obtain relevant and reliable audit evidence sufficient to draw reasonable conclusions therefrom. The relationship between tests of control and substantive procedures applies as much in a computer-based accounting system as it does in a manual system: if the auditor obtains reasonable assurance from testing the controls the substantive work can be limited.

5.2 THE RELATIONSHIP BETWEEN INFORMATION PROCESSING CONTROLS AND GENERAL CONTROLS

It may be appropriate for the auditor to concentrate upon information processing controls before deciding how far to proceed with examining general controls. The reasons for this are as follows:

(a) Information processing controls can be more easily related to a specific control objective, and therefore a specific audit objective, than can general controls.

(b) Information processing controls can be more easily tested by using specific transactions to act as a medium for the test which is then performed either clerically or by using computer-assisted audit techniques (see later in this chapter).

(c) As a result of (a) and (b) the testing of information processing controls may be more effective than general controls.

There are, however, certain reasons for still considering general controls to be highly relevant to the auditor:

(a) If information processing controls become concentrated in the computer department, the environment within which the information processing controls function will be fundamental. Furthermore if general controls are weak these can undermine strong information processing controls.

(b) If certain information processing controls are lacking the auditor may attempt to limit his substantive testing by placing more reliance on general controls.

From the above it is possible to set out basic rules relating to audit testing of controls:

(a) The auditor can test and rely on general controls alone without having to test information processing controls.

(b) The auditor can test and rely on manual information processing controls alone without having to test general controls.

(c) In order to rely on programmed information processing controls the auditor must first be satisfied with general controls. As stated earlier, if the controls covering the whole computer environment are poor, then the programmed information processing controls within it will be worthless.

5.3 AUDIT DOCUMENTATION

You have seen that auditors are likely to wish to rely upon controls as a source of audit evidence. To do so they must record the system and carry out a preliminary evaluation. Their work will be assisted by the use of existing client documentation to help identify the internal controls on which they may wish to place reliance.

The documentation may take a variety of forms but two particular methods will often form an important part of the audit documentation.

(a) **An audit control file or systems file**

This file contains important details of both manual and programmed procedures. It must be reviewed and updated regularly. The auditor should ask to be notified of all procedural changes. The file might typically contain:

(i) Copies of documents used in the system with details of checks performed on them.

(ii) Description of how source documents are converted into input, with associated control procedures.

(iii) Details of information processing controls in each area of the system.

(iv) Flowcharts of system operations.

(v) Details of all data files including storage media, organisation, labelling, storage arrangements, back-up facilities.

(vi) Details and copies of output documents.

(vii) The results of the auditor's review of the system and the effectiveness of the controls within it.

(b) **Internal control questionnaire (ICQ)**

The ascertainment and evaluation of both information processing and general controls will be assisted by the use of specially designed ICQs. The ICQ would include questions covering both manual and programmed controls as both types are likely to be relied upon by the auditor.

ACTIVITY 5

When auditing computerised systems, the auditors need to consider both general and information processing controls. They also need to consider the relationship between the two types. Explain why this is the case.

For a suggested answer, see the 'Answers' section at the end of the book.

6 AUTOMATED TOOLS AND TECHNIQUES

6.1 THE ROLE OF AUTOMATED TOOLS AND TECHNIQUES

Shown below is our simple representation of a computer system showing the main elements of input, processing and output.

In the early days of auditing computer-based systems, the auditor did not have the tools available to audit the (electronic) processing of the data. The audit process therefore had to focus on the input and the output, largely ignoring the processing that produced the final figures. This became known as auditing around the computer. The principal problem is that it did not guarantee that the audit work would detect errors in the computer programs that carried out the processing.

The modern approach to auditing computer-based systems is known as **auditing through the computer** – the auditor examines all three elements shown above i.e. processing as well as input and output.

In order to do this, the auditor needed to be able to get inside the computer – it was the development of automated tools and techniques which allowed the auditor to do this. These are sometimes known as computer assisted audit techniques or CAATs. CAATs can be defined as a series of techniques which allow the auditor to use the client's computer system to generate audit evidence.

In practice, automated tools and techniques can take a wide variety of forms. However, the two major categories that we shall focus on here, together with the role they play for the auditor, can be summarised as follows:

Test data	Audit software	Data analytics
The auditor supervises the process of running data through the client's own system (either dummy data or real data).	Audit software makes use of the auditor's own specialised software (either an off-the-shelf package or a tailor-made system).	When used to obtain audit evidence in a financial statement audit, data analytics is the science and art of discovering and analysing patterns, deviations and inconsistencies, and extracting other useful information in the data underlying or related to the subject matter of an audit through analysis, remodelling and visualisation for the purpose of planning and performing the audit. (Source: FRC, 2017)
The results tell the auditor whether the internal controls within the system are operating effectively.	It works on the basis of interrogating the client's system and extracting and analysing information.	
This is therefore a test of control.	A range of substantive procedures can be carried out.	

Each of these is dealt with in more detail, below.

6.2 TEST DATA

Definition   **Audit test data** consists of data submitted by the auditor for processing by the client's computer-based accounting system. The actual output produced by the computer is compared by the auditor with the expected (correct) data. It may be processed during a normal processing run (running test data 'live') or during a special run at a point in time outside the normal cycle (running the test data 'dead').

Test data could be held in the form of a batch of documents put through the system to test both manual and computer controls. It is more often used to refer to data stored in electronic form used to test programmed controls. Its primary use is in the testing of information processing controls.

Use of test data

There are three major approaches:

(i) **Using live data**

At its simplest level the auditors could use real data that has been processed which involves the controls they want to test. They should then predetermine the results which they would expect from the processing of the data. They later check that the actual processing has been carried out in the expected way and investigate any differences.

This method is not usually feasible as the auditors will usually want to use a collection of normal, exceptional and even absurd data to test controls. They are unlikely to find all these conditions in a batch of data and therefore are likely to design their own (dummy) data.

(ii) **Dummy data in a normal processing run**

The auditor constructs a series of dummy transactions which contain the required information to check all the controls which the auditor wants to check. These are processed along with normal data. Actual results are then compared with predetermined results.

This method has the advantage of producing a realistic test environment. The client's actual programs and data files are being used in the test.

The dangers of this method are, however, considerable. It must be ensured that the dummy data does not affect the actual data. Great care is needed in planning and controlling the test.

(iii) **Dummy data in a special run**

In this method the auditor creates special data and uses it against copies of the client's data files. The dangers associated with 'live' testing are therefore largely eliminated although the interaction of one file with another must still be carefully considered.

It is still essential to obtain the client's permission which reduces the independence of the test. It is also necessary to obtain assurance that the programs being used in the test run are identical to those used by the client for production runs and not special programs kept aside for the auditor's use!

Difficulties in using audit test data

(i) **Costs**

There may be considerable costs involved in ascertaining the relevant controls and in constructing test data from scratch. It may be very difficult to identify all relevant conditions. The need to predetermine the results manually may be both time-consuming and tedious. These costs, however, are normally substantially less than for audit software.

(ii) **Objectives of the test**

Test data is likely to be confined to tests of control and therefore may be less valuable in audit terms than using audit software.

(iii) **Dangers of live testing**

Careful planning and control is needed to separate the test data from the records.

(iv) **Dangers of testing during a special run**

If special test runs are used, an artificial testing environment is created. Assurance is needed that the normal programs and files have been used.

(v) **Recording**

Working papers should include details of the controls to be tested, an explanation of how they are to be tested, details of the transactions and files used, details of the predicted results, the actual results and evidence of the predicted and actual results having being compared.

6.3 AUDIT SOFTWARE

Definition **Audit software** comprises computer programs used by auditors to examine an enterprise's computer files. It may consist of generalised package programs, specially written programs or the client's own programs.

(i) **Generalised package programs**

These are programs already written either by the auditor or a specialist software company which are designed to be used on different types of computer system. They need to be tailored to each specific system by defining the format of the files to be interrogated and by specifying the parameters of output data required and the form of that output. In some cases additional programming is required to tailor the package to the auditor's requirements/client's circumstances.

(ii) **Specially written programs**

In some cases it is not possible to adapt a package program due to the type of machine, processing or file organisation used. In such cases a purpose-written program is required. It could be written by the auditor, by a software specialist or by the client acting on the instructions of the auditor. In all cases it should be fully tested before being used 'live'.

(iii) **The client's own programs ('enquiry programs')**

These can often be useful to the auditor when obtaining specific information such as 'sales during a period'. These are unlikely to provide all information required but will supplement other techniques. The auditor must satisfy himself when using client programs that the controls within the programs are satisfactory.

Use of audit software

Audit software may be used during many audit testing procedures. Its use is particularly appropriate during substantive testing of transactions and balances, as it may scrutinise large volumes of data and extract information leaving skilled manual resources to concentrate upon the investigation of the results.

Typical uses of such programs include:

(i) **Calculation checks**

e.g. the program adds the value of open items on a file to ensure that they agree with control records which are maintained.

(ii) **Detecting violation of systems rules**

e.g. the program checks all accounts on the receivables ledger to ensure that no customer has a balance above a specified credit limit.

(iii) **Detecting unreasonable items**

e.g. a check that no customer is allowed trade discount of more than 50%, or that no receivables ledger balance is more than total sales made to that customer.

(iv) **Conducting new calculations and analyses**

e.g. obtaining a statistical analysis of inventory movements to identify slow-moving items.

(v) **Selection of items for audit testing**

e.g. obtaining a stratified sample of receivables ledger balances to be used as a basis for a receivables circularisation.

(vi) **Completeness checks**

e.g. checking continuity of sales invoices to ensure they are all accounted for and that they all have unique numbers.

Difficulties in using audit software

(i) **Costs**

There will be substantial set-up costs even in using a generalised package. This is because the client's procedures and files need to be investigated thoroughly prior to identifying audit tests and identifying whether or not they are compatible with the audit software. The use of specially written programs will be even more expensive.

(ii) **Changes to client's systems**

These can mean costly alterations to the programs or at least require the programs to be run regularly during the year to test the system at different dates.

(iii) **Small installations**

There may be no suitable audit software package for use on mini-computer or PC installations. Software documentation may be incomplete so that it is very difficult to identify all procedures. It may be impossible to justify and hence recover the cost of specially written audit software.

(iv) **Over-elaboration**

There may be a tendency to produce over-elaborate enquiry programs which are expensive to develop, take up considerable computer running time and extensive reviewing time. The auditor should be able to justify the costs of using the programs to the benefits in audit terms of its use.

(v) **Quantities of output**

An enquiry program may produce huge quantities of output. This may be because the system is wrong or the enquiry program was badly designed. To avoid this problem some packages can be set to terminate after a given number of items have been included in the count. The auditor must distinguish between cases where the parameters were misjudged and too large a sample was obtained and cases where the print-out is long because lots of items are wrong. In the latter case the auditor must follow the audit work through and consider the implications of the problems encountered.

(vi) **Version of files used in the test**

The audit software only tests the files against which it is run. It is therefore preferable to use the software on the actual files of the client. The permission of the client is needed and the software must be carefully tested prior to its use on 'live' data to ensure that it does not affect the live data.

An alternative approach is to run the programs against copies of the data files which is much safer. To be valid there must be adequate general controls to ensure that the client uses the same files. Provided this is so the use of copy files enables the auditor to be more flexible in deciding when to test and to retain the copy files for further testing.

6.4 DATA ANALYTICS

Definition   **Data analytics** is a process of inspecting, cleansing, transforming and modelling data with the goal of discovering useful information, informing conclusion and supporting decision-making.

Data analytics is a very hot topic in the auditing profession, and can be seen as part of the broader revolution of 'big data'. Complex analysis can be performed on data, without the need to create tailor-made software. Standard data analytics techniques can be applied to client's data in order to generate intuitive visualisations of very complex data e.g. bubble charts, pie charts, bar graphs which can then be used by the auditor in their analysis to spot trends that might otherwise have been missed.

Data analytics techniques are increasingly being adopted by auditors worldwide to perform techniques, for example:

- analysing all transactions in a population, stratifying that population and identifying outliers for further examination.
- comparing entity data to externally obtained data
- analysing of revenue trends split by product or region

FAU: FOUNDATIONS IN AUDIT

- matching orders to cash and purchases to payments
- three-way matching between purchase/ sales orders, goods received/ despatched documentation and invoices
- assisting in segregation of duties testing.

Audit Data Analytics (ADA) is the science and art of discovering and analysing patterns, deviations and inconsistencies, and extracting other useful information in the data of underlying or related subject matter of an audit through analysis, modelling, visualisation for the purpose of planning and performing the audit.

Big data refers to data sets that are large or complex.

Big data technology allows the auditor to perform procedures on very large or complete sets of data rather than samples.

Example

The auditor may use ADA to analyse journals posted to identify:

- The total number of journals posted.
- The number of journals posted manually.
- The number of journals posted automatically by the system.
- The number of people processing journals.
- The time of day the journals are posted.

The auditor may conclude there is a higher risk of fraud this year compared with last if:

- The number of manual versus automatic journals increases significantly.
- The number of people processing journals increases.
- Journals are posted outside of normal working hours.

The quality of the audit can be enhanced by the use of ADA. ADA enables the auditor to obtain a greater understanding of the entity and its environment. Professional scepticism and professional judgment are improved when the auditor has a better understanding.

6.5 OTHER TECHNIQUES

Although test data, audit software and data analytics are the principal methods used by the auditor, other techniques are becoming increasingly widely used which are more sophisticated. You need only have a general appreciation of these techniques; do not attempt to learn all the points of detail!

(a) **Integrated test facilities (ITF)**

Definition An **ITF** uses test data input as part of a normal run which is then applied to dummy records set up by the auditor on the client's master files.

The auditor can use ITF to carry out regular testing of the system e.g. at each month end without using a special test run and indeed without being present during processing.

ITF is used largely to test information processing controls.

(b) **Embedded audit facilities**

Definition This consists of a module of a computer program written by the auditor which is incorporated into the client's computer system either temporarily or permanently. This technique allows tests to be made at the time the data is being processed.

It is 'real time auditing'. It is useful where the audit trail is deficient so that historical audit work is difficult, or where files are constantly being updated e.g. in a real time or database system. The facilities may allow results to be printed immediately or to be written onto tape or disk for later evaluation by the auditor.

This technique may achieve the following objectives:

(i) To store information as it is processed for subsequent audit review.

(ii) To check the integrity of files which are being processed.

(iii) To identify and report items which are of some special audit interest, as previously defined by the auditor.

(c) **Systems software data analysis**

Most systems software provides facilities for logging information relating to computer activity. For example, details may be kept of invalid passwords used, attempts to gain unauthorised access to data, operator interventions or keying errors.

The data produced by this software may be analysed to provide evidence during the audit testing of general controls. It may be particularly useful in systems which allow easy access to data through terminals but which have sophisticated software available to protect such data.

(d) **Application program examination**

This involves detailed examination of the program instructions within the client's system.

It can be done manually but there are also some specially written computer programs which can be used to assist in this task.

The auditor may wish to check that a program is operating in the way that it should be. For example, the program code which performs a complex discount calculation may be examined to ensure that the discounts are properly computed. This would be done as part of the audit testing of the information processing controls.

Alternatively the auditors may examine programs as part of the testing of general controls. For example, in testing the controls that ensure that all program changes are adequately tested and documented, they may use software to compare two versions of the program in the production library before and after the changes and check them against the authorised program change documentation.

(e) **Parallel simulation**

This is a technique whereby the auditor writes a program which is intended to perform the same operation as a client's program.

Identical data is submitted to each program and the results are compared. Obviously they should be identical: if they are not then it means that one of the programs is not operating correctly.

(f) **Tracing**

Tracing involves following a transaction through its processing from start to finish to determine which program instructions are executed. This is a means of determining how the system operates.

Emerging technologies

Many firms are now using smartphone technology to increase audit efficiency e.g. apps which auditors can use to follow and record the results of inventory count procedures.

Several are using robotic process automation (e.g. to populate audit working papers from a set of underlying audit evidence) and predictive analysis (where the auditor forms an independent expectation of events, conditions or outcomes) to improve efficiency and audit quality.

The use of drones (to inspect and verify assets in inaccessible places), natural language processing (extracting and structuring information from source documents (largely unstructured text) into audit working papers for further analysis), process mining, and machine learning (identifying unusual patterns in populations of data) are in research or pilot stages by many firms. The use of drones specifically may be limited in future as laws and regulations surrounding the use of drones are developing rapidly, rules being tightened and some countries banning their use altogether.

6.6 THE ADVANTAGES OF AUTOMATED TOOLS AND TECHNIQUES TO THE AUDITOR

(a) In a computer-based system the large volume of transactions is likely to force the auditor to rely upon programmed controls. Automated tools and techniques are likely to be the only effective way of testing programmed controls which, of course, operate within the computer programs.

(b) The use of automated tools and techniques enable auditors to test a much larger number of items quickly and accurately.

(c) Automated tools and techniques enable auditors to test the accounting system and its records (i.e. the tapes and disk files) rather than relying upon testing printouts of what they believe to be a copy of those records.

(d) Once set up, automated tools and techniques are likely to be a cost effective way of obtaining audit evidence provided that the enterprise does not regularly change its systems.

(e) Careful planning by auditors should enable the results of their work using automated tools and techniques to be compared with results from the traditional clerical audit work to increase confidence.

6.7 THE DISADVANTAGES OF THE USE OF AUTOMATED TOOLS AND TECHNIQUES TO THE AUDITOR

(a) The use of automated tools and techniques may require extensive investment in to both software and training of staff.

(b) The use of automated tools and techniques often requires a computer specialist on the audit team.

(c) The use of automated tools and techniques once a year (in the form of test data) may not provide evidence that the system is functioning throughout the period of the audit.

(d) Test data may corrupt a client's system if the live system is used.

ACTIVITY 6

(a) What do the initials CAAT stand for?

(b) How is the use of automated tools and techniques advantageous to auditors?

(c) Describe two main types of automated tools and techniques used by the auditor.

For a suggested answer, see the 'Answers' section at the end of the book.

7 THE INTERNET

The increasing use of the internet within organisations has also had implications for the auditor both in the audit of clients and also for assisting with the audit work itself. The internet has provided the auditor with an extensive source of material and collective knowledge/experience which he can draw upon for use with his audit work. External databases exist which the auditor can use for planning and risk assessment, and provide the auditor with industry data for use with analytical review. It provides an excellent mechanism to the auditor for ensuring that their knowledge is up to date and gives them access to new techniques and methods.

The internet has significantly improved communications between the audit firm's head office and the audit staff for example with email facilities especially where the client is physically located some distance away from the audit head office. It has reduced the need for senior staff to keep travelling between locations to review work which can now be emailed between locations. It has also improved communications between auditors and their clients for example with videoconferencing and conference calling which saves time and therefore costs.

The auditor needs to be aware of control and security issues related to use of the internet, particularly with the ease with which computer viruses are transmitted between computers. Viruses can infect and destroy data; this makes back up procedures all the more important. The client should also have adequate virus protection in place, together with firewalls to prevent 'hacking' of data.

The rise in the number of people working from home, due to the Covid-19 pandemic, has increased the importance of using the internet, making the aforementioned points even more relevant in today's society.

8 APPENDIX: SOME CONTROL TERMINOLOGY EXPLAINED

Manual controls (i.e. controls which operate outside the computer system)

Physical controls

Many of the simpler controls are largely a matter of common sense. For example, the computer room should be kept locked when not in use, keys should only be provided to authorised personnel, and extreme variations in temperature and humidity should be avoided. In addition, fire precautions should be taken and contingency arrangements should be made to cater for emergencies such as system failure.

Back-up disks

The creation and updating of an identical back-up disk for every disk in the system (this means data files **and** program files) is a fundamental control in all systems. The back-up disks should be stored in an entirely separate place to where the main disks are kept. This covers not only local damage to one or a few disks, but also more drastic circumstances such as a fire in the computer room that destroys all the main disks kept there.

Having created a back-up copy of a disk, it is essential that it is updated every time any change is made to the main disk.

Data filing

Having established a set of source and back-up disks, the need for a filing system is obvious. Each disk should be labelled clearly, following a set pattern so that the data stored on it can be identified immediately making it less likely that a disk full of vital information will be over written in mistake for a blank disk. Printed labels are often used to enhance identification controls.

The labelled disks should be filed in special disk boxes to provide a degree of protection against liquid being spilt on the disks or their being bent or folded (all of which is likely to damage them and ruin the data that they contain) and then placed in a secure location.

The appointment of a disk librarian in larger computer systems is essential to control the filing and movement of disks.

Documentation

This is as vital as any of the other system controls shown above as it provides both a support system for work already stored on disk and filed, and a progress report on data currently being processed or updated. An automated chart is usually generated by the system to monitor the progress of data on, or being put onto disk – a hard copy may be printed daily; otherwise it will be utilised on an online basis. This should be maintained by the media librarian, or if one does not exist then someone who is sufficiently independent from the operations function and has a clear understanding of the processes involved. It will then be possible to see at a glance the stage reached by any items of data.

Each process should also be documented and a job sheet, clearly explaining the tasks that are to be done, should be completed (usually online) and passed to the person responsible for completing them.

A list of all the files on a disk and their contents, as well as the dates on which the files were originated and updated and the name of the persons responsible for this, can be recorded on an online information file.

Staff training

It is important that all staff involved are adequately trained so that they understand the system and the reasoning behind the controls to which they must adhere; they are then more likely to comply with them. They must be aware too of the need for careful handling of the disks themselves (e.g. a fingerprint on a floppy disk can spoil the data stored on it). They should also be made aware of the necessity for data management and version control, so the correct data is used at all times.

Proofing

Proofing is generally carried out by two persons keying the same data i.e. initial input then verification to ensure that the data has been correctly input.

Passwords

Passwords are commonly used to restrict access to data to authorised individuals only (for example, data concerning salaries on personnel files should not be widely available). They should be unique, known only to the individual and frequently changed.

Date/time stamps

Definition The user is asked to confirm the date and time when the relevant program is loaded; the date and time are then stamped on each file created or updated until the program is removed or the computer turned off. This feature is very useful, especially when comparing two versions of the same data, as it will show immediately which is the more recent.

Prompts

Definition The process which asks the user to confirm that the action selected was correct. For example, when requesting deletion of a file, a prompt will be issued to ask 'Are you sure?' This control also prevents two files being created with identical names.

Check digits

Definition A means of control which ascertains whether or not a number (for example, an International Standard Book Number) is valid.

A formula is used to calculate the digit which is attached to the end of the number itself. Modulus 11 is a common system and works as follows:

Number say,	32153
Multiply by weightings (see below)	65432
Results	18/10/4/15/6
Results total	53
Results total ÷ modulus	53 ÷ 11 = 4
Remainder	9
Modulus minus remainder	11 – 9 = 2
Check digit	2
Number now becomes	321532

The weightings to use are in ascending order starting on the right. The check digit will be assigned weighting 1 so start with weight 2 at the first stage above.

If there is no remainder the check digit is 0, if the remainder is 10 the check digit is shown as X.

The check digit is initially calculated by the computer and then becomes an integral part of the number. The example above could be a customer account number.

The computer will then detect if the number is ever input incorrectly e.g. a transposition error resulting in 231532. The computer performs the modulus 11 calculation on 23153 and gets a check digit of 11 – 8 = 3 (check it yourself to confirm this) instead of 2. An error message will then be sent to the operator.

Batch totals and hash totals

Definition   A **batch (or control) total** is the sum of one of the numerical fields on the documents in the batch e.g. total of the sales invoice values. This total is calculated manually and the documents are then input to the computer. The computer then calculates the batch total and this is compared with the manually calculated total. If they are different then an error has occurred. The input clerk is alerted to the error and can then investigate and correct it.

These controls are often used in batch processing systems whereby documents are grouped (batched) together and processed in a single block.

Definition   A **hash total** works in exactly the same way as a batch total but a different type of field is used. A typical hash total would be the total of customer account numbers: unlike the batch total the value of the hash total is meaningless but it is still useful for control purposes to detect errors on input or omissions.

Reasonableness checks

Definition   A check to ensure that the data input is reasonable given the type of input it is.

An example on a payroll system would be to check that hours recorded for the week fall within the range 30 to 50.

Existence checks

Definition   A check to ensure that the data input is valid by checking that the entity already exists on the system e.g. check to ensure that an employee number input already exists on the system.

Dependency checks

Definition   The comparison of data input fields with other fields for reasonableness e.g. check that the VAT (or other sales tax) amount input is in line with the net amount keyed.

CONCLUSION

Auditors now often use portable, laptop computers to assist in the management and performance of the audit and to complete the audit work. This has significantly improved the efficiency of the audit, and control of the audit process.

In addition, most clients maintain their accounting records on computer-based systems. It is important that appropriate general, and information processing controls are in operation over these systems – the controls should, as usual be tested and evaluated by the auditor.

In order to effectively audit the input, processing and output the auditors use automated tools and techniques of three main types – **audit software** to extract data from the client's computer files, **test data** to test of information processing controls, and **data analytics**.

The increasingly wide use of networked and standalone PC systems by clients may give the auditor additional problems to consider in the process of planning and performing the audit.

Finally, do bear in mind that this area (and this chapter) is of necessity rather detailed and technical – aim for a reasonable general understanding and appreciation of the approach to computer audits, rather than an in depth knowledge.

EXAM-STYLE QUESTION 1

ROTHWELL

On making arrangements to commence the final audit work at Rothwell, the company accountant informs you that the company has acquired a desktop computer for processing transactions and preparing financial statements. He had not seen fit to discuss the matter with you as the computer salesman had run a demonstration which seemed to show that the introduction of the system would cause very few problems. However, whilst you are carrying out your final audit tests, the company accountant informs you that he cannot access the computerised accounting data. The only response which he is able to receive from the computerised system is that 'the system is active'. You inform him that this means that the data disks have been corrupted either because of a malfunction in the software or because of a 'user error'.

You are required to:

(a) describe the audit implications of the introduction of the computer system in the period between the interim audit visit and the year-end date **(6 marks)**

(b) describe the controls which the company should have installed in order to ensure that this corruption of the data files did not cause a major accounting breakdown.
(9 marks)

(Total: 15 marks)

For a suggested answer, see the 'Answers' section at the end of the book.

FAU: FOUNDATIONS IN AUDIT

EXAM-STYLE QUESTION 2

ROTHWELL

On making arrangements to commence the final audit work at Rothwell, the company accountant informs you that the company has acquired a desktop computer for processing transactions and preparing financial statements. He had not seen fit to discuss the matter with you as the computer salesman had run a demonstration which seemed to show that the introduction of the system would cause very few problems. However, whilst you are carrying out your final audit tests, the company accountant informs you that he cannot access the computerised accounting data. The only response which he is able to receive from the computerised system is that 'the system is active'. You inform him that this means that the data disks have been corrupted either because of a malfunction in the software or because of a 'user error'.

You are required to:

Describe the audit implications in the year that the corruption of data files has taken place, assuming that the company has not maintained adequate safeguards over computer-generated data. **(Total: 10 marks)**

For a suggested answer, see the 'Answers' section at the end of the book.

EXAM-STYLE QUESTION 3

AUDITING IN A COMPUTER ENVIRONMENT

The following comments have been made in a discussion of auditing in a computer environment:

(i) Computer systems give rise to 'such possibilities as a lack of visible evidence and systematic errors'.

(ii) 'The nature of computer-based accounting systems is such that the auditor is afforded opportunities to use the enterprise's computer . . . to assist him in the performance of his audit work.'

(iii) 'In choosing the appropriate combination of computer assisted audit techniques and manual procedures, the auditor will need . . . to take (a number of factors) into account . . .'

(iv) 'In performing tests on information processing or general controls, the auditor should obtain evidence which is relevant to the control being tested.'

Required:

Explain each of the phrases 'lack of visible evidence' and 'systematic errors' referred to in (i) above and state in respect of each THREE ways in which the auditor might attempt to overcome the problems arising from these two possibilities. You should illustrate your answer by reference to an inventory control system. **(Total 10 marks)**

For a suggested answer, see the 'Answers' section at the end of the book.

EXAM-STYLE QUESTION 4

AUDITING IN A COMPUTER ENVIRONMENT

The following comments have been made in a discussion of auditing in a computer environment:

(i) Computer systems give rise to 'such possibilities as a lack of visible evidence and systematic errors'.

(ii) 'The nature of computer-based accounting systems is such that the auditor is afforded opportunities to use the enterprise's computer . . . to assist him in the performance of his audit work.'

(iii) 'In choosing the appropriate combination of computer assisted audit techniques and manual procedures, the auditor will need . . . to take (a number of factors) into account . . .'

(iv) 'In performing tests on information processing or general controls, the auditor should obtain evidence which is relevant to the control being tested.'

Required:

(a) Describe briefly TWO automated tools and techniques which the auditor can use in the enterprise's audit. (Refer to (ii) above.) **(4 marks)**

(b) State and explain FIVE factors which the auditor will need to take into account in choosing the appropriate combination of computer assisted audit techniques and manual procedures. (Refer to (iii) above.) **(5 marks)**

(c) Explain the words 'information processing control' and 'general control' in the computer audit context. Illustrate your answer by outlining one relevant audit test on:

  (i) an information processing control

  (ii) a general control.

(Refer to (iv) above.) **(6 marks)**

(Total: 15 marks)

For a suggested answer, see the 'Answers' section at the end of the book.

Chapter 15

THE FINAL REVIEW STAGE

INTRODUCTION

In following through the time structure of an audit, we have dealt with the appointment process, the audit planning, the audit work on accounting systems and the audit testing. We have also dealt with two specialist techniques which the auditor may need to use – sampling and computer auditing techniques.

Before the auditor's report can be signed, the audit work needs to be reviewed.

The purpose of the review is to check that sufficient work has been done, there are no major errors in the work and that the objectives have been achieved.

Standard auditing practice requires that auditors carry out a review of the audit before the auditor's report is issued – this review involves a number of elements and is the subject matter of this chapter.

This chapter covers syllabus areas C (4), E (1), E (2) and E (3).

CONTENTS

1   The overall review of the financial statements

2   Analytical procedures

3   The going concern review

4   Subsequent events

5   Written representations

6   Reports to management

FAU: FOUNDATIONS IN AUDIT

LEARNING OUTCOMES

At the end of this chapter, you should be able to:

- appreciate the role of the final audit review process
- apply appropriate analytical procedures at the audit review stage
- assess the going concern status of an enterprise
- understand the importance of auditing events taking place after the date of the statement of financial position
- understand the significance to the audit of written representations
- draft reports to management.

1 THE OVERALL REVIEW OF THE FINANCIAL STATEMENTS

1.1 INTRODUCTION

Once the auditors have completed the majority of the substantive procedures they should have a draft set of financial statements which are supported by sufficient, relevant and reliable audit evidence. The final audit review will then take place.

Auditors should carry out such a review of the financial statements as is sufficient, in conjunction with the conclusions drawn from the other audit evidence obtained, to give them a reasonable basis for their opinion on the financial statements.

Note that the review stage is seen as an integral part of the overall audit process.

The elements of this overall review process are explained more fully below.

1.2 ACCOUNTING POLICIES

The auditors should consider whether the information presented in the financial statements is in accordance with statutory requirements and that the accounting policies employed are in accordance with accounting standards, properly disclosed, consistently applied and appropriate to the entity.

The auditor should take a number of factors into consideration when reviewing the accounting policies adopted by the client, as follows:

- whether similar policies are used by other companies in the same industry
- whether the policies used are widely recognised as acceptable
- whether any departures are necessary to give a true and fair view
- whether the financial statements reflect the true substance of the transactions.

If the company has used policies inconsistent with accounting standards then, in a note to the financial statements, the company is required to give details of the departure, reasons for it and the financial effect(s).

1.3 CONSISTENCY OF THE FINANCIAL STATEMENTS

In addition, auditors should consider whether the financial statements as a whole and the assertions contained therein are consistent with their knowledge of the entity's business and with the results of other audit procedures, and the manner of disclosure is fair.

The auditors should therefore conduct a detailed review of the financial statements to ensure that:

(a) the individual amounts are consistent with each other and with comparative figures

(b) the amounts appearing in the financial statements are consistent with internal data such as management accounts, budget statements or forecasts.

1.4 PRESENTATION AND DISCLOSURE

The auditor should ensure that information in the financial statements is properly presented and disclosed in accordance with company law requirements and relevant accounting standards.

It is important that you appreciate that the presentation of numerical and other information can affect the true and fair view as much as the information itself.

2 ANALYTICAL PROCEDURES

2.1 SUMMARY

ISA 520 *Analytical Procedures* requires that analytical review procedures must be used at both the planning and at the final review stages of the audit. In addition to using analytical review at the planning and final review stages, the auditor typically makes use of such procedures as part of substantive testing during the audit.

When completing the audit, auditors should apply analytical procedures in forming an overall conclusion as to whether the financial statements as a whole are consistent with their knowledge and understanding of the entity's business.

If necessary, you should refer back to chapter 5 of this publication to remind yourself of the definition, purpose of methods of performing analytical review procedures.

2.2 ANALYTICAL PROCEDURES AT THE FINAL REVIEW STAGE

At this stage, the focus will be upon ensuring that all work required was satisfactorily performed, reviewed and concluded upon. Examples of issues that will be included within analytical review work at this stage will include:

- was the audit plan followed, completed and documented?

- have any problems encountered during the audit been satisfactorily documented and concluded upon in the working papers?

- do the financial statements comply with the relevant reporting framework of law, reporting standards and other relevant regulation?

- have other final review requirements been completed, such as review of going concern and subsequent events?

- does the audit evidence collected support the auditor's report opinion?

3 THE GOING CONCERN REVIEW

3.1 THE GOING CONCERN BASIS OF ACCOUNTING

The going concern concept is defined as the assumption that the enterprise will continue in operational existence for the foreseeable future. This means in particular that the statements of financial position and comprehensive income assume no intention or necessity to liquidate or curtail significantly the scale of operations.

Note that financial statements can be assumed by the reader to be prepared under this assumption unless there is a clear statement in the financial statements to the contrary.

If financial statements are prepared on a going concern basis and this is inappropriate, it is almost certain that those statements will not present a true and fair view, as on a going concern basis, non-current assets are normally shown at cost less depreciation. If the enterprise is not a going concern, non-current assets should be valued at realisable value – the differences could be massive!

It is therefore a fundamental stage in every audit for the auditor to review the going concern status of the enterprise. Clearly, a going concern review inevitably involves an assessment of the future. Any consideration involving the foreseeable future involves making a judgement about future events which are inherently uncertain. Uncertainty increases with time and the judgement can only be made on the basis of information available at the time. Subsequent events can overturn that judgement.

The auditors should generally look ahead at least one year from the date of the directors' approval of the accounts, in assessing the validity of the going concern basis, but there may be circumstances in which it is appropriate to look further ahead. This depends on the nature of the business and the associated risks.

The auditors will need to satisfy themselves that the going concern assumption is reasonable.

Auditors should not assume that the going concern concept will continue to apply but need to conduct a specific examination of the relevant factors to reach a decision. This will involve an overall review of financial factors, preferably before the client's year end, in order to establish whether there are factors which cast doubt on the going concern basis. If there are, further investigation is required.

3.2 ISA 570 GOING CONCERN

The fundamental principle within the standard states:

'When performing risk assessment procedures, the auditor shall consider whether events or conditions exist that may cast significant doubt on the entity's ability to continue as a going concern.'

ISA 570 emphasises the point made in IAS 1 that it is management's responsibility to assess the validity of the going concern status of the entity. The auditor then evaluates management's assessment as explained below.

Auditors should consider the entity's ability to continue as a going concern and any relevant disclosures in the financial statements. They should also assess the adequacy of the means by which *directors* have satisfied themselves that:

(a) the going concern basis of accounting is appropriate

(b) the financial statements contain appropriate disclosures, if any.

Auditors should make 'enquiries' of directors and should plan and perform procedures designed to identify matters which could indicate concern about the entity's ability to continue as a going concern.

The volume of work that is required depends on the auditors' knowledge of the business and its size. Many of the matters referred to below will be inappropriate to a small business for example.

Auditors should consider:

(a) Whether the period the directors have considered in coming to a conclusion on the going concern status is appropriate.

(b) Any systems that exist to provide timely warnings of future risks (for example, management information systems).

(c) Budget and forecast information and the procedures for keeping this up to date, and the sensitivity of that information to factors which the directors may not be able to control, such as inflation and exchange rates.

(d) Whether any obligations or guarantees have been given to other organisations which could cause the collapse of the client being audited (for example, companies in a group often cross guarantee each other's bank commitment. If one of those companies becomes insolvent it can cause the collapse of other group companies).

(e) The existence, adequacy and terms of borrowing facilities and the directors' plans to deal with matters giving rise to concern.

These matters are examined in more detail below.

3.3 INDICATORS OF GOING CONCERN PROBLEMS

There are a number of both financial and non-financial indicators which assist the directors and the auditor to assess the going concern status of an enterprise. The major factors are listed below:

Financial:

(a) liabilities are greater than assets in total or based on current items

(b) necessary borrowing facilities have not been agreed

(c) defaults on loans, breach of loan covenants

(d) significant liquidity or cash flow problems

(e) substantial sales of non-current assets which are not to be replaced

(f) major restructuring of debt

(g) denial of trade credit by suppliers

(h) inability to pay debts as they fall due.

Non-financial:

(a) changes in the market or technology to which the entity is unable to adapt

(b) reductions in operations through legislation

(c) loss of key management or staff, labour difficulties or excessive dependence on a few product lines where the market is depressed

(d) loss of key suppliers or customers or obsolescence of a product

(e) major litigation.

3.4 AUDIT PROCEDURES ON GOING CONCERN

(a) **Cash flow forecasts**

Cash flow forecasts should normally be prepared by management as a matter of course. In situations where there is doubt about the applicability of the going concern basis of accounting, and such forecasts are not prepared, the auditors should request that they be prepared.

Where a cash forecast is prepared, the auditors will review it critically, and consider whether the cash requirements indicated will in fact be available.

(b) **Availability of financial support**

Where the cash forecasts indicate borrowing requirements beyond those currently available, the auditors will need to satisfy themselves that such funds will be available. Assurances that such funds will be available should be in writing and if they are not, because negotiations with the bank are continuing, a modified auditor's report may arise.

The auditor will also need to consider:

(i) the company's ability to maintain its financial viability

(ii) limits on the company's borrowing powers imposed by trust deeds, Articles of Association, and so on.

(c) **Evidence from directors**

Auditors should consider the need to obtain *written* representations from directors with regard to the appropriateness of the going concern basis of accounting and the adequacy of disclosures (representation letters are dealt with later in this chapter).

These may be necessary where there is concern over the applicability of the going concern basis of accounting and the directors' representations should be consistent with the auditor's other evidence obtained.

3.5 REPORTING IMPLICATIONS OF GOING CONCERN

Note that audit modifications are examined in more detail in a later chapter. This section is designed to give a brief introduction to this matter in the context of the going concern concept.

When reporting on the financial statements the auditors give their opinion as to whether or not the financial statements give a true and fair view. The process followed by the auditors in arriving at their opinion is dealt with in a later chapter. It is important that the users have a clear understanding of the status of the company. Where the auditors are 'significantly concerned' about the client's ability to continue as a going concern but they do not disagree with the preparation of the financial statements on a going concern basis they should consider whether the disclosures are satisfactory. If they are satisfied with the extent of information provided they should refer to those in the auditor's report. This is known as a **'significant uncertainty'**; it does not constitute an audit qualification.

If the auditors consider that the disclosures are inadequate then they should modify the report using a **'qualified'** or an **'adverse'** opinion.

If the client has prepared the financial statements on a going concern basis, and the auditor disagrees with this then he should modify using an **'adverse'** opinion.

We will consider the different auditor's reports in the next chapter.

ACTIVITY 1

You have just completed the audit of a client who is experiencing financial problems. The accounts have been prepared on a going concern basis, but there is a significant level of concern as to whether they will continue as a going concern.

Required:

State what information you could expect to be presented in the financial statements in order for such disclosures to be considered adequate for reporting purposes.

For a suggested answer, see the 'Answers' section at the end of the book.

4 SUBSEQUENT EVENTS

4.1 INTRODUCTION

Definition   **Subsequent events** are events occurring and facts discovered between the period end and the laying of financial statements before members.

From a financial accounting point of view IAS 10 *Events after the Reporting Date* identifies two types of events which are 'adjusting events' and 'non-adjusting events'.

(a) **Adjusting events** are those events after the reporting period that provide additional evidence relating to conditions existing at the reporting date. Such events require adjustments in the financial statements. Examples include:

    (i) Where a receivable existed at the year end, which became evident after the year end that it would not be paid.

    (ii) Amounts received or receivable in respect of insurance claims which were being negotiated at the reporting date.

(iii) The determination of the purchase or sale price of non-current assets purchased or sold before the year end.

(b) **'Non-adjusting events'** are those events after the reporting period that concern conditions which did not exist at the reporting date but which may be of such materiality that their *disclosure* is required to ensure that the financial statements are not misleading.

Examples of non-adjusting events include:

(i) the issue of new share or loan capital

(ii) major changes in the composition of the group (for example, mergers, acquisitions or reconstructions)

(iii) financial consequences of losses of non-current assets or inventory as a result of fires or floods

(iv) major changes in the nature of the business

(v) strikes, government action such as nationalisation, and declines in the value of non-current assets or non-current asset investments.

4.2 ACCOUNTING AND DISCLOSURE (IAS 10)

(a) A material event after the reporting period requires *recording* (in the financial statements themselves) where:

(i) it is an adjusting event, or

(ii) it indicates that application of the going concern concept to the company is not appropriate.

(b) A material event after the reporting period should be *disclosed* (in notes to the financial statements) where it is a non-adjusting event of such materiality that its non-disclosure would affect the ability of the users of financial statements to reach a proper understanding of the financial position.

(c) In respect of each event after the reporting date which is required to be disclosed the following information should be stated by way of notes in financial statements:

(i) the nature of the event, and

(ii) an estimate of the financial effect, or a statement that it is not practicable to make such an estimate.

4.3 AUDIT GUIDANCE

ISA 560 *Subsequent Events* provides the auditor with guidance in this area and states that auditors should consider the effect of subsequent events on the financial statements and on their report.

The ISA considers three categories of subsequent events:

(a) between the period end and the date of the auditors' report

(b) between the date of the auditors' report and the issue of the financial statements

(c) after the financial statements have been issued, but before they are presented to the members.

4.4 AUDIT PROCEDURES UP TO THE DATE OF THE AUDITOR'S REPORT

Auditors should perform procedures to identify subsequent events that might require adjustment or disclosure, **up to the date of their auditor's report**. Auditors have an active duty to identify subsequent events up to the date the auditor's report is signed.

Procedures include:

(a) enquiring into management procedures for the identification of subsequent events

(b) reading minutes of members' and directors' meetings and of audit and executive committee meetings, and enquiring about matters not yet minuted

(c) reviewing accounting records including budgets, forecasts and interim information

(d) making enquiries of directors

(e) normal work after the reporting date performed in order to verify year end balances

(f) obtaining written representations. This will be dealt with later in this chapter.

4.5 PROCEDURES AFTER THE DATE OF THE AUDITOR'S REPORT

The auditors do not have a duty to search for evidence of events occurring after the date of the auditor's report but before the date of the general meeting at which the accounts are presented to members, **but they should not ignore any knowledge which they acquire, from whatever source**. If they feel that the information would have altered their audit opinion, had they been aware of it prior to the date of their report, then they should discuss the matter with the directors.

Directors should be requested to amend financial statements where required if they have not yet been sent to members and auditors should issue a new auditor's report on the new financial statements.

If financial statements have already been sent to members, directors may be permitted in certain circumstances to revise the accounts. In such circumstances, auditors are required to issue a new auditor's report and also to report on whether the financial statements have been revised correctly in accordance with the legislation.

Whenever a new auditor's report is issued, the auditors should extend their review of subsequent events up to the date of the new report.

Where directors refuse to amend financial statements where auditors consider this to be necessary, auditors should consider speaking at the relevant Annual General Meeting, taking legal advice and consider the possibility of withdrawing their auditor's report. The last option is rarely used in practice.

The auditors have *no* duty to consider the effect of events occurring *after* the general meeting, but they should inform the directors of any event materially affecting the financial statements. They may also wish to consider taking legal advice on their own position.

ACTIVITY 2

You are auditing the financial statements of Hope Engineering Ltd for the year ended 31 March 20X3. The partner in charge of the audit instructs you to carry out a review of the company's activities since the financial year end. Mr Smith, the managing director of Hope Engineering Ltd overhears the conversation with the partner and is surprised that you are examining accounting information which relates to the next accounting period.

Mr Smith had been appointed on 1 March 20X3 as a result of which the contract of the previous managing director, Mr Jones, was terminated. Compensation of $50,000 had been paid to Mr Jones on 2 March 20X3.

As a result of your investigations you find that the company is going to bring an action against Mr Jones for the recovery of the compensation paid to him, as it had come to light that two months prior to his dismissal, he had contractually agreed to join the board of directors of a rival company. The company's solicitor has informed Hope Engineering Ltd that Mr Jones' actions constituted a breach of his contract with them, and that an action could be brought against the former managing director for the recovery of the moneys paid to him.

Required:

(a) Explain the nature and purpose of a review of subsequent events.

(b) List the audit procedures which would be carried out in order to identify any material events after the reporting period.

(c) Discuss the audit implications of the company's decision to sue Mr Jones for the recovery of the compensation paid to him.

For a suggested answer, see the 'Answers' section at the end of the book.

5 WRITTEN REPRESENTATIONS

5.1 INTRODUCTION

Definition   **Written representations** are statements made to the auditor during the course of the audit which provide audit evidence in respect of specific (or general) matters.

You will recall that one of the audit testing procedures used to generate evidence on the financial statement assertions is enquiry – the process of seeking information from management on matters relevant to the audit.

Initially, this information may be provided by management in verbal form but as this may be an important part of audit evidence in the audit of companies of all sizes such information should be documented and confirmed as accurate by management.

This is reinforced in ISA 580 *Written Representations* which starts by saying that auditors should obtain written confirmation of appropriate representations from management before their report is issued.

Representations are required:

(a) to ensure directors acknowledge their collective responsibility for the preparation of financial statements and to confirm that they agree with what they have stated (it ensures that confusion and disagreement is avoided)

(b) to confirm matters material to the financial statements where the representations are critical.

Of course, where possible, auditors should always try to obtain written external evidence, this being the most reliable form of evidence. However, there will be circumstances where evidence from external sources is not available or is inadequate for audit purposes. In these situations, the auditor will seek written representations from the directors.

Critical representations will typically relate to those matters where knowledge of the facts is confined to management (e.g. management's intention to dispose of a business segment), and those where the matter is principally one of judgement and opinion (e.g. with respect to litigation in progress or on the trading position of a particular customer, or on the appropriateness of a change in accounting policy).

Representations are *not* a substitute for other evidence that should be available and auditors should ensure that representations are reasonable and consistent with the auditor's knowledge of the business. Any contradiction of other audit evidence should be thoroughly investigated.

5.2 THE WRITTEN REPRESENTATIONS LETTER

The usual means of the auditor obtaining appropriate representations from management is in the form of a **representations letter**. This is typically a letter signed by the directors, addressed to the auditor which gives written assurance on a number of matters of significance to the audit. The letter will be drafted by the auditors and presented to the directors for signature.

(a) **Arrangements for signing letter**

Written representations should be signed by persons with an appropriate level of authority – normally by one or more of the executive directors (for example, by the chief executive and the financial director), on behalf of the whole board. The persons signing the letter should ensure that they fully understand the nature of the matter(s) contained in the letter. Matters contained in the letter would have been discussed in detail with the directors, prior to the letter being prepared.

(b) **Actions if management refuse to sign letter**

If management disagrees with the auditor's statement of representations, discussions should be held to clarify the matters in doubt and, if necessary, a revised statement prepared and agreed. Should management fail to reply, the auditors should follow the matter up to try to ensure that their understanding of the position, as set out in their statement, is correct.

If management refuses to provide written confirmation of a representation that the auditors consider necessary, the auditors should consider the implications for their report.

(c) Modification of the auditor's report

There may be circumstances where the auditors are unable to obtain the written representations which they require. This may be because of a refusal by management to cooperate, or because management declines to give the written representations required on the grounds of their own uncertainty regarding the particular matter. In either case if the auditors are unable to satisfy themselves, they may have to conclude that they have not received all the information and explanations that they require, and consequently may need to consider modifying their auditor's report.

(d) Dating of the written representations

The formal record of representations by management should be dated on the same day that financial statements are approved by the directors. It should never be dated after the auditor's report since it is part of the evidence on which the auditor's opinion is based.

(e) Contents and wording

The precise scope of the formal record of representations should be appropriate to the circumstances of each particular audit. The representations will be necessary where there are matters which are material to the financial statements, in respect of which the auditor cannot obtain independent corroborative evidence and could not reasonably expect it to be available, as indicated above.

Example of written representations

Set out below is an example of written representations which relates to matters which are material to financial statements, and to circumstances where the auditor cannot obtain independent corroborative evidence and could not reasonably expect it to be available. It is not intended to be a standard letter because representations by management can be expected to vary not only from one enterprise to another, but also from one year to another in the case of the same audit client. This example is based on one provided in an appendix to the ISA.

In reviewing this letter, remember that it is drafted by the auditors (they know the areas on which they need representations), addressed to the auditors, signed by the Board of directors or individual directors acting on behalf of the Board. You will note that point (a) below reinforces the directors' responsibilities in connection with the financial statements. The other points are gaining written assurances from management on key judgmental areas of the audit.

> Dear Sirs,
>
> We confirm to the best of our knowledge and belief, and having made appropriate enquiries of other directors and officials of the company, the following representations given to you in connection with your audit of the company's financial statements for the year ended 31 December . . .
>
> (a) We acknowledge as directors our responsibility for the financial statements, which you have prepared for the company. All the accounting records have been made available to you for the purpose of your audit and all the transactions undertaken by the company have been properly reflected and recorded in the accounting records. All other records and related information, including minutes of all management and shareholders' meetings, have been made available to you.
>
> (b) The legal claim by Mr G H . . . . . has been settled out of court by the company paying him $38,000. No further amounts are expected to be paid, and no similar claims by employees or former employees have been received or are expected to be received.
>
> (c) We have no plans or intentions that may materially alter the carrying value of assets and liabilities reflected in the financial statements.
>
> (d) The company has had at no time during the year any arrangement, transaction or agreement to provide credit facilities (including loans, quasi-loans or credit transactions) for directors nor to guarantee or provide security for such matters.
>
> (e) There have been no events since the reporting date which necessitate revision of the figures included in the financial statements or inclusion of a note thereto.
>
> As minuted by the board of directors at its meeting on . . . . (date)
>
> . . . . (Chairman)   . . . . Secretary)

ACTIVITY 3

Explain why it is important for the auditors to discuss the contents of the written representations with management at an early stage of the audit.

For a suggested answer, see the 'Answers' section at the end of the book.

6 REPORTS TO MANAGEMENT

6.1 THE REPORT TO MANAGEMENT

Definition   The **report to management** is the means by which the auditor communicates to management any deficiencies discovered in the system of internal control, and is usually sent at the end of both the interim and final audits.

During the course of the audit work, the auditor may well identify matters which indicate that the company's control systems are deficient in one or more areas, or that controls are not operating or that inappropriate accounting policies or methods are being applied by the company. These are matters which may not be material such that they affect the audit opinion but should be addressed.

It is seen to be an appropriate aspect of client service that matters of this type are formally brought to the attention of management by the auditor. This is usually done in the form of a **report to management**.

The report to management is sometimes called the letter of weakness, the internal control memorandum, the letter of recommendations, the management letter or the constructive service letter. Reporting such matters is a requirement of ISA 265 *Communicating Deficiencies in Internal Controls to Those Charged with Governance and Management*.

6.2 THE CONTENTS OF THE REPORT TO MANAGEMENT

The report to management covers three main areas:

(a) Significant deficiencies in the design and the operation of the accounting and internal control system together with constructive recommendations for improvement.

The deficiencies will be identified by examining, recording and testing the controls in the accounting systems. Where the auditors report these deficiencies they will usually explain why these should be prevented (i.e. stating the effect or implication of the deficiency) and provide recommendations to ensure that such deficiencies are prevented in future.

Definition A **deficiency in internal control** exists when:

(i) a control is designed, implemented or operated in such a way that it is unable to prevent, or detect and correct misstatements in the financial statements on a timely basis; or

(ii) a control necessary to prevent, or detect and correct misstatements in the financial statements on a timely basis is missing.

Definition The **significant deficiency in internal control** is a deficiency or combination of deficiencies in internal control that, in the auditor's professional judgement, is of sufficient importance to merit the attention of those charged with governance.

(b) Other constructive business advice on economies and efficiencies which may be available in running the business.

(c) Comments on accounting policies and unadjusted errors in the financial statements.

6.3 OTHER POINTS

To be effective, the letter should be drafted as soon as possible after completion of the audit procedures giving rise to the need to comment.

Prior to issuing the letter the auditor should discuss all the points with management to ensure their complete accuracy and to avoid any misunderstandings. It also enables discussion of the recommendations or alternative solutions in further detail.

The auditor should request a formal response to the report to management by a specified date stating what action management propose to take or have already taken. The auditor should consider the previous year's report to management, the responses and actions taken at the planning stage of the subsequent audit. The importance with which management treat the document will also assist the auditor in evaluating inherent risk of the organisation i.e. are management control conscious?

ISA 260 *Communication with Those Charged with Governance* also requires that auditors communicate the following matters on a timely basis:

- the auditor's responsibilities in relation to the financial statements audit

- the planned scope and timing of the audit

- significant findings from the audit; and

- matters affecting auditor independence.

6.4 THIRD PARTIES INTERESTED IN REPORTS TO MANAGEMENT

The auditors should treat any report issued to management as confidential; they should not disclose any of its contents without the consent of management.

Once the report has been issued the auditor has little control over what happens to it and management may provide third parties with a copy e.g. their bank.

The auditor can use a disclaimer of liability against unforeseen liability to third parties, but this may not give full protection from liability where the auditor knows or ought to know that a report to management may be passed to a third party who would rely on it.

6.5 EXAMPLE OF A REPORT TO MANAGEMENT

An example of a typical letter is shown below; there is no prescribed format. There are other acceptable layouts which you may have seen in practice; columnar formats with the headings ' deficiency', 'implication' and 'recommendation' are common. Again it is not necessary to learn this example, as the points would not be appropriate for all enterprises. Note however the type of points made, and the disclaimer used at the beginning of the letter.

PRIVATE AND CONFIDENTIAL

The Directors
Upper Crust Inc
Lower Court
Little Town

15 May 20X3

Dear Sirs

Upper Crust Inc
Audit for the year ended 31 December 20X2

In accordance with our normal practice, we are writing to you with regard to matters arising out of our audit for the year ended 31 December 20X3 which we consider should be brought to your attention.

Our responsibilities as auditors are governed by company law and principally require us to report on the accounts laid before the company in general meeting.

This report has been prepared for the sole use of the directors of Upper Crust Inc. None of its contents may be disclosed to third parties without our written consent. Bloggs & Co assumes no liability to any other persons.

The matters detailed in this report reflect matters coming to our attention during the course of our audit. They are not intended to be a comprehensive statement of all deficiencies that may exist or of all improvements that could be made. We set out below those matters which we consider to be of fundamental importance. Other matters of lesser significance, but which nevertheless require your attention, are dealt with in note form in the attached Appendix.

(a) **Management reporting**

A fundamental requirement to allow proper control over your business is the regular and timely preparation of accurate management accounts. Preferably these should be prepared monthly, compared with budgets and submitted for formal consideration and adoption by the full board of directors. At the moment no such system exists.

(b) **Internal control – accounting system**

(i) The company exercises no control over the input, processing or output of information processed by the computer bureau. Reliance is placed on the computer bureau to ensure complete and accurate processing of accounting information. In our opinion the directors should ensure that the company effects proper control over the completeness and accuracy of information processed.

(ii) There are other areas covering aspects of inventory, non-current assets and receivables where control is lacking or inadequate which are dealt with in the Appendix attached.

(iii) Our audit work was made considerably more difficult by the absence of care in filing supporting documentation which was therefore difficult to trace. The proper maintenance of records is not only a requirement of company law but is also necessary for the efficient running of your business.

(c) **Preparation of accounts**

The quality of the draft statutory accounts submitted to us for audit was poor.

(i) The accounts were produced late without proper support. When support was provided in some cases it failed to agree with the amounts stated in the draft accounts.

(ii) A number of items required to be disclosed were omitted. Extensive discussions were necessary with you to ascertain the information to be disclosed in respect of directors' interests and capital expenditure.

To reduce the time spent on the audit, and thus the cost to you, all supporting documentation should agree with the accounts and statutory disclosure information should be assembled prior to our examination.

We would be pleased to discuss these points with you at your convenience.

Yours faithfully

Bloggs & Co

Appendix
Upper Crust Inc – year ended 31 December 20X2

(a) **Computer processing**

Deficiency:

Lack of control exercised over computer processing.

Implications:

The completeness, accuracy and validity of the accounting records may be undermined.

Recommendations:

(i) Authorisation of input especially journals not arising from books of prime entry.

(ii) Batch controls using registers over all input in terms of value and number of documents/transactions processed.

(iii) Use of hash totals.

(iv) Management control over master file amendments.

(v) Reconciliation to control accounts.

(vi) Clear audit trail for the correction and resubmission of any rejected transactions.

(vii) All financial information processed at one location.

(viii) A back-up system should be available if the bureau is unable to process the input.

(b) **Payroll**

Deficiency:

No evidence of approval.

Implications:

Unauthorised changes may occur.

Recommendations:

Management should evidence their approval of the payroll, changes in rates of pay and the employment of new staff.

(c) **Inventory**

Deficiency:

Lack of physical and financial control over inventory.

Cut-off errors were discovered for widgets despatched prior to the year end but uninvoiced.

Overhead allocation in valuation of widgets lacked support.

Implications:

Inventory could be misappropriated.

The year-end inventory figure could be misstated.

FAU: FOUNDATIONS IN AUDIT

Recommendations:

(i) A simple system of perpetual inventory should be implemented at each location. This should be used to check for the despatch and receipt of inventory and would provide good overall control to enable a comparison of:

- expected use to actual by comparison with orders, and
- book inventory to actual after regular inventory checks.

(ii) Improvements should be made to the system of control to facilitate a review of the despatches at the year end to ensure that a proper cut-off is achieved.

(iii) The valuation of widgets depends on the estimated throughput during the year. It is important that the number of widgets produced is properly recorded and that consideration is given to normal production levels to allow compliance with IAS 2.

(d) **Non-current assets**

Deficiency:

Lack of physical control.

Lack of clear capitalisation policy.

Assets with nil net book value were subject to a depreciation charge.

Implications:

Portable assets could be misappropriated.

Items could be incorrectly capitalised.

The depreciation figures in the accounts could be overstated.

Recommendations:

(i) A register should be introduced to record all assets at cost together with associated depreciation.

(ii) In previous years capital additions, notably the improvements to the leasehold premises, have been written off. Also, assets scrapped have not been written off. The effects of these cancel out and therefore we have not proposed an adjustment to opening figures. A capitalisation policy should be laid down and adhered to.

(iii) A register would enable the identification of fully depreciated assets and allow them to be excluded from the depreciation calculations.

(e) **Purchases payments**

Deficiency:

Lack of proper allocation of costs.

Lack of supporting documents.

Lack of control over cheque books.

Unauthorised charges.

Poor control over unrecorded liabilities.

Implications:

Purchases in the accounts may be misstated.

Payables may be understated if unrecorded liabilities are not controlled.

Recommendations:

(i) All charges incurred should be allocated to the relevant cost centre to promote accountability of these centres.

(ii) Proper supporting documents for all payments must be retained and properly filed for easy retrieval.

(iii) Control over payments would be improved if only one cheque book was in use at any one time.

(iv) Documents supporting charges should be authorised by an appropriate level of management.

(v) A purchase day book should be introduced. Payments should be marked off. This would provide control over unpaid invoices and a means for regular control account reconciliation.

ACTIVITY 4

Explain why the auditors provide the client with a report to management.

For a suggested answer, see the 'Answers' section at the end of the book.

FAU: FOUNDATIONS IN AUDIT

CONCLUSION

The audit review stage is an important step in the audit process. The auditor has an opportunity to make an overall examination of the financial statements, before finally coming to a decision on the appropriate form of the auditor's report. Two elements included at the overall review stage are the review of subsequent events and going concern. You should note that these are linked – in assessing the going concern status of the enterprise, the audit will need to consider events which take place after the reporting period.

Written representations by the directors are a key document providing evidence from the directors of issues where the auditor is unable to obtain independent, external, third party evidence. He should always seek to obtain corroboratory evidence of such issues and consider the consistency of information related to such points.

The report to management produced by the auditor is an internal document detailing control deficiencies; it is not generally a statutory requirement but is considered to be part of the service provided to management.

KEY TERMS

Analytical procedures – The analysis of relationships:

(a) between items of financial data and non-financial data deriving from the same period

(b) between comparable financial information deriving from different periods or different entities.

in order to identify consistencies, predicted patterns or significant fluctuations, unexpected relationships, and the results of investigations thereof.

The going concern concept – The assumption that the enterprise will continue in operational existence for the foreseeable future. This means in particular that the statements of financial position and comprehensive income assume no intention or necessity to liquidate or curtail significantly the scale of operations.

Subsequent events – Events occurring and facts discovered between the period end and the laying of financial statements before members.

Adjusting events after the reporting period – Events providing additional evidence relating to conditions existing at the reporting date.

Non-adjusting events after the reporting period – Events concerning conditions which did not exist at the reporting date but which may be of such materiality that their disclosure is required to ensure that the financial statements are not misleading.

Written representations – Statements made to the auditor during the course of the audit which provide audit evidence in respect of specific (or general) matters.

Report to Management – The means by which the auditor communicates to management any deficiencies discovered in the system of internal control or the use of inappropriate accounting policies or procedures.

SELF TEST QUESTIONS

Paragraph

1	What procedures should the auditor follow in carrying out an overall review of the financial statements?	1.1, 1.2, 1.3, 1.4
2	What does the term 'analytical procedures' encompass?	2.1
3	What are the issues covered during analytical review procedures at the final review stage?	2.2
4	What is the definition of the going concern concept?	3.1
5	What is a non-adjusting event?	4.1
6	What is meant by written representations?	5.1
7	What are the three main areas covered by the report to management?	6.2

FAU: FOUNDATIONS IN AUDIT

PRACTICE QUESTION

BIRCHINLESS

You are engaged in the final examination of the financial statements of Birchinless for the year to 30 June 20X7, a company engaged in the purchase and resale of earthenware and crockery products. You are aware that the company has increased its trading activity substantially during the year, that it has plans for future expansion and that it intends to request a considerable extension in overdraft facilities with its bank following issue of the audited financial statements.

Summarised draft financial statements for the year to 30 June 20X7, together with comparative figures are set out below.

Income Statement

	20X7 £	20X7 £	20X6 £	20X6 £
Turnover		24,000,000		13,875,000
Cost of sales		(14,500,000)		(9,712,500)
Gross profit		9,500,000		4,162,500
Distribution costs	(3,280,000)		(1,110,000)	
Administrative expenses	(1,300,000)		(1,200,000)	
Loss on disposal of Non-current assets	(2,000,000)		(200,000)	
Interest payable	(80,000)		–	
Income from trade investments	50,000		75,000	
		(6,610,000)		(2,435,000)
Profit before taxation		2,890,000		1,727,500
Taxation		(300,000)		(900,000)
Profit after taxation		2,590,000		827,500
Dividends proposed		(150,000)		(150,000)
Profit retained		2,440,000		677,500
Profit brought forward		5,720,000		5,042,500
		8,160,000		5,720,000

	£	£
Depreciation has been included in the above headings as follows:		
Cost of sales	180,000	140,000
Distribution costs	60,000	50,000
Administrative expenses	60,000	50,000
	300,000	240,000

Statement of financial position

	20X7			20X6		
	Cost £	Dep'n £	Balance £	Cost £	Dep'n £	Balance £
Non-current assets:						
Tangible assets	4,300,000	530,000	3,770,000	5,000,000	1,330,000	3,670,000
Trade investments			2,600,000			2,600,000
			6,370,000			6,270,000
Current assets:						
Inventory		4,500,000			1,500,000	
Trade receivables		3,900,000			1,700,000	
Bank		–			400,000	
		8,400,000			3,600,000	
Current liabilities:						
Trade payables	(3,500,000)			(1,100,000)		
Taxation	(300,000)			(900,000)		
Dividends	(150,000)			(150,000)		
Bank overdraft	(660,000)			–		
		(4,610,000)			(2,150,000)	
Net current assets			3,790,000			1,450,000
Net assets employed			10,160,000			7,720,000
Financed by:						
Share capital			2,000,000			2,000,000
Income statement			8,160,000			5,720,000
			10,160,000			7,720,000

Required:

(a) Following careful review of the financial statements:

    (i) state FOUR matters you would wish, as auditor, to raise with management

    (4 marks)

    (ii) briefly discuss why you would raise each matter   **(6 marks)**

    (iii) in respect of each matter give TWO questions you would put to management during your audit.   **(10 marks)**

(b) Using your review of the financial statements of Birchinless as an example, explain why an analytical review of the final financial statements is a necessary part of the auditor's work.   **(5 marks)**

(Total: 25 marks)

For a suggested answer, see the 'Answers' section at the end of the book.

FAU: FOUNDATIONS IN AUDIT

EXAM-STYLE QUESTION 1

REPRESENTATIONS

Written representations are an important source of audit evidence. These representations may be oral or written, and may be obtained either on an informal or formal basis. The auditor will include information obtained in this manner in his audit working papers where it forms part of his total audit evidence.

Required:

(a) Explain the nature and role of written representations. **(9 marks)**

(b) Explain why it is important for the auditor to discuss the contents of the written representations at an early stage of the audit. **(6 marks)**

(Total: 15 marks)

For a suggested answer, see the 'Answers' section at the end of the book.

EXAM-STYLE QUESTION 2

REPRESENTATIONS

Written representations are an important source of audit evidence. These representations may be oral or written, and may be obtained either on an informal or formal basis. The auditor will include information obtained in this manner in his audit working papers where it forms part of his total audit evidence.

Required:

(a) Explain why standard letters of representation are becoming less frequently used by the auditing profession. **(6 marks)**

(b) Discuss the implications for the auditor of a small company, if the directors refuse to sign the written representations. **(9 marks)**

(Total: 15 marks)

For a suggested answer, see the 'Answers' section at the end of the book.

Chapter 16

THE AUDITOR'S REPORT

INTRODUCTION

This chapter looks in detail at the end result of the audit – the auditor's report issued to the members of the client company.

We looked at the report as a means of communication between the auditor and the members earlier. This chapter looks in more detail at the unmodified auditor's report i.e. where the auditor's report gives a true and fair view opinion, and also deals with modified reports and opinions available where the auditor is not in a position to give a true and fair view opinion.

In preparing an auditor's report as in many other aspects of the audit process, a high level of judgement will be required. The ultimate decision lies with the partner in charge of the audit assignment. Your task as an accounting technician might be to draft what you consider to be an appropriate report for consideration by your superiors. You need a sound understanding of the types of report available in a range of circumstances in order to be able to perform this type of task.

This chapter covers syllabus areas E (4).

CONTENTS

1 The auditors' report revisited

2 The modified auditor's report

3 Forming an audit opinion

LEARNING OUTCOMES

At the end of this chapter, you should be able to:

- understand the form and content of an independent auditor's report including an unmodified opinion

- appreciate the circumstances in which the auditor should express a modified opinion in the auditor's report

- identify the type of opinion which it is appropriate to express, based on the given circumstances.

1 THE AUDITORS' REPORT REVISITED

1.1 UNCORRECTED MISSTATEMENTS

The auditor must consider the effect of misstatements on both the audit procedures performed and ultimately, if uncorrected, on the financial statements as a whole. Guidance on how this is performed is given in ISA 450 *Evaluation of Misstatements Identified During the Audit.*

The auditor should accumulate a record of all misstatements identified during the audit, unless they are clearly trivial. In the first instance they must consider if the existence of such misstatements indicates that others may exist, which, when aggregated with other misstatements, could be considered material. If so the audit plan and strategy may need to be revised and further procedures may be necessary to obtain more evidence.

All misstatements identified during the course of the audit should be reported to an appropriate level of management on a timely basis. Importantly, the auditor should request that all misstatements are corrected.

If management refuses to correct some or all of the misstatements the auditor should consider their reasons for refusal and take these into account when considering if the financial statements are free from material misstatement.

Evaluation of Uncorrected Misstatement

Before misstatements are evaluated the auditor should revisit their assessment of materiality to determine whether, according to their judgement, it is still appropriate in the circumstances. Following this they can then determine whether the unrecorded misstatements, either individually or in aggregate, are material to the financial statements as a whole.

In so doing the auditor must consider both the size and nature of the misstatements and the effect of misstatements related to prior periods (e.g. on corresponding figures, comparatives and opening balances).

Following this consideration the auditor should report the uncorrected misstatements to those charged with governance and explain the effect this will have upon the audit opinion. At the same time they should request a written representation from those charged with governance that they believe the effects of uncorrected misstatements are immaterial.

The ultimate impact on the auditor's report must be considered.

1.2 THE UNMODIFIED AUDITOR'S REPORT

Definition The **unmodified auditor's report** provides assurance that an independent examination of the accounts has not discovered any unadjusted material misstatements and that the financial statements give a true and fair view.

The main elements of the auditor's report, as stated in ISA 700 *Forming an Opinion and Reporting on Financial Statements* are:

(a) a title identifying the person(s) to whom the report is addressed

(b) the auditors' opinion on the financial statements

(c) the basis of the auditors' opinion

(d) key audit matters

(e) responsibilities of management

(f) responsibilities of the auditor

(g) the auditors' signature and address

(h) the date of the auditor's report.

An example of an unmodified auditor's report which you saw in an earlier chapter is shown below as a reminder. A commentary on the various elements comprising the report is also given in the section which follows.

INDEPENDENT AUDITOR'S REPORT TO...................[appropriate addressee]

Opinion

We have audited the financial statements of ABC Company (the Company), which comprise the statement of financial position as at December 31, 20X1, and the statement of comprehensive income, statement of changes in equity and statement of cash flows for the year then ended, and notes to the financial statements, including a summary of significant accounting policies.

In our opinion, the accompanying financial statements present fairly, in all material respects, (*or give a true and fair view of*) the financial position of the Company as at December 31, 20X1, and (*of*) its financial performance and its cash flows for the year then ended in accordance with International Financial Reporting Standards (IFRSs).

Basis for Opinion

We conducted our audit in accordance with International Standards on Auditing (ISAs). Our responsibilities under those standards are further described in the Auditor's Responsibilities for the Audit of the Financial Statements section of our report. We are independent of the Company in accordance with the International Ethics Standards Board for Accountants' Code of Ethics for Professional Accountants (IESBA Code) together with the ethical requirements that are relevant to our audit of the financial statements in [jurisdiction], and have fulfilled our other ethical responsibilities in accordance with these requirements and the IESBA Code. We believe that the audit evidence we have obtained is sufficient and appropriate to provide a basis for our opinion.

Key Audit Matters

Key audit matters are those matters that, in our professional judgment, were of most significance in our audit of the financial statements of the current period. These matters were addressed in the context of our audit of the financial statements as a whole, and in forming our opinion thereon, and we do not provide a separate opinion on these matters.

[Description of each key audit matter in accordance with ISA 701]

Responsibilities of Management and Those Charged with Governance for the Financial Statements

Management is responsible for the preparation and fair presentation of these financial statements in accordance with IFRSs, and for such internal control as management determines is necessary to enable the preparation of financial statements that are free from material misstatement, whether due to fraud or error.

In preparing the financial statements, management is responsible for assessing the Company's ability to continue as a going concern, disclosing, as applicable, matters related to going concern and using the going concern basis of accounting unless management either intends to liquidate the Company or to cease operations, or has no realistic alternative but to do so.

Those charged with governance are responsible for overseeing the Company's financial reporting process.

Auditor's Responsibilities for the Audit of the Financial Statements

Our objectives are to obtain reasonable assurance about whether the financial statements as a whole are free from material misstatement, whether due to fraud or error, and to issue an auditor's report that includes our opinion. Reasonable assurance is a high level of assurance, but is not a guarantee that an audit conducted in accordance with ISAs will always detect a material misstatement when it exists. Misstatements can arise from fraud or error and are considered material if, individually or in the aggregate, they could reasonably be expected to influence the economic decisions of users taken on the basis of these financial statements.

[Auditor's signature]

[Date of the auditor's report]

[Auditor's address]

1.3 PREPARING A FORMAL AUDITOR'S REPORT

To prepare a formal auditor's report the following elements need to be considered.

It may help to refer to the example above as you consider the following sections to ensure you fully understand each point.

Title

The auditor's report should have an appropriate title. It will usually be appropriate to use the term 'Independent Auditor' in the title to distinguish the auditor's report from reports that might be issued by others, such as by officers of the entity or the board of directors, or from the reports of other auditors who may not have to abide by the same ethical requirements as the independent auditor.

Addressee

The auditor's report should be appropriately addressed as required by the circumstances of the engagement and local regulations. The report is ordinarily addressed either to the shareholders or the board of directors of the entity whose financial statements are being audited.

Introductory paragraph

The auditor's report should identify the financial statements of the entity that have been audited, including the date of and period covered by the financial statements.

Opinion paragraph

The auditor's report should clearly state the auditor's opinion as to whether the financial statements give a true and fair view (or are presented fairly, in all material respects) in accordance with the financial reporting framework and, where appropriate, whether the financial statements comply with statutory requirements.

The terms used to express the auditor's opinion are 'give a true and fair view' or 'present fairly, in all material respects', and are equivalent. Both terms indicate, amongst other things, that the auditor considers only those matters that are material to the financial statements.

The financial reporting framework is determined by IFRSs, rules issued by professional bodies, and the development of general practice within a country, with an appropriate consideration of fairness and with due regard to local legislation. To advise the reader of the context in which 'fairness' is expressed, the auditor's opinion would indicate the framework upon which the financial statements are based by using words such as 'in accordance with (indicate IFRSs or relevant national standards)'.

In addition to an opinion of the true and fair view (or fair presentation, in all material respects), the auditor's report may need to include an opinion as to whether the financial statements comply with other requirements specified by relevant statutes or law.

Basis of audit opinion

The auditor's report should describe the scope of the audit by stating that the audit was conducted in accordance with ISAs or in accordance with the relevant national standards or practices, as appropriate. 'Scope' refers to the auditor's ability to perform audit procedures deemed necessary in the circumstances. The reader needs this as an assurance that the audit has been carried out in accordance with established standards or practices. Unless otherwise stated, the auditing standards or practices followed are presumed to be those of the country indicated by the auditor's address.

The report should include a statement that the audit was planned and performed to obtain reasonable assurance about whether the financial statements are free of material misstatement.

The auditor's report should describe the audit as including:

- examining the evidence to support the financial statement amounts and disclosures

- assessing the accounting principles used in the preparation of the financial statements

- assessing the significant estimates made by management in the preparation of the financial statements

- evaluating the overall financial statement presentation.

The report should include a statement by the auditor that the audit provides a reasonable basis for the opinion.

Management's and auditor's responsibility

The report should include a statement that the financial statements are the responsibility of the entity's management, and a statement that the responsibility of the auditor is to express an opinion on the financial statements based on the audit.

Financial statements are the representations of management. The preparation of such statements requires management to make significant accounting estimates and judgements, as well as to determine the appropriate accounting principles, and methods used in preparation of the financial statements. In contrast, the auditor's responsibility is to audit these financial statements in order to express an opinion thereon.

Date of report

The auditor should date the report as of the completion date of the audit. This informs the reader that the auditor has considered the effect on the financial statements and on the report of events and transactions of which the auditor became aware and that occurred up to that date.

Since the auditor's responsibility is to report on the financial statements as prepared and presented by management, the auditor should not date the report earlier than the date on which the financial statements are signed or approved by management.

Auditor's address

The report should name a specific location, which is ordinarily the city where the auditor who has responsibility for the audit maintains his office.

Auditor's signature

The report should be signed in the name of the audit firm, the personal name of the auditor or both, as appropriate. The auditor's report is ordinarily signed in the name of the firm because the firm assumes responsibility for the audit.

1.4 PROPER ACCOUNTING RECORDS

Legislation will often require auditors to form an opinion as to whether the company has maintained proper accounting records, as required by the relevant company law.

The auditor therefore must be aware of what constitutes proper accounting records.

The general principle

Subject to any specific local statutory requirements, the accounting system should be adequate to enable the financial statements to be prepared. What is considered to be adequate will depend on the size, nature and complexity of the organisation. Obviously a small company with few customers and suppliers would only require very simple records such as a cashbook together with details of unpaid invoices.

The detailed requirements

Precise rules as to what constitutes proper accounting records will vary internationally. The following may be taken as a general guide.

(a) Every company should keep accounting records which are sufficient to show and explain the company's transactions and are such that they:

    (i) disclose the financial position of the company at that time, and

    (ii) enable the directors to ensure that the statements of financial position and comprehensive income comply with the requirements of relevant company law.

(b) The accounting records shall contain:

    (i) entries from day to day of all sums of money received and expended by the company, and the matters in respect of which the receipt and expenditure takes place, and

    (ii) a record of the assets and liabilities of the company.

(c) If the company's business involves dealing in goods, the accounting records shall contain:

    (i) statements of inventories held by the company at the end of each financial year of the company

    (ii) all statements of inventory counted from which any such statement of inventory as is mentioned in point (i) has been or is to be prepared, and

    (iii) except in the case of goods sold by way of retail, statements of all goods sold and purchased, showing the goods, buyers and sellers in sufficient detail to enable all these to be identified.

ACTIVITY 1

What matters should be disclosed in an unmodified auditor's report?

For a suggested answer, see the 'Answers' section at the end of the book

2 THE MODIFIED AUDITOR'S REPORT

2.1 CIRCUMSTANCES REQUIRING MODIFICATION

It is important to recognise that auditor's opinions should only be modified **as a last resort** – the majority of auditor's opinions are unmodified.

Whenever the auditors are concerned about their opinion they should discuss the matter with management to try and resolve the issue(s), thus avoiding modification.

The final decision on the appropriate report to be issued lies with the audit partner, acting upon information gained from his review of the audit files and discussions with the audit manager and other members of the audit team.

This is one of the critical roles of the audit working papers, containing evidence gathered during the audit which will be used as the basis for the formulation of the audit opinion.

Of particular significance within the audit working papers will be:

- the conclusions reached by the members of the audit team on each of the audit areas

- errors or omissions discovered during the audit and the audit team's assessment of their impact (materiality again!).

2.2 THE FORM OF AUDIT OPINION MODIFICATIONS

ISA 705 *Modifications to the opinion in the Independent Auditor's Report* states that all modifications arise from either material misstatements in the financial statements or an inability to obtain sufficient appropriate evidence, which can be material or pervasive (refer to paragraphs below which examine these terms in more detail).

The 'grid' below is a useful summary of the decisions the auditor has to make in drafting a modified auditor's report opinion.

Reason for modification	Material	Pervasive
Inability to obtain sufficient appropriate evidence The auditor is unable to obtain sufficient appropriate evidence e.g. a lack of accounting records that have been lost or destroyed, or a lack of adequate information and explanations from directors	Qualified ('Except for') opinion	The auditor is unable to form an opinion and *does not know* whether the financial statements give a true and fair view. This gives rise to a 'Disclaimer' of opinion
Material misstatement in the financial statements The auditor identifies a material misstatement in the financial statements, such as the non-provision for a doubtful debt	Qualified ('Except for') opinion	The financial statements *do not* give a true and fair view. This gives rise to an 'Adverse' opinion

We have already dealt at length with the concept of materiality. In an auditor's report context, the materiality column above will come into play when the auditor encounters a material problem with one or more specific items in the financial statements (e.g. inventory or revenue), but the remaining items and the financial statements as a whole comply with the true and fair view criterion.

A 'pervasive' modification is one that relates to the **overall true and fair view** given by the financial statements. In the case of material misstatements it is one that renders the financial statements seriously misleading; in the case of the inability to obtain sufficient appropriate evidence, it renders the auditor unable to form an opinion.

The difference between a material and a pervasive modification is a matter of judgement. There are no absolute cut-off points and what is material to one auditor may be pervasive to another. Pervasive modifications are very rare in practice, adverse opinions are almost unheard of! The issue of a modified opinion often has certain legal effects such as the requirement for additional auditors' reports if the company wishes to pay dividends.

In all cases where a modified opinion is issued, the auditor should adequately describe and quantify if possible the reason for the modification.

2.3 EXAMPLES OF MODIFIED AUDITOR'S REPORT OPINIONS

(a) An example of a qualified opinion relating to a material misstatement in the financial statements.

INDEPENDENT AUDITORS' REPORT TO THE SHAREHOLDERS OF XYZ

Opening paragraphs – as normal.

Qualified opinion

In our opinion, except for the effects of the matter described in the Basis for Qualified Opinion section of our report,, the financial statements give a true and fair view of the financial position of XYZ as at December 31 20X1, and of its financial performance and its cash flows for the year then ended in accordance with International Accounting Standards.

Basis for qualified opinion

Included in the trade receivables shown in the statement of financial position is an amount of $Y due from a company which has ceased trading. XYZ has no security for this debt. In our opinion the company is unlikely to receive any payment and full provision of $Y should have been made, reducing profit before tax and net assets by that amount.

Closing paragraphs – as normal.

Registered auditors   Address

Date

(b) An example of an 'adverse' opinion relating to a pervasive misstatement in the financial statements.

INDEPENDENT AUDITORS' REPORT TO THE SHAREHOLDERS OF XYZ

Opening paragraphs – as normal.

Adverse opinion

In our opinion, because of the significance of the matter discussed in the Basis for Adverse Opinion section of our report, the financial statements do not give a true and fair view of the financial position of XYZ as at December 31 20X1, and of its financial performance and its cash flows for the year then ended in accordance with International Accounting Standards.

Basis of adverse opinion

As more fully explained in note . . . no provision has been made for losses expected to arise on certain long-term contracts currently in progress, as the directors consider that such losses should be offset against amounts recoverable on other construction contracts. In our opinion, provision should be made for foreseeable losses on individual contracts as required by International Accounting Standard 11. If losses had been so recognised the effect would have been to reduce the profit before and after tax for the year and the contract work in progress at December 31 20X1 by $. .

Closing paragraphs – as normal.

Registered auditors   Address

Date

(c) An example of a qualified opinion relating to an inability to obtain sufficient appropriate evidence which is considered to be material.

INDEPENDENT AUDITORS' REPORT TO THE SHAREHOLDERS OF XYZ

Opening paragraphs — as normal.

Qualified opinion

In our opinion, except for the possible effects of the matter described in the Basis for Qualified Opinion section of our report,, the financial statements give a true and fair view........*(remainder as normal)*

Basis of qualified opinion

Our responsibility is to express an opinion on these financial statements based on our audit. Except as discussed in the following paragraph, we conducted our audit in accordance with...*remainder of this section as normal, followed by:)*

We did not observe the counting of the physical inventories as of December 31 20X1, since that date was prior to the time we were initially engaged as auditors for the company. Owing to the nature of the company's records, we were unable to satisfy ourselves as to inventory quantities by other audit procedures.

Closing paragraphs — as normal.

Registered auditors   Address

Date

(d) An example of a 'disclaimer' of opinion relating to an inability to obtain sufficient appropriate evidence which is considered to be pervasive.

INDEPENDENT AUDITORS' REPORT TO THE SHAREHOLDERS OF XYZ

Opening paragraphs as normal

Disclaimer of opinion

We were engaged to audit the accompanying financial statements................
(Remainder of this paragraph as normal)

We do not express an opinion on the accompanying consolidated financial statements of the Group. Because of the significance of the matter described in the Basis for Disclaimer of Opinion section of our report, we have not been able to obtain sufficient appropriate audit evidence to provide a basis for an audit opinion on these consolidated financial statements.

Basis of disclaimer of opinion

The Group's investment in its joint venture XYZ Company is carried at xxx on the Group's consolidated statement of financial position, which represents over 90% of the Group's net assets as at December 31, 20X1. We were not allowed access to the management and the auditors of XYZ Company, including XYZ Company's auditors' audit documentation. As a result, we were unable to determine whether any adjustments were necessary in respect of the Group's proportional share of XYZ Company's assets that it controls jointly, its proportional share of XYZ Company's liabilities for which it is jointly responsible, its proportional share of XYZ's income and expenses for the year, and the elements making up the consolidated statement of changes in equity and the consolidated cash flow statement.

Closing paragraphs — as normal

Registered auditors   Address

Date

2.4 EMPHASIS OF MATTER PARAGRAPH

A fundamental uncertainty relates to an uncertain future event, in much the same way as a provision or a contingent liability. However, if fundamental uncertainties are so significant, directors are required to disclose such matters in the financial statements in accordance with IAS 1.

If they are adequately disclosed in the notes to the financial statements, the auditors need not modify the audit opinion (as there would be no misstatement of the accounts). However, because they are of such importance to the users of the accounts the auditor can draw attention to such disclosures in their auditor's report.

These additional narratives in the auditor's report are referred to as 'emphasis of matter paragraphs.' If an emphasis of matter paragraph is included in an auditor's report, the report would be regarded as modified.

2.5 MATERIAL UNCERTAINTY RELATING TO GOING CONCERN

If the fundamental uncertainty impacts the going concern status of the client, as per ISA 570, the auditor's report would be amended with a separate paragraph, headed up 'Material uncertainty related to going concern'. (This is not to be an emphasis of matter paragraph.)

The disclosure should explain:

- the principal events or conditions that cast significant doubt on the entity's ability to continue as a going concern and management's plans to deal with them
- the company may be unable to realise its assets and discharge its liabilities in the normal course of business.

Example of a modified auditor's report containing an emphasis of matter paragraph. The auditor's opinion will remain unmodified.

INDEPENDENT AUDITORS' REPORT TO THE SHAREHOLDERS OF XYZ LTD

Opening paragraphs as normal.

Basis of audit opinion

As normal

Opinion

As normal

Emphasis of matter – possible outcome of a lawsuit

In forming our opinion, we have considered the adequacy of the disclosures made in the financial statements concerning the possible outcome to litigation against B Limited, a subsidiary undertaking of the company, for an alleged breach of environmental regulations. The future settlement of this litigation could result in additional liabilities and the closure of B Limited's business, whose net assets included in the consolidated statement of financial position total £ . . . and whose profit before tax for the year is £ . . . Details of the circumstances relating to this emphasis of matter are described in note . . . Our opinion is not qualified in this respect.

Closing paragraphs as normal.

ACTIVITY 2

Modifications

(a) What are the four types of modified auditor's report opinion?

(b) Give an example of when each type of report would be appropriate.

For a suggested answer, see the 'Answers' section at the end of the book.

3 FORMING AN AUDIT OPINION

The flowchart below may be helpful in deciding the action(s) auditors should take in respect of their report. Do not attempt to learn this – it should simply help you to see how the various types of audit opinion to which we have now referred are arrived at.

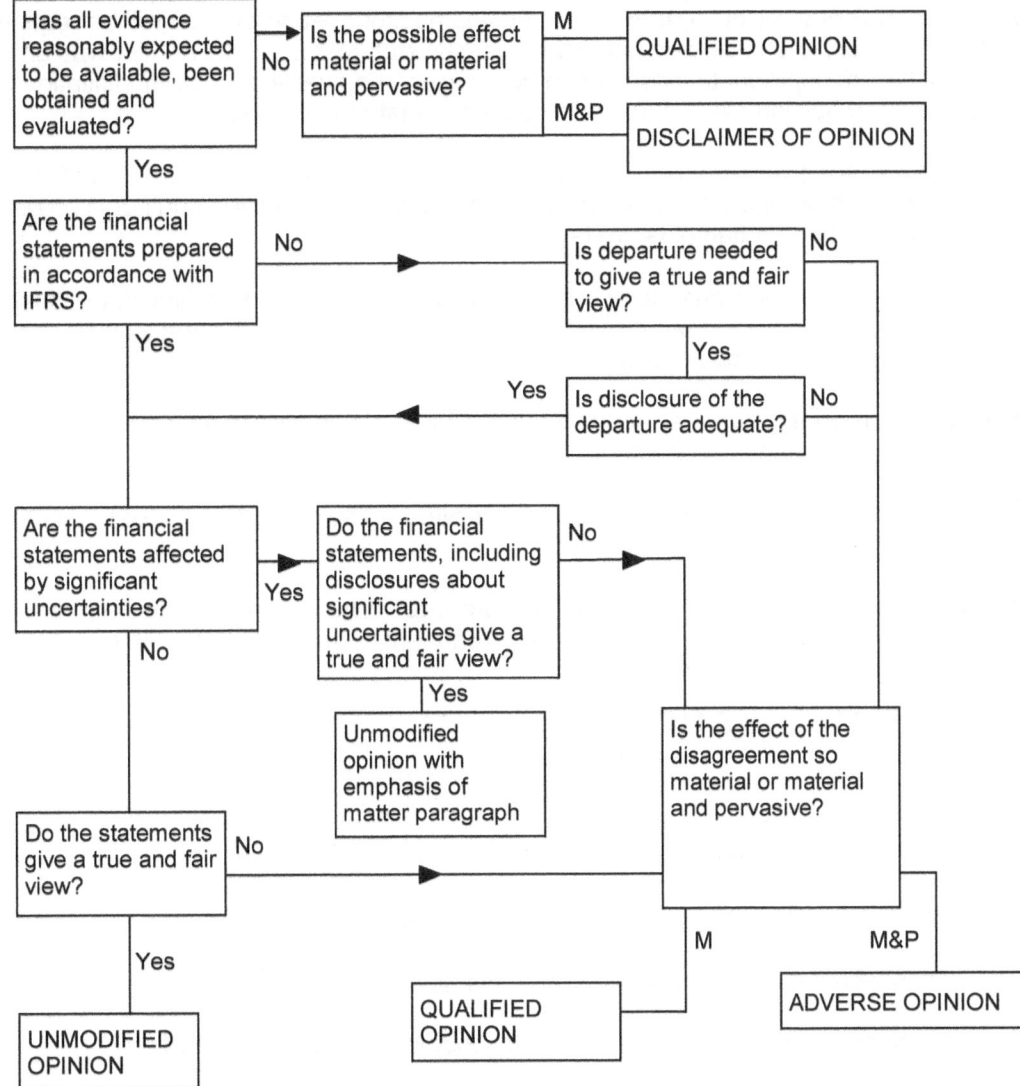

CONCLUSION

We have now come to the end of the audit process – the issue by the auditor of an appropriate opinion on the truth and fairness of the client's financial statements.

You may be involved in drafting an auditor's report which appropriately reflects the opinion which has been formed on the financial statements under review. It is therefore important that you are aware of the format and content of the unmodified report and the various types of modified reports available to the auditor.

Always remember the significance of the auditor's report – it is the only formal means of communication between the auditor and the shareholders. The type of report and its contents needs to be carefully considered – a modification in the auditor's report should be seen as a last resort!

FAU: FOUNDATIONS IN AUDIT

KEY TERMS

Unmodified auditor's report opinion – A report from the auditor to the members of the client company providing assurance that an independent examination of the accounts has been carried out and that the accounts do give a true and fair view.

Modified auditor's report opinion – A modified auditor's report opinion will be required when there is either a misstatement in the financial statements, or the auditor was unable to collect sufficient appropriate evidence. In both cases, the qualification or modification to the auditor's report opinion may be judged to be either material or pervasive.

Modified auditor's report – A modified auditor's report relates to an emphasis of matter included within that report. Such a report may still give an unmodified audit opinion on whether the financial statements are fairly stated.

Pervasive – A material matter is regarded as pervasive if it is fundamental to the financial statements and, if there is a pervasive misstatement, will result in the financial statements as a whole being regarded as unreliable.

A pervasive modification – A modified audit opinion that relates to the overall true and fair view given by the financial statements.

Inability to obtain sufficient appropriate evidence – The auditor is unable to carry out procedures because of a lack of evidence.

Material misstatement in the financial statements – The auditor identifies a material misstatement with regards to the accounting treatment or disclosure of a matter.

SELF TEST QUESTIONS

		Paragraph
1	To whom is an auditor's report addressed?	1.4
2	What should be referred to with the auditor's signature?	1.4
3	Suggest some examples of material misstatements?	2.2, 2.3
4	A pervasive misstatement gives rise to what form of audit modification?	2.2

PRACTICE QUESTION

AUDITOR'S REPORT TERMINOLOGY

Explain the meaning of each of the following terms which are used in connection with auditor's reports:

(a) circumstances of uncertainty

(b) disclaimer of opinion

(c) circumstances of material misstatements in the financial statements

(d) a qualified ('except for') opinion.

(8 marks)

For a suggested answer, see the 'Answers' section at the end of the book.

EXAM-STYLE QUESTION 1

EASTERN ENGINEERING

The following table of tangible non-current assets appeared in the draft final accounts of Eastern Engineering, a medium-sized manufacturing concern, at 31 March 20X6:

	Land and buildings	Plant and equipment	Assets in course of construction	Total
	$000	$000	$000	$000
Cost:				
Balances at 1 April 20X5	161	976	13	1,150
Additions	6	124	35	165
Transfers	3	29	(32)	–
Disposals	(1)	(18)	–	(19)
Total cost at 31 March 20X6	169	1,111	16	1,296
Depreciation:				
Balances at 1 April 20X5	30	397	–	427
Charge for year	5	88	–	93
Disposals	–	(18)	–	(18)
Total depreciation at 31 March 20X6	35	467	–	502
Carrying value at 31 March 20X6	134	644	15	794
Carrying value at 31 March 20X5	131	579	13	723

Notes:

The carrying value of land and buildings at 31 March 20X6 comprised:

	$000
Freeholds	116
Long leases (over 50 years unexpired)	8
Short leases	10
	134

The company's statement of accounting policies included the following:

(a) Tangible non-current assets are stated at historical cost less depreciation. Where assets are constructed by the company's employees, cost includes materials, direct labour and related overheads.

(b) Depreciation of plant and equipment is provided on a straight line basis from the time assets are brought into use, so as to write off their historical costs over their estimated useful lives.

The company's directors' report included the following:

'Following a professional valuation of a proportion of the company's land and buildings the directors are of the opinion that there was no significant difference between market and book values at 31 March 20X6.'

The company's statement of comprehensive income for the year ended 31 March 20X6 included the following:

Profit before taxation is $100,000.

During the course of your audit of the non-current assets of Eastern Engineering at 31 March 20X6 two problems have arisen:

(a) The calculations of the cost of direct labour incurred on assets in course of construction by the company's employees have been accidentally destroyed for the early part of the year. The direct labour cost involved is $10,000.

(b) The company has received a government grant of $25,000 towards the cost of plant and equipment acquired during the year and expected to last for ten years. The grant has been credited in full to profits as exceptional income which is not in accordance with accounting standards which require that such grants be deferred to the statement of financial position and credited to income over the useful life of the related asset.

Required:

(a) List the general forms of modification available to auditors in drafting their report and state the circumstances in which each is appropriate. **(5 marks)**

(b) State whether you feel that a modified auditor's report would be necessary for each of the two circumstances outlined above, giving reasons in each case. **(10 marks)**

(Total: 15 marks)

For a suggested answer, see the 'Answers' section at the end of the book.

THE AUDITOR'S REPORT : CHAPTER 16

EXAM-STYLE QUESTION 2

EASTERN ENGINEERING

The following table of tangible non-current assets appeared in the draft final accounts of Eastern Engineering, a medium-sized manufacturing concern, at 31 March 20X6:

	Land and buildings	Plant and equipment	Assets in course of construction	Total
	$000	$000	$000	$000
Cost:				
Balances at 1 April 20X5	161	976	13	1,150
Additions	6	124	35	165
Transfers	3	29	(32)	–
Disposals	(1)	(18)	–	(19)
Total cost at 31 March 20X6	169	1,111	16	1,296
Depreciation:				
Balances at 1 April 20X5	30	397	–	427
Charge for year	5	88	–	93
Disposals	–	(18)	–	(18)
Total depreciation at 31 March 20X6	35	467	–	502
Carrying value at 31 March 20X6	134	644	15	794
Carrying value at 31 March 20X5	131	579	13	723

Notes:

The carrying value of land and buildings at 31 March 20X6 comprised:

	$000
Freeholds	116
Long leases (over 50 years unexpired)	8
Short leases	10
	134

The company's statement of accounting policies included the following:

(a) Tangible non-current assets are stated at historical cost less depreciation. Where assets are constructed by the company's employees, cost includes materials, direct labour and related overheads.

(b) Depreciation of plant and equipment is provided on a straight line basis from the time assets are brought into use, so as to write off their historical costs over their estimated useful lives.

FAU: FOUNDATIONS IN AUDIT

The company's directors' report included the following:

'Following a professional valuation of a proportion of the company's land and buildings the directors are of the opinion that there was no significant difference between market and book values at 31 March 20X6.'

The company's statement of comprehensive income for the year ended 31 March 20X6 included the following:

Profit before taxation is $100,000.

During the course of your audit of the non-current assets of Eastern Engineering at 31 March 20X6 two problems have arisen:

(a) The calculations of the cost of direct labour incurred on assets in course of construction by the company's employees have been accidentally destroyed for the early part of the year. The direct labour cost involved is $10,000.

(b) The company has received a government grant of $25,000 towards the cost of plant and equipment acquired during the year and expected to last for ten years. The grant has been credited in full to profits as exceptional income which is not in accordance with accounting standards which require that such grants be deferred to the statement of financial position and credited to income over the useful life of the related asset.

Required:

(a) On the assumption that you decide that a modified auditor's report opinion is necessary with respect to the treatment of the government grant, draft the section of the report describing the matter (the whole report is not required). **(6 marks)**

(b) Outline the auditor's general responsibility with regard to the statement in the directors' report concerning the valuation of land and buildings. **(4 marks)**

(Total: 10 marks)

For a suggested answer, see the 'Answers' section at the end of the book.

Chapter 17

THE AUDITOR'S LIABILITY

INTRODUCTION

The major legal problem that arises for auditors is the possibility of claims being made against them for negligence i.e. where the audit has not been adequately performed. Claims may be made by either the client company or external third parties (banks, and other creditors or shareholders) claiming that they have suffered some financial loss as a consequence of the auditors' actions.

Of course, in any given case, auditors may well be successful in defending any legal action brought against them. Even if the auditor loses the case, damages claims may be covered by professional indemnity insurance. However, it is better to prevent the problem arising in the first place as legal claims against the auditor result in loss of credibility to the auditor. It is therefore important to ensure that the audit work is of the highest quality; we have already covered this topic when dealing with planning, recording and controlling the audit. Quality control is mentioned briefly again here, in the context of prevention of legal claims arising against the auditor.

It is also important to bear in mind that the way in which the law of negligence operates will differ internationally – you will not be expected to demonstrate a detailed knowledge of the law applicable in any particular country. The objective of this chapter is to give you a general understanding of the auditors' possible liability to the client company and to others (third parties) if the auditor is careless in performing the audit work.

You should also note that the legal framework within which auditors operate in a given country may make them legally liable under a number of provisions in addition to negligence. A typical example is the situation where the auditors commit offences related to the liquidation of a company. Some of these may impose a criminal liability on the auditor, with penalties taking the form of fines or imprisonment – these are not covered here.

There have been numerous discussions recently regarding limitation of auditor liability due to legal cases that have arisen where the amounts paid by auditors have been significant.

This chapter covers syllabus area A (4).

CONTENTS

1. Negligence and the auditor

2. Solutions to the negligence problem

3. Quality control

FAU: FOUNDATIONS IN AUDIT

LEARNING OUTCOMES

At the end of this chapter, you should be able to:

- appreciate the extent to which negligence claims may be made against auditors both by clients and others

- appreciate the significance of quality control procedures in limiting the scope for legal claims being made against the auditor.

1 NEGLIGENCE AND THE AUDITOR

1.1 INTRODUCTION

The possibility of claims being made against the auditor as a result of careless auditing is the major legal threat faced by the auditing profession. The analysis which follows is designed to give you an appreciation of the legal principles involved, based on English law. Although the main points at issue will be similar, the points of detail in the application of the principles are likely to vary internationally. For examination purpose, you are advised to focus on the general principles involved. The case decisions summarised below are designed to show the development of the legal issues.

Definition **Negligence** is some act or omission which occurs because the person concerned has failed to exercise the degree of care and skill appropriate to the circumstances.

In simple terms, negligence is the legal term for carelessness.

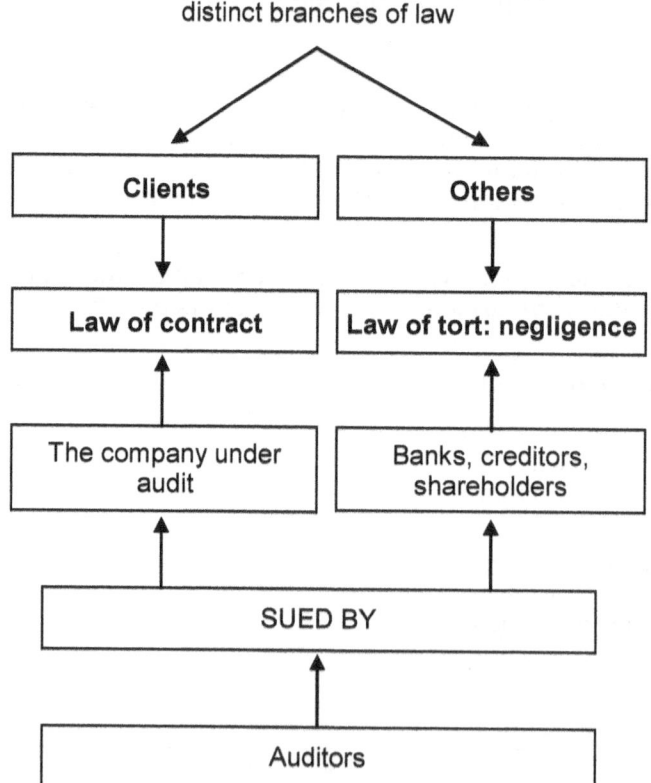

The legal principles at play here are examined more fully below.

Note that shareholders do not have a contract with the auditor so shareholders cannot sue in contract.

The auditors may also be liable to others who have relied on the financial statements upon which they expressed an opinion even if they did not know that the financial statements were specifically being relied upon (this is examined later in this chapter).

1.2 DUTY OF CARE UNDER CONTRACT LAW

The client company has a contract with the auditor and hence can sue the auditor for breach of contract if the auditor is negligent in carrying out the terms of the contract. Note that only the company can sue the auditor under contract law as other people, such as banks, creditors and shareholders, are not in a contractual relationship with the company.

When carrying out their duties the auditors must exercise reasonable care and skill. This is required by the accountants' Rules of Professional Conduct; each accountancy body has their own detailed set of rules and members agree to abide by those rules. Any members found in breach of the rules can face disciplinary action from the relevant body to which they belong.

ACCA rules state that 'members should carry out their professional work with *due skill, care, diligence and expedition* and with proper regard for the technical and professional standards expected of them as members'.

The degree of skill and care expected of an auditor in a particular situation depends on the circumstances. There is no general standard of skill and care; the auditor is expected to react to the individual situation and circumstances he is facing.

The outcomes of individual legal cases are summarised below and are designed to give an appreciation of the view the courts have taken of the degree of skill and care owed by an auditor to the client under contract law. Note that these are UK cases, so the decision reached in another country may have been different where the legislation varies.

(a) **Re London and General Bank (No 2) (1895)**

It is the duty of an auditor to bring to bear on the work he has to perform that skill, care and caution which a reasonably careful and cautious auditor would use. What is reasonable skill, care and caution must depend on the particular circumstances of each case.

It should, however, be appreciated that decisions in old cases will tend to under-state rather than over-state the degree of care and skill required, since what is regarded as reasonable by the courts will necessarily be affected by current standards of auditing practice. Also, more reliance will be placed on subsequent cases as these are more current and therefore more relevant.

(b) **Re Kingston Cotton Mill (1896)**

An auditor is not bound to be a detective or to approach his work with suspicion or with a foregone conclusion that there is something wrong. He is a watch-dog, but not a bloodhound.

(c) **Re Thomas Gerrard & Son (1968)**

C, the managing director of the company, falsified the accounts to conceal company losses causing dividends to be paid either wholly or partially out of capital over a number of years. He had done this by including non-existing inventory and altering invoices which the auditors discovered and pursued no further.

Held. The discovery of the altered invoices should have put the auditors on enquiry, they were no longer entitled to be content with the assurances of the officers of the company. Their suspicions should have been aroused and enquiries should have been made to suppliers to verify those assurances. They were therefore negligent.

In the absence of suspicious circumstances, the auditor is entitled to accept the word of a responsible company official unless there is evidence to the contrary. The auditor should always seek to obtain the best evidence available, he also needs to consider the materiality of the item and whether the evidence is sufficient. But once an auditor's suspicions have been aroused there is a duty to investigate the matter until it is satisfactorily resolved.

Overall, if auditors have complied with generally accepted auditing standards and can demonstrate this in their working papers they will not usually be found guilty of negligence. This is why it is so important for the auditors to ensure that they adequately maintain their working papers and obtain sufficient, relevant and reliable evidence to support the audit opinion. Compliance with relevant ISAs is also important in this area.

There have been a number of significant corporate scandals that resulted in their subsequent failure in the last few years e.g. WorldCom, Adelphia and Enron. These resulted in the Public Company Accounting Reform and Investor Protection Act (Sarbanes Oxley) in the US to try and prevent further corporate fraud. This has increased the costs to public companies in order to comply with requirements of the Act, and as a result a number of companies are seeking to revert to private company status. Clearly this has resulted in a 'conflict' of issues. It is vital that investors are protected, but if this is to the extent where the costs of providing that protection are so onerous such that corporations feel it is not worth having investment by the general public and remove themselves from the stock market, then the investors suffer from the lack of investment opportunities.

The harmonisation of accounting and auditing standards internationally should improve consistency of accounting practice and ensure that the regulatory environment is one that is rigorous on a worldwide basis.

1.3 LIABILITY IN TORT

Only the client company can sue the auditor in the law of contract – because only the company is in a contractual relationship with the auditor. Others who feel they may have suffered as a result of careless auditing have to rely on a different branch of law – the law of tort.

A tort can be defined as a 'civil wrong other than that arising under contract law, giving rise to a claim for damages.'

Negligence is one of many branches of tort.

If a person is to successfully make a claim against the auditor in the tort of negligence, three conditions must be satisfied:

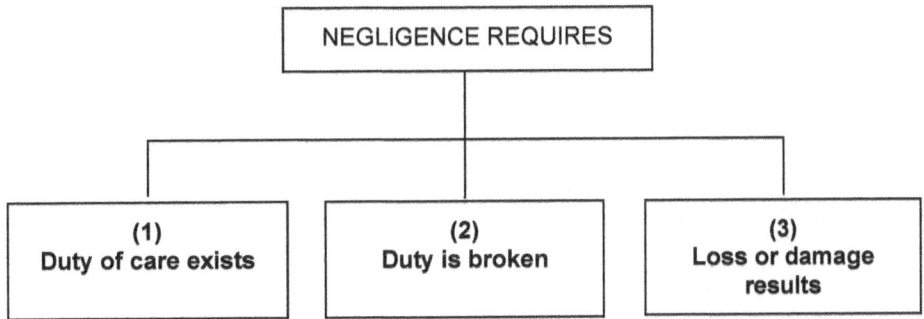

Condition (1) – the existence of a duty of care, has proved the most troublesome of the three conditions in cases brought before the courts – this is dealt with more fully below.

Condition (2) – the duty is broken – the party bringing the claim against the auditor would have to show that the auditor did not exercise a reasonable degree of skill and care in the circumstances. A typical approach to this in court cases is to call another firm of auditors as expert witnesses who will be asked to give their view on whether a proper audit was performed.

Condition (3) – loss or damage results – is usually a question of demonstrating that the person making the claim suffered a financial loss as a result of negligent/careless auditing. For example, a bank lent money to a company on the basis of audited accounts which were subsequently found to contain material errors or omissions.

The auditor's duty of care

Most of the major court cases on auditor negligence have been concerned with the question of whether the auditor owed a duty of care to the plaintiff – the person making the claim. The cases summarised below show the historical development of the view the courts have taken on this question. Note the principles which have developed rather than the details of the case – some of the cases do not deal specifically with auditors.

1   *Candler v Crane Christmas* (1951)

   In this case Candler sued the accountants Crane Christmas when he lost money he had invested in a company, the accounts of which Crane Christmas had prepared. The court ruling was that although the accounts were negligently prepared, Candler could not recoup his losses from the accountants because he did not have a contract with them. There was therefore no duty of care owed to third parties not in a contractual relationship with the auditor.

2   *Hedley Byrne v Heller & Partners* (1964)

   Although this is a case dealing with banks, it is seen to be relevant to all professionals, including auditors and accountants. The plaintiff lost money when a bank reference from the defendant turned out to have been negligently produced. The bank indicated that a mutual client was a good credit risk when this was not the case. The court ruled that Hedley Byrne, although they did not have a contract with the bank Heller & Partners, could recoup their losses due to the negligence and loss involved. However, the bank did not have to pay any damages due to a general disclaimer in its letter absolving it from any liability.

The decision affected accountants in that if a third party can show that it relied on the work of an accountant which later turned out to be wrong, it can claim damages. However, this principle was only extended to plaintiffs whom the auditor actually knew by name. Unidentified third parties would not be able to claim against the auditor.

3 *JEB Fasteners v Marks Bloom* (1980)

The plaintiff acquired the share capital of the company. The audited accounts, due to the negligence of the auditors, did not show a true and fair view of the state of affairs of the company. It was accepted that at the time of the audit the defendant auditors did know of the plaintiffs but did not know that they were contemplating a take-over bid.

Held. Whilst recognising that the auditors owed a duty of care in this situation, it was decided that the auditors were not liable because the plaintiff had not suffered any loss. It was proved that the plaintiffs would have bought the share capital of the company at the agreed price whatever the accounts had said. Therefore, whether or not a duty of care existed was not directly relevant to the decision.

4 *Caparo Industries v Dickman and Touche Ross & Co* (1989)

This is seen to be the leading case in the area of 'to whom does the auditor owe a duty of care'.

Fidelity plc was taken over by Caparo Industries. Fidelity's accounts had been audited by Touche Ross. Caparo alleged that the accounts overstated the profits of Fidelity plc and that its purchases of shares and takeover bid were all made in reliance on the audited accounts.

Held by the House of Lords, that a duty of care was not owed to potential investors in, or takeover bidders for, the company because of:

(a) the lack of proximity (closeness of relationship) between auditor and potential investor

(b) the fact that it would not be just and reasonable to impose a duty on the auditor to such investors.

In the above case, the House of Lords identified the auditors' functions as being:

(a) to protect the company itself from errors and wrongdoing; not its owners, the shareholders

(b) to provide shareholders with information such that they can scrutinise the conduct of a company's affairs and remove or reward those responsible i.e. the directors.

The decision in Caparo clarified the extent of auditors' liability by defining three criteria for the imposition of a duty of care as follows:

- it must be reasonably foreseeable by the defendant that the statements will be relied on by the plaintiff

- there has to be a relevant degree of proximity between the parties

- it must be just and reasonable to impose a duty of care on the part of the defendant to the plaintiff.

It followed that the auditors, although they do not owe a duty of care to shareholders individually or potential investors, they have a duty to shareholders as a group.

5 BBH v ADT (1995)

A further case, since **Caparo**, which is of relevance to third party liability is that of *BBH v ADT*, the facts of which are as follows:

The former BDO Binder Hamlyn (BBH) partnership had audited the 1988/89 accounts of BSG which ADT (an electronic security group) had acquired for £105m in 1990. BSG was later found to be worth only £40m rather than £105m.

Usually, the auditors do not owe a duty of care in general to third parties, however, in this case one of the audit partners had verbally confirmed the accuracy of BSG's accounts during a meeting. At this point he therefore took on a verbal contract with ADT.

In December 1995, ADT were awarded £65m damages plus interest and costs for negligence, against BBH. BBH appealed this decision and an out of court settlement was reached with ADT.

ACTIVITY 1

Read accounting magazines and other financial publications on a frequent (ideally weekly) basis and note any new cases or developments in existing cases in respect of auditor liability.

There is no feedback to this activity.

1.4 SPECIALIST ADVICE

When expressing an opinion or giving advice on difficult or complex matters the auditor should consider the extent of financial consequences/financial loss for their client if that advice/opinion is incorrect. Where appropriate, if the accountant considers that he does not have sufficient technical knowledge/skills or competence to be able to provide satisfactory advice on the matter then he should consider consulting a specialist. In such situations the accountant would seek prior approval from the client. In *Sayers v Clarke Walker (2002)* an accountant failed to advise his client on how to maximise his tax advantages when purchasing shares in a company. The accountant had suggested to the client that specialist tax advice should be sought but that was not sufficient to absolve him from his obligation to give the client competent advice. Advice on how to maximise the tax advantages should have been within the practitioner's general competence and his failure to advise accordingly amounted to negligence. This case made it clear that members can never absolve themselves of the obligation to give competent general advice.

2 SOLUTIONS TO THE NEGLIGENCE PROBLEM

The original reaction of the auditing profession to the negligence problem was to improve quality control procedures (discussed below). Legislation reinforced this action by introducing monitoring provisions. These are solutions in the sense that no negligence therefore arises in the first place.

The other reaction has been to fight cases on the grounds that no duty of care arises to the plaintiff (i.e. as in the Caparo case). This is somewhat of an unsatisfactory solution as the public look upon the auditor escaping liability on a 'technicality' of the law while they have not proved that they have not been negligent.

In practice many negligence claims do not come to court because of the costs and possible bad publicity resulting to the audit firms. Settlements have been made for a reduced sum of damages 'out of court' with most of the money coming from the persons who insured the audit firms against damages arising out of liability to negligence claims. This, for a time, was regarded as a 'solution' as a part of gross income of the auditing firms was paid to insurers as **professional indemnity insurance**. Costs were therefore known and it was the insurers who were taking the risk for negligence claims.

The overall result of this however has been an ever increasing trend of claims for larger and larger amounts so that insurers do not cover all the claim and the premiums payable have become very expensive.

The current remedy suggested by the large audit firms is that the firm should be allowed as part of its contract with the client company to set a liability on the size of any claim – i.e. a liability cap. Auditors are now able to practise as limited companies. This gives the partners the protection of limited liability, but it does not stop the firm being sued for large amounts of money and the firm being wound up.

This solution does not of course remove the cause of the problem i.e. that the auditor may have been negligent but many argue that few auditors are negligent. They point out that the main reason that auditors are subject to so many negligence claims is the result of a 'deep pocket syndrome' i.e. the auditors are sued because they have to be well insured, which the directors do not. Ultimately, it is the directors who have the responsibility for the accuracy of the internal controls and therefore the accounting records, this is the justification behind the supporters of limited auditor liability.

Many people consider that the current climate places a disproportionate liability burden on the auditor, and it also has a negative impact on the auditor's behaviour, for instance:

- audit firms are unwilling to provide advice outside the limits of the assignment; whereas users increasingly want more detailed information

- there are few firms who will/can undertake the audit of large organisations due to the level of insurance required. This also significantly increases the audit fee and reduces competitiveness and choice within the audit market

- auditors are likely to be reluctant to undertake new types of assurance activity.

Proportional liability and/or liability capping exist or are being introduced in many countries. The US has proportionate liability and Germany has statutory limitation of the amount. In the US a 'Model Business Act' provides that directors must discharge their duties with the care that a person in a like position would reasonably believe appropriate under the circumstances. Also, in many states this duty is subject to a business judgement rule which is used to analyse whether a board decision can be successfully challenged or a director held personally responsible. The Courts would then consider whether or not the director acted in good faith and whether the decision made was in the best interests of the corporation. The Act has a provision to allow a corporation to eliminate/limit the liability of directors for money damages for breach of their duty of care if it can be seen that the directors acted in good faith. In Barbados however, it is considered that the management of resident companies are not sufficiently regulated by legislation such that they can 'get away' with attempting to mislead auditors or with hiding negative financial information.

So you can see that the worldwide position in respect of auditor liability varies significantly in different countries. You are not expected to have a detailed knowledge of the rules in any one particular location but need to have an overall appreciation of the situation and be able to demonstrate your understanding of the issues.

One way in which auditors may seek to avoid liability for non-statutory work is to use 'disclaimers of liability' such as:

'While every care has been taken in the preparation of this document, it may contain errors for which we cannot be held responsible.'

3 QUALITY CONTROL

3.1 INTRODUCTION

This subject was examined in an earlier chapter. However, it is relevant to mention it at this stage as it is important in ensuring that audit work is performed to a high standard, thus avoiding the risk of negligence claims arising.

All firms should establish and monitor quality control procedures and policies to ensure that audits are conducted in accordance with auditing standards. The policies and procedures should be communicated to all staff, via policy statements, audit manuals and informal briefings. It is important that they are then monitored to ensure that they are implemented.

3.2 QUALITY CONTROL PROCEDURES

The key areas which the firm's procedures should cover are reiterated below in summary form:

(a) providing guidance on professional requirements

(b) ensuring staff are sufficiently skilled and competent to perform their work

(c) evaluation of prospective clients and ensuring reappointment is only taken where appropriate

(d) proper assignment of work to suitable staff

(e) proper delegation of work which is adequately directed, supervised and reviewed

(f) consultation between audit staff as required to avoid uncertainties and to resolve any matters requiring the use of judgement

(g) adequate monitoring to ensure that the professional standards of the firm are properly and effectively reviewed.

CONCLUSION

The auditors may have civil and criminal liabilities as a consequence of carrying out their work. Negligence under the law of tort is however, the most important form of potential liability.

Over time case decisions have modified the view which the courts take on the question of *to whom does an auditor owe a duty of care?* Currently, the position is that a duty of care is owed to a third party where it is foreseen that a statement will be relied upon – there is a relevant degree of proximity between the parties and it must be just and reasonable to impose a duty of care.

In order to minimise the risk of negligence claims, the audit firm should have satisfactory quality control procedures.

KEY TERMS

Civil law – Individuals who may have suffered some loss as a result of the actions of another individual take action through the courts. If the claim is successful, damages may be awarded.

Criminal law – The State takes action acting on behalf of society as a whole. Penalties may include fines or imprisonment.

Tort – A civil wrong other than that arising under contract law, giving rise to a claim for damages.

Negligence – A tort in which a person who owes another a duty of care fails to take reasonable care as a result of which the other person suffers some loss or damage.

SELF TEST QUESTIONS

		Paragraph
1	Can shareholders sue the auditor under contract law?	1.3
2	What three things must a person claiming for negligence prove in order to be successful?	1.3
3	What was the outcome in the Caparo case?	1.3
4	When a firm is appointed as an auditor, what factors should be borne in mind in relation to quality control?	3.2

THE AUDITOR'S LIABILITY : CHAPTER 17

EXAM-STYLE QUESTION 1

DUTY OF CARE

For many years the law had adopted an approach whereby no action for negligence could be brought if the parties concerned had no contractual relationship with each other. Thus, the auditor had a contractual relationship with his client company only and owed a duty of care to it alone. However, the courts have increasingly sought to extend the liability of the auditor to other (even potential) users of financial statements. The view of the judiciary appears to be that the time is ripe for the auditing profession to assume a greater responsibility for its actions. The risk attaching to the users of audited financial statements has been reduced and, at the same time, there has been an increase in the risk carried by the auditing profession.

You are required to describe the judicial decisions which have altered the range of the auditors' duty of care to third parties.

(Total: 15 marks)

For a suggested answer, see the 'Answers' section at the end of the book.

EXAM-STYLE QUESTION 2

DUTY OF CARE

For many years the law had adopted an approach whereby no action for negligence could be brought if the parties concerned had no contractual relationship with each other. Thus, the auditor had a contractual relationship with his client company only and owed a duty of care to it alone. However, the courts have increasingly sought to extend the liability of the auditor to other (even potential) users of financial statements. The view of the judiciary appears to be that the time is ripe for the auditing profession to assume a greater responsibility for its actions. The risk attaching to the users of audited financial statements has been reduced and, at the same time, there has been an increase in the risk carried by the auditing profession.

You are required to:

(a) explain how the auditor can ensure that the risk attaching to an audit is reduced to a minimum **(9 marks)**

(b) comment on the view that much of the litigation and allegations of negligence directed against the auditors may be more appropriately aimed at the directors of a company.
(6 marks)

(Total: 15 marks)

For a suggested answer, see the 'Answers' section at the end of the book.

ANSWERS TO ACTIVITIES AND QUESTIONS

CHAPTER 1

ACTIVITY 1

The main points to be made are:

1. Some companies and other organisations are required by law to have their accounts audited. This, however, is unlikely to apply to you as a sole trader, though ultimately it depends on the law of the country in which you are operating.

2. An audit can identify deficiencies in the accounting system and lead to recommendations for their improvement.

3. A satisfactory auditor's report can be used to provide evidence of a well-run business when seeking to raise external finance.

4. It can be useful for businesses wanting to change their current ownership, such as forming a partnership, or incorporating to form a limited company.

PRACTICE QUESTION 1

KID BROTHER

Tutorial note: Imagine yourself here talking to your 'brother' about accountancy, assuming that your brother was at the same stage as you a few years ago i.e. considering accountancy as a career. This should indicate the level to pitch your letter at. Note the importance of responding to the examiner's specific requirements – here, a letter!

1108 Leicester Road, Capital City, W2

12 October 20X9

Dear Guy

I received your letter this morning and was pleased to read that you are contemplating accountancy as a career. As requested, I shall explain the nature and purposes of the audit.

(a) **The legal position and the purpose of the audit**

The most common form of business entity in many countries is the limited company.

In a limited company the 'owners' of the company (the shareholders) appoint the 'directors' to run the company on their behalf. At certain times (usually annually) the directors produce accounts for the shareholders showing the financial position of the company at that time (the statement of financial position) and the results for the period just ended (the statement of comprehensive income). The information to be disclosed to the shareholders is usually detailed in legislation and certain professional publications known as accounting standards.

The shareholders appoint the auditor to conduct an independent examination of the accounts in order to form an opinion as to whether adequate books and records have been kept, that the accounts comply with the legal requirements and that they give a true and fair view (an undefined term, usually taken to mean 'not misleading'). It is generally a legal requirement that all limited companies over a certain size should be subject to audit, and have an auditor's report on the annual accounts.

After the completion of the audit the auditor writes a report to the shareholders indicating whether in his opinion the accounts comply with these requirements. He would also ensure that the accounts comply with any relevant accounting standards issued by the accountancy bodies.

The auditor's report lends credibility to the accounts since it is the opinion of an independent expert – the auditor – so third parties, e.g. suppliers or providers of loans, can rely on the accounts. Thus, the primary purpose of the audit is to conduct such tests and enquiries as the auditor considers necessary to form his opinion. There are other (secondary) purposes of the audit: detection of fraud and error (although not usually a purpose specified by legislation); being of help to management by giving advice; and so on.

(b) **Practical points as to the nature of the audit**

The directors are responsible for the day-to-day running of the company (safeguarding assets, keeping adequate records). To help them in this, they institute various 'methods' or 'systems' to deal with the types of transactions in which the company is involved (buying, selling, keeping inventories). To assist in ensuring that the possibility of fraud or error in the records is reduced, the directors set up a system of internal control'. This in very basic terms means various checks and procedures to control the recording of the business transactions.

The actual audit is usually performed at the client's premises as a two-stage operation for each year. The first stage is referred to as an interim, or systems, audit. This is usually conducted before the year end. The emphasis is on evaluating the accounting systems and system of internal control to see if they appear to be adequate for the preparation of accounts. This involves discussion with staff, preparation of detailed notes (sometimes in the form of flowcharts), completing questionnaires and actually checking or testing the recording of transactions.

The second, and final, stage is concerned with directly verifying items in the final accounts. The extent of verification work is determined by the auditor's assessment of the adequacy of the system of internal control. This builds on work performed at the earlier stage, but the emphasis is on direct verification. For example, part of the verification of the item of inventory would require the auditor to actually attend the inventory-counting.

Audits are performed by an audit team. This would vary according to the size of the client, but would include staff under training and qualified accountants. The audit is directly controlled by a manager. The actual auditor's report is signed in the name of the professional firm by one of its partners. The partner relies upon the work carried out by the audit team, as shown by the working papers and notes on the audit files.

This letter is, of course, only a very general outline of the nature of the work, and I do not think you should rely on one letter to choose your future career. If I can give you any further help or guidance please let me know.

Yours

Emma

ANSWERS TO ACTIVITIES AND QUESTIONS

PRACTICE QUESTION 2

(a) An audit can be described as the independent examination of evidence from which the financial statements of an enterprise are derived in order to give the reader of those statements confidence as to the *'truth and fairness'* of the state of affairs which they disclose. The objective of an audit has been described as being to enable auditors to express an opinion whether the financial statements give a true and fair view and have been properly prepared in accordance with the applicable reporting framework.

Independent – an auditor should be, and be seen to be, independent of the enterprise on which he is expressing an audit opinion.

Examination – there is a separation of audit and accountancy functions, with audit being the examination of the financial statements.

Opinion – the auditor does not certify that the financial statements are correct; he merely expresses an opinion.

Financial statements – this term includes statements of financial position and comprehensive income, statement of changes in equity, statement of cash flows and any supporting notes.

Applicable reporting framework – the audit is carried out in accordance with relevant legislation and accounting standards (e.g. IASs and IFRSs).

CHAPTER 2

ACTIVITY 1

There is a possible danger that objectivity or independence may be threatened by the acceptance of hospitality from a client and thus the acceptance of 'undue hospitality' poses a threat to the objectivity principle.

However, this does not preclude all hospitality, only excessive hospitality. In the circumstances outlined it is reasonable to conclude that the invitation can be accepted.

ACTIVITY 2

This is confidential client information and should not be supplied to Y unless X gives its consent.

FAU: FOUNDATIONS IN AUDIT

EXAM-STYLE QUESTION 1

BRIEFING NOTES – ACCA RULES

AUDITOR INDEPENDENCE

The ACCA rules in respect of auditor independence are as follows:

(i) An established practice should ensure that the recurring fees from one client (or group of clients) do not exceed 15% of the gross income of the practice.

(ii) An auditor should ensure that personal relationships do not affect his objectivity.

(iii) A partner in a practice or his spouse or minor child or any member of staff employed on the audit should not hold shares in the client company except in special cases (see (vii) below).

(iv) A practice should not make a loan to a client nor guarantee a client's borrowings. Neither should it accept a loan from a client or have its borrowings guaranteed by a client. This also applies to a partner in a practice or spouse or minor child.

(v) A partner or his spouse or minor child or any employee of the firm should not accept goods or services from a client unless the value is modest. Acceptance of undue hospitality can also threaten independence.

(vi) Auditors should take care where involved in litigation with their clients. A minor dispute over fees may not cause a problem; a writ for negligence almost certainly will.

(vii) Where any shares are held in an audit client company due to special cases they should not be voted at any general meeting in any matters concerning the role of the auditor. These special cases are:

- Where shares are acquired involuntarily (for example, a bequest). These should be disposed of at the earliest opportunity.

- Where legislation or a company's constitution require an auditor to hold shares, the auditor should hold the minimum necessary.

If you have any queries, please do not hesitate to contact me.

EXAM-STYLE QUESTION 2

MEMORANDUM

To   Audit Partner

From   Audit Junior

Date   XX/XX/XX

Subject   **Further measures to enhance auditor independence**

INTRODUCTION

Further to your request, I have summarised further ways in which the independence of the auditor could be improved. These are additional to those already required in the ACCA rules.

POSSIBLE ENHANCEMENTS

Non-audit services

The independence of the auditor might be strengthened and improved in several ways and there has been much recent discussion among the accountancy bodies on this subject. One area for discussion is whether the provision of other services detracts from an objective approach to an audit. These other services could include accountancy, consultancy, taxation, etc. Such services should be charged separately from audit work and the auditor's involvement must be advisory only. He must not perform executive functions or take executive decisions. The prohibition of other services would clearly affect the small company particularly in a detrimental way as it often relies on its auditors for this type of support.

Audit committees

A further suggestion has been the compulsory setting up of audit committees which are becoming increasingly common. These audit committees consist primarily of non-executive directors who are able to view a company's affairs in a detached and independent way and can liaise effectively between the main board of directors and the external auditors. An audit committee can increase public confidence in the credibility and objectivity of published financial information.

Other measures

Other changes proposed include the rotation of auditors on, say, a three year cycle. However, this would prove costly as additional time would be required at the start of each new cycle for each firm to familiarise itself with the client and its systems, staff etc.

Independent reviews are now also quite common in practice. This is the process whereby the audit work and the relationship between auditor and client are reviewed by an audit partner other than the one responsible for the audit. This could be another partner in the same office or a partner from another office of the same firm.

Please let me know if you require any further information.

CHAPTER 3

ACTIVITY 1

The auditors' overall duty is to express an opinion on the truth and fairness of the financial statements. Two more specific duties which may apply, subject to local legislation are:

(a) To consider whether other information contained in the published annual report, such as the Directors' Report is consistent with that in the accounts.

(b) To report to the members as to whether the company's financial statements have been prepared in accordance with appropriate legislation.

Two specific rights granted to the auditors to enable them to perform their duties are:

(a) The right of access at all times to the books, records, documents and accounts of the company.

(b) The right to require from the officers of the company such information and explanations necessary for the performance of their audit.

EXAM-STYLE QUESTION 1

THE GROWFAST COMPANY

Tutorial note: A question where it is easy to pick up marks if the basic facts are known. Remember that some questions in the examination are factual and that you will score highly if the basic facts have been learnt before the exam.

(a) The need for an audit arises from the division in many companies between ownership of the company, and the day-to-day running of the company.

In many companies, the owners of the company, that is the shareholders, will not normally be involved in the actual running of the company. The company will be run by the directors, who are elected or appointed by the shareholders. The owners of the company thus buy shares in the company, and expect a return on their investment in the company in the form of dividends, whilst the directors run the company and are paid a salary for doing this.

At the end of each year, the directors will produce the financial statements to show the results of the company. The shareholders need confidence that these financial statements are correct i.e. that the directors have actually told the truth regarding the company's results. To ensure that the financial statements are correct the shareholders employ an auditor. The job of the auditor is to 'audit' or check the financial statements, and then report back to the shareholders whether these financial statements are correct, or show a 'true and fair view'. By having this independent check the shareholders gain confidence that the accounts are reliable and therefore that their investment in terms of money, is being handled properly.

(b) The responsibilities of the directors in relation to the accounting function of the company are as follows:

(i) to safeguard the company's assets and to prevent fraud and errors in the company

(ii) to ensure that the company keeps proper accounting records as defined in appropriate legislation

(iii) to prepare annual financial statements to show the results of the company for the year and the state of affairs of the company at the reporting date. These accounts must show a true and fair view

(iv) to deliver to the regulatory authority a copy of the company's audited financial statements within any prescribed statutory time limit

(v) to set up a system of internal control in the company to ensure that all of the above are carried out. The directors cannot run the company by themselves; they must employ staff to carry out many of the accounting and other duties in the company. The system of internal control tries to ensure that the directors' other responsibilities above are met.

CHAPTER 4

ACTIVITY 2

There is no statutory or professional definition of true and fair.

True and fair is a technical term and the phrase must be looked at as an entirety.

To show a true and fair view accounts must be prepared:

(a) in accordance with generally accepted accounting principles

(b) on a consistent basis, and

(c) so as not to be misleading.

ACTIVITY 3

The correction of both errors would reduce the net asset value of the company.

The inventory error would reduce net assets by $3m, one third of the figure shown in the draft accounts. This may well change my decision to buy the company, or, at least, reduce significantly the price which I am prepared to pay. As knowledge of this error is likely to change my behaviour and decision, it would almost certainly be seen to be material.

The $0.1m error relating to accrued liabilities is not so likely to affect my decision to buy the company and I may well still pay $10m for it – especially as accruals are a notoriously subjective area. This error is less likely to be seen as material.

ACTIVITY 4

The main considerations when determining whether something is material are:

(a) the size of the item

(b) the nature of the item

(c) the likely impact of the item.

PRACTICE QUESTION

CONCEPT OF MATERIALITY

Tutorial note: It is normal to give a definition and discussion in this sort of question to make some relevant points about the term being queried.

It is the auditor's chief duty to express an opinion as to whether the financial statements which he audits show a true and fair view. The true and fair concept is a general one and the auditor is often faced with deciding if a particular error or omission is such that it prevents a true and fair view being shown. If so, the item is said to be material.

Before an auditor issues a modified auditor's report he must, therefore, consider whether or not the points on which he is not satisfied are material or not. To do this, the following points must be considered:

(a) Is the item so fundamental that the accounts can no longer be said to show a true and fair view?

(b) Materiality is a relative factor and the item must be considered in relation to the accounts as a whole, the total of which it would form part and the corresponding amount in the previous years.

(c) Some items are capable of exact calculation. Others such as depreciation are merely estimated and, providing the estimate is reasonable, should be acceptable.

Under statutory and professional accounting regulations the disclosure of certain items depends upon whether or not they are material e.g. amount of contingent liabilities, capital commitments, transfer to reserves, hire of plant and machinery. Other items, however, are often specifically required to be shown e.g. directors' emoluments and the audit fee. If these are incorrect, the items must be material since the accounts will not then comply with the legislation.

In conclusion, therefore, an auditor must take into account the degree of approximation necessary in calculating a particular item, the size of the company and the level of its profits and its significance in relation to the company as a whole.

The basic question to be answered is 'does the misstatement or omission of this item impair the true and fair view principle?'

CHAPTER 5

ACTIVITY 1

Analytical review procedures should be used during the planning, testing and review stage of the audit, to isolate account areas which merit further investigation or trends which seem unusual. Procedures will include ratio analysis, exception reporting and comparison with industry and competitor standards. The auditor will consider current and historical data and trends. The reconciliation of purchases, sales and inventory by volume and quantity can be a useful technique.

The review forms part of the basis for the auditor's conclusion on the financial statements as well as useful and time-saving information to assist in the planning and conduct of future audits.

ANSWERS TO ACTIVITIES AND QUESTIONS

ACTIVITY 2

The main areas that the auditor would consider are as follows:

- Business and financial environment:
    - any deterioration in operations
    - profit analysis of different operational divisions/departments
    - reasons for continuing to operate unprofitable segments
    - range and diversity of products
    - extent and nature of financial reports
    - effectiveness of financial management
    - range of business financial planning.

- Personnel environment:
    - state of morale and motivation
    - opportunity for fraud
    - control over recruitment
    - level of expertise and qualifications
    - clear and appropriate organisation structure.

- Accounting environment:
    - efficiency and effectiveness of accounting system(s)
    - adequacy of staff.

- Management environment:
    - management attitude and competence in preparing the financial statements
    - style of decision making
    - risk levels
    - source of remuneration
    - acceptance of change
    - susceptibility to window dressing.

- Professional environment:
    - limitation of scope in the audit work
    - audit pressures
    - possible independence conflicts
    - modified auditor's report previously
    - previous auditor conflicts
    - risk of current audit qualification
    - state of relations between client and third parties e.g. bank, solicitors.

ACTIVITY 3

The objectivity of the department, including its freedom from conflicting responsibilities and the level of management it reports to. In this case, you know that the internal auditors report directly to the board of directors, so the department has an important status in the company. You would also consider whether there is any limitation on the assignments carried out, and to what extent recommendations are acted upon by management.

The competence of the people carrying out the work. In this case it would be necessary to inquire about the competence of the members of the internal audit team; for example, are they qualified accountants?.

The application of a systematic and disciplined approach. The external auditors should review the work carried out by the internal auditors to check that it was documented in the first place, and to assess whether it was planned and whether there is evidence of its being supervised and reviewed.

Communication with external audit. You would need to enquire what arrangements have been put in place to enable internal audit to communicate freely and effectively with external audit.

ACTIVITY 4

Knowledge of the business may be obtained from sources such as:

(a) the previous auditor

(b) prior year working papers

(c) industry statistics

(d) press reports

(e) bankers and other advisers

(f) prior year financial statements

(g) the client himself e.g. management accounts, budgets, meetings with directors and managers.

ANSWERS TO ACTIVITIES AND QUESTIONS

ACTIVITY 5

(a) The objectives of audit planning are:

    (i)   To ensure that appropriate attention is paid to the different areas of the audit. This involves, for example, ensuring that adequate time is devoted to the audit of inventories, which are usually higher risk, and that petty cash, which is usually lower risk, is not over audited.

    (ii)   To ensure that potential problem areas are identified, such as deficiencies in the control over payables which might lead to a material understatement, and ensure sufficient attention is devoted to the relevant area(s).

    (iii)   To facilitate review.

Planning also assists in the proper allocation of work to the audit team and the co-ordination of work done by other auditors and experts.

(b) **Planning procedures may include the following (amongst others):**

    (i)   Review of points raised in previous year's audit.

    (ii)   Assess the effects of changes in legislation or accounting practice.

    (iii)   Analytical review of management accounts.

    (iv)   Review of significant changes in systems.

    (v)   Preparation of a timetable of audit work and a budget.

    (vi)   Consideration of the extent to which client's staff can assist in accounting matters.

ACTIVITY 6

The audit partner's typical responsibilities will be:

(a) to agree the audit fees to be charged with the client

(b) to review the audit and ensure the audit objectives have been achieved, and form the audit opinion

(c) to sign the auditor's report (after the accounts have been approved by the directors).

ACTIVITY 7

The working papers would be filed as follows:

Permanent Audit File	**Current Audit File**
– Memorandum and Articles	– Audit programme for receivables
– Details of accounting policies	– Ratio analysis. The permanent file would be updated with this information
– Bank account details	– Minutes of board meetings
– Organisation charts	
– Product pricing policy	– Report to management

ACTIVITY 8

A firm's quality control procedures should cover:

(a) professional (ethical) requirements

(b) skills and competence of audit staff via appropriate training procedures

(c) acceptance and retention of clients

(d) assignment of work to audit staff and to outside experts where appropriate

(e) delegation of work

(f) consultation with partners and others (to resolve audit issues)

(g) monitoring and reviewing of audit work to ensure compliance with standards.

PRACTICE QUESTION

KOALA LIMITED

	OVERALL AUDIT PLAN
To:	Mr X (Partner in charge)
From:	Ms Y
Date:	X-X-20XX
Subject:	The Koala Company
	Audit planning – year end 30 September 20X7

(a) (i) **Knowledge of the business**

The main point arising in 20X6 was the continuing weakness in internal control over expenses. This led to our spending considerable time on detailed substantive testing in this area.

No particular problems were discovered during the testing however, and there are no other specific matters of continuing importance.

(ii) **Changes during the year to 30-9-X7**

The most significant change this year was the appointment of Miss Jones late in 20X6 as Chief Accountant.

Miss Jones has considerably strengthened the systems for payment and recording of expenses with new systems being fully operational from 1 January.

There are no changes in legislation or best accounting practice which affect the company.

(b) **Risk and materiality**

(i) **Systems evaluation and tests of control**

Obviously this is most critical for the systems which have changed, but we will need to confirm that other systems may still be relied on.

(ii) **Salesmen's expenses**

As always this is a critical expense in the statement of profit or loss and other comprehensive income.

(c) **Nature, timing and extent of procedures**

In all areas except purchases, wages and salesmen's expenses the approach adopted will be exactly as in 20X6. We will place reliance on the effective operation of internal controls to reduce the level of substantive testing.

In relation to purchases, wages and salesmen's expenses we will carry out our testing in three sections.

In testing transactions up to 31 December we will adopt the purely substantive approach used in 20X6.

For the nine month period from 1 January to 30 September however we will perform tests of controls, evaluating and testing the systems, then aiming to place reliance on the controls to reduce our substantive testing.

We will carry out some additional work on the changeover period where there is the greatest chance of errors occurring.

We will carry out a receivables' circularisation as at 30 September 20X7.

We will attend the annual inventory count on 20 September 20X7.

(d) **Co-ordination, direction and review**

July	18	Interim visit – systems work and detailed testing of transactions.
July	22	Systems work completed: End of interim visit.
August	5	Report to management sent.
September	19	Audit confirmation letters sent.
September	20	Inventory count.
October	20	Final audit visit.

The client would like the accounts signed by Christmas.

Miss Jones is under pressure in this new job but we must seek her assistance in preparing statement of financial position schedules, inventory summaries, aged inventory and receivables' analyses etc. With this co-operation I propose the following budget for audit hours.

Partner	5 hours
Manager	10 hours
Senior	100 hours
Junior	70 hours

Senior and Junior includes 35 extra hours each in relation to extra systems evaluation work this year.

I shall be in the office all next week if you wish to discuss any of the points raised in this memorandum.

Tutorial note: The structure of this answer covers all the areas to be considered relating to audit planning:

(a) the auditor's knowledge of the business

(b) risk and materiality

(c) the nature, timing and extent of procedures

(d) co-ordination, direction, supervision and review.

In this way you can demonstrate your knowledge of auditing principles. The examiner would also be looking to see that you had taken note of the information in the question; note how these details have been incorporated into the answer.

CHAPTER 6

ACTIVITY 2

The following methods may be used to record the client's system:

(a) **Narrative systems notes**

This is a simple convenient way of recording a system – the quickest approach in a small unsophisticated system.

However, it suffers from the disadvantages that:

(i) it will be cumbersome in a large system

(ii) it may be difficult to interpret and review

(iii) it may be difficult to alter if the system changes

(iv) it may be easy to miss 'loose ends' or even to miss out whole sections of the system.

(b) **Organisation charts**

These are a convenient way of showing the individuals in an organisation and the lines for reporting and delegation of responsibilities between those individuals; useful to indicate who should report to whom.

However, they do not deal with informal relationships and do not indicate the detailed reporting procedures involved. They cannot, therefore, replace the other recording methods, but only supplement them.

(c) **Internal control questionnaire**

The ICQ is a pre-printed document used widely in practice to ascertain controls in a client's system. It helps to ensure a formal approach to systems recording. The auditor's attention should be drawn to the need for controls in the system. It is easy to cross reference to other working papers.

It has few disadvantages except that it may be used improperly. The auditor may waste time asking unnecessary questions using a standard ICQ. It may encourage auditors to perform work in a mechanical fashion without considering the circumstances of a particular client.

(d) **Flowcharts**

Being a diagrammatic representation of the system, they are not only easy to understand but also better facilitate spotting deficiencies and inefficiencies in internal controls than other narrative forms.

They provide a permanent record which is easy to update. They also allow rapid independent review.

Limitations of flowcharts are that they are time consuming and of little use in small systems.

FAU: FOUNDATIONS IN AUDIT

ACTIVITY 3

An ICQ (Internal Control Questionnaire) is a formal document which is often standardised by many audit firms and comprises a list of questions (to which the answer is usually either 'yes' or 'no'. The main objectives of the ICQ are:

(a) to ascertain a client's systems of accounting and internal control

(b) to evaluate the systems of internal control

(c) to highlight control strengths which the auditor intends to rely on

(d) to identify control deficiencies which should be tested in detail and reported to management.

ACTIVITY 4

An ICQ is designed to identify whether controls exist which meet specific control objectives, whereas ICEs are designed to determine whether controls exist which prevent or detect specified errors or omissions.

For example:

(a) an ICQ may ask 'are all invoice payments authorised?'

(b) an ICE for the same area would ask 'Is there reasonable assurance that all payments are properly authorised?'

PRACTICE QUESTION 1

INTERNAL CONTROLS

(a) A system of internal control should have the following objectives:

  (i) ensure that the business of the enterprise is carried on in an orderly and efficient manner

  (ii) ensure adherence to internal policies

  (iii) prevent and detect fraud and error

  (iv) safeguard the assets

  (v) secure, as far as possible, the completeness and accuracy of the records

  (vi) secure the timely preparation of reliable financial information.

(b) The main categories of internal control are:

  (i) approval and control of documents

  (ii) controls over computerised applications and the IT environment

  (iii) checking the arithmetical accuracy of the records

  (iv) maintaining and reviewing control accounts and trial balances

  (v) comparing the results of cash, security and inventory counts with the accounting records

  (vi) comparing internal data with external sources of information

  (vii) limiting direct physical access to assets and records.

ANSWERS TO ACTIVITIES AND QUESTIONS

PRACTICE QUESTION 2

WAGES AND SALARIES

The objectives of the system of internal control dealing with wages and salaries include the following:

1   To ensure that only valid and authorised employees are paid.

2   To ensure that employees are paid at the correct rate for the time worked.

3   To ensure that statutory payroll deductions have been correctly calculated and made, and then paid over to the appropriate third party e.g. tax authorities.

4   to ensure that any voluntary payroll deductions have been properly authorised, calculated and made, and then paid over to the appropriate third party e.g. charitable donations.

5   To ensure that individual wages and salary costs have been correctly calculated.

6   To ensure that the payments are made to the right employees.

7   To ensure that all transactions relating to wages and salaries are included in the accounting records.

(Any five of the above is acceptable or other appropriate objectives.)

PRACTICE QUESTION 3

SALES AND RECEIVABLES

The objectives of the system of internal control dealing with sales and receivables include the following:

1   To ensure that customer orders are authorised before the order is fulfilled.

2   To ensure that the correct goods are despatched to fulfil approved customer orders.

3   To ensure that customers are invoiced at the right price for goods ordered and subsequently despatched.

4   To ensure that any goods returned by customers are recorded and examined to determine the validity of any customer claims for refunds or credit notes.

5   To ensure that invoices and credit notes raised are authorised before the transactions are recorded in the accounting records.

6   To ensure that sales invoices are paid by applying effective credit control procedures.

7   To ensure that any amounts due but considered to be doubtful or bad are written down to their expected recoverable amount.

(Any five of the above is acceptable or other appropriate objectives.)

CHAPTER 7

ACTIVITY 1

- An invoice from a supplier of an item of plant to the client

    This is written evidence from an external source. Provided the invoice is an original, not a copy, it would be treated as reliable evidence.

- A calculation of the depreciation for the year prepared by the auditor

    This is evidence produced by the auditor himself and would therefore be viewed as reliable evidence.

- A verbal statement from the managing director of the client that the market value of the company's factory premises amounts to $20 million

    This is verbal, internal evidence. It would not normally be treated as being sufficiently reliable for audit purposes. The auditor would seek additional evidence in this area, perhaps in the form of a report from an expert valuer.

ACTIVITY 2

Test of control to be performed, both based on the auditing testing procedure of inspection are (only two required):

(a) Review control accounts for the last 12 months to examine whether evidence existed to show that they reconciled to the ledgers e.g. a signature and date from a responsible person on the control account.

(b) Review the accounts to verify that the control account reconciliations had been performed at the month end, and that evidence existed of review by the section supervisor or manager.

(c) Review the control account reconciliation performed by a member for evidence that it has been checked and signed off by a supervisor.

ANSWERS TO ACTIVITIES AND QUESTIONS

ACTIVITY 3

AUDIT PROGRAMME

Client name: Performed by:
Period: Date:
  Reviewed by:
  Date:

Test: Tests of control – sales system

Detailed tests

W/P Ref:

(1) Perform sequence checks on invoices, credit notes, despatch notes and orders. Ensure all items are included and none are omitted

(2) Check authorisation exists at the following stages in the sales process:

　(a) acceptance of the order

　(b) despatch of the goods

　(c) raising of invoice or credit note

　(d) pricing (and discounts if applicable)

　(e) write off of irrecoverable debts

(3) At each authorisation point, check that the relevant signature exists and that the control has been applied

(4) Obtain evidence that the arithmetical accuracy of invoices, credit notes and sales tax has been checked (e.g. by signatures)

ACTIVITY 4

XY Audit firm
123 Little Street
Brightown
XP11 8QD

XX December 20XX

Dear Sir

Further to your request for advice on purchases system control procedures, the relevant details are specified below:

1. The key areas to be controlled within the purchases cycle are:

    - ordering of goods
    - receipt of goods
    - invoicing
    - returns
    - payables ledger control.

2. The control procedures required over invoicing are as follows:

    (a) Purchase invoices should be stamped with an approval grid and given a unique serial number to ensure that all are accounted for.

    (b) Purchase invoices should be matched with goods received notes and should not be processed until this is done.

    (c) Invoices should be checked against the order and the GRN, and its arithmetical accuracy should be checked (it should be cast and cross cast).

    (d) All invoices should be approved by a responsible official who is independent of the receipt and ordering function. This approval should be evidenced by a signature for example.

    (e) Invoice sequential numbers should be checked against the day book.

    (f) Input VAT/ other recoverable taxes should be segregated from the actual expense item.

    (g) Invoices should be correctly allocated to appropriate general ledger accounts.

    (h) Batch controls should be used to ensure the accuracy of postings to the purchases day book, general ledger and payables ledger.

    (i) Details of goods returned should be recorded and checked to credit notes received.

ANSWERS TO ACTIVITIES AND QUESTIONS

ACTIVITY 5

The main controls that would be expected in a payroll system include the following:

(a) Personnel records should be kept similar to those for hourly paid employees.

(b) Written authority should be required to employ or dismiss an employee or change salary rate.

(c) Overtime (if any) should be authorised by someone outside the payroll department.

(d) The usual checks on deductions are required.

(e) When an employee has been absent for a significant period his entitlement to salary should be checked against personnel details and the employer's policy in this area.

(f) Direct bank transfers should also be signed and checked regularly against details on personnel files.

ACTIVITY 6

(a) Information to be recorded in the non-current asset register would be as follows:

- unique asset number (sequential number allocated)
- date of purchase and supplier
- description
- classification of asset (e.g. motor vehicle, fixtures and fittings)
- location
- date of sale (where applicable)
- purchase price
- depreciation rate
- depreciation amount
- net book value.

(b) Typical control procedures that should be performed are as follows:

- the register should be amended/updated by someone independent of the purchase/sale function, and this should only be performed on receipt of proper authorisation by a responsible official
- the register should be checked to the non-current assets periodically to ensure that none have gone missing
- the register should be regularly reconciled e.g. monthly to the general ledger.

KAPLAN PUBLISHING

PRACTICE QUESTION 1

STICKY BAR CHOCOLATES

Tutorial note: A relatively short question that could give time pressure problems due to the many sub-parts. State the definitions quickly, and then list the other information required to speed up the writing of the answer i.e. don't write long paragraphs when point form answers are sufficient and clearer too.

(a) **Shortcomings**

  (i) There is no check that the expenses claimed by the salesmen actually represent money spent on behalf of the company.

  (ii) There is no check that the expenses were properly incurred by the salesmen in carrying out their duties.

  (iii) The deputy chief accountant could easily perpetrate a fraud either alone or in collusion with a sales representative.

  Improvements

  (i) Each sales representative should complete a weekly log showing calls made and mileage covered. The logs and the expense claims should be submitted to the sales manager who should check and sign the log before passing it to the deputy chief accountant.

  (ii) At intervals a member of the accounts staff should verify that claimed mileage is consistent with the mileage shown on the cars' mileage recorders.

  (iii) The directors should verify that complete and signed documentation is attached to and is consistent with the cheques presented to them. They should cancel the presented documents to prevent a second presentation.

(b) Tests of control are those tests which seek to provide audit evidence that internal control procedures are being properly applied throughout the period under review.

  The tests of control that could be performed are:

  (i) Check that expense claim forms are signed by the rep, and countersigned by the deputy chief accountant as authorisation of the claim.

  (ii) Check that there is evidence that the cheque signatory has reviewed supporting documentation re validity of the payment made to the reps e.g. countersigning the claim form.

ANSWERS TO ACTIVITIES AND QUESTIONS

PRACTICE QUESTION 2

(a) Substantive procedures are those procedures which seek to provide audit evidence as to the financial statement assertions of completeness, existence, measurement, valuation, etc.

The substantive procedures that could be performed are:

(i) Completeness – examine expense claims paid after the reporting date to ensure that all outstanding claims are included.

(ii) Measurement and valuation – review mileage claims with mileage records obtained from inspection of cars or repair invoices. Verify that sales representatives who have made claims are legitimate employees of the company. Select a sample of hotel and entertaining expenses and verify that they are prima facie valid e.g. that the sales representative operates in the area and the customers entertained are customers of the company. Test the analysis of bank payments to ensure that all expense payments and no other payments are correctly charged to the account. Review previous years' accounts, directors' minutes and budgets, if any, to seek evidence of the validity of the total.

(b) Auditor's actions on discovering the false claim:

(i) Inform the management verbally immediately and in writing in the report to management.

(ii) Consider whether the discovery casts doubt on the effectiveness of the system, hence whether further tests may be necessary.

(iii) Consider whether the discovery casts doubt on the company's records in general and hence whether further work may be necessary in other areas.

EXAM-STYLE QUESTION 1

HOWDEN – 1

Tutorial note: (a) should be straightforward; (b) is more demanding, therefore try to think of any general principles that you know that could be of assistance.

(a) The following duties should be performed by different people:

(i) initiation of a transaction

(ii) custody or handling of the related asset

(iii) recording the transaction.

If these duties are segregated, then no one person is in a position to execute a complete transaction and therefore collusion would be required for a fraud to be perpetrated.

(b) Requisition notes for purchases should be authorised to confirm their validity.

Re-order levels and quantities should be pre-set and preferably recorded in advance on the requisition note. Re-order levels and quantities should be subject to review and there should be evidence of the review, signed by an appropriate person.

All orders should be recorded on official documents showing the suppliers' names, quantities ordered and price and authorised by a responsible official whose authority limits should be predefined.

Major items e.g. capital expenditure, should be authorised by the board, with authorisation noted in the board minutes.

Copies of orders should be retained as a method of following up late deliveries by suppliers.

EXAM-STYLE QUESTION 2

HOWDEN – 2

Tutorial note: (a) should be straightforward; (b) is more demanding, therefore try to think of any general principles that you know that could be of assistance.

(a) Goods inwards centres should be identified to deal with the receipt of all goods.

All goods should be checked for quantity and quality. Goods received notes should be raised for all goods accepted. The GRN should be signed by a responsible official.

Goods received notes should be checked against purchase orders and procedures should exist to notify the supplier of under- or over-deliveries.

A record of goods returned should be kept and checked to the credit notes received from suppliers.

(b) Purchase invoices received should be stamped with an approval grid and given a unique serial number to ensure purchase invoices do not go astray.

The invoices should be checked against the order and the GRN, and casts and extensions should also be checked.

The invoices should be signed as approved for payment by a responsible official independent of the ordering and receipt of goods functions.

Invoices should be properly allocated to the general ledger accounts, perhaps by allocating expenditure codes. A portion of such coding should be checked independently.

Input VAT/other recoverable taxes should be separated from the expense.

Payables ledger records should be kept by persons independent of the receiving of goods, invoice authorisation and payment routines.

Invoice sequential numbers should be checked against purchase day book details.

A payables ledger control account should be maintained and regularly checked against balances in the ledger by an independent official.

Statements from suppliers should be checked against the payables ledger account.

(c) Unused cheques should be held in a secure place.

The person who prepares cheques should have no responsibility over payables ledger or receivables ledger.

Cheques should be signed only when evidence of a properly approved transaction is available. Such evidence may take the form of invoices, payroll, petty cash book, etc.

This check should be evidenced by signing the supporting documentation.

In a large concern those approving the original document should be independent of those signing cheques.

Cheque signatories should be restricted to the minimum practical number.

Two signatories should be required except perhaps for cheques of small amounts.

The signing of blank cheques and cheques in favour of the signatory should be prohibited.

Cheques should be crossed before being signed.

Supporting documents should be cancelled as paid to prevent their use to support further cheque payments. This cancellation could be done by the cashier before the cheque is signed (providing the cancellation identifies the cheque number) or by the cheque signatory at the time of signing the cheque.

Cheques should preferably be despatched immediately. If not, they should be held in a safe place.

Returned cheques may be obtained from the bank and a sample checked against cash book entries and supporting documentation.

EXAM-STYLE QUESTION 3

THE QUICKSAND COMPANY

Tutorial note: A straightforward question requiring the candidate to simply list the expected internal controls, which a good candidate will have memorised! As long as sufficient controls are listed (at one mark per control a minimum of nine each for cheque payments and petty cash would be expected) then a pass should be obtained. Finally, note the letter format, marks would be awarded for good style here.

(a)

Kirk & Co
Certified Accountants
1701 Enterprise Road
Logtown

A Black Esq
Managing Director
The Quicksand Company
Freeman Industrial Estate
Longtown

14 February 20X7

Dear Sir

Internal control procedures for petty cash

Following our discussions of last week, I have set out below my recommendations for internal control procedures for the petty cash systems in your company.

The over-riding requirement of these systems is that money expended is in respect of valid transactions of the company. Petty cash given out when valid authorised vouchers are presented to the appropriate official. Detailed internal controls are as follows:

Petty cash payments

(i) Petty cash should be kept on an imprest system with the level of the cash float and its location being formally agreed. As the level of petty cash expenditure is around $300 per month a float of $350 should be maintained to meet this; $600 appears to be excessive here.

(ii) Only authorised persons should have access to the cash. In this case only the cashier and one director should have the petty cash tin key.

(iii) The cash should be held in a secure location e.g. the company safe.

(iv) Before cash is given out, the cashier should receive an authorised expense voucher signed by a responsible official. This official should not be the cashier.

(v) With the use of the imprest system, the cash in the petty cash tin together with the expense vouchers should always equal the amount of the float. Spot checks by a director not involved with petty cash payments could be carried out to ensure that this is the case.

(vi) When the petty cash float is to be reimbursed at the end of the month, the amount of the cheque required should be supported by the vouchers received during the month.

(vii) The vouchers in (vi) should be cancelled after the reimbursement is made to ensure that they are not used twice. Similarly the petty cash book will be signed to confirm the amount of the reimbursement.

(viii) The cashing of IOUs and cheques for individuals within the company should be prohibited except on express permission of the directors. Similarly a limit can be placed on the amount of any one petty cash payment which can only be amended by the directors.

(ix) The petty cash book should be reviewed regularly by a director not involved with the petty cash system, the castings should be checked along with the analysis of payments and the postings into the general ledger.

I hope that these procedures will be of use to you. Should you require any further advice or assistance please do not hesitate to contact me.

Yours faithfully

L McCoy

Partner

(b) The managing directors of many companies may decide not to become involved in the day-to-day running of the company and therefore leave this function to other staff and directors who have more skill in this area. Mr Black has apparently decided to follow this route. There is though some value in being involved to some degree in the cash payments of the company, because by signing cheques the director gains knowledge of what the company is paying for, and can exercise some control over the cash payments of the company. It is therefore unusual that Mr Black does not want to involve himself in this respect.

A satisfactory compromise is for Mr Black not to be involved in the smaller cheque payments, and not to be involved at all with the petty cash payments. Larger payments over a pre-determined amount could require his signature so that Mr Black can be familiar with the company's payments and maintain some control over these payments.

CHAPTER 8

ACTIVITY 1

The components of audit risk are:

IR = Inherent risk

CR = Control risk

DR = Detection risk

Sampling risk forms part of detection risk which is the risk that the audit procedures do not detect material errors or omissions in the financial statements. This may result from the use of inappropriate sampling techniques.

ACTIVITY 2

(a) **Tolerable error** is a monetary amount set by the auditor in order to obtain an appropriate level of assurance that the monetary amount set is not exceeded by the actual misstatement.

(b) **Expected error** is the amount of error that the auditor anticipates exists in the population.

(c) **Confidence level** is the degree of certainty that the auditor requires from the testing.

(d) **Precision limits** are the parameters within which the auditor is prepared to work i.e. it is the number of errors that the auditor is willing to accept in a population and still be satisfied it is correct.

The auditor commonly uses sampling as an audit technique where there are a high number of similar transactions; it would not be cost effective to examine all transactions.

ACTIVITY 3

Statistical sampling uses probability theory and requires the use of random number selection. It also enables the sample results to be evaluated quantitatively. In contrast, non-statistical sampling is more subjective and does not rely on probability theory.

FAU: FOUNDATIONS IN AUDIT

PRACTICE QUESTION

Tutorial note: A detailed knowledge of the mathematics underlying statistical sampling is NOT expected, but students should understand the basic techniques involved.

(a) The main advantages derived by an auditor from the successful employment of statistical sampling are listed below:

    (i) It is possible to state, with a stipulated degree of confidence, that the sample result is not further away from the true condition of the population than some specified amount.

    (ii) The result obtained by the sample is not subject to the complaint of bias i.e. that the auditor has looked at the worst items.

    (iii) The method provides means of knowing in advance the size of the maximum sample needed. If the auditor has decided on the degree of risk he is prepared to accept, then he is relieved of the onus of determining sample sizes arbitrarily. Justification is provided for the size of the sample used and thus for the time spent on the audit work.

    (iv) Statistical sampling can be more accurate than an examination of every item in a large population. Examining a high volume of data involves tedious detailed work, causing carelessness and different interpretations, and errors may arise.

    (v) The evaluation of results is simplified, but great care is necessary, firstly, to ensure that each characteristic being tested is evaluated separately and, secondly, that in fixing an 'acceptable error rate'. For example, a low error rate may be serious if the errors represent irregularities or serious evasions of internal control but, on the other hand, a relatively high error rate may not give concern if the errors are of a random nature, showing no particular trend and indicating no specific control weakness.

It is clear that statistical sampling has many advantages. It is difficult, however, to say that statistical sampling is to be preferred to non-statistical sampling. The auditor must still use his judgement to decide what confidence level and precision limits are acceptable. Furthermore, there are many tests which the auditor will wish to perform where the sample will require selection by judgement. Examples would include a receivables' circularisation.

Finally, statistical techniques often take longer to apply than tests using non-statistical sampling. The auditor must be careful that the benefits are not outweighed by the additional costs.

(b) Statistical sampling is likely to prove most successful under the following conditions:

    (i) Where every potential sampling unit has the appropriate chance of selection and where systematic bias is avoided. This is most likely to apply to source documents which are subjected to standard internal control procedures.

    (ii) Where the sample size is large enough so that any chance departure from the typical is not significant.

    (iii) Where the set-up time and selection time are reasonable in relation to the time needed to verify the items and follow up discrepancies i.e. large material populations.

    (iv) Where records of the entire population are reasonably accessible e.g. sales/purchase invoices.

    (v) The attribute to be sampled is easily identified.

    (vi) The drawing of the statistical sample is facilitated by computerised records.

ANSWERS TO ACTIVITIES AND QUESTIONS

CHAPTER 9

ACTIVITY 1

Note that your answer should focus on the assertion of existence.

The principal audit technique used would be physical inspection. A sample of non-current assets would be selected from the non-current asset register and physically checked to ensure that they existed. At the same time it is likely that a sample of assets would be selected and checked to the register; this would assist in achieving the objective of completeness.

It is important that the sample is representative, and the auditors should also ensure that they are certain of what they are inspecting. If they are not then they should consider seeking expert help to verify what the asset is.

ACTIVITY 2

The audit assertions tested are as follows:

1   Items selected in the warehouse and traced to ensure accurate inclusion in the inventory count sheets helps to verify **completeness**.

2   Items selected from the inventory count sheets and traced to ensure inclusion in the inventory count sheets helps to verify **existence**.

3   Items inspected for evidence of obsolescence or damage helps to verify the **valuation** of those items.

4   Attendance at inventory counts are the premises of third parties who hold inventory on behalf of your client helps to verify **completeness and existence** of inventory.

ACTIVITY 3

The audit assertions tested are as follows:

1   Inspection of the bank confirmation latter for loan accounts held test the assertions of **completeness, classification** and **rights and obligations**.

2   Reconciliation of a sample of supplier statements to purchase ledger balances helps to verify both **completeness** and **existence**.

3   Ensuring that trade payables and accruals are classified as current liabilities helps to verify **classification** and **presentation**.

4   Review of the list of trade payables and accruals to compare with earlier year(s) helps to verify **completeness**.

FAU: FOUNDATIONS IN AUDIT

ACTIVITY 4

Audit assertions relevant to the audit of prepayments include:

(a) Existence – the prepayments exist as at the year-end date by reference to payments made during the year.

(b) Completeness – no material prepayments have been omitted or misstated as at the year-end date.

(c) Classification – the prepayments have been correctly classified as current assets in the statement of financial position.

(d) Accuracy, valuation and allocation – the prepayments have been calculated or estimated on an accurate or reasonable basis for inclusion in the financial statements.

(e) Cut-off – the prepayments include only those amounts which were paid during the year and which relate to the following accounting period.

ACTIVITY 5

Audit assertions relevant to the reporting of vehicle running expenses include:

(a) Occurrence – the reported costs actually occurred and relate to the company being audited.

(b) Completeness – the reported costs are complete and there are no other omitted vehicle running costs to be accounted for.

(c) Accuracy – the reported costs accurately reflect the total vehicle running costs for the year under audit.

(d) Cut-off – the reported costs include only those costs incurred during the accounting year being audited.

(e) Classification – the reported costs have been correctly classified as vehicle running costs in the financial statements subject to audit.

ACTIVITY 6

An accounting estimate is a monetary amount for which the measurement, in accordance with the requirements of the applicable financial reporting framework, is subject to estimation uncertainty'.

Examples of such estimates are:

Tutorial note: The question only asked for three examples – additional items are given for information purposes.

- provisions for depreciation
- allowances to reduce inventories and receivables to their estimated realisable value
- accrued revenue
- provisions for losses in a legal dispute
- profits/losses on long term contract work
- provisions to meet warranty claims.

EXAM-STYLE QUESTION 1

Tutorial note: Part (a) of the question relates to material found in the earlier chapters of the text book; it is important to clearly understand the nature of the audit, and is a useful exercise to remind yourself at this stage.

(a) The audit of the financial statements is an exercise whose objective is to enable auditors to express an independent opinion on whether the financial statements give a true and fair view of the entity's affairs as at the period end, and of its cash flow and profit or loss for the period then ended and have been properly prepared in accordance with the appropriate reporting framework (e.g. legislation and accounting standards) or, where statutory or other requirements prescribe the terms, whether the financial statements thus 'present fairly'.

(b) The financial statement assertions are the representations of the directors that are embodied in the financial statements. By approving the financial statements, the directors are making representations about the information contained within them. These assertions can be defined as follows:

 (i) **Completeness**

 There are no unrecorded assets, liabilities, transactions, events or undisclosed items.

 (ii) **Occurrence**

 Transactions and events are recorded in the proper period.

 (iii) **Existence**

 All assets and liabilities exist at a specific date.

 (iv) **Rights and obligations**

 All assets and liabilities pertain to the entity at a specific date.

 (v) **Accuracy, valuation and allocation**

 Transactions and events are recorded at the proper amounts.

 (vi) **Classification**

 All items are recorded in the proper accounts.

 (vii) **Presentation**

 Transactions and events are appropriately aggregated or disaggregated and clearly described, and related disclosures are relevant and understandable in the context of the applicable financial reporting framework.

FAU: FOUNDATIONS IN AUDIT

EXAM-STYLE QUESTION 2

The directors and management of a company are responsible for making estimates included within the financial statements. Examples of such estimates are:

(i)   provisions for losses on long-term contracts

(ii)   provisions for profits on long-term contracts

(iii)   provisions for depreciation

(iv)   provisions for doubtful debts

(v)   provisions for obsolescence of inventory

(vi)   provisions for losses in legal disputes

(vii) accrued revenue

(viii) provisions to meet warranty claims.

Note: Only five examples were required.

EXAM-STYLE QUESTION 3

Examples of audit procedures which could be used to support each of the financial statement assertions relating to property, plant and equipment include:

Assertion	Audit procedure
Accuracy and valuation	• Select a sample of property, plant and equipment additions in the year and agree cost to supplier invoice. • Physically inspect a sample of items of property, plant and equipment for evidence of obsolescence or damage. • For revalued items of property, plant and equipment inspect the valour's report to confirm revalued amount and required accounting treatment of revaluation amount.
Existence	• Select a sample of assets from the property, plant and equipment register and physically inspect them to confirm existence. • Review the list of property, plant and equipment additions in the year and confirm that all are eligible to be capitalised and that none relate to repairs and renewals.
Completeness	• Review the repairs and maintenance expense account for evidence of amounts and transactions that should be capitalised. • Select a sample of physical items of property, plant and equipment and confirm their inclusion in the property, plant and equipment register.

CHAPTER 10

ACTIVITY 1

Continuous inventory counting is where each item of inventory is counted throughout the year, and each item is physically counted at least once a year. The frequency will be determined according to the risk level of the inventory item. This method requires that records are maintained up to date; these will be amended as a result of physical inspection where any errors are identified.

Periodic inventory counting is where all inventories are counted at the same time, once a year, usually at the financial year end.

ACTIVITY 2

The auditor's attendance at the inventory count is a key step in the audit process. Inventory is often a material statement of financial position item and the auditors will want to assess the effectiveness of the client's inventory counting procedures. By doing this they will obtain confirmation as to whether controls are working effectively and they can then decide the extent of their reliance on such controls.

If the client's inventory counting procedures are not being followed, the auditor should raise the matter with management immediately so that action can be taken on the occasion of the count to ensure that adequate audit evidence is obtained.

ACTIVITY 3

Production overheads should be allocated to inventory based on the normal activity level of the company. Management will estimate what this level is and allocate the overheads accordingly.

If less than the 'normal' level is produced then the unallocated overheads should be written off as an expense. If significantly more than the 'normal' level is produced then overheads should be reapportioned to ensure not too much overhead cost is included in inventory.

For example if a company normally produces 50 units of product X and the factory rent – the only overhead cost considered here – is $1,000, then the amount of rent allocated to each product would be $20. If only 40 were produced in a particular period then $200 should be written off to profit and loss.

If 60 were produced, then overheads should be reapportioned so that each item only includes overheads of $16.67 ($1,000/60). If this were not done, then inventory would include overheads of $1,200.

EXAM-STYLE QUESTION 1

NERO SCRAP AND HAULAGE COMPANY

(a) **Instructions regarding unpressed scrap:**

   (i) All movements of scrap should, if possible, cease during the inventory counting. Any scrap entering the yard during the day of inventory counting should be stored separately.

   (ii) The yard should be divided into areas during the inventory count.

   (iii) Once inventory has been assessed in an area, a marker should be placed to show that the area has been counted. Inventory movements between areas should be prohibited during the inventory count.

   (iv) The assessment should be carried out by two persons. One should be familiar with quantities and types of ferrous scrap. The other should be from an independent department.

   (v) The last numbers of input and output documents should be noted to ensure adequate cut-off procedures are applied.

   (vi) Inventory sheets should be pre-numbered and their issue and return should be recorded and controlled.

   (vii) All inventory count results should be noted and signed.

(b) **Valuation of inventory of scrap:**

   (i) Inventory should be valued at the lower of cost and net realisable value.

   (ii) Cost might be calculated on an actual basis related to invoices where inventory is separately identifiable. A FIFO or average cost basis might be simpler to apply.

   (iii) Net realisable value could be estimated from actual prices received in the post-reporting period. The cost of transport to the steelworks would need to be deducted from the selling price.

(c) **Verification of value:**

   (i) Ascertain the policies used to estimate cost and net realisable value. Ensure that these policies are consistent with the principles of IAS 2.

   (ii) Test a sample of inventory prices with purchase invoices or other input documents.

   (iii) Test that the prices used are consistent with the accounting policies.

   (iv) Review prices received from the steel mill for goods in inventory at the reporting date. Ensure provision is made when NRV is below cost.

   (v) Examine inventory count records for evidence of slow-moving or unsaleable inventories. Test that provision is made for losses.

   (vi) Test the arithmetical accuracy of calculations, additions and summaries.

ANSWERS TO ACTIVITIES AND QUESTIONS

EXAM-STYLE QUESTION 2

NERO SCRAP AND HAULAGE COMPANY

(a) **Transport manager's commission:**

    (i)   This matter appears prima facie to be a corrupt practice but should be investigated carefully by the auditor to see if the matter is material.

    (ii)   He should examine the invoices and delivery notes from the tyre suppliers and ensure that prices are reasonable and deliveries and payments are matched.

    (iii)   The auditor should draw the matter to the attention of the management.

    (iv)   The auditor may need to consider if any evidence appears of other doubtful practices which may have implications for the financial statements.

(b) **Audit programme covering haulage charges:**

    (i)   Ascertain and record the system for logging journeys and invoicing the customers.

    (ii)   Evaluate the strengths and deficiencies in the system.

    (iii)   Design and carry out tests of control which could include the following:

        • Inspection of loading documents related to vehicle journey log books and delivery notes.

        • Relate delivery notes to specific invoices made to the steel wholesaler customers. This would include a check against agreed prices and arithmetical checks of invoices.

    (iv)   Ascertain correct cut-off between delivery costs and charges to customers.

    (v)   Check invoice totals to day book and to the recording of sales and receivables.

EXAM-STYLE QUESTION 3

CAMRY PRODUCTS

Tutorial note: Inventory is a favourite examination area. Part (a) simply concerned normal planning activities with which candidates involved in auditing inventory should be familiar.

Principal procedures in planning attendance at an inventory count

The following procedures will normally be followed by the auditor during the planning stage of an attendance at the inventory count:

(i)   Review prior year's working papers to gain knowledge of the client and the type and location of inventory, and also to identify any problem areas encountered last year to direct additional attention to those areas this year.

(ii) Contact client to:

- obtain copy of inventory count instructions to be issued to client's staff. These should be reviewed and any potential problem areas brought to the client's attention immediately

- agree inventory count date

- confirm location of inventory including any new locations and location of material quantities

- discuss internal control over inventory counting

- obtain management accounts to identify large inventory types if possible e.g. large orders in progress.

(iii) Book required staff to attend the inventory count.

(iv) Consider whether the internal audit department at the company can be relied upon by the external auditors. Reviewing last year's file will give some information on this.

(v) Brief staff due to attend the inventory count on material areas to investigate.

(vi) Assess need for specialist advice if inventories are of a technical or complex nature, either to count or to value.

(vii) Ensure that if there are any inventories held at third parties an appropriate confirmation letter is sent, and that staff are booked to visit the location if the inventory there is material.

EXAM-STYLE QUESTION 4

CAMRY PRODUCTS

Tutorial note: Inventory is a favourite examination area. Parts (a) and (b), however, required detailed use of the information in the question due to the difficult system in use at the company. Candidates who ignored this information, but gave general comments about procedures and cut-off, will have found it difficult to gain sufficient marks to attain a pass.

(a) **Procedures to be adopted by client to ensure that all inventories are counted once but once only**

These procedures are important for Camry Products because production will continue throughout the inventory count, increasing the risk of double-counting or of excluding items from inventory.

Procedures to adopt include:

(i) One individual given authority over the whole inventory count. Ensure that all employees know who this individual is and that all queries are referred back to him.

(ii) Divide the inventory into a definite number of areas and assign teams of two counters to each area. These teams should be impressed that they must count all inventory in their area, and no inventory from any other area.

(iii) Issue lists to each team of the inventory that they can expect to count in each area. In some cases, such as raw material stores, pre-printed sheets showing all inventory lines can be issued, although in production and finished goods that is unlikely to be possible. In these cases pre-numbered sheets will be issued and the sequence agreed for completeness both before and after the count has taken place.

(iv) As each inventory item is counted it should be identified as being counted by some unique mark. The attaching of an appropriately coloured tag is one method of doing this, with different coloured tags for each location. Thus if inventory does move between locations, the colour of the tag will readily identify this.

(v) Movement of inventory should be kept to a minimum. Certainly movement between production and finished goods should not be allowed, while the number of emergency requisition notes should be kept to a small number if possible. Each emergency requisition note issued should be listed by the store man. The official responsible for the inventory count may then ensure that the inventory items are not included on the store sheets as they will be included in work in progress.

(vi) The work in progress area could be counted at the end of work for that day. This will assist the count as items in production will not be continually moving around the shop floor. If both stores and finished goods are counted by this time, then staff will be available to count work in progress in a reasonable time. Care will be needed, however, to assess correctly the state of completion of each inventory line, and guidance must be given to counters on this matter. Production staff could assist by being available for, say, one hour after normal work finishes in return for some bonus payment.

(vii) Goods received during the day must be kept in a separate location and counted there so as not to be double-counted within stores.

(viii) Goods despatched should be sent out with the normal documentation from the finished goods store. If the good is tagged to indicate that it has already been counted, this should be recorded on a separate sheet. The official in charge of the inventory count must ensure at the end of the count that the finished goods sheets are reviewed and these items eliminated from inventory.

(b) **Audit procedures on the accuracy of cut-off at inventory count**

Normal audit procedures to ensure the accuracy of cut-off will include:

(i) Review the client's system in operation:

- ensure that goods entering the client's premises are separated from inventory already present and counted separately

- ensure that as goods are despatched a note is made of any tag attached to them, that this is recorded on the appropriate sheet and that these items are eliminated from inventory later by the responsible official

- check that any emergency requisitions are recorded in the stores and that these goods are eliminated from inventory later by the responsible official.

(ii) Ensure that no transfers of goods take place from the production area to the finished goods store.

FAU: FOUNDATIONS IN AUDIT

(iii) List the last goods inwards note, the last goods outwards note along with any numbers noted as unused in numeric sequence before these. After the inventory count normally on the final audit, the auditor will then:

- ensure that goods despatched numbers prior to the last number are excluded from inventory and that those after this last number are included in inventory; and

- ensure that goods received numbers prior to the last number noted are included in inventory and that those after this last number are excluded from inventory.

(iv) Discuss with management any exceptions noted to (i) or (ii) above or problems found with (iii) and ensure that appropriate adjustments are made to the inventory quantities.

CHAPTER 11

ACTIVITY 1

Controls expected in a non-current asset system include:

(a) Authorisation limits and procedures, including board approval for major items.

(b) Estimates obtained for major items.

(c) All non-current assets recorded in a register which is regularly reconciled with the general ledger.

(d) Regular physical checking of assets against the register.

(e) Procedures for the disposal of non-current assets.

(f) Procedures to ensure that depreciation rates are appropriate and correctly calculated.

(g) Procedures to ensure that impairments in value are detected and correctly accounted for.

ACTIVITY 2

Details or headings to include in a non-current asset register include:

(a) Date of purchase of the asset e.g. 1 April 20X5

(b) Supplier name e.g. Office Suppliers Ltd

(c) Brief description of the asset e.g. photocopier model number AZ-32

(d) Cost of the asset e.g. $600-00

(e) Sequential asset register or serial number 1350

(f) Location of the asset e.g. Liverpool office, accounts department

(g) Depreciation method and/or rate to be applied to the asset e.g. 25% straight-line

(h) Annual depreciation charge and net carrying value for each accounting year e.g. $150

(i) Disposal information (when applicable) – date, proceeds, gain/loss on disposal.

ACTIVITY 3

AUDIT PROGRAMME   WP REF:

CLIENT NAME: XY LTD   PREPARED BY:

                                        DATE:

                                        Y/E DATE: 31/X/XX

                                        REVIEWED BY:

                                        DATE:

TEST: Valuation of tangible non-current assets

OBJECTIVE: To ensure all tangible non-current assets are included in the financial statements at the correct valuation

TEST	W/P REF:
(1) Select a sample of entries in the non-current asset register and trace back to source documentation to ensure stated at cost as per the source documentation (e.g. invoice).	
(2) Review assets generally and consider whether there have been any impairments in value which require write-down in the accounts. (This should be discussed with directors.)	
(3) Review the company policies for depreciation and consider whether they are appropriate (obtain information in respect of assets useful lives e.g. profits/losses on disposals of past assets).	
(4) Identify cases where VAT or similar taxes is irrecoverable and ensure this has been capitalised as part of the asset's cost.	

FAU: FOUNDATIONS IN AUDIT

EXAM-STYLE QUESTION 1

ENGINEERING COMPANY

Tutorial note: In reaching a decision on each of the points in your answer, remember to give **reasons** why you decide on a certain answer. Reasons for the proposed treatment must also be considered, for example, obsolescence problems. Note should also be made that assets not in use may deteriorate – non-depreciation is therefore not appropriate except in a few isolated circumstances.

(a) The purchase of non-current assets should normally be authorised at two separate stages in the accounting cycle. Firstly, the company should prepare capital budgets. In the capital budget all expected future expenditure on non-current assets should be detailed as to type of asset, estimated cost and expected date of purchase. This budget should be approved by the directors. The auditor should ensure that he has a copy of the budget and proof that the directors have approved the anticipated expenditure (normally through a copy of the minutes of the board meeting). The purchase of all non-current assets should be checked to the budget.

The second stage of authorisation comes when the asset is actually ordered. The directors will establish levels of authority for managers to authorise the purchase of assets. Major items should require the signature of a director. The auditor should ensure that the purchase requisition requesting purchase of the plant is duly authorised by the responsible official. He should ensure that the invoice has been matched to the appropriate goods inward note, purchase order and purchase requisition and approval for payment made by the appropriate official. He should also ensure that the asset has been received in good condition and is being used in the business of the company.

By checking the budget approval and by ensuring that the necessary purchase approvals have been adhered to, the auditor has checked that all major non-current asset expenditure has been authorised.

(b) A non-current asset register is a list of all the non-current assets owned by a company. It may be in the form of a hand-written ledger, machine card system or maintained on a computer. The company requires a non-current asset register in order to control and identify all the non-current assets which it owns. The register should show:

   (i) the plant number allocated to the asset (ideally, each asset should have its own unique identity number)

   (ii) details of the type and specification

   (iii) name of the supplier and date of purchase

   (iv) cost

   (v) rate of depreciation and total depreciation charged to date

   (vi) location

   (vii) expenditure incurred by way of maintenance and repair charges.

Every year the auditor should select some items from the non-current asset register and physically check their existence and condition. This ensures that items shown in the statement of financial position are still in existence and are in good condition and have not been scrapped without a record being made in the accounting records. The company should also require that individual assets are checked against the non-current asset register on a regular basis and that periodically the register is reconciled to the general ledger, as part of its system of internal control.

EXAM-STYLE QUESTION 2

ENGINEERING COMPANY

Tutorial note: In reaching a decision on each of the points in your answer, remember to give **reasons** why you decide on a certain answer. For example, simply stating that a company should depreciate assets would be insufficient for part (c). Reasons for the proposed treatment must also be considered, for example, obsolescence problems. Note should also be made that assets not in use may deteriorate – non-depreciation is therefore not appropriate except in a few isolated circumstances.

(a) The procedures for scrapping plant should be detailed in writing and approved by the directors. All scrapping of plant should be on a systematic basis and should be included in the capital budget in order that replacement assets can be ordered (if necessary). Any major item of plant should be examined prior to scrapping by an engineer to ensure that it is not worth repairing the machine and keeping it for a longer period of time. All major items which are scrapped should be approved by the directors, but they may delegate the authority to scrap small items of plant to the works manager or his equivalent. If the plant is still in good working order, the directors should ensure that they sell it for its current market value. These prices may be obtainable in the trade press. If the machine is sold as scrap metal, the directors should ensure that the value received is in line with current scrap metal prices.

(b) All rates of depreciation should be approved by the directors. It is not necessary to allocate rates by individual machine, but generally by type of machine based on its estimated useful life. The auditor should review the rates and check whether the machines are fully depreciated at the end of their useful lives.

The auditor should review profits and losses on disposal of assets. If these show high losses, then it would indicate that the rate of depreciation is too low. If losses are minimal, then the rates would appear to be reasonable.

If the company measures profitability by individual machines, it may be possible that methods of depreciation other than straight line may be applicable; if this is so, then the auditor should review these alternative methods of depreciation to ascertain their validity.

(c) If the asset has been purchased recently and the machine is still in the process of installation prior to commencement of use, then it can be reasonably argued that as no revenue is accruing to the company, no expense should be charged. In these circumstances it can be acceptable not to charge depreciation on assets not in use.

However, if the asset is not in use due to bad trading conditions and if there is no indication that these conditions will necessarily improve, then it is less valid to argue that as no revenue accrues, no charges should be made. In these circumstances the machine will be losing value merely due to the passage of time. It may well become obsolete.

The auditor should examine all the circumstances surrounding the non-use of the asset and recommend that, if the valuation is likely to deteriorate merely through the passage of time, then appropriate depreciation should be charged. If it is known that the asset is likely to become obsolete and scrapped, then the auditor should recommend that the machine is written down to its expected realisable value immediately.

CHAPTER 12

ACTIVITY 1

Note that the requirement here is to deal with procedures relating to trade receivables – not prepayments.

The auditor would usually perform the following analytical procedures:

(a) Calculate receivables collection period and compare to previous year(s) and/or budget figures. This is calculated by $\frac{receivables}{sales} \times 365$ and indicates the average number of days that customers are taking to pay their debts.

This is an important ratio for the auditor as it can indicate possible financial problems which have caused the company to relax their credit terms which can in turn result in irrecoverable debts. It would indicate a potential liquidity problem if the company is having to pay payables before they receive the money from their customers.

(b) Obtain an aged receivables listing and analyse the information by comparing the proportions in the different age bands (e.g. less than 30 days, 30 days to 60 days, 60 days to 90 days and greater than 90 days).

This would indicate any problems with the collectability of debts and identify those which are potentially bad. It is important that a provision for such debts is set up. If it is confirmed that the debt is bad then it should be immediately written off against income – assets must not be overstated.

ACTIVITY 2

Substantive tests for the audit of trade receivables would be as follows:

(a) Obtain a list of sales ledger balances and agree the total of the balances to the sales ledger control account and the general ledger.

(b) Check the cast on the list of balances.

(c) Agree a sample of the balances to the individual ledger accounts.

(d) Carry out a circularisation to obtain direct confirmation of a sample of balances.

(e) Review the balances for old/disputed debts and ensure that adequate provision has been made for these.

(f) Ensure that contras with the purchase ledger have been authorised.

(g) Review after-date credit notes for items which should be reversed.

(h) Check that the cut-off at the yearend between sales and inventory is correct.

(i) Ensure that all receivables are collectable and that the disclosure in the financial statements is appropriate.

ANSWERS TO ACTIVITIES AND QUESTIONS

ACTIVITY 3

The main contents of a bank confirmation letter are shown below. (These are the main headings shown in bold type in the standard letter).

(a) **Bank accounts**

This refers to all accounts held including loans and joint accounts, and also encompasses accrued charges and the bank's right of set-off (i.e. the bank's right to offset debit and credit balances).

(b) **Customer's assets held as security**

This refers to mortgages, share certificates, bills of exchange and any other assets the bank is holding as security for its loans.

(c) **Customer's other assets held**

A common response to this request is 'safe deposit box, contents unknown'.

(d) **Contingent liabilities**

This includes bills of exchange discounted, guarantees and indemnities and certain foreign exchange information.

(e) **Other information**

This is where the auditor seeks to find unrecorded assets or liabilities by asking the bank whether it is aware of any other branches or banks where the client holds an account.

PRACTICE QUESTION 1

ASKWITH

Tutorial note: A relatively straightforward question on receivables. The answer should state clearly the information required, and also use the question information where possible to make the answer relevant to the question asked.

(a)

> Smith Manufacturing
> Jones Street
> Latherton
>
> Date:
>
> Dear Sirs
>
> This is not a request for payment. It is a request for confirmation of your balance with us as at 31 December 20X7 for audit purposes.
>
> Balance owed to us at 31 December 20X7 $ . . . .
>
> If you are in agreement with the above amount, please write directly to our auditors (not to us) at the following address, for which purpose a prepaid envelope is enclosed:
>
> Dobbins & Co
> Mule Street
> London ECl

> If you are not in agreement, please write to our auditors, explaining the breakdown of the balance you have at 31 December 20X7, for which purpose the reverse side of this letter may be used.
>
> Thank you for your co-operation.
>
> Yours faithfully
>
> D Smith
>
> Company Secretary
>
> ---
>
> Balance agreed/Not agreed*
>
> Signature . . . . Position . . . . Date . . . .
>
> * Delete as applicable.

(b) If no reply is received to the initial circularisation letter, a second request should be sent. In addition, the customer could be contacted by telephone and asked to confirm the balances (provided the client grants permission).

If direct confirmation still proves impossible, the following alternative procedures might be used:

(i) review cash received after the year-end to see if the balances have been cleared

(ii) agree individual outstanding invoices to independent evidence such as delivery notes signed by the customer

(iii) review credit notes issued after the year-end to ensure the receivables balance should not be reduced

(iv) review make-up of the balance and ensure that it consists of recent invoices

(v) check authorisation for unusual entries (journals, contras) in the accounts.

(c) Cut-off tests are intended to provide evidence that transactions have been recorded in the correct period. Companies may wish to manipulate their records to treat transactions as having occurred in an earlier period, so as to improve the appearance of the financial statements.

The following tests would be appropriate to ensure cut-off was correct:

(i) agree a sample of despatch notes, from either side of the year-end to invoices to ensure that the dates agree (details of the last despatch notes would usually be taken at the inventory count)

(ii) review credit notes issued after the year-end and check that they do not relate to inventory returned before the year-end, etc.

(iii) check that cash received has been allocated to the correct period.

ANSWERS TO ACTIVITIES AND QUESTIONS

PRACTICE QUESTION 2

DEFAULTERS

Tutorial note: This question required the re-drafting of a bank reconciliation to show a potential cash theft. If you could not do this, then it would be advisable to revise the preparation of bank reconciliations. Audit tests related to the bank reconciliation were required in (a); look down the reconciliation and try and give a test for each item appearing there. By doing this you will ensure that the audit tests given are relevant to the question and that all items on the reconciliation are audited.

(a) **Audit schedule showing amount of cash missing from Defaulters Cash Book at 31 May 20X1**

		$	$
Balance per statement			31,100
Less: Unpresented cheques			
	134	232	
	183	300	
	284	506	
	861	380	
	862	412	
	863	290	
			(2,120)
			28,980
Less: Lodgement on bank statement not yet in cash book			(200)
			28,780
Add: Lodgement to enter into cash book			7,588
Expected cash book balance			36,368
Less: Actual cash book balance			(37,802)
Cash difference			1,434

Audit tests on cash difference statement above.

(i) Agree bank balance to bank statement.

(ii) Agree unpresented cheques recorded in cash book before 31 May, and to bank statements dated after this date.

(iii) Investigate why cheques 134, 183 and 284 have not been presented to the bank. Discuss with client whether the bank balance requires adjustment if these cheques will not be presented.

(iv) Agree lodgement of $200 to bank statement before 31 May and cash book after this date.

(v) Ensure that the undeposited receipts are banked in early June. Agree entries for these items in the cash book and bank statements.

(vi) Agree cash book balance to the cash book.

(vii) Agree a number of cash book entries to the bank statement during the year.

(viii) Check casting of the cash book and the bank reconciliation above.

(ix) Request the working papers of the chief accountant on the bank balance to confirm amount of work done in this area.

(b) The cashier attempted to conceal the possible theft of cash in three ways.

(i) Not all the unpresented cheques were included in the bank reconciliation. This understated the deduction from the bank balance making it possible to show a higher cash book balance than actually existed.

(ii) The petty cash float was included in the bank reconciliation. The float is reimbursed on an imprest basis, the cheques for which will have already been entered in the cash book; the float does not need including in the bank reconciliation.

(iii) The unrecorded credit was treated incorrectly. It should have been deducted from the cash book figure in the client's reconciliation not added to it as in the cashier's reconciliation.

(c) Internal control deficiencies that could have assisted the theft of cash by the cashier are:

(i) The cash is banked by the cashier without apparent checking by any other member of staff. If the cashier is to bank the cash then the paying-in slip stamped by the bank should be agreed by an independent official to the listing of cash received on that day. Any differences should be investigated. The cash should also be banked on a daily basis rather than being left for a few days as appears to be the case at the moment.

(ii) The cashier is responsible for the custody of the cash, and also for the preparation of the bank reconciliation. Although this does indicate some lack of internal control, this can be rectified by the bank reconciliation being reviewed in depth by an independent responsible person. Again, any differences should be immediately investigated.

(d) The actions that the auditor should take on the discovery of potential improprieties are as follows:

(i) Extend audit testing in that area to try and ascertain whether any impropriety has actually occurred.

(ii) Quantify the effect of the potential impropriety discovered as a result of the extended testing above.

(iii) Discuss the matter with management. The discussion should include the findings of the auditor and agree actions to be taken by management.

(iv) Confirm the discussions, and agreed actions, if any, in a report to management either during or at the end of the audit.

(v) Ascertain at a later date what action has been taken by management. If appropriate action has not been taken remind management again that action is necessary. If no action is forthcoming the auditor may wish to obtain legal advice on whether the matter should be disclosed further (i.e. to third parties).

CHAPTER 13

ACTIVITY 1

(a) A company should ensure it has a proper system of internal control over its payables for the following reasons:

- to ensure all goods/services purchased are authorised

- to ensure goods/services purchased are only ordered for business purposes and from appropriate suppliers

- to ensure all goods/services received are inspected as to quality and quantity

- to ensure all invoices and supporting documentation are checked and approved to ensure their validity

- to ensure only valid transactions are accurately processed.

(b) When verifying individual payables balances, the auditor should consider the following factors:

- whether or not the balance comprises items outstanding within a reasonable timescale

- whether the outstanding items have been authorised for payment

- whether the amount can be reconciled to the supplier's statements

- whether a payables' circularisation is required

- whether payments made to suppliers just after year end relate to specific outstanding items.

FAU: FOUNDATIONS IN AUDIT

PRACTICE QUESTION 1

Tutorial note: Apply the basic audit tests for purchases and supplier balances to the particular situation in the question. Consider the need for any additional tests required specific to the type of business concerned.

It is important to provide a complete answer here, therefore think of what happens in a normal purchases and payables audit and list these tests. If you can then make any relevant comments concerning the fashion store then do so, but the question does not have any specific factual information, and so specific examples are difficult to bring into your answer. Note that the tests marked * are tests of controls.

Notes for audit programme for purchases and year-end suppliers' balances for a medium-sized retail fashion store.

Purchases

(a) Using the firm's standard statistical sampling techniques, select a sample of entries in the purchases account in the general ledger, after first having checked the cast of this account.

(b) Agree each item selected with the purchase day book summary totals.

(c) For each summary total checked, check the cast of the list of invoices making up the total.

(d) Using the firm's standard statistical sampling techniques, select a sample of entries in the purchase day book.

(e) Agree the amounts with the relevant purchase invoices.

(f) Check that each purchase invoice shows evidence of having been passed for payment.*

(g) Check that the level of authority passing the invoices for payment accords with the client's regulations.*

(h) Check the cast, extension and coding of each invoice.

(i) Check the details on the invoice with the goods received note.

(j) Check the details on the invoice with the purchase order.

(k) Examine the invoice for evidence that the above two procedures were carried out by the client.*

(l) Check that the purchase order carries the correct level of authority according to the client's regulations.*

Suppliers' balances

(a) Agree or reconcile the balance on the control account with the total of the list of balances, and agree the total to the draft financial statements.

(b) Check the cast of the list of balances.

(c) Using the firm's standard statistical sampling techniques, obtain a sample of balances, and check these to balances on ledger cards.

(d) Select a sample of major suppliers from a list of opening balances, where these suppliers do not have a closing balance.

ANSWERS TO ACTIVITIES AND QUESTIONS

(e) If there are any suppliers with whom the client has done a significant amount of business during the year and who do not have a closing balance, select a sample from these.

(f) Circularise these suppliers requesting that they confirm directly to the auditors' address the balances shown in the client's records. The firm's standard payables circularisation letters should be used for this. Insert on each letter the name and address of the supplier, the balance to be confirmed and the date at which the balance exists. Ensure that the client gives permission for this and that each request letter is signed by the client.

(g) Send the letters independently of the client.

(h) If the balances are disputed, the reasons for this should be ascertained and balances reconciled.

(i) If a reply is not received, a second request should be sent.

(j) Summarise the results. The summary should show the total number of payables and the total balance, the number and amount of payables' balances circularised, the number and amount replying, the number and amount agreeing, the number and amount reconciling, and the number and amount disagreeing and being incapable of reconciliation. Each summary should express number and amount as a percentage of the total amount.

(k) Select a sample of payables and reconcile the account with the suppliers' statement. Summarise the results in a way similar to (j) above.

(l) Select a sample of goods received notes and ensure that for every item selected the correct entry is ultimately made in the supplier's account.

(m) Select a sample of goods received notes dated shortly before the year-end, and check that, unless the items shown thereon had been paid for prior to the year-end, they were shown as a liability in the supplier's account or had been separately accrued.

(n) Select a sample of goods returned shortly before the reporting date and ensure that the related amounts were deducted from suppliers' balances at the year-end or otherwise correctly treated.

(o) Select a sample of goods received notes dated shortly after the year-end and check that these did not result in items being included in payables at the year-end.

(p) Select a sample of goods returned shortly after the reporting date and ensure that no amounts in respect of these were deducted from suppliers' balances before the year-end.

(q) Check invoices received after the year-end for items received before the year-end. Check that the amounts relating to these were included in payables.

(r) Check payments made to suppliers either side of the year-end to ensure that these were dealt with in the correct accounting period as far as the payables' balances were concerned.

(s) For payments made before the year-end, check when these appeared on the client's bank statement. If any significant delay has arisen request that the client obtains the cheque from the bank. Examine the cheque and check its date and the payee.

(t) Compare the total balance with last year and also compare the ratio of the total to the total purchases for the year.

(u) Obtain representations from management that all known amounts owing to suppliers have been provided for in the financial statements.

CHAPTER 14

ACTIVITY 1

The auditor can use computers to enhance audit work in the following ways:

(a) Documenting the client's systems through the use of flowcharting packages and word processing software.

(b) Evaluating audit risk components (i.e. inherent risk and control risk) for individual transactions and balances.

(c) Preparing audit programmes through use of databases and word processing software.

(d) Analytical review such as ratio analysis using spreadsheet software.

(e) Preparing audit working papers.

(f) The audit review process.

(g) Communication between the audit location and the auditor's offices, or between offices.

(h) Recording and managing time spent on the audit.

ACTIVITY 2

When auditing computer-based systems, the auditor needs to take into account the following additional factors when auditing computerised, rather than manual, systems:

(a) Controls are often concentrated in the computer department rather than being dispersed across the organisation as a whole.

(b) Data is often entered direct onto computer systems, hence there is a loss of primary records.

(c) Data is usually encoded and cannot be read by the human eye – it must be decoded first.

(d) There is frequently a loss of audit trail.

(e) Transaction data may have a short retention period, and therefore may not be available for audit purposes.

(f) Program controls are of more importance in ensuring the accuracy and completeness of data.

(g) The auditor may have insufficient expertise to be able to use/interrogate the client's system(s) and may therefore have to employ the use of an expert.

(h) Computer time may only be available to the auditor at certain specified periods; this will impact on the audit plan.

ANSWERS TO ACTIVITIES AND QUESTIONS

ACTIVITY 3

(a) Master files data relating to trade receivables would normally include the following:

- Customer account number
- Customer name and contact details (postal address, telephone, email etc.)
- Customer authorised credit limit
- Customer authorised credit period
- Customer key terms of business e.g. eligibility for discounts and preferential prices
- Customer trading history or activity
- Product price lists
- Customer discount
- Any restrictions on making sales, such as unpaid or disputed invoices.

(b) Controls expected to operate on master files include:

- Restricted access to master files to only authorised individuals e.g. by password.
- Master files can only be amended following proper authorisation by a responsible person.
- There should be segregation of duties between the authorisation of amendments to master files and the processing of those amendments.
- A sequential record or log should be maintained of all amendments to master files.
- Periodic review of amendments to master files to confirm their validity.
- Periodic review of the content of master files to confirm validity of the files by tracing back to documentation for proper authorisation.

ACTIVITY 4

Information processing controls are those which apply to specific applications such as the payroll, sales ledger, purchase ledger systems. They consist of controls over input, processing, output and master files.

General controls are those which relate to the environment in which all applications operate. Examples of information processing controls are:

- batch controls
- hash totals
- reasonableness checks
- run to run controls
- record counts.

Note: The question only required two examples.

Examples of general controls are:

- job scheduling
- password protection
- back up procedures
- segregation of duties
- physical protection of files.

ACTIVITY 5

The interaction between general and information processing controls is fundamental to the auditor's evaluation of control and determination of the extent of substantive testing. When testing controls they should consider the following:

(a) Information processing controls may be concentrated within the computer department. The strength of the general controls in operation is therefore fundamental to the success or otherwise of the information processing controls.

(b) If information processing controls are insufficient to prevent/detect all errors, compensating general controls may exist.

ACTIVITY 6

(a) Computer Assisted Audit Technique.

(b) Automated tools and techniques are of use to auditors in the following ways:

    (i) In a computer-based system the sheer volume of transactions is likely to force auditors to rely upon programmed controls. Automated tools and techniques are likely to be the only effective way of testing programmed controls.

    (ii) The use of automated tools and techniques will enable auditors to test a much larger number of items quickly and accurately.

    (iii) Automated tools and techniques enable auditors to test the accounting system and its records rather than relying upon testing print-outs of what they believe to be a copy of those records.

    (iv) Once set up, automated tools and techniques are likely to be a cost-effective way of obtaining audit evidence.

    (v) Careful planning by auditors should enable the results of their work using automated tools and techniques to be compared with results from the traditional clerical audit work to increase confidence.

(c) (i) Audit software comprises computer programs used by auditors to examine an enterprise's computer files. It may consist of generalised package programs, specially written programs or the client's own programs.

ANSWERS TO ACTIVITIES AND QUESTIONS

Audit software may be used during both tests of control and substantive procedures, although it is particularly appropriate for use in the substantive testing of transactions and balances as it may scrutinise large volumes of data and extract information leaving skilled manual resources to concentrate upon investigation of the results.

(ii) Test data consists of data submitted by the auditors for processing by the enterprise's computer-based accounting system. It may be processed during a normal production run ('live' test data) or during a special run at a point in time outside the normal cycle ('dead' test data).

EXAM-STYLE QUESTION 1

ROTHWELL

Tutorial note: Part (a) is asking about the systems change, so any information about system changeover (e.g. parallel running) and the evaluation of new systems for audit trail can be incorporated into an answer.

Part (b) requires some thought, although 'standard' items like back-up, staffing and service contracts can be used effectively.

Part (c) requires detail not only on whether the situation can be remedied, but also the final effect of this – a potential modification.

(a) The introduction of the computer will require the auditor to evaluate and test the internal controls relating to the new system, in order to assess the level of additional testing and procedures required to ensure the accuracy of the accounting records in the period between the interim audit and the year end.

The auditor will have to assess whether the installation procedures adopted were satisfactory and whether adequate audit trail is available from the system. He will check the systems controls using tests of control, having regard to the previous assessment of controls, the length of the interim period, the volume of transactions in that period and the fact that the system has suffered a breakdown since the year end.

(b) The controls necessary to protect against corruption of data files are those relating to data file and program security. The controls which would have been required for this company are:

   (i) Procedures to ensure the quality of documentation, including manuals laying down the content of program files and hard copies of important documents at various stages of the processing cycle.

   (ii) Back-up procedures in the event of disaster including the use of alternative hardware.

   (iii) Maintenance of back-up copies of all the data files and the software program files to replace the originals in the event of corruption. All back-up files should be clearly marked as to content, date and time, and must be stored securely and in fire-proof storage facilities. Additional copies should be kept at a location outside the company's premises.

   (iv) The company should have a service agreement with the manufacturer or the supplier of the system covering the effect of major corruption and the assistance offered in such circumstances.

(v) The accounting staff should have been given proper training in the use of the hardware and software including procedures in the case of emergencies and other 'helpline' facilities.

(vi) The introduction of the system should be properly planned over a realistic timescale including a period of parallel running during which both systems will be operated and the results from both compared for accuracy and completeness. This period should continue until all operational and systems problems have been overcome.

EXAM-STYLE QUESTION 2

ROTHWELL

The audit implications of data file corruption depend upon the extent to which the missing data and transactions can be reconstructed. Partial reconstruction may be assisted by supplementary manual records or controls, batch totals, control totals, etc.

The client should be informed of the audit implications of lack of evidence and audit trail, since considerable extra work and expense may be involved in the reconstruction. Modification of the auditor's report may be required with a partial reconstruction and will certainly result if records cannot be reconstructed, on the grounds of limitation in the scope of the audit.

The form of modification will depend on the materiality of the missing records. The auditor should ensure that the cause of the corruption is ascertained. System failures may require a partial or full rewrite of the software. Hardware failure or user error can be corrected quickly though additional or improved training may be required.

EXAM-STYLE QUESTION 3

AUDITING IN A COMPUTER ENVIRONMENT

'Lack of visible evidence' refers to the fact that in a computerised system the intermediate stages between input and output are not evidenced by hard copies.

In an inventory control system, there may be no detailed breakdown of individual transactions thus causing problems with cut-off at period ends.

The problems may be overcome by:

(i) arranging with the client for special purpose audit print-outs to be provided

(ii) clerical re-creation of the data

(iii) performance of alternative audit tests.

'Systematic errors' are those which arise from a basic weakness in the system, and therefore they may recur frequently.

In an inventory control system, a systematic error may be the failure to restrict access to authorised personnel (by means of passwords), thus enabling the data to be tampered with.

ANSWERS TO ACTIVITIES AND QUESTIONS

The auditor can attempt to detect systematic errors by:

(i)   checking that systems development and testing procedures are fully documented

(ii) testing the general controls which operate within the computer department

(iii) using automated tools and techniques to test the processing of data.

EXAM-STYLE QUESTION 4

AUDITING IN A COMPUTER ENVIRONMENT

(a) The two most common types of automated tools and techniques are:

    (i)   audit software – programs used to examine the enterprise's computer files

    (ii) test data – data submitted by the auditor for processing by the enterprise's computer-based accounting system.

(b) In choosing the appropriate combination of automated tools and techniques and manual procedures, the auditor will need to take the following into account:

    (i)   if the computer program performs functions for which no visible evidence is available, then it may not be practicable for the auditor to perform tests manually

    (ii) the efficiency of the alternatives, taking into account the extent of testing achieved, the pattern of costs, and the ability to use the automated tools and techniques for a number of different audit tests

    (iii) the reporting time scale (automated tools and techniques tend to be quicker to apply)

    (iv) availability of computer time, files and programs

    (v)   Automated tools and techniques performed by the client staff may be relied upon, depending upon the auditor's assessment of that department's effectiveness.

(c) (i)   'Information processing controls' relate to the transactions and standing data of each application: they ensure the completeness and accuracy of the accounting records. An audit test appropriate to an information processing control would be the use of test data with documents missing to ensure a sequence check control was operating correctly.

    (ii) 'General controls' relate to the environment within which computer-based accounting systems are developed, maintained and operated. An appropriate audit test would be to check that all program changes were authorised.

FAU: FOUNDATIONS IN AUDIT

CHAPTER 15

ACTIVITY 1

The following matters should be included in the financial statements for disclosure to be regarded as adequate:

(a) a statement that the financial statements have been prepared on a going concern basis

(b) a statement of the relevant factors

(c) the nature of the concern(s)

(d) a statement of the assumptions adopted by the directors

(e) a statement regarding the directors' plans for resolving the matters giving rise to the concern(s) (if appropriate)

(f) details of any relevant actions by the directors.

ACTIVITY 2

(a) Financial statements should be prepared on the basis of conditions existing at the reporting date but consideration must be given to events and transactions which have or will occur after the reporting date since these may have a material effect on the financial position or viability at that date.

An 'adjusting event' is one which is important enough to require the financial statements at the recent, or previous, yearend to be amended. These arise from additional evidence on conditions existing at the reporting date which provides a basis for more realistic estimates or provisions including inventory valuation, irrecoverable debts, insurance claims and changes in taxation law.

Certain events may not concern amounts included in the financial statements but their effect in the future may require some form of additional disclosure by way of note or pro forma statement of financial position to prevent a misleading position being shown. Such non-adjusting events include changes in share capital or the composition of the group or company (e.g. from acquisitions or disposals).

In order to identify events after the reporting period the auditor should perform a review that covers all significant events up to the date of his report and he should ensure that such events, if material, are accounted for or disclosed in the financial statements. Such a review should encompass all sources of knowledge available to him and should be adequately recorded in the working papers.

(b) (i) Review interim financial statements for period since year end to detect trends and potential trading difficulties.

(ii) Investigate material differences between valuation of audited statement of financial position figures and latest statement of financial position figures.

(iii) Review major entries in general ledgers or journal records since year end and agree to supporting evidence.

(iv) Review after date cash from customers and credit notes issued for sales returns and allowances.

(v) Check the bank reconciliation to ensure all 'unpresented cheques' and 'outstanding lodgements' have been cleared.

(vi) Check market prices or material prices for impact on inventory valuation.

(vii) Review the cash book for evidence of large loans or financing arrangements, significant sales of non-current assets or other unusual transactions.

(viii) Review minutes of the meetings of shareholders and board of directors in the period since the reporting date.

(ix) Review contingencies and provisions included in the financial statements in the light of the latest available information to determine whether adjustment is required.

(x) Obtain details from the company or its legal counsel concerning pending litigation, settlements, claims or contractual charges.

(xi) Consider the need to obtain written representation concerning events which may have occurred.

(c) The compensation paid to Mr Jones will be included in the 'directors' emoluments' note to the financial statements at 31 March 20X8. The potential recovery of the compensation from Mr Jones requires the auditor to consider whether the event will determine the value of 'compensation for loss of director's office' in the financial statements and thus be an 'adjusting event'. Alternatively, since the outcome of the case is uncertain, it could be disclosed as a 'non-adjusting event', giving the nature of the event and an estimate of the amount to be received (net of legal fees). However, possible gains should not be accrued in the financial statements unless it is very likely that the gain will be realised. If realisation is probable then the gain should be disclosed by way of note with a prudent estimate of the financial effect.

In order to assess the potential outcome, the auditor should consult both the client's counsel and independent legal advice, as well as checking the resolution to take action and the opinion of the directors, from the board minutes.

ACTIVITY 3

Written representations from the directors are an important part of audit evidence and should be considered at an early stage in the audit in order that the auditors become aware of the areas in which representations may be required. It also acts as an indicator to management of potential areas of concern, which they may have to give attention to. If significant matters are left until the end of the audit it does not provide for a good working relationship as if such matters had been highlighted earlier management could have taken necessary action to avoid them being included in the written representations (e.g. obtain sufficient corroboratory evidence).

FAU: FOUNDATIONS IN AUDIT

ACTIVITY 4

The auditor provides the client with a report to management for the following reasons:

(a) to highlight deficiencies in the system of internal control

(b) to identify areas where improvements in efficiency could be made

(c) to verify or comment on compliance with specific requirements laid down by relevant regulatory organisations, for example housing associations

(d) to provide management with any other constructive advice

(e) to identify matters which could have an effect on future audits.

PRACTICE QUESTION

BIRCHINLESS

Tutorial note: The answers given to (a) and (b) cover more points than would be required (the question asks for four points in (a).)

Don't panic about the volume of information. Look for the more obvious problem areas like cash and profit, or lack of them, and comment on these. There may well also be more than the required number of points that you spot; stick to the number given and ensure that these are well explained. This will maximise your marks.

(a) (i) Matters which would be raised with management include the following:

- revenue has increased by 73%, and gross profit percentage has increased from 30% to 40%

- distribution costs have risen dramatically by nearly 200% whereas administrative expenses have only increased by 8%

- considerable loss made on sale of non-current assets ($2m)

- the return on trade investments is very small (approx. 2%)

- the current ratio has risen from 1.67 to 1.82, and the quick ratio has fallen from 0.98 to 0.85

- the credit period allowed to customers has increased from 45 to 59 days. Similarly, credit taken has increased from 41 to 88 days.

(ii) (iii)

Changes in revenue and gross profit percentage

The auditor will need to be satisfied that revenue and cost of sales are correctly stated. Comparison with prior periods is one way to obtain assurance.	Is cut off accurate? Has inventory counting and valuation been accurately and consistently carried out? Have all liabilities been recorded?

Changes in distribution costs and administrative expenses

The auditor will need to be satisfied that costs have been correctly recorded and allocated to the various expense headings.	Is the system for allocating costs to statement of profit or loss and other comprehensive income headings adequate? Are management of the opinion that administrative expenses have remained fairly constant? Is it costing the company considerably more to sell and distribute its products?

Loss on sale of non-current assets

The auditor will need to be satisfied that the loss has been correctly calculated and disclosed. The life of non-current assets and the depreciation policy are also related to this item.	Have the proceeds been correctly recorded and received? Was the depreciation rate set at too low a level? Is the loss exceptional?

Return on trade investments

This item is of importance both for the statement of profit or loss and other comprehensive income and the valuation of the trade investments in the statement of financial position. It may be that there has been a fall in value of the investments.	Has all income due been correctly recorded? Should the value of the investments be reduced to reflect a fall in value?

Inventory turnover

An increasing inventory turnover period may indicate that inventories are obsolete or slow-moving, or that inventory has been inaccurately quantified or valued. The auditor will need to be satisfied that inventory is correctly valued in the financial statements (i.e. at net realisable value if that is below cost).	Is any inventory obsolete or slow-moving and, if so, have appropriate write-downs to the cost been made? Was inventory accurately counted and valued? Is cut-off correct?

Current ratio and quick ratio

The going concern concept is a fundamental accounting concept. If the going concern assumption does not apply, then assets should be valued on a break-up basis, and thus the matter is of considerable importance to the auditor. Decreasing liquidity is an indicator of going concern problems.	Are there short-term arrangements with the bank for maintaining overdraft facilities? Are there plans for improving liquidity in the near future?

Credit given and taken

Poor collection of debts may indicate that the doubtful debt provision is inadequate. Increases in the credit period taken may indicate liquidity problems. Both may also be due to incorrect cut-off.	Has the age and collectability of debts been prudently assessed? Has payment to suppliers been delayed as a matter of policy? Is cut-off accurate?

(b) The auditor is required to express an opinion on the financial statements of an enterprise. Evidence is collected on each individual element in those financial statements, but they must also be reviewed as a whole to ensure that they present the correct picture, that disclosure is adequate, etc. The review can also be useful for highlighting any potential problem areas, as in the case of Birchinless.

FAU: FOUNDATIONS IN AUDIT

EXAM-STYLE QUESTION 1

REPRESENTATIONS

Tutorial note: Do not mix up this letter with an engagement letter; the two letters may appear to have similar points being made in them, but their purposes are different.

(a) Written representations are prepared by the directors of a company to the auditors of that company, normally towards the end of an audit, before the auditor signs his auditor's report. The letter confirms verbal representations made by the directors during the audit, as well as providing audit evidence on areas where other audit evidence is not available. An example of this could be where a company settles a legal claim out of court; the directors would then provide representations to the auditor that they know of no other claims on the company in this area. 'Normal' audit evidence on this matter could be difficult to obtain.

The written representations will also have the following functions:

(i) it reminds the directors of their duties concerning the financial statements. In the letter the directors acknowledge their responsibility for the preparation of the financial statements, even though the auditor may have assisted in this area

(ii) it provides the auditor with a further source of audit evidence. The auditor can normally rely on the letter because company law usually makes it an offence to give the auditor false information. This does not in any way relieve the auditor of his responsibilities; he must still ensure that he has sufficient audit evidence to form his opinion on the financial statements.

(b) It is important for the auditor to discuss the contents of the written representations with the directors at an early stage in the audit for a number of reasons:

(i) it provides time for the directors to consider what representations are going to be required of them, and therefore to raise queries on these areas in good time

(ii) it facilitates the ending of the audit. The directors will already be aware of the contents of the representation letter, the signing of the auditor's report will therefore not be delayed by last minute queries or refusal to sign the letter on the part of the directors

(iii) it will assist the auditor in the planning and control of his audit. The auditor can identify at an early stage in the audit the sources of audit evidence available to him and plan his work accordingly

(iv) when the directors become aware of the representations required of them, they may decide to provide the auditor with other audit evidence rather than the representation letter in certain areas

(v) keeping the directors informed of the auditor's work will hopefully promote good relations between the auditor and the directors.

ANSWERS TO ACTIVITIES AND QUESTIONS

EXAM-STYLE QUESTION 2

REPRESENTATIONS

Tutorial note: Do not mix up this letter with an engagement letter; the two letters may appear to have similar points being made in them, but their purposes are different.

Part (a) may seem unusual; to get relevant points consider why standard documentation is a problem anywhere. Items such as not allowing for change, and the documentation being ignored may then be thought of.

(a) Standard representation letters are being used less frequently by the auditing profession because:

   (i) audits are becoming more individually tailored to specific clients; the use of a standard letter is therefore not appropriate

   (ii) a standard letter will lose its impact after a number of years, and the directors may therefore not fully appreciate what they are signing

   (iii) the auditor would find the use of a standard letter for a number of years difficult to justify in court if he had not kept pace with changes at his audit client

   (iv) changes in audit methods and client circumstances each year will necessitate the rewriting of the representation letter.

(b) A representation letter is of particular importance in a small company due to the influence that the directors can have over the running of the company. Confirmations regarding the completeness of the company's transactions in the books and records and other representations like the directors being responsible for the financial statements, even when the auditor acting as accountant has completely prepared the accounts, become very important.

The lack of representations may also put the auditor on enquiry regarding the quality of the other audit evidence received, especially if the company is dominated by the directors.

If the directors refuse to sign the representation letter, then the auditor has a number of options available to him.

   (i) The auditor could discuss the matter with the directors and try and resolve their problems with the letter.

   (ii) The auditor could write a representation letter for the directors, then send this to the directors and ask them to sign it.

   (iii) If the auditor considers that he has not received all the information and explanations required for his audit, then the auditor's report should be modified. The auditor will need to state the reason for the modification, which will be due to the uncertainty of amounts and balances in the financial statements, and state his modification accordingly. An 'except for' qualification for the material uncertainty is the most likely form of modification, although a disclaimer may be necessary if the lack of representations means that the financial statements are potentially meaningless.

Before taking these actions, the auditor should explain to the directors the consequences of not signing the representation letter to try and avoid a confrontation.

Even if the letter is subsequently signed, then the auditor will still have to evaluate the reliability of this evidence. If, in his opinion, the letter does not provide sufficient and reliable evidence in those areas required, then a modification will still be required.

CHAPTER 16

ACTIVITY 1

An unmodified auditor's report should state:

(i) a title identifying the person or persons to whom the report is addressed

(b) the auditors' opinion on the financial statements

(c) the basis of the auditors' opinion

(d) key audit matters

(e) responsibilities of management

(f) responsibilities of the auditor

(g) the auditors' signature and address

(h) the date of the auditor's report.

ACTIVITY 2

(a) The four types of modified auditor's report opinion are summarised in the grid below:

	Material	Pervasive
Inability to obtain sufficient appropriate evidence	Qualified	Disclaimer
Material misstatement in the financial statements	Qualified	Adverse

(b) **Inability to obtain sufficient appropriate evidence – material**

No inventory count carried out at a branch.

Inability to obtain sufficient appropriate evidence – pervasive

Destruction of accounting records.

Material misstatement in the financial statements – material

Difference of opinion between directors and auditor as to whether to provide for a doubtful debt.

Material misstatement in the financial statements – pervasive

Non-compliance with an accounting standard, and the auditor does not agree with the non-compliance.

ANSWERS TO ACTIVITIES AND QUESTIONS

PRACTICE QUESTION

AUDITOR'S REPORT TERMINOLOGY

(a) **Circumstances of uncertainty**

Uncertainty can arise from:

(i) an inability to obtain sufficient appropriate evidence caused by a failure to obtain all the information and explanations considered necessary; or

(ii) an inherent uncertainty resulting from circumstances in which it is not possible to reach an objective conclusion as to the outcome of a situation due to the circumstances themselves. Such uncertainties relate to matters where considerable judgement is required as regards the likely outcome and the probable outcome is not sufficiently capable of estimation.

Items under (i) may lead to modification. Items under (ii) may lead to an explanatory paragraph (emphasis of matter) in the auditor's report.

(b) **A disclaimer of opinion**

This arises where there is a pervasive uncertainty relating to the scope of the audit and the auditor is unable to form an opinion on whether a true and fair view is given by the financial statements. For a matter to be pervasive it should have an impact so great as to render the financial statements as a whole meaningless. It is, therefore, only used as a last resort.

(c) **Circumstances of material misstatement**

(i) departures from acceptable accounting practices:

- failure to follow an accounting standard

- an unacceptable policy not covered by an accounting standard

- compliance with accounting standards where this does not in the circumstances give a true and fair view

(ii) disagreement as to facts or amounts included in financial statements

(iii) disagreement as to the manner or extent of disclosure of facts or amounts

(iv) failure to comply with legislation

and may result in an 'except for' or an adverse opinion.

(d) **An 'except for' opinion**

This arises on a particular matter which, while being material to the true and fair view given by the financial statements, is not so pervasive as to render them totally misleading. The 'except for' opinion, therefore, indicates that, with the exception of the particular matter, the financial statements do give a true and fair view.

FAU: FOUNDATIONS IN AUDIT

EXAM-STYLE QUESTION 1

EASTERN ENGINEERING

Tutorial note: Ensure that all sub-parts of the question are answered fully, giving reference to relevant guidance where necessary e.g. the Auditing Standards. Also ensure that all parts of the question are read carefully; part (b) actually has two parts to it although they are not stated on two separate lines.

(a)   'Except for' – material but not pervasive

       Disclaimer – pervasive inability to obtain sufficient appropriate evidence

       Adverse – pervasive material misstatement in the financial statements

(b) (i) **Records destroyed**

If there is no other evidence available to support the direct labour calculations, then the auditor will be uncertain as to the accuracy of figures included in the financial statements. He is therefore unable to obtain sufficient appropriate evidence.

The question of the materiality of the $10,000 then arises. The labour cost represents approximately 30% of the cost of assets constructed during the year, 6% of total non-current asset additions, and only 1% of the year-end net book value. An item is considered to be material when knowledge of it would be likely to influence the user of financial statements. Any error in the calculation of the $10,000 is unlikely to be considered material in relation to the profit figure of $100,000. In such circumstances, a modification may not be necessary.

      (ii) **Government grant**

Accounting standards state that grants received in respect of non-current assets should be credited to profits over the expected useful life of the non-current asset. The auditor has therefore spotted a material misstatement in the financial statements.

The amount of $22,500 ($25,000 less the $2,500 to be written off each year) does appear to be material. A material misstatement becomes pervasive when the amount is such as to render the financial statements misleading; such is not the case in this example. A qualified (except for) opinion is therefore appropriate.

(c) Independent auditors' report to the shareholders of Eastern Engineering (extract):

A government grant received during the year in respect of the purchase of non-current assets has been credited in full to profits instead of being apportioned over the life of the assets. As a result, profits for the year, together with retained earnings, have been increased by $22,500.

In our opinion, except for . . .

(d) Legislation may extend the statutory responsibilities of an auditor to require him to consider whether the directors' report is consistent with the financial statements. If not consistent, the auditor should state that fact in his report.

ANSWERS TO ACTIVITIES AND QUESTIONS

EXAM-STYLE QUESTION 2

EASTERN ENGINEERING

Tutorial note: Ensure that all sub-parts of the question are answered fully, giving reference to relevant guidance where necessary e.g. the Auditing Standards. Also ensure that all parts of the question are read carefully; part (b) actually has two parts to it although they are not stated on two separate lines.

(a) Independent auditors' report to the shareholders of Eastern Engineering (extract):

A government grant received during the year in respect of the purchase of non-current assets has been credited in full to profits instead of being apportioned over the life of the assets. As a result, profits for the year, together with retained earnings, have been increased by $22,500.

In our opinion, except for . . .

(b) Legislation may extend the statutory responsibilities of an auditor to require him to consider whether the directors' report is consistent with the financial statements. If not consistent, the auditor should state that fact in his report.

CHAPTER 17

EXAM-STYLE QUESTION 1

DUTY OF CARE

Tutorial note: Although this answer does go into a lot of detail to explain fully the trend in case law, the examiner's report states that candidates would gain good marks for presenting the facts and stating why they were relevant. A difficult question in the time available. Try to ensure that all cases are mentioned rather than going into detail about one only; a broad answer will gain many more marks than a narrow one.

Auditor's duty of care to third parties

The auditor's contract is with the company he is auditing. The company can therefore sue the auditor for breach of contract if the audit is carried out incorrectly.

Until recently a third party has not been able to sue the auditor. The tests to be shown in court are that:

(i) there was a duty of care to the third party by the auditor, and

(ii) there was a breach of this duty, and

(iii) the third party suffered financial loss as a result of this breach of duty.

How the auditor's liability has been extended, taking into account the above tests, is best shown by looking at some important cases in chronological order.

(i) **Candler v Crane Christmas (1951)**

In this case Candler sued the accountants Crane Christmas when he lost money he had invested in a company, the accounts of which Crane Christmas had prepared. The court ruling was that although the accounts were negligently prepared, Candler could not recoup his losses from the accountants because he did not have a contract with them. There was therefore no duty of care owed to third parties.

(ii) **Hedley Byrne v Heller & Partners (1964)**

Although this is a case dealing with banks, it is relevant for accountants. The plaintiff lost money when a bank reference from the defendant turned out to have been negligently produced. Basically the bank indicated that a mutual client was a good credit risk when this was not the case. The court ruled that Hedley Byrne, although they did not have a contract with the bank Heller & Partners, could recoup their losses due to the negligence and loss involved. The three tests noted above were therefore met and satisfied. However, the bank did not have to pay any damages due to a general disclaimer in its letter absolving it from any liability.

The decision affected accountants in that if a third party can show that it relied on the work of an accountant which later turned out to be wrong, it can claim damages. However, this principle was only extended to plaintiffs whom the auditor actually knew by name. Unidentified third parties would still not be able to claim against the auditor.

(iii) **JEB Fasteners v Marks Bloom & Co (1980)**

In this case JEB Fasteners lost money when the company in which they had invested, BG Fasteners went into liquidation. The plaintiff had used the latest set of audited accounts of BG Fasteners to assist in the investment decision and these accounts were agreed in court to have been audited negligently. The defendants considered that their defence was good because they did not know about JEB Fasteners by name at the time the auditor's report was signed. The auditors were therefore under Hedley Byrne not liable to the plaintiff for damages.

Woolf J also noted, however, that the defendants should have realised that BG Fasteners would accept a bidder for the business, given its loss-making state. He therefore ruled that Marks Bloom & Co were liable to JEB Fasteners on the grounds of reasonable foresight i.e. that they should have realised that a company such as JEB Fasteners would be making an offer, and therefore they were liable to this company.

Damages were not awarded because JEB Fasteners could not prove sufficient reliance on the audited financial statements. Nevertheless, the principle remained that auditors were liable to third parties they should be able to reasonably foresee.

(iv) **Lloyd Cheyham v Littlejohn de Paula (1985)**

Littlejohn de Paula successfully defended themselves against a negligence claim in this case by showing:

- that they had followed the standard expected of the normal auditor i.e. that in Accounting Standards and Auditing Standards

- that their working papers were good enough to show consideration of the problems raised by the plaintiff and reasonable decisions made after consideration

ANSWERS TO ACTIVITIES AND QUESTIONS

- that the plaintiff had not made all the reasonable enquiries one could expect when, in this case, purchasing a company e.g. a review of the business was not undertaken upon investigating the purchase but only after purchase.

The judge, therefore, held that far too much reliance was placed on the accounts by the plaintiff and he awarded costs against the plaintiff to the defendant.

(v) *Caparo Industries v Dickman and others* (1989)

This case investigated the auditor's relationship to shareholders and third parties who purchase shares in a company and then lose money as a result of a foreseen fall in the share price – foreseeable that is by the auditor.

The decision here indicates that the auditor will not be liable to potential investors or to individual shareholders but only to shareholders as a group.

Recent decisions, therefore, have attempted to extend auditor liability to third parties. As long as the auditor follows the steps in the Littlejohn case (above), it would appear to be unlikely that he will be found guilty of negligence.

EXAM-STYLE QUESTION 2

DUTY OF CARE

(a) **Ensuring that audit risk is minimised**

Audit risk may be minimised in two basic ways – by ensuring that planning is adequate and by ensuring that audit work is of a satisfactory quality.

(i) **Planning**

If an auditor plans an audit properly, those areas of the audit that are potentially risky will have been identified, and the auditor can ensure that resources are devoted to those areas to minimise the risk of misstatement in the financial statements.

- Ensuring that the audit objectives are known e.g. statutory audit only, and therefore ensure that the client accepts this by sending a signed copy of the engagement letter back to the auditor. The auditor is not looking for any immaterial fraud as this would not affect the true and fair view given by the financial statements.

- Planning the audit will ensure that work is directed to cover the whole of the company's accounting systems. Thus reviewing last year's files and discussions with management will identify all the accounting systems – adequate audit programmes can then be written to cover all of these systems.

- If particularly difficult or critical areas come to light, then additional resources will be devoted to these to investigate the problem fully. Thus last year's file may note a difficult inventory count; therefore an experienced senior may be sent to attend this year rather than a semi-senior or junior staff member.

The aim of planning, therefore, is to identify risk areas early in the audit and to ensure that appropriate action is taken to minimise the potential risk that they pose.

(ii) **Other areas**

If the auditor ensures that all jobs are done to a high standard, this of itself will minimise the amount of risk involved to the auditor. A complete, well presented and referenced audit file is likely to prove of much more value in court than a shoddy and only partly referenced file.

Particular procedures to employ to ensure that audit work is of a high standard include:

- observing all Auditing Standards

- before accepting any appointment, ensuring that there are no conflicts of interest between the firm's duty as auditors and other non-professional situations e.g. client being a close relative

- following from above, also ensuring that potential clients are of a good standing e.g. not potentially insolvent

- ensuring that the firm has the skills necessary to perform the service for the client e.g. detailed use of computer auditing if the client has a highly computerised accounting system

- ensuring that consultative procedures are available to reconcile problems between staff and partners

- ensuring that full file reviews are carried out either by another auditing firm, or by another office of the same firm.

If these procedures are followed the firm should be less liable to negligence claims as noted above.

(b) **Litigation directed at auditors or directors of company**

The directors of a company are required to prepare accounts which show a true and fair view. If therefore the financial statements do not show a true and fair view, the directors have breached their duty under the Act. The fact that at least one director signs the accounts indicates that they are aware of this requirement.

The auditor of a company then reports on the accuracy of the financial statements i.e. does he concur with the directors' opinion that the financial statements show a true and fair view? In doing this he also reports on the stewardship function of the directors; the members own the company but do not run it – they employ the directors. The auditor therefore in effect reports that what the directors say is correct.

Both the directors and the auditor therefore in some way confirm the accuracy of the financial statements. It can be argued that both should share the blame if the financial statements are found to be incorrect. Unfortunately, because the auditor has insurance against being sued, it is more likely that he will be the subject of litigation because some financial benefit is seen from suing him rather than the directors who do not have insurance.

REFERENCES

The Board (2020) *IAS 2 Inventories*. London: IFRS Foundation.

The Board (2020) *IAS 10 Events after the Reporting Date*. London: IFRS Foundation.

The Board (2020) *IAS 16 Property, Plant and Equipment*. London: IFRS Foundation.

The Board (2020) *IAS 37 Provisions, Contingent Liabilities and Contingent Assets*. London: IFRS Foundation.

The Board (2020) *IAS 39 Financial Instruments: Recognition and Measurement*. London: IFRS Foundation.

INDEX

A

ACCA Code of Ethics and Conduct, 15

Acceptable error, 149, 151

Accounting
  estimate, 168
  policies, 266
  records, 2
  system, 94

Accruals, 224

Accuracy, 164, 242
  valuation and allocation, 164

Adjusting events, 271

Advantages of an audit, 7

Adverse opinion, 296

Advocacy threats, 28

Analytical procedures, 58, 124, 163, 203, 235, 267

Application controls, 240, 241

Application program examination, 255

Assets, 167

Attribute sampling, 157

Audit
  definition, 3
  documentation, 76, 248
  evidence, 75, 120, 229
  objectives, 163
  opinion, 301
  opinion modifications, 296
  plan, 54
  programme, 73, 234
  review, 235
  risk, 54
  sampling, 146
  software, 251
  strategy, 53
  testing procedures, 123
  verification techniques, 162
  working papers, 76

Auditing around the computer, 249

Auditing in a computer environment, 239

Auditing through the computer, 249

Auditor's expert, 197

Auditor's report, 4, 290

Authorisation, 242

Automated tools and techniques, 249

B

Back-up disks, 258

Bank
  and cash, 138, 210
  certificate, 211
  loans, 225
  overdrafts, 224
  reconciliation, 215

Basis for opinion, 5

Batch totals, 260

Benefits of internal control, 90

Big data, 254

Block sampling, 153

Briefing meetings, 72

C

Caparo industries, 312

Cash balances, 216

Check digits, 259

Circularisation of receivables, 205

Circularisation, 164, 194, 205

'Cold' review, 83

Completeness, 164, 175, 194, 242

Computer-based systems, 237

Computers in audit, 234

Confidence level, 148

Confidentiality, 15, 16, 80

Conflict of interest, 17

Contingency, 228

Contingent liability, 228

Control account, 202

Control activities, 88, 90, 92, 124, 125, 128, 131, 135, 136, 139

Control environment, 88

Control objectives, 111, 124, 125, 128, 131, 134, 136, 138

Control risk, 55

Credit notes, 204
Current file, 76
Current liabilities, 222
Cut-off, 164, 180

D

Data filing, 258
Debenture loan, 225
Deficiency in internal control, 278
Dependency checks, 260
Depreciation, 192
Detection risk, 55
Difference between internal and external auditors, 64
Difference between tests of control and substantive tests, 124
Direct bank confirmation, 211
Disadvantages of an audit, 8
Disclaimer of opinion, 296
Disclosure of provisions, 227
Documentation, 258
Documenting the internal control system, 96
Dummy data, 250
Duties of the auditor, 32, 35
Duty of care, 309

E

Embedded audit facilities, 255
Emphasis of matter paragraph, 299
Engagement partner, 82
Enquiry, 163
Evaluation of audit results, 170
'Except for' opinion, 296
Existence, 164, 174, 194
Existence checks, 260
Expected error, 149, 151
Expert, 197
External audit, 64
External auditor's report, 40
External confirmation(s), 123, 163, 205

F

Familiarity threats, 22
Fiduciary' relationship, 6
Final review stage, 267
Financial statement assertions, 163
Financial statements, 2, 167
Finished goods, 182
Flowcharts, 97, 234
Freehold and leasehold land and buildings, 195
Fundamental ethical principles, 15

G

Gains and losses, 167
General controls, 245
Going concern
    basis of accounting, 268
    review, 268

H

Haphazard selection, 153
Hash totals, 260
'Hot' review, 83

I

IFAC Code of Ethics and Conduct, 9
Independence, 15, 17
Independent auditor's report, 291
Information system, 89
Information technology and documentation, 80
Inherent limitations of internal controls, 115
Inherent risk, 55
Inquiry, 123
Inspection, 123, 162
Integrated test facilities (ITF), 254
Integrity, 15, 17
Internal audit, 64
Internal control(s), 88, 92, 202, 210, 222, 240
    evaluation questionnaires (ICEQs), 97, 110
    questionnaire(s) (ICQs), 97, 106, 248
    system, 105, 278

International auditing practice statements (IAPSs), 9

International standards on auditing (ISAs), 9

International standards on quality control (ISQCs), 9

Intimidation threats, 28

Inventory, 134, 174
    cost, 175
    count, 176
    quantities, 175
    valuation, 175, 181

Irrecoverable debts, 203

ISA 402 *Audit Considerations Relating to Entities using Service Organisations*, 240

J

Judgement
    sampling, 148, 155
    selection, 153

K

Key audit matters, 5

L

Liabilities, 167

Liability cap, 314

Liability in tort, 310

Loss of audit trail, 238

M

Management accounts, 2

Manual systems flowcharts, 98

Material and pervasive, 296

Material misstatement, 296

Material uncertainty relating to going concern, 300

Materiality, 44, 63, 296

Misstatements, 290

Modified auditor's report, 295
    opinions, 297

Monetary unit sampling (MUS), 152, 158

Monitoring of controls, 93

N

Negligence, 308

Net realisable value, 175, 183

Non-adjusting events, 272

Non-current asset(s), 136, 190
    register, 194

Non-current liabilities, 222

Non-statistical sampling, 155

Non-statistical techniques, 148

O

Objectivity, 15, 17

Observation, 123, 162

Occurrence, 164, 194

Opinion paragraph, 293

Organisation charts, 97

Overhead allocation, 183

Overheads, 183

Owners' equity, 167

P

Parallel simulation, 256

Passwords, 259

Payables, 128, 222

Payables/ purchasing system, 93

Peer review, 83

Performance materiality, 48

Permanent file, 76

Physical controls, 92

Planning, 52, 67

Planning memorandum, 68

Population, 146, 149

Post-audit review, 83

Precision limit, 148

Prepayments, 204

Presentation, 164, 194

Professional
    behaviour, 15
    competence and due care, 15
    ethics, 14
    indemnity insurance, 314
    judgement, 46, 48
    scepticism, 48

Proper accounting records, 294

Provision, 226

Purchases, 222
  system, 128

Q

Qualified ('except for') opinion, 296

Quality control, 81, 315

R

Random selection, 151

Ratios, 60

Reasonable assurance, 44

Reasonableness checks, 260

Recalculation, 123, 163

Receivables, 125, 202

Recording the internal control system, 96

Reliability of audit evidence, 122

Reperformance, 123, 163

Report to management, 277, 279

Responsibilities, 5

Returns inwards, 204

Review of financial statements, 167, 266

Review procedures, 81

Rights and obligations, 164, 174, 194

Rights of the auditor, 33, 34

Risk assessment, 54
  process, 89

Risk-based audit approach, 54

S

Sales system, 125

Sample
  design, 148
  selection, 151
  size, 149

Sampling, 146
  risk, 147, 150

Sarbanes Oxley, 310

Segregation of duties, 92

Self interest threats, 18

Self-review threats, 24

Significant deficiency in internal control, 278

Software, 235

Stakeholders, 2

Standardised audit programme, 74

Statistical sampling, 148, 155

Statutory regulation of auditors, 31

Stratification, 149

Subsequent events, 271

Substantive procedure, 124

Sufficient, appropriate evidence, 121

Symbols, 100

Systematic selection, 152

Systems software data analysis, 255

T

Tangible non-current assets, 194

Test data, 250

Test of control, 124, 127, 130, 133, 136, 138, 139

Threats to integrity, objectivity and independence, 18

Tolerable error, 149

Tort, 310

Tracing, 256

Trade payables, 222

True and fair, 42
  view, 296

U

Uncorrected misstatements, 290

Understanding the entity, 56

Unmodified auditor's report, 40, 290

V

Valuation, 175

Value weighted selection, 152

Variables sampling, 157

Virus protection, 257

W

Wages and salaries system, 131

Work in progress, 174

Working papers, 76, 235

Written representations, 274
  letter, 275